ENCHANTMENT AND SORROW

ENCHANTMENT AND SORROW

The Autobiography of Gabrielle Roy

Translated by Patricia Claxton

LESTER
&ORPEN
DENNYS
PUBLISHERS

Originally published in French under the title *La Détresse et l'enchantement* by Les Editions du Boréal Express, copyright © Fonds Gabrielle Roy, 1984

FIRST EDITION

Canadian Cataloguing in Publication Data

Roy, Gabrielle, 1909–1983
Enchantment and sorrow

Translation of: La Détresse et l'enchantement.
ISBN 0-88619-101-7 (bound) ISBN 0-88619-167-X (pbk.)

1. Roy, Gabrielle, 1909–1983 — Biography.
2. Authors, Canadian (French) — 20th century — Biography.* I. Title.

PS8535.095Z5313 1987   C843'.54   C87-094273-5
PQ3919.R74Z46613 1987

The Publisher wishes to thank the Canada Council for its support in the translation of this book.

Design by Gordon Robertson
Typeset in 11 pt Aldus by Q Composition Inc.

Printed and bound in Canada by Metropole Litho Inc. for

Lester & Orpen Dennys Limited
78 Sullivan Street
Toronto, Ontario M5T 1C1

Foreword

THIS BOOK is the last that Gabrielle Roy wrote, the autobiography in two parts which she began in 1976 and at which she worked virtually until she died in 1983. It completes her literary estate – consisting of all her works – which she bequeathed to the Fonds Gabrielle Roy, a non-profit trust established to administer the estate and distribute its revenues to various charities.

Of the three or four parts she initially planned, she was able to complete only the first two before illness forced her to cease her work. These two, "The Governor's Ball" and "A Bird Knows Its Song", retrace what might be called her formative years, from her Franco-Manitoban childhood to her return from Europe on the eve of the Second World War. She began her first novel, *Bonheur d'occasion* (*The Tin Flute*), three or four years later.

This, then, is the story of the first thirty years of Gabrielle Roy's life, her discovery of herself as an individual and, gradually, her vocation as a writer. The story is interwoven with memories: in the first part, memories of her family, especially her mother, and the milieu in which she taught school, took part in amateur theatre productions, and became aware of her identity; in the second, of Europe in the late thirties and the two years she spent there, which for her were decisive. Much of this story has been hitherto unknown.

Gabrielle Roy was most anxious that this book be considered an *autobiography*, not memoirs, for what she wanted to write was not a historical reconstitution of a time gone by, but rather a re-creation or re-enactment of the past from memory and imagination, strongly flavoured with emotion and subjectivity: a past that never fails to quicken and live in the very process of its recall.

v

Foreword

The original French text of the autobiography was taken directly from the typewritten manuscript, of which she left two copies, corrected by the author's own hand. She entrusted one of these to me shortly before her death; the other was found among her papers. When it was first published in Montreal in the autumn of 1984, the book was enthusiastically acclaimed by critics and public alike.

Patricia Claxton's translation has been patiently researched and thoughtfully rendered. No finer tribute could be paid to Gabrielle Roy and her work.

FRANÇOIS RICARD
Executive Director
Fonds Gabrielle Roy

Translator's Note

A FEELING of urgency underlies this book, an anxiety to set down, before time runs out, as much as possible of the things that Gabrielle Roy wanted the world to know about her life, her urge to seek beyond an increasingly confining milieu, her large and small discoveries, and above all, perhaps, about the strong, often conflicting emotional forces at work in her – the things that led her, or drove her, towards the vocation she was destined for.

A translator has a curious position in such an intensely personal book. Although I met and talked to Gabrielle Roy at some length years ago, in a context of no importance here, I would not for a moment imagine that I knew her personally. Yet for more than a year I lived in her left-hand pocket, so to speak, and now must remind myself that I really did not know her, that she really was not there in the flesh sometimes, telling me her story so I could pass it on.

The first French edition of *La détresse et l'enchantement*, published in 1984, reproduced Gabrielle Roy's personally corrected typescript almost exactly as she left it, which is to say, without editing of any kind except for minor spelling and grammatical tidying. From time to time the author expresses worry that her dervish will fail to finish what he has started. Indeed, there was only time to complete part of what she had planned, and as this translation progressed it became clear that time had run out also for the honing and polishing her work habitually received. For instance, in dialogue spoken in 1938, before the outbreak of the Second World War, characters speak of the "First World War".

Such potentially distracting anomalies have been corrected in the course of translation.

I have also added first names on first mention of real people, which is more customary in English than French, and the names of authors of most books and plays, since French works will be less familiar to English readers. Proper names have been verified for spelling and some have been corrected.

Readers with an academic bent would no doubt like to see footnotes to justify such apparent divergences from the underlying text, or to add interesting information. If this were a scholarly work it would bristle with indexes and footnotes, which would be only proper. But that was not the kind of book Gabrielle Roy was so anxious to leave.

It would be a pity, nevertheless, not to share at least a few gleanings from my research and reflection. For instance, I was puzzled by the way in which Gabrielle Roy speaks of "Pembina Mountain". I learned that this, in the early days of Manitoba, was the name used collectively for a group of small settlements on the slopes of the Pembina Escarpment, although I found no other reference to an elevation by that name. I also learned that on the Canadian prairies the berries called "pembinas", from which pembina jelly is made, are also known as "mooseberries", and are elsewhere more prosaically called "highbush cranberries".

The need for research has occasionally been more apparent for a person of English heritage than of French. The line of investigation and resolution has often been circuitous. For example, since Charing Cross is at one side of Trafalgar Square, a bus leaving Trafalgar Square and heading north towards Epping Forest will not pass Charing Cross ten minutes or so later, though it will almost certainly pass King's Cross. To Gabrielle Roy, "Saxon" appears to mean "old English" in a broad sense, but "Saxon" cottages, thatched and half-timbered, are more accurately Tudor, and Boadicea lived before the coming of the Saxons and was therefore not a Saxon but a British queen. Still, designating Boadicea as "British" might allow an impression that she was a rather recent queen, whereas if she is identified with the ancient Britons her antiquity is no longer in doubt. Similarly, in 1938 Zambia was Northern Rhodesia; however, in the context it is not so much the name as its exotic aura that is important, and so the missionary with whom Esther corresponds is located in neither Zambia nor Northern Rhodesia in the translation, but "somewhere up the Zambezi", which fits both the tone and the geography.

Where details in the French text are at variance with strict accuracy, a decision on how fastidious to be with correction has sometimes been difficult. In general, errors of indisputable fact are corrected, whereas those in grey areas involving Gabrielle Roy's opinion or impression are left intact. For instance, in a reconstructed conversation, Esther remarks that the Queen belongs to the "High Church"; but in 1938 King George VI was on the throne and therefore "Queen" should more properly be "King and Queen". On the other hand, the significance given to "High Church" and "Low Church" is supposition on the author's part, and so this remains unchanged. When a Swedish girl's parents are mentioned as being in Oslo, the placename appears to be an error; in this case, since nothing whatever depends on the placename, the least obtrusive solution is for it simply to disappear. A morning's walk from just outside Nice to St-Tropez is clearly intended to telescope a distance of some hundred kilometres. Still, such a walk rather severely taxes the imagination for one who may know the region; the solution is merely to allow a slightly vaguer impression of the length of the ride by *micheline* before the walk begins. More complex is the use of the name "Provence" as a synonym for the Midi or South of France in general. This, while not strictly accurate, is a common practice among the French themselves, and furthermore it is "Provence" in this sense that is so dear to Gabrielle Roy's heart; "Provence" is therefore the term that remains, except when Ruby's thoughts are being expressed.

Certain socio-cultural situations and allusions have needed pondering and even gentle nudging in order not to leave some readers thoroughly perplexed. One of these is Madame Jouve's abhorrence of being labelled a "landlady". Another occurs with the appearance of Sir John Henry Dunn, Bart, where the comma after "Dunn" and the period after "Bart" were lost in the French printing, and where the distinction between a peer and a baronet, no doubt incomprehensible to most French-speaking people, will be important to many English-speaking readers. In another vein, a *château* is not necessarily a castle. As to Lillie Road, why the name should "smack of perdition" remains a mystery, but I suspect that Gladys

ix

planted the notion, the street perhaps having been named for Lillie Langtry, the "Jersey Lily", who was both admired and scorned as an actress, great beauty, and long-time favourite of Edward, Prince of Wales in the late nineteenth century.

Finally, Gabrielle Roy often obtains emphasis or sharpened impression by using tautologies; after due reflection, a few of these have been omitted if, instead of adding something to the text in translation, they intruded to the point of weakening it.

All decisions of an editorial nature have been approved by François Ricard, Gabrielle Roy's literary executor, and have benefited from the opinion of Joyce Marshall, who was general editor for this book. I am indebted to both for their wisdom and guidance on these and other matters. Joyce, who knew Gabrielle Roy and translated three of her books, for example pointed out, when I was inclined to use the word "garret", that an "attic" figures quite prominently in other of Gabrielle Roy's books, notably *Street of Riches*, and recalled that Gabrielle Roy was particularly fond of the word "horizon" and would certainly have preferred it where in some instance I had initially used "skyline".

I have also had occasion to call upon the special expertise of a number of others and could not finish without expressing my gratitude for their generous assistance. I wish in particular to thank Mary and Jack Plaice, Joan Rolland, Anthony Abbott of Debrett's in London, and Vaughan and Sally Turner of London.

PATRICIA CLAXTON

This translation is dedicated
to Jim

I

THE
GOVERNOR'S
BALL

I

WHEN DID IT first dawn on me that I was one of those people destined to be treated as inferiors in their own country? I don't think it was during any of the frequent forays that Maman and I made to Winnipeg, leaving our little French city of St-Boniface and crossing the Red River by the Provencher Bridge. It would be easy to suppose so, since our capital city never really received us otherwise than as foreigners, but when I was a child I rather liked the feeling of crossing a border and being in a strange place, light years away but right next door to home. I think it opened my eyes, trained me to observe things and stimulated my imagination.

Generally we set out early, Maman and I, and if it was summer we went on foot. We didn't do it just to save money. We did it because all of us were natural walkers and loved to stride along with our eyes free to roam, our minds wherever they wished and our thoughts unfettered – and so we do still, those of us who are still of this world.

We almost always set off in high spirits and full of expectation. Maman would have read in the paper or heard from a neighbour that Eaton's was having a sale of curtain-lace, or printed cottons suitable for making aprons or house-dresses, or maybe children's shoes. Always, as we began these shopping expeditions, we were drawn by the hope that so warms the hearts of poor people, that of turning up a real find at the bargain counter. It occurs to me now that we hardly ever ventured into the rich metropolis next door except on buying trips. This was where a good portion of our hard-earned money went – and it was pennies from the pockets of poor people like us that made the city such an arrogant and intimidating neighbour. Later I often went to Winnipeg for a lot of other

3

reasons, but in my childhood, as I recall, it was almost exclusively for bargain hunting.

As we left, Maman was most often bubbling with merriment and inclined to optimism, even wishful thinking, as if she was set free by leaving the house and city behind along with the usual trammel of constraints and obligations. From that point on she had that capacity for enjoyment which is the lot of every footloose adventurer. To tell the truth, Maman had only to step outside her familiar routine and she was at once on an adventure and open to the whole world.

On the way, she'd talk to me about the things she'd buy if the discounts were really big. But she always let herself imagine much more than our means would allow, thinking perhaps of a rug for the living room, or a new set of china. Since she hadn't yet dipped into the little sum she'd set by for the day, it always felt like enough to satisfy all the wants long kept in check, plus some more that emerged on the spur of the moment. So when we crossed the bridge, we were rich, with all our possible acquisitions still intact in our heads.

But as soon as we were on the other side, we'd undergo a kind of transformation that made us draw together, as though solidarity would help us face a kind of shadow that had fallen over us. It was partly because we were now on dismal Water Street beside the railway sorting yards, undoubtedly the most woebegone part of Winnipeg, full of drunkards, the wails of crying children and the hiss of escaping steam; the hideous face which the haughty city couldn't hide, a mere stone's throw from its broad airy avenues. But there was more to it than that; our discomfort came partly from inside us too. We'd suddenly be less sure of ourselves, the money we were going to spend wouldn't seem so inexhaustible, and our plans for it would have come back down to earth.

We'd arrive at Portage Avenue, which was so inordinately broad it could swallow a throng of thousands without showing it. We'd still be speaking French, of course, but perhaps less audibly, particularly after two or three passersby turned around and stared at us. The humiliation of having someone turn to stare when I was speaking French in a Winnipeg street was something I'd felt so often as a child that I no longer realized it was humiliation. Besides,

4

I'd often turned around myself to stare at some immigrant whose soft Slavic voice or Scandinavian accent I'd heard. I got so used to it eventually that I suppose I thought of it as natural for us all to feel more or less like foreigners on someone else's ground. That is, until I came around to thinking that if everyone was a foreigner, then none of us was.

Only when we arrived at Eaton's was it decided whether or not there would be a confrontation. It all depended on Maman's frame of mind. Sometimes she'd begin by calling for a saleswoman who spoke our language to serve us. In our patriotic moments, we of St-Boniface claimed it was our right and even our duty to make a point of doing so, and that if all of us did this, industry and department stores would be obliged to hire our people.

So if Maman was having one of her good days, if her confidence was up and her tongue felt nimble, she'd take the offensive and demand one of our compatriots to wait on us. The more forceful she was, I'd observed, the more accommodating the floorwalker would be. He'd lose no time sending for Miss or Mrs. So-and-so, who often turned out to be someone we knew, sometimes even a neighbour. Amid the hustle and bustle of strangers on all sides, the most cordial and composed of conversations would ensue.

"Ah, Madame Phaneuf," Maman would say. "How are you? And how's your father? Is he still living in the country?"

"Madame Roy!" the saleslady would exclaim. "How are you? What can I do for you? It's always such a pleasure to help you."

It seems to me we poor people of St-Boniface had a gift for neighbourly warmth when thrown together, handed down from some gracious society of olden times.

On days like that we probably bought more than we should have, being so grateful to be doing it in our own language that the money slipped through our fingers even faster than usual.

But there were also times when Maman felt beaten before she began, weary of a struggle that had to be taken up again and again and was never won for good and all; at such times she found it simpler and less taxing to "bring out" her English, as she used to say.

We'd move from counter to counter. Using her hands and facial expressions to help, she really managed pretty well, though some-

5

times a real problem arose, like the time she wanted some chamois ("shammy" to the English) to line a coat, and asked for "a yard or two of Chinese skin to put under the coat."

When a saleswoman failed to understand her, she would call another to help, and sometimes that one would call a third. Passing customers would stop to help too, for Winnipeg, while it treated us as foreigners, was nothing if not quick to fly to our assistance the moment we found ourselves in a fix. These confabulations were intended to solve our predicament, but to us they were pure torture. Sometimes we'd slip away in the middle of it all. Then we'd be overcome with mirth at the thought of all those good-hearted folk no doubt still arguing over how to rescue us, with us already far from the scene.

Once, when she was even more upset than usual by the barrage of solicitousness, Maman opened her umbrella as we escaped, and we ran down the aisles of the store as though caught in a downpour. Only when we got outside to find a beaming sun did she think of closing it, which lent an air of provocation to the harmless escapade. I know now that the paroxysms of laughter she infected me with despite myself were a blessing, an antidote for the bleakness in our lives, but at the time I was quite embarrassed.

In fact, after the umbrella episode – a good few minutes after – I became angry and told Maman that we might both have been laughing, but we'd been making ourselves a laughing stock too.

To which Maman retorted, somewhat stung, that it was not for me to lecture her; I'd had every kind of opportunity for education, while she'd only been able to stay in school long enough to finish sixth grade at her little country school in St-Alphonse-de-Rodriguez, where the teacher herself didn't know much more than the pupils, and how could she, poor girl, when all she earned was four hundred dollars a year. I was the one, with my quick mind and my brain not broken down already from constant figuring, who ought to start learning English so I could make up for all the rest of us. Later, when I came to Montreal and found things no different in that city's west end department stores, I was dumbfounded and began to feel there was no cure for the misfortune of being French Canadian.

Never had Maman been so voluble on the subject. I was taken aback. I think this was the first time I ever realized that she'd suffered cruelly from her condition in life and had found comfort only in imagining her children established in circumstances she would have liked for herself.

WE CAME HOME from our expeditions to Winnipeg dog-tired and, in truth, almost always depressed. Either we'd been sane and sensible and had bought only what was essential (and who ever reaped joy from sticking to essentials?), or else we'd done something idiotic (like buying the hat that suited me so well but cost the earth), and then we felt guilty; we'd have to make it up somewhere else, Maman would say, and besides, she would hint, not let Papa know what we'd paid. Being so strapped for money all the time meant that sooner or later we'd overspend and then we'd be more strapped than ever.

In any event, though we crossed the bridge on the way out with our heads full of plans as if we were rich, we never recrossed it feeling anything but poor, three-quarters of our money having slipped through our fingers, very often without our being able to say where it had gone.

"My, how fast it goes!" Maman would sigh. "That's what money's for, of course, but your father's going to say – again – that I can let it go faster than anyone else."

Soon, on the other side of the bridge, we'd see the towers of the cathedral, then the dome of the Jesuit College, then spires and other church towers. The familiar outline of our little city against the intense Manitoba sky revealed much more attachment to prayer and education than to business, and it always gave us comfort. It reminded us that we'd been created for eternity and would be recompensed for having been so hard put to make ends meet.

A few steps more and we'd be on home ground. We may not have been numerous in our pious and studious little city, but this helped us feel of one heart. Now Maman and I would be speaking our own language with all the confidence in the world, neither in whispers nor too loudly as we would in Winnipeg, where our behaviour was governed by our self-consciousness, or by the shame of it. And we'd be hearing the sound of other French voices in harmony with ours. In our relief at being back in our natural surroundings we'd find ourselves greeting almost everyone we met, though it's true that between us we knew practically everyone in the city, at least by name. The farther we went, the more people Maman would recognize as friends, exchanging greetings and snatches of personal news with this one and that.

There were times, once we were back in our own city, when she'd look up at the tall sky with a kind of rapture. Often the weariness would vanish from her face as if by magic and she'd declare, as if calling me to witness: "It's good to be home!"

At last we'd arrive at Deschambault Street. We must have felt it was something like a miracle to find our house still intact and standing guard over our French way of life, protecting it from the hurly-burly and disparity of the Canadian West, for in the last minute we'd hurry towards it, as though we might arrive to find it had been snatched away from us.

It was a pleasing but unpretentious house, with dormers in the attic, lots of big windows on the second floor, and a wide veranda with a row of white columns around the front and west sides. We always came back to it as though returning from a harrowing expedition. Yet those expeditions from St-Boniface to Winnipeg, however revealing, were not what really opened my eyes to our lot in life, we French Canadians of Manitoba. That happened at another and much more trying time.

II

I HAD BEEN ill with one severe case of indigestion after another, and my stomach still hurt. The day I began to feel a little better, Maman decided to take me to the doctor, as many people in our condition would have done, no doubt. After the questions and the examination, which in those days consisted mostly of palpations, she and I waited on tenterhooks for the verdict. The doctor took a very long time to deliver it. Finally he looked straight at Maman and said crisply and a bit reproachfully:

"Madame, this child will have to have an operation. As soon as possible. Without delay."

I turned my head a mite to glance at Maman and saw her shudder, as though accused of a crime. She turned white, then I think I remember her turning red, and all this time she seemed to be looking for words that wouldn't come. At last she found the usual ones, the ones that came most naturally to us. I can still hear her. I'll always be able to hear her say in that stifled voice:

"How much? How much will it be, Doctor?"

We might have been at the grocer's or the butcher's, but I had the impression that Maman was steeling herself for a much closer contest than with the merchants, with whom she easily had the upper hand.

The doctor shuffled his papers, pen, blotter, as uncomfortable, it seemed, as Maman.

"Well now, in the normal course of these things, for an operation of this kind it's a hundred and fifty dollars."

He must have seen the consternation on Maman's face because he quickly held up his hands, adding, "But..., but...."

Having calmed her a little he continued.

9

"For you, since I know your circumstances, it'll be a hundred dollars."

I could see that this didn't do much to help Maman relax. With a little groan she repeated as if to herself, not complainingly to him, "A hundred dollars! A hundred dollars!"

Helplessly, the doctor gave a shrug. Then I realized she was going to recite the story of our life, which she brought out in public only when she really had nothing else to fall back on, and which always filled me with such shame and distress that I could neither cry nor speak. I wished I could stop her, shut her up somehow, but the time for that had already run out. Sitting on the edge of her chair, her hands clasped tightly in her lap, without once raising her eyes towards the doctor so as not to be distracted in any way from what she had to say, she began.

"My husband was a civil servant with the federal government. He was persecuted behind his back for not hiding his political loyalties. To make it short, he was given the sack, dismissed just six months before he reached retirement age, which meant he would get no pension. So you see, in our old age we were suddenly penniless, with nothing we could count on coming in. We had to live on what we'd been able to put by, which didn't go far as you can imagine, plus some help from my grown children, and whatever I could earn myself from sewing...."

The story went on and the doctor listened. Perhaps he was bored, for his eyes would stray to the ceiling at times, come to rest on me for a moment or two, unsmiling, then turn away again. He'd spoken to me only once, at the beginning of the consultation. "How old are you, little girl?" he'd asked. "Twelve? You don't look it. More like ten, I'd say." And he'd said to Maman sternly, "You should have brought this child to me six months ago."

Now he was looking at me unamiably, one would say. What an absurd idea of Maman's to have me seen by the most expensive doctor in the city!

Now she came to the most painful details, which I couldn't hear without wanting to hide my face in my hands: the mending and alterations she'd sit down to at night after her normal day was over, and which brought in quite a bit of money, she said with curious emphasis, as if the doctor might have household mending jobs to pass along to her in return for his services.

There were times when I really didn't understand Maman. This proudest of women would spend nights on end making dresses for her daughters that were as beautiful as any worn by the daughters of the city's richest and most important figures, and find money Lord knows where for our piano lessons. This most stoical of women, too, never in my hearing admitted to the least physical pain, nor even, at a later time, to the terrible hurt of loneliness. Yet the moment the health, well-being, or future of her children might have been in jeopardy, she could easily have become a street-corner beggar.

Finally, when he could stand no more of her story, which was perhaps much like many others he'd heard in this very place, the doctor raised his hands to silence her.

"Please, Madame, please.... If you can't pay me my fee all at once, then do it bit by bit, as you're able to."

Then she unwound a little.

The moment a monetary obligation – however large – could be broken up and settled in small instalments, she felt she had it beaten. After all, she'd been doing this for years, she'd been trained to it: so much this month for the sewing machine (though sometimes when she was feeling low she'd admit that the machine would probably wear out before it belonged to us); so much for the silverware (as I recall this was only fifty cents every fortnight, but we almost never had it when the salesman came to collect); so much for the ice-box. Having understood that my operation could be fitted into this category, she was immediately soothed and turned to me with a look that seemed to say, "There, you see? We'll manage this too." In her relief, her face even showed a gentle little smile, which included both the doctor and me and made her look almost happy for all her distress. She was like a fine, full-flowing river whose bed is strewn from beginning to end with obstacles – boulders, rocks, and reefs – amid which she'd keep flowing, around them, over them, or wishful-thinking them away. And in the brief spells between obstacles, before the next turbulence caught her, you could hear her calm-water song.

"Well, Doctor, in that case please be assured that I'll manage to pay you...."

The doctor stood up, cutting short her promises. We stood up too. Then she remembered.

"When will the operation be? In a few weeks?"

"What can you be thinking of, Madame! I'm going to telephone the hospital immediately. I want her admitted this evening. Tomorrow at the latest."

"Oh, tomorrow, please!" Maman begged.

With the business end of it put in order – or put off – she could at last think of her concern for me and her own anxiety on other counts. She began to plead for more time. Time to make me some clothing suitable for the hospital. Time to get my father used to the idea of the operation. And, who knows, perhaps even to work things out without it, if she was granted enough time.

"We've already waited far too long," snapped the doctor. "We're dealing with a serious crisis that could lead to a ruptured appendix. I'll operate on your child the day after tomorrow at the latest."

WE LEFT. Which little tree-shaded street we came out on, I really don't know. I do remember the day was one of the loveliest that summer can bring – gentle and filled with a breeze that caresses your face. On a day like this it seemed odd to be so taken up with making ends meet, with our terror of hospitals, and our anxiety about what Papa was going to say. Where we should have been, we agreed, was in the country somewhere, sitting on the grass under a tree, having a picnic or just looking at the sky and daydreaming. But with perfectly healthy bodies.

Maman took my hand and asked if I wasn't too tired. "Because," she said, "if you feel strong enough I'd like to walk a bit." We were in an area of small streets where we'd have had to walk farther to find a streetcar than if we went straight home. She must have been really preoccupied not to have considered this. "I'd like to have time," she said, "to think over how I'm going to tell your father."

I tried to talk her into not telling him at all. I told her I was better, that it didn't hurt any more, anywhere. And it was true. Anxiety had galvanized me, borrowed strength for the moment from goodness knows where. There was nothing new about a reaction like that for me, either. A toothache that had kept me awake all night would promptly disappear when I was taken to the dentist. Maman therefore paid no attention to what I was saying. She continued her line of thought.

12

"He's always had a horror of debts, even when he was earning enough to support us, so you can imagine how they terrify him now. Still, when you can pay a bit each month debts aren't the end of the world, it seems to me."

I must have taken after my father on that point because they terrified me too. I'd made up my mind.

"I don't want the operation," I declared. "We can't afford it. And Papa will be against it."

Maman stopped abruptly and shook me gently by the shoulders.

"Don't you ever say such a thing! Your father won't be against it. All I have to do is make him see that this debt's no worse than any other. But it's a tight spot we're in. Don't take away my courage," she begged, "not just when I need it most to get us out of this."

"But we're always in a tight spot," I reminded her.

To my surprise she began to chuckle, as if reviewing all her feats of ingenuity from a distance.

"We've got out of lots of tight spots before."

"It wasn't the same," I insisted, and I couldn't resist a conspiratorial smile.

We'd turned the corner of one quiet little street and were walking down another, which was lined like the first with trees whose leaves we could hear rustling gently despite our preoccupation. One lovely thing about our life was that Nature hardly ever failed to leave a benign mark on us throughout our trials and tribulations. Or perhaps it was because we kept looking to Nature for consolation that she always granted it.

Then, as though talking to herself, Maman astonished me with a sudden admission of defeat.

"Yes, it's true, things have been going hard with us for ages. We'd probably have to go a long way back to find out how it all started. It's a long story."

Stories were so dear to my heart, even in the depths of misery, that I was all ears.

"Tell me," I begged.

She gave me a wry smile which said: it's time I did, here goes.

Then, despite our troubles of the present, a tale of woes from the past began to come forth in snatches, stirred up no doubt by the scene in the doctor's office – at least, that's the way it seemed to me. For suddenly, there in that peaceful street, we were joined by a host of kith and kin, all beset with troubles, and all long dead, yet still living in us. As I listened to Maman, I had the curious impression that our predicament of the moment had summoned hundreds of others, and that all of them were walking with us along the deserted street, they perhaps consoled to find we still cared about them, though they were long gone, and we to find we weren't alone.

"It all started," recounted Maman, "when the English stole our land – the farms we had back there in our first home, when we had one – because they saw how good it was there in the land of Evangeline. So they could get those rich farms for themselves, they rounded us up, tricked us, put us on leaky ships, then took us far away and left us in places we'd never seen before."

"We were Acadians?"

Perhaps she'd already told me the story and I hadn't remembered. Or perhaps I hadn't been ready to listen to awful things like that and hadn't paid much attention.

"That's how our troubles began, a very long time ago," she said. "I don't know the whole story. Only bits, handed down from one generation to another."

"Where were they taken to, Maman?"

"Oh, here and there in America. They didn't even know the language where they ended up. They had to get along however they could. With great difficulty, one group managed to get back together in Connecticut. They used to work in factories, in the bush, and on the railways, wherever there was hard work to be done cheap. But they looked out for each other, and were a comfort to each other in their homesickness."

This was the point in Maman's story at which I began to worry about the notion of home, about what exactly it meant, collectively speaking. In any event, I caught her off-base by asking her point blank if we had a home.

"Why, yes," she replied. Then as soon as she'd said it she didn't seem so sure herself, and she put a hand on my forehead and said, "You haven't got a fever, have you?"

I protested that I hadn't, then persisted in wanting to know what had happened to our people in Connecticut.

"It's a sad old tale and this isn't the moment to make me tell

14

it," she sighed. "I'm discouraged enough as it is. I've got to pack your things for the hospital...." Then with a little groan, "the hospital," she said again, and quickly assured me I'd be all right there..., and then she was back with our people in Connecticut. "In those days," she said, "there were priests called colonizers, whose whole lives you'd swear depended on finding lost flocks and bringing home as many sheep as possible. One of them came to us in Connecticut."

She'd begun to say "we" when she talked of our distant fore-fathers, and it gave me a funny warm feeling.

"In our little church there he preached to us in French. And he told us we'd be welcomed with open arms in Quebec and that land would be granted in a fertile township not far from Joliette, if we wanted to come back."

"So Quebec was our home?"

"Yes and no," said Maman. "It's pretty hard to explain." Then she continued, "There was a split among us. Some said, 'We'll make a home here. We're already half American. Our children will speak English. It's only common sense. If we move around all our lives we'll never get anywhere.' But others were all for giving the Quebec adventure a try. 'They're our brothers up there,' they said. 'We speak the same language. We have the same faith. Let's go and put ourselves in their hands.' "

"So what did they decide?"

"My, how this story's got you interested all of a sudden!" she exclaimed, then continued, "Well, some stayed, so we ought to have some distant cousins in Connecticut, and some came and settled in the lovely, fertile parish of St-Jacques-l'Achigan."

At that point we saw a bench at a street corner under a rustling tree, and Maman said, "Let's sit down for a bit so you can rest." And the gently stirring leaves whispered to us of respite and a moment of cheer in the lives of the exiles.

"You've still got no pain?" Maman asked.

I shook my head, and it was true that I felt none – only the pain in my ancestors' hearts.

"Were our people happy in St-Jacques-l'Achigan?"

"Yes and no," she said again. "They had lots of children. All our relatives brought up big families. Our priests used to tell us it was the price of winning back our place in the sun. In St-Jacques-l'Achigan they were soon pretty cramped for room. Not far north there was a line of barren hills, where the land was poor and full of rocks and all spiky with dark evergreens. But that's where your grandfather Elie and grandmother Emilie went to settle. Nobody on earth ever worked harder than those two," she said with a faraway look, as though still suffering herself from their long, hard labours. "They cleared the trees, they dug thousands of stones from the ground, built fences with some and put the rest in piles, and they planted several fields of oats and buckwheat. They soon replaced their first cabin with the house I was born in, the one you've seen in the album. Your grandfather was good with his hands and it was a fine house. We ate buckwheat cakes more often than white bread, but I think I was a happy little girl in that house."

I heaved a sigh of contentment, I was so glad Maman had been a happy little girl before her troubles began. I wanted to know what had made her happy, and she replied that she didn't remember but she thought children were generally happy because it didn't take much to make them so. Then she felt sorry for me because I was looking at her and wanting to cry, though she'd got me wrong and didn't know it was for her I wanted to cry. She stroked my brow and told me I was going to get better, and then I'd be back at my games and I'd be happy again.

"If you were happy at St-Alphonse-de-Rodriguez, why did you ever leave?" I wanted to know.

"Maybe wandering was in our blood, we'd moved around so much," she replied. "Though nowadays nobody wants to stay put once and for all more than I do. Your grandfather Elie was an adventurous soul. He felt he was too hemmed in by those barren hills and wouldn't be able to settle his sons around him. Then another of those colonizing priests came our way, this time to tell us wonderful things about Manitoba and how we'd be made to feel at home here. He talked about beautiful rich land and all the Canadian West where we should hurry to go and get established before the Scots and English, who were arriving in droves in those days. He told us the whole country from ocean to ocean belonged to us, we of French blood, because of the French explorers who'd been all over it first. Our rights to our language and our religion would be respected. The government of the new province would grant a quarter-section to each family head and each of his male children who'd turned eighteen. It was tempting for people like us. Your grandfather was all excited. You're like him, the way your imagination can run away with you," she said, stroking my cheek, then she went on, "Your grandmother was the only one against it. But in the end she gave in, and there we were on the move again. You know the rest of the story, I've told it to you a hundred times. They were granted land in the Pembina Mountain settlements."

"And they could take it easy then?"

"Oh, my heavens, they were a long way from taking it easy. They had to start all over again. Your grandfather built the new house exactly like the one at St-Alphonse, your grandmother made all new furniture, the cupboards, the dough-box...."

"And the settle-bed," I put in, remembering.

"When you were little and we went to visit, you'd cry if we wouldn't let you spend the night in the settle-bed.... I always wondered why you so loved sleeping in that thing. It's like a coffin!"

I think I remember feeling totally safe there, as though the hands that had made the rustic old piece held the power to keep away all danger.

"After a few years everything could have been wonderful at St-Léon," said Maman, "because the land was ours. Counting the boys' land, we had a square mile in all. Grandmother used to grow the same flowers in her garden that she'd had in Quebec, the only language we heard spoken around us was the one we knew, and at last we were almost prosperous, and then the Manitoba government turned against us. It passed that dreadful law forbidding French to be taught in our schools. We were trapped, far away from our second home. We couldn't afford to leave, and besides, where would we have gone?"

"So we were without a home again?"

"We still had our land, our customs, our houses...and our language, which we weren't ready to have taken away from us. But that's what ruined us too — that long struggle, and all the money we had to spend to keep our schools. Have you rested enough?" she asked. "We should go. Your father will be worried not to see us back by now."

When the leaves parted they showed us a patch of high, clear blue sky. We sat watching it side by side, and it made us smile. And Maman continued.

"Your father, now, it was the terrible poverty of his people near Beaumont that drove him away. He had to start working when he was a young child and soon went to the States, like so many of us that Quebec couldn't support. He worked at everything under the sun, but all the time he read and studied, and prepared to do something important when he came back to his country. He ended up in Manitoba. Like the colonizing priest of the old days, when I met him at St-Léon he believed that the whole of the West would be dotted with little colonies, and at least half French from sea to sea. Then he got to know Laurier, who was to become prime minister soon after, and who asked him to work for his election. From that point on your father gave his life to that man, he had so much faith and confidence in him. When Laurier was prime minister and wouldn't take sides in the Manitoba French issue because it was a provincial matter, he kept on believing in him. 'He has his reasons,' he used to say. Religious soul that he was, what really hurt him was hearing an anathema pronounced on Laurier's supporters from the pulpit, and Laurier declared a traitor because of the language quarrel. In the end his political loyalty cost him his job as settlement officer, because just before he reached retirement age he lost it. It was the ruin of us, and I've reasons to suspect it was the doing of our own people, our Manitoba French. You know, perhaps the saddest part of our story is that we still aren't united after all we've been through."

Then she looked at the ground by her feet and spoke without raising her eyes.

"Now perhaps you can begin to understand why I talked about those things to the doctor. I didn't like doing it, I can tell you."

I felt so bad for her, for my father, for all those people we'd been talking about, I couldn't have replied if I'd known how. When she asked me again if we hadn't better get along home and I stood up to follow her, we might have been taking our places in the interminable exodus. Where would we get to by the end of the end?

Suddenly, without any connective, she said, "When I met him your father wasn't young any more, but he had lots of energy and great ideals, a very attractive man, and full of fun when the mood was on him."

Then I remembered that when we were in his consulting room the doctor had asked her, "How old were you when she was born?" and Maman had seemed embarrassed. As though she wasn't sure, she'd answered, "Forty...forty-two, or -three."

"And your husband?"

"Fifty-nine, Doctor."

As if in answer to my unspoken question, she now assured me, "Your father was proud and happy when you came into the world.... They say," she continued, "that the children of older parents are frail and have delicate health, but it seems they're the most gifted too."

At this point we couldn't have been far from the cathedral, because she had a suggestion: "Shall we go in on the way and pray for everything to go right?"

After the daylight, the high-vaulted nave seemed very dark. It seemed to be lit only by the votive candles on stands at the back of the church.

Maman took me almost to the front pews, near the choir. This was where we used to come and pray when we were in desperate need of help, as if here we'd have more chance of being seen and heard. We knelt down. I prayed, I suppose, but most of all I watched Maman pray. I've since seen a few, a very few others pray as she prayed that day, but this was the first time, and my heart ached to see it. She stayed totally motionless, not a muscle moving, yet everything was taut, her face, her eyes, her lips, even her hands as she held them in front of her in suppliant attitude. It was then, I believe I remember correctly, that I resolved in the depths of my soul to make good for her. Or rather, it was then that my resolution must have taken shape from all my impotence and weakness.

When we came out, the brightness of the daylight hurt our eyes, and our souls too. I was beginning to drag, so Maman slowed her step, which normally was so brisk in those days. She scolded herself for having kept me talking so long, for having made me walk a few steps more to get to the church. I was near the end of my strength but my head was still full of my little plan to make good for her. I'd make good for my father, too, and my Beaumont

19

relatives and my St-Jacques-l'Achigan relatives and my Connecticut ancestors before them. I was far away in the past discovering the hardship of my forebears, and from this I drew the will to place one foot after the other.

BUT IN the hospital, behind a screen which a nun had set in place, when the old priest sat near me and began to talk about life, death, and eternity, I changed my mind. It would be better, I thought, if I died and spared my parents further expense than if I lived, perhaps, only perhaps, to make good for them some day, which at that point looked pretty difficult.

The old missionary was temporarily in the city, having come perhaps from the North. Sometimes I think fate must have had a hand in sending him to me. He talked to me softly, enveloping me with a calm, kindly gaze, his eyes shining from a bearded face in the nightlight's dim incandescence. He talked to me about death without stripping it of solemnity and seriousness, as he might have done since I was a child, and it's perhaps because I heard this old man speak of it with dignity and candour when I was very young that death has lost much of its power of terror over me. He told me that I would almost certainly get better, but that all would happen as God wished it. Tomorrow, when they put me to sleep, I would be like a little bird that the Lord held in His hand. Either He would release me so I could go back to playing and laughing and having fun with other children, or else He would keep me in His mysterious abode.

I'd discovered what I wanted; I asked the old priest to explain what that mysterious abode was like. Today I still bless Heaven for having put someone near me who made no pretence of understanding the inexplicable, but just imagined it.

"Oh, my child," he said, "if only we knew, eh? But then making the long journey wouldn't be worth much, and not very interesting either, don't you think? All I can foresee or imagine myself is that our lives will open into infinity, and all of us want that, I think."

Ah, just to hear him talk about it made me want it myself. I asked him whether we were still responsible for our debts in infinity.

What kind of debts, he wanted to know. Dishonourable debts, which you take on deliberately knowing perfectly well you'll never be able to repay them? Or poor people's debts, which they have hanging over them because they really can't do otherwise?

I had trouble finding an answer. It seemed to me that our debts didn't fit cleanly into either category, and were perhaps a bit of both.

He stroked my forehead gently and told me not to worry about it. He told me to rest in the Lord and to put all my problems in His hands. I think I'd always known that when you came down to it there was no one else to help us, but it seemed to me, too, that He wasn't doing it. How could that be? Was it because we were too far away from Him, or He from us? I began to imagine that when I arrived in the abode of the Most High, as He was called, I'd be close enough to tell our whole story right into His ear. Then He'd see that you had to take Maman with a grain of salt. How could she pay five dollars a month towards my operation when she already had three to pay for the sewing machine, four for my piano lessons, which she refused flatly to give up, plus arrears at the grocer's, the coal merchant's, and practically all the other tradesmen? Besides, she'd just promised me a new coat as a reward for getting better – made out of an old one, it's true, but she was going to give it an astrakhan collar, bought from one of the city's better furriers. If anything was keeping me a mite attached to life it was that coat, and my curiosity to see how Maman was going to manage it as well as everything else.

On the other hand, I still wanted to quit life so I'd stop being an expense to Maman, and that was the substance of what I expected to be my final prayer, which I think really expressed a desire to escape. For thinking about my death – oddly but on the other hand perhaps quite logically – had given me a glimpse of what life might hold for me, and it had frightened me. In order to make good for Maman, I realized that once I was back at school I'd have to work twice as hard, always come first in French and English and all the other subjects, win medals and other kinds of prizes, and keep bringing her trophies. Then I couldn't see anything clear-cut and identifiable before me beyond the end of my studies, only a road leading upward, seemingly deserted, going off into some desolate distance beneath a cloudy sky. My courage failed me.

I'd always loved prairie roads with a passion. They allowed you to see far ahead and all around because everything was flat; the road of my future as I saw it that night was nothing but steep hills and twists and turns that all disappeared in darkness and never allowed me to look ahead and see where I was going. At a later time, I was to stand one day on a slight rise in the prairie and look out along a little dirt road bathed in sunlight, which seemed to me to have a mysterious connection with my life, buoying me up with a rush of elation. But in the hospital that time, the road of my life – or of any life, perhaps – looked like a road to nowhere, and the terror of it remained with me for many years.

A nun came and gave me a sedative. Soon I felt almost happy, in a waiting state that no longer rattled my nerves. I would go to sleep and wake up in what the old priest called the wonderful abode. The next morning I was in the same tranquil state when they wheeled me into the operating room. I wondered only if God came out to meet people who were dying, or whether He waited for them without budging from His doorstep. Just one step towards them would be reassuring, I thought. When Maman was expecting some-one she really loved, she'd watch at the living-room window or sometimes on the veranda, and when they appeared at the end of the street she'd run down the steps and often to the gate. You'd be hugged tight against her breast. You'd hear another heart joy-fully beating against yours. You'd be home at last. Had I known that happiness? Or had I only imagined it?

"Breathe deeply, dear," said a strange voice, and I felt myself dissolve.

I CAN'T DENY it was disappointing at first to open my eyes and find I was still of this world. And how very much the world I knew too well became immediately apparent. Beside me there stood a man in white, whom I saw dimly owing to the continuing effects of the anaesthetic. He was talking to me and his voice seemed to come from a great way off.

"I was the one who put you to sleep, dear," he was saying. "When your mother comes, will you give her this? It's my bill. Anaesthesia's separate."

How can anaesthesia be separate? Nobody told us that. I was sure for a minute I'd said it aloud. In fact, I didn't have the strength to bring the words to my lips, and they stayed inside, resting heavily on my stomach.

Then I noticed he'd slipped a piece of paper between my fingers.

"Don't forget, dear. Anaesthesia's separate, and generally that's what you pay first."

I nodded and groped for somewhere to hide, but where can you hide when you've been sent back to Earth by the Lord Himself after being an inch from His doorstep? Someone came and gave me an ice-cube to suck, then Maman arrived, and I knew I was glad to be still of this world after all. The minute our eyes met, all our cares and troubles were swept away in an outpouring of happiness at being reunited. But when she bent over me, her face very close to mine, I could see the weariness of her life, as if through a magnifying glass, the scars of adding and subtracting, the lines left by evenings of mending and alterations, and it was more than I could bear. I closed my eyes and tried to go back to where there were no expenses, costs, or fees. Alas, I remembered the slip left by the anaesthetist and handed it to her.

She unfolded it, saying, "I'd have thought he could have waited a bit...," then fell silent, with a familiar crease in her forehead.

"Is it much?" I asked, full of apprehension.

She forced a smile.

"No, it's not too bad." Then she tucked the bill away in her handbag.

In a cheerful voice, sitting close to me, she began at once to tell me the good news.

"Listen to this, now. Yesterday, as I was leaving the hospital, who d'you think I met? Madame Bérubé, whose daughter's getting married next month. She needs a dress for the wedding and so does her sister-in-law. So there I am with two big orders, just because I went out by one door rather than another, which God probably put me up to. He gets a finger in the pie sometimes, you know."

I wasn't so sure of that since He'd turned me back from His paradise. Besides, if Maman had got those orders, it was probably more because she was going to do them cheap. But today I didn't have the strength to stand up to her.

"The anaesthetist's bill's going to put a dent in my order before it's even started," she said, then seemed to find it funny that our money was always spent before it was earned.

Out of a grocery bag she took three oranges. She must have spent ages choosing them because it seemed to me I'd never seen oranges rounder, more flawless, or more perfectly matched.

"You bought them at Mr. Trossi's!" I declared, knowing at once, and my thoughts smiled with me in my affection for the poor immigrant who always treated me like a princess whenever Maman sent me to his shop to buy *à la graine*, as we used to say – one or two of this or that.

A little sadly, she then admitted she'd only bought two, Mr. Trossi having added the third as a present from him to "the little sick girl who has to get better quick if she wants to do her Italian friend a favour." I must have shown more pleasure over the Italian's present than hers, because she seemed a bit jealous, observing that it was curious I should be so fond of someone we really hardly knew.

But that day she had no time to spare for either joy or resentment. She barely seemed to have arrived when she was telling me she'd have to leave and begin her sewing if she was going to finish her order in time and get paid the money we needed so badly. All the same, she delayed going a few moments, long enough to arrange my pillows and give me some encouragement: the doctor had said I'd soon be on my feet and everything would be fine. She asked me several times if I was suffering and I shook my head, and it was partly true; throughout the illness which left such an indelible mark on my life, search my memory as I may, I can recall no trace of physical pain, perhaps because one easily forgets that kind of pain. But I do remember having lived what seemed years in those few days.

Finally Maman fled, so to speak. Perhaps because I hadn't seen her from behind for so long, or else because my illness had given me eyes to see with, her silhouette seemed old, quite different from the one I thought I knew, almost like Grandmother's not long before she died. I couldn't stand it and found voice to call her back. At my feeble call she stopped, hesitated, long enough to compose herself, I think, then turned and came back to me.

"Is there something you want?"

I don't know what I'd had in mind to say to her, but when I saw traces of the distress she hadn't quite had time to banish from her face, I thought of committing myself to the one promise I was sure would bring back her courage. So I announced that at school from then on I'd always come first in my class...though it was a promise I was far from believing I would keep.

She leaned over me and stroked my hair, and her face, which a moment before had looked so drawn, was now radiant. In her brown eyes shone the pride I so loved to see there.

"If you come first," she promised in return, "you won't only have a new coat in the fall; I'll make you a lovely little skirt, too... the kind you like, a flared one...so full it'll fly...."

Thereupon I could picture the undulations of the light-as-gossamer skirt, I could see it fly up around me as I spun on my heel, my eyes were filled with the graceful image. And the other children in the ward looked on, blind or envious, not understanding how rich we were, Maman and I, for all our poverty.

III

TOWARDS THE END of the day, a time he found soothing, when the light was fading and the outlines of things were beginning to blur, wavering as they do in dreams perhaps, and life seemed less difficult, my father appeared.

He stopped at the door, looked at each of the little girls in the four corners of the hospital ward in turn, then slowly came over to me. For a long moment he stood still and silent by my bedside, looking forlorn.

Yet he couldn't have known that the night before last I'd been hiding outside near the door to the summer kitchen, a kind of small building backed against the house, where my father loved to sit alone on warm evenings. Maman had joined him there and I'd heard them talking about me. Under the low branches of the gooseberry bush, I held my breath the better to hear them.

"What did he say?" my father asked.

"It's an operation, Léon," my mother answered.

I'd noticed that when things were bad they were quite likely to address each other by name, as though a full measure of identity was appropriate to such solemn moments.

There were some murmured words that I missed, but I grasped the subject and it was what I'd expected; such a familiar subject, yet it never failed to deal me a blow.

"How much is it, Mélina? What's he asking?"

I heard in the tone of her voice that Maman was trying to avoid alarming my father.

"He says he'll give us a good price, Léon."

"A good price! What's he mean by 'good'?"

In the end, of course, Maman had to state the figure. Something like a short groan from my father came to my ears.

I could see him without needing to be there. He'd be sitting in the faint light of the little old stove Maman kept there for cooking on in summer if the day was torrid, which helped keep the main house cool. For some time now she'd hardly ever used this room, saying at first that there was always something missing when she needed it, and finally that the inconveniences of preparing meals there outweighed the possible advantages. My father was practically the only one to set foot in it any more and remained strangely attached to the place. Often in the evening we'd go looking for him all over and then find him there, sitting quietly in the darkness with the door open to the back yard, to the gentle rustlings of night. Though it was joined to the main house by a door, this squat little structure was quite different, rather rustic, really a kind of shack which seemed to us like the country or even a cabin in the wilds, with its rough cupboards and exposed beams in the ceiling. Perhaps it gave my father the same feeling he'd had for the crude shelters in settlement areas in his days of arduous travels. In any event, he could stay there for hours, sitting on a little low chair near the stove, which he'd keep just barely lit.

When Maman had joined him she'd been careful not to put on a light, so they weren't really able to see each other as they talked quietly.

"A hundred dollars, Mélina! How are we going to do it?"

Maman's voice was reassuring.

"We'll find it, Léon. Money can always be found. I won't say all at once, but little by little."

Papa seemed to take some courage from this and made a suggestion.

"Maybe I could sell our garden vegetables to the neighbours and not just give them away. That's what you've always told me I should do, Mélina, though I couldn't ever bring myself to...."

Apparently they finally agreed to ask modest prices for the produce of Papa's long summer labours, those beautiful vegetables he'd been so happy to distribute as presents to almost everyone around us.

And now he was standing by my bedside with an anxious look on his face, perhaps not knowing how to talk to children any more. He seemed so old I thought I'd never find the right words to reach him. Yet when I was little I'd loved to make up games to play with old people.

I glanced at him in puzzlement. How old was he then? Seventy-one...seventy-two? When he'd fathered me he was already old. Did he sometimes think of this with a kind of regret and, could it be, a certain embarrassment? Was that what stopped him from opening his heart when he talked to me? I've never known. We never revealed any of our deep feelings to one another, he and I – like most human beings living in close proximity, I imagine.

Yet according to what I've been told, when I came into the world he was still full of energy if not in robust health, and sure of the usefulness of his life and his work. I often heard that he was committed in those days to the idea that French Canadians should come in great numbers to the West, despite all the difficulties, in order to ensure the happy balance between French and English that is so assiduously sought today. He'd just founded one of his most impressive settlements, Dollard in Saskatchewan, composed almost entirely of compatriots from the county of Dorchester in Quebec, where he was born, and the rest repatriated from the United States. I was the only one of his children who hadn't known him as a man of great plans, fine accomplishments, and profound hopes which gave life to his clear blue eyes. Or at least, I was so young I could only have had the most tenuous, most shadowy memories of him while he was still that way.

Drowsy with sedative, I dozed off briefly as he stood beside me, or else I had a dream while only half asleep. I thought I was back in the days before I began to be frightened by the aura of tragedy surrounding him. I was still very small. I used to run to him quite happily, not so he'd pick me up and cuddle me, which little children love so much, but just to be near him, sharing a strange kind of solemnity. I think this pleased him. Being in his sixties, he could have felt it unbefitting his advanced age, I suppose, to give me the cuddling that most fathers lavish on their very young children. And yet I seem to recall he'd readily take his grandsons into his arms, my sister Anna's children, the eldest exactly my age, whereas with me all he'd ever do was put his hand on my head and stroke my hair. But in the kind of dream I was drifting in, one day when I had run to him as he was working in the garden, he'd put down his hoe, picked me up and sat me in the wheelbarrow, then pushed me several times round the house, with me clutching my fat grey cat to my chest. The strange, slow ride had shown me several totally new things about a landscape I knew better than anything else in the world. I was so enthralled I begged for "More!" after the third turn, and off we went again, my old father puffing a bit harder than before. That day being so bright a flower amid all the dark ones, the reawakening of the memory must have caused me more pain than happiness, for I couldn't hold back a moan.

With a distraught look, my father asked at once if I was suffering that much. I told him no, all I felt was a little burning where they'd opened me up.

Then he urged me to eat well as soon as I could so I'd soon get my strength back, and reminded me I'd have to avoid too-vigorous games for a time. And he even dared report to me part of what the doctor had told him, that I'd be weak for quite some time, and that I'd have to look after my health because it would always be fragile.

I was a little more awake now and turned my head towards him, trying to give him a reassuring smile. I saw then that he was holding three roses. They were the kind we used to call "cemetery roses" because he'd bought some roots to plant on the graves of the two little girls named Agnès in our family plot, and they'd flowered so successfully that he'd taken some cuttings to plant around the house. Maman didn't like them and neither did I. Nobody in our house liked them, in fact, except my father. What did we have against them? Probably the fact that they came from the cemetery, but not only that. They weren't really very pretty. They had a lot of small petals which curled too tightly against each other, they faded as soon as they bloomed, and became blotched for no reason, a drop of rain or a brisker wind than usual. They really didn't have anything to recommend them except their smell, and even that was sickly sweet and reminded us of flowers at funerals.

None the less, to me that day, those roses in my father's hand were beautiful. Perhaps I realized he must have chosen them with as much care as Maman had her oranges. Or else I'd learned how to see at last. I was sorry now I'd never helped him care for them. They didn't need much, I remembered, only the soapy water poured over them after you'd washed your hands, which had an insecticidal effect. I reflected that I'd hardly ever bothered to do so, either because I forgot or because I didn't want to put myself out for flowers which to my mind didn't deserve it. But at the moment I was moved by their eagerness to live despite our indifference, and I promised Papa I really would try to collect soapy water for them in the future.

"It doesn't take much effort," he replied, "and the soap that's so dear gets used twice that way."

I remembered then that as the days went by I'd seen him being careful not to waste things, though he was never mean about it, and working hard to acquire skills that weren't entirely natural to him, like gardening. The thought crossed my mind that now, perhaps more than when he was admired, he was showing nobility. Having fallen low, his hopes fled, he'd been devoting himself to such modest endeavour as might still be useful. Was fever making me ten times more perceptive that day about people and things? Or was the sedative blunting my natural heartache, allowing me to see more clearly than usual? With his callused hands, his lined face, and his stooped back, my father seemed to have a courage that even yesterday I'd been incapable of seeing. I'd have liked to tell him so but didn't know how.

When he'd put the three roses in my water glass, their heads already drooping a little, he walked slowly away, looking rather like those tired roses, I thought. I buried my face in my pillow, trying to hide from the pain so it wouldn't ever find me again.

IV

WHY IS IT that we who were so often unhappy could also be so happy? That's what astonishes me most, even today. Just as I also find the coming of happiness more surprising than the coming of sorrow, not because it's more unusual but perhaps because it's less easily explained.

Happiness came to us like the wind, from nothing and from everything. Summer was a festival in itself for us. When I was a child I didn't know anyone who cherished summer as we did. Whatever worries or sorrows Maman had, as soon as summer came she'd drop everything to gather up the geraniums and fuchsias that had spent the winter on the windowsills and plant them in the earth around the house. We'd soon see the pale, sickly things return to health. Papa used to plant a big vacant lot not far from our house, having obtained permission from the municipal council to cultivate it until it was sold, which couldn't have happened for a long time because I seem to remember our always having that big, beautiful vegetable garden. And summer repaid our efforts. Our fruit trees gave us sweet-smelling flowers and then tart little apples from which Maman made an exquisite jelly, and also cherries and small blue plums. Our yard behind the house was surrounded by a wooden fence and was always full of robins and sparrows, which sang so loudly and cheerfully we couldn't help hearing them, even when our troubles were many. It wasn't a very big yard but it bordered a lane which in turn bordered an unsubdivided meadow, so that all the open space behind the house looked just like a glimpse of green prairie. My father would sit in the half-darkness by the open door of the little summer kitchen and contemplate it endlessly. And sometimes you could see a red glow in the sky between two street corners beyond, mysteriously deepening the narrow cleft

31

between the houses and making it seem to reach into a kind of limitless space, right in the middle of the city. If we ever went to talk to Papa at that hour as he sat at his observation post, there was a strange and surprising peacefulness in his voice. It was as if we'd brought him back from some infinite distance, from his youthful excursions in the wilds, perhaps.

But it was the summer holidays above all that used to bring us the most intense happiness. We'd set off, Maman and children and later just Maman and I together, for Pembina Mountain. Papa would stay behind to watch the house, quite happy to have it to himself, I think, to be free to wander from room to room, engrossed in the reveries often encouraged by solitude. Then, probably, those dreams that still dared stir his heart seemed less surely doomed.

I think now I can see what it was that made us the way we were, and in a sense made things so hard for us. Just as we were rich although poor, we were unfortunate people with a flair for happiness.

In the time I remember best, we used to spend the summer holidays with my uncle Excide, the youngest of the Landry sons.

We used to take the train at the domed CN station, which we called *le dépôt*, though I don't know why. In no time we'd reach the flat land around Winnipeg. From above, the train must have looked like some black caterpillar crawling into eternity beneath the immense prairie sky. I loved the open prairie; I've always been fascinated by it. For all its reticence, it's always had more to say to me than any other landscape. But on these train trips to the settlement area called Pembina Mountain, the centre of attraction to which all our thoughts turned was the mountain itself. About an hour out of Winnipeg, shadowy hills would begin to show against the pale blue sky. A little later the train would enter those hills so gradually that we wouldn't notice it. Only when we were in the middle of them would we realize we were in broken and even mountainous country, or so it seemed to us, who were so used to flatness. We'd come to a place of no importance called Babcock. The train would stop for a minute or two, and I still wonder why, for as I recall there was nothing there except a shack and an abandoned quarry. But also the mountain. Just an elevation really, crowded against the railway line, its flanks forming rocky escarpments. To see its summit, Maman and I would crouch till we were almost kneeling, our eyes level with the bottom of the window. That way we could see all of it. It took our breath away. Such altitude! Such soaring height! On the way there, we'd talk about nothing else, Maman and I. We'd be watching for it from the moment the train left the station. Afterwards it so dominated what we remembered of the ride that it banished all other recollection. On a visit to Manitoba a few years ago, I felt an intense desire to see the mountain that had stirred my soul more, I'm sure, than the Rocky Mountains did later, or even perhaps the Alps. I found myself in a tiny out-of-the-way place closed in by heaps of quarried stone left lying about and hiding the skyline. But I could see absolutely no mountain! Finally, among the piles of stone, I did distinguish a more or less natural butte.

I'm still not sure who had the better vision, the impassioned child with her nose pressed against the train window, or the seasoned traveller who had to have a real mountain before her eyes to believe in it.

After Babcock we'd leave the little hills almost immediately. Now another kind of prairie unfolded before us, rolling towards infinity in wide, flowing undulations. We'd arrive at the village of Somerset. On one of these trips it was here that I heard the jangle of a handbell being rung on the doorstep of the hotel next to the station, signalling that the noonday meal was about to be served. This was a detail I used in *Enchanted Summer*. The Somerset of those days has become very dim in my mind, but if I retained nothing else, this would be enough to make me remember it with affection.

My uncle Excide with his big black moustache would be waiting for us, pacing up and down the wooden platform, as high-strung as he'd always been. He'd drive us to the farm, which wasn't much more than two miles from the village, in his little high Ford with mica windows in its canvas doors. But our hearts lightened because we were really going much, much farther than two miles, back into time past, through the generations, almost to the beginnings of our family. We were finding something from the old days still alive in the brisker air of the plateaux, here in the third of the homes our forebears had built since they began their wanderings.

This third home in fact began near the village of St-Léon, six or seven miles beyond the farm. It was there that Grandfather obtained his concession and built his house, which was exactly like

33

the one at St-Alphonse-de-Rodriguez, with a wing of the same shape but smaller and lower. Those people were amazing, I must say; they'd leave everything behind, then begin all over again to make everything just the way it had been at the other end of the earth. I've always been touched by this. It reminds me of the birds, who always build the same nest wherever they go in the vast expanses open to them.

Grandmother, who was as good at working with wood as with dough or yarns, soon turned out cupboards, hutches, and a dough-box patterned after those she remembered from years past. Their neighbours, almost all compatriots from Quebec, spoke only French; in all the years she spent in Manitoba, I doubt that Grandmother learned more than a dozen words of English, and from those she fashioned others for her own use, words like *ouaguine* (for wagon), *mitaine* (a Protestant church, from "meeting"), *bécosse* (outhouse, from "backhouse").... The neighbours' names were Lafrénière, Labossière, Rondeau, Major, Généreux, Lussier. Oddly enough, they had a parish priest from France, Théobald Bitsche, born in Nieder-Bernhaupt in the diocese of Strasbourg, and later, for the education of their daughters, a religious community from France, the Chanoinesses Régulières. Out in the country, they had a counterpart of the little country school in Quebec, called *l'école Théobald* after the parish priest, which was often the custom in Quebec. My eldest sister, Anna, attended it when she was very young, before my parents moved with their children to St-Boniface.

I came to know and love the third home of the Landrys long after those early days. I was fourteen or fifteen. Grandfather had been dead for about ten years. With the help of his sons, in a little more than a generation he'd brought a whole section under cultivation, which is to say a square mile of marvellously black earth, the wheat-growing soil of the West, which yielded prodigiously. He'd built an impressive farm with its house and barn, fine outbuildings, a well with a rim, and silos, and he must have died happy in the belief that he'd left his descendants a lasting home. After he died Grandmother went to live in the village of Somerset in a little house that her sons built for her just the way she wanted it. I knew that little house. This was the one I had more or less in mind when I wrote "My Almighty Grandmother" in *The Road past Altamont*. It too was in the French-Canadian style, once again

34

perpetuating the memory of the beloved house in St-Alphonse which Grandmother had left with such regret, but which had never really been left behind, since it was reborn twice on faraway soil. As I recall, it had a mansard roof and a smaller, lower wing in the same style. From its chimney to the plants around it, it proclaimed Quebec very loudly in Somerset, which in those days was at least half English.

When the railway was built to pass through here rather than St-Léon, Somerset's growth was assured, to the detriment of the little French-Canadian village, which thereupon began to decline.

My grandmother lived alone until she was very old in her little Quebec house in Somerset. Immediately after her death a buyer came forward who'd had his eye on that house for some time, without wishing Grandmother's demise I should hope, but keeping himself posted nevertheless. He was an elderly retired Englishman for whom, it seems, Grandmother's house was a strong reminder of the dear old England he'd left years before. He surrounded it with honeysuckle and planted rosemary where Grandmother's dill had been and lived happily there without any other change. Thus the house that had comforted Grandmother in her homesickness gave him comfort in his. All of which made me also want to buy the house that had been such a haven. The last time I was in Manitoba I learned that Grandmother's successor had finally died. I hadn't exactly wished for his death, but I'd been waiting my turn with some impatience, since the old Englishman lived to be very old indeed.

I arrived in Somerset. I managed to find the house on my own. By now it was only a tumble-down ruin. And yet, deserted and mournful though it was, surrounded by high yellow autumn grasses and long-overgrown honeysuckle, there seemed to be some mysterious collusion between that house and nostalgic stirrings of my own which I'd never really admitted to myself. I came close to buying it. Then my cousin pointed out that it was only good for taking down and I'd have to rebuild from scratch if I really wanted a house in Somerset.

"And what would you do with a house here when you live in Quebec?" he wanted to know.

I had to give in to reason. Nevertheless, the deserted house long reproached me for having abandoned it. But more than the crumbling house I'd so wanted to buy because it touched the very heart of my most precious memories, perhaps it was the sound of the wind that voiced all those generations of longing for a home so often sought and so often lost, a gentle, wistful September wind I heard plucking at the vestiges of Grandmother's garden, one day when I passed that way.

It seems to me sometimes as if the episode of our existence in Manitoba had no more substance than dreams that blow away with the wind, and if anything's left of it, it can only be in dreams.

AT THE TIME I myself remember best, we found the spirit of my pioneer grandparents still almost intact in Uncle Excide. For all that, he'd given up the much-loved paternal house and built one to his own liking on a new farm just a few miles from Somerset. And so we began to oscillate between Somerset for reasons of business, which was done mostly in English, and St-Léon for the good of our souls. Sometimes we'd go to one and sometimes to the other, and finally we went to Somerset almost always; it was closer and really more convenient.

My uncle, who'd become a widower at a very young age, was always happy to see Maman arrive. She'd at once take the running of the house in hand, much to the relief of my cousin Léa, who at the age of fourteen had found that weighty responsibility on her shoulders. The house was spacious, pleasant, and very comfortable for the time, with a hand pump which brought water inside from a well under the summer kitchen, and central heating too. It was in the middle of a little wood, which my uncle had long sought, he'd so missed having trees over his head as at St-Alphonse. Though he'd left there when very young, only five, he'd apparently been longing ever since to have at least a grove of trees around him.

In truth, the little wood around my uncle's house played almost as important a role in my life as did the mountain at Babcock. It was probably rather sparse as woods go, composed mostly of poplars and small oaks, but for years it was the archetypal forest to me, embodying all the shadowy and magical things I used to imagine about a forest. I loved it, but I think most of all I loved the contrast it provided, always renewing the feeling of space you'd get from the open prairie beyond. When you came out of that little wood at the end of the farm road, you'd instantly feel you were entering infinity. From there the prairie stretched away as far as you could see; in one immense, rolling plain it unfolded in a series of long, fluid waves sweeping unendingly to the horizon. I've seen nothing more harmonious anywhere, except perhaps where the downs of Dorset flow down to the sea.

In that permanence in constant motion, in that tranquil yet beckoning immensity, there was a beauty that tugged at my heart like a magnet, even when I was still very young. I kept returning to that vista as if it might get away from me if I left it alone too long. I'd arrive at the end of the farm road, reach the place where the trees parted, and the vast, magnetic expanse would appear, and each time it was the world laid at my feet again. But really much more than the world, I know that now.

Eventually I discovered another road I could take to find that unaccountable excitement. A little section road bordering my uncle's farm climbed a slope to a high point from which the view across the prairie was even more breathtaking. I told no one of my discovery. I'd pretend I was going there to gather hazelnuts and wild cherries. The happiness awaiting me at the end of my walk was so mysterious I seemed to feel I'd risk losing it if I talked to anyone at all about it; perhaps even if I admitted it to myself.

I'd set off along that rutted little road. Nothing was more ordinary. It consisted only of two cart tracks with weeds growing rife between them and bushes on either side. There was no horizon, nothing but the sound of the wind imprisoned in the dense shrubbery, intoning a kind of tedium. Then all at once the revelation, the magnitude, the endless unfolding of naked earth! That little road to nowhere took me to the edge of eternity. A wave of inexplicable joy would sweep over me. Where it came from, why it was granted me, what it was made of, I don't know and I've never known.

For a long time I believed the excitement I was promised, there at the end of the little dirt road when I was sixteen, was a joy of this world, to be seized while I was alive. Now I'm not so sure. Perhaps that kind of joy awaits us elsewhere.

THOUGH we still felt at home in the high country near the sky, little by little the things that made it home were eroding, wasting away, without our really doing much about it. When we went into

Somerset we'd see how many of our people were defecting, putting up signs in English only and taking the initiative in speaking first in that language to almost everyone. The young men were going to Winnipeg, Chicago, or Vancouver; nearly all my uncle's sons settled permanently in one or another. The poles of attraction were the West and the United States. We would come back to the farm discouraged and depleted. The comforting vastness, as if suffused with dreams, would take us in hand and bring us a kind of confidence – or forgetfulness – with the sound of a gently plaintive wind. In my mind I can still hear that wind from the high plateaux, one that unfailingly seemed to soothe the pain of great but fruitless efforts.

Often I'd go alone to where my dead grandparents had felt at home. I'd learned to ride a little roan mare that I'd trained myself. I'd gallop off, crossing an old dried-up lake bed at the bottom of my uncle's farm, then skirting some other little lakes whose beds were barely wet and were ringed with tattered bulrushes – a curious landscape in the midst of the rich wheat farms – and soon reach the village of St-Léon. It was so sleepy and deserted it might have been under some grim kind of spell. The only time I ever saw it wake up and show signs of life was after high mass on Sundays. Yet when the colonists arrived in my grandparents' day it must have been bustling with life. Then progress passed it by and established its banks, its trade, and the railway in Somerset. There was no longer even a hotel in St-Léon, or a single shop or store of any consequence. Yet there stood a presbytery better suited to a city than this isolated country setting, along with the church and the convent. The three of them were so dominant you really saw nothing else. At the end of the main street, the only street in the village, I'd come to a house of considerable size but unfinished, covered in black insulating paper. It stayed that way through all the time I knew it. That house alone, better than anything else, showed the depth of despondency that must have weighed on that poor village shorn of its expectations. For St-Léon had been something of a Ville-Marie of Manitoba, destined to grow into the Montreal of the West under the guidance of stern priests with visions, I have no doubt, of human communities that would be rigorously pure.

The tarpapered house was a friendly place for me, despite all. This was where the Majors lived, the parents of Uncle Excide's dead wife whom we'd loved so much, the gentle, tender-hearted Luzina whose name I gave in affection to one of the most lovable of all the characters in my books. Luzina had died young but her old mother was still living, and everyone in the village called her "Mémère", meaning "Granny". I almost always found her making blood pudding or soap in an enormous black cauldron over a brush fire. Here, against the Manitoba sky that was so very blue, everything was black: the cauldron, the billows of smoke escaping from under it, the house, the old woman in her long skirts. I'd always supposed she had a bit of gypsy in her, but it must have been the effect of the outdoor life she loved that made it seem so, or perhaps a nomadic instinct that was rare in those days in our old people, whose hardships in early life had made them more inclined to seek all the comfort possible. She alone seemed to take pleasure – for a few months of the year at least – in living the way my grandmother probably had when she first came to St-Léon. She used to keep some of her kitchen pots hung on the outer walls of the house so they'd be at hand when the spirit moved her to take her knitting outdoors in summer. Her laundry tub was also hung up outside, and all kinds of utensils and other objects were strewn around her as if she were camping.

With her eyes reddened by the smoke, Mémère glared at me.

"Who's that riding this way like Saint Michael at the end of the world for the Last Judgement?" she demanded.

That bantering manner alone told me she'd recognized me. I didn't say a word. At last she greeted me in her characteristic way.

"Black damnation! If it isn't Elie Landry's wife Emilie Jeansonne's girl Mélina's girl! And where is it you've come from galloping hell-bent on your great black steed?"

She knew my little mare wasn't black, or damnation either, and I didn't bother to put her right, I was so entranced with her colourful language and the kind of rich earthy spirit it showed. Besides, I'd come for quite a different reason. I dismounted from my little Nell and approached the old woman.

"Tell me my fortune with your cards, Mémère Major," I begged. "Tell me what's in the future for me."

39

"What's in the future for you, my little charmer of the highways and byways, I can tell you that without cards! You're going to live, get old, and die."

That sent chills down my spine.

"No, no, my own future, Mémère!" I insisted.

She burst out laughing, sounding like a cackling hen.

"What's the matter with you young people, wanting to know what's in the future, you that's got a future. It'll come anyway, it'll come, then one day you'll turn round and it'll be gone. Serve you right, too!"

Sometimes she'd consent to peer into my open palm, her old face crackled like gumbo in a drought. I'd catch the still-bright sparkle in her old, worn eyes.

"Yes, I see," she'd say, raising my expectations, then she'd continue, "You'll travel...you'll make friends with young men...fair-haired ones...and dark-haired ones...."

I wonder what it was that made me want so much to have my future predicted by this ancient matriarch who never did anything but poke fun at me about it, unless it was the persistent rumour that she was capable of seeing everything that was going to happen...if she really wanted to...once in a while....

But in the end I was drawn to her perhaps more because of the past than the future. Mémère Major, who was so different from my tidy grandmother and just a little older, had been her friend and remembered hundreds of details from a time long before I'd known her, and I never tired of hearing her tell me about them. Tight-lipped though she was about my future, she didn't have to be asked twice to recount what had gone before me. She'd relate the story of the journey from St-Norbert by ox-cart, the clouds of mosquitoes around the tent they'd just pitched, the darkness of the prairie pierced only by the travellers' campfire, the first winter at St-Léon which six families spent under one roof, the squabbles, the kindnesses exchanged, the help from God, the devil's tricks....

There weren't many left of those Mémère Major talked about, only a few frail old relics. They made me think of survivors of a long-ago shipwreck. I used to love those poor old souls from Quebec who were living out their days here in the middle of nowhere; who, though they still spoke only their own language among themselves, had watched many of their children switch irrevocably to English, and their children's children grow up unable to communicate with their old grandmother or grandfather. They seemed so isolated, as the anchorites of Patmos seemed to me later. Their extreme fragility made me cherish them; they were like leaves held just barely to a branch, which the first little shake will carry away. I realize now that what drew me to them was their past, which would soon be vanishing with them. Their gentleness and resignation have stayed as indelibly in my heart as the intense blue of the sky above their pensive faces, and the wind lamenting round them, recounting tales of wasted lives, it seemed to me. So many times they'd been brought to the middle of nowhere, there to disappear without a sound and almost without a trace.

I'D COME BACK from those trips to St-Léon wrapped in thought and bearing affectionate messages as if from a much-loved distant country. We were too close to write letters and too far away to see each other very often. My uncle was glad to have the fresh news I'd bring back to him. Soon, though, he began to look at me and frown. The idea of a girl in pants riding through the pious little village scandalized him. He said as much to Maman. She, whom I'd had such trouble winning over, now stood up to her brother in my defence. "For goodness' sake, Excide, don't be such an old fogey! If she's going to ride, better she do it in pants than a skirt flying in the wind."

When I'd first talked to her about a pair of riding jodhpurs, though, she'd been against it, then one day she changed her mind: "Let's go and see how they're made, it won't do any harm." And there we were in a very exclusive shop catering to a small carriage trade. In those days there weren't many riders in Winnipeg. We'd never been so out of place. Yet Maman looked around and very quickly singled out the finest ensemble in the shop, and probably the most expensive too. She asked to have me try it on. The saleslady consented but not with good grace. She'd unmasked us immediately, perhaps because we were speaking French, though quietly between ourselves, but more probably because Maman didn't even ask the price, being so certain she wouldn't be tempted to buy anything there. I could have sunk through the floor, but I wanted a pair of jodhpurs so badly that in the end I put them on, then came and modelled them in the light of a bay window overlooking

41

the street, watched with sudden enthusiasm by Maman and disdain by the pinch-lipped saleslady. To prepare her retreat, Maman then began to find fault with them. "They wrinkle here, they bulge there."

We were barely outside when she told me they suited me beautifully, that she'd had time to really study the cut and thought she remembered it and could make me a pair exactly like them from some old putty-coloured trousers of my brother Rodolphe's, the material being still in very good condition. And she did, so successfully that no one in the world would ever have recognized Rodolphe's old trousers in my jodhpurs. I used to wear them with a pastel blouse open at the neck and a little kerchief knotted cowboy style, with the ends blowing in the wind. When I wore the outfit I felt ready to face the world, ready to cope with life, and it gave me confidence. When Maman saw the effect it had on me, making me stand straighter and hold my head higher, she came to love it too.

So my uncle's criticism didn't bother either of us very much. We knew he was a grouch about propriety, boy-girl friendships, and young folk in general, who he felt had too much freedom, though really he was far from ill-disposed towards them. There was a puritan streak in him, tempered by a merry disposition, a love of life, and a healthy sexual urge.

How he managed to reconcile those conflicting inclinations was rather odd. For example, in order not to disobey the village priest, who forbade parents to allow their children to dance under their roofs, he'd declare an absolute ban to his children, then go out square-dancing himself in the houses of less punctilious neighbours; when called upon to swing his partner, he'd grasp her with gusto and squeeze her so tight against his chest he'd half stifle her.

His widowed state was certainly hard on him. More than once he was on the point of remarrying, but in the end he wouldn't allow himself to, remaining faithful to his gentle Luzina whose idealized image he carried in his heart all his life, and also for fear of giving his children a stepmother they might not like.

If there was no dance in the neighbourhood in the evening, after the interminable family prayers were done he'd take up his violin and for hours on end try to play rollicking tunes like "Turkey in the Straw" by ear, though all his bow ever produced were doleful lays with practically no melody at all. Even at summer's end after the exhausting work of harvesting, rare were the evenings when he failed to try his hand at playing jolly tunes, which, alas, always turned so diabolically into laments.

He was a handsome man, tall, well built, and dark-complexioned, with glossy black hair parted in the middle and a superb black moustache. His eyes were black too, like shiny dark marbles, and he was constantly casting them about, as if following a thought that darted first in one direction, then another. Watching him pursue his thoughts like that, dogging them this way and that, became obsessive after a while.

He could be full of fun one minute, telling hilarious jokes to us children, then suddenly become moody and glum for a time, during which no one could get a word out of him; then just as suddenly his eyes would begin to turn this way and that again, and he'd be out of his spell of depression as quickly as he'd fallen into it.

I was very fond of him just as he was. When I came to read the Russian authors I found him, with his bouts of giddy merriment and a moody side plunging him abruptly into devastating silences, to be the image of so many of their characters, excessive at one minute in their devotions and equally excessive the next in letting off steam.

Later I used to wonder what he was seeing so far away during those moody contemplations, whether it was the future lying in store for his people and his family. His children, if anything, spoke better English than French, while he knew only a few words of English at most. Towards the end of his life, this last of the Landry sons who'd come to Manitoba from Quebec began recalling the faint memories he had of St-Alphonse-de-Rodriguez. The older he became, the more came back to him. He became obsessed with a desire to go back to the village of his ancestors before he died. He used to talk about it often, but as if it were a joy too great to be attained in this world. When, at the age of eighty-four, he died where he'd spent his whole life except his early childhood, he did so, one might say, with his soul turned towards his almost-forgotten source.

A FEW YEARS ago when I was in Manitoba attending to my sister Clémence, who lives in a home, I took time to run up to Somerset.

The fascination the village and its surroundings had and still have for me always outweighs the disillusionments they've brought me. The few relatives who are still there complain that if I find the time to go there it's always to see places first, and people after. It was true again this time. My first visit was to my uncle Excide's farm, which, while one couldn't say it was abandoned, was now a lonely place.

My uncle's eldest son lives in the village two and a half miles away and comes there every day at a fixed time, like a civil servant going to the office, to plough, harrow, and seed the fields, and, when appropriate, to mow and harvest the crops, all by machine, of course. Except on rare occasions, he can do it all himself. So work that used to require an army of farm labourers is now done in uncanny silence, without a sound other than that of a motor, in an atmosphere that's almost other-worldly. It numbs the mind to see a man just sitting at the controls of a tractor – his sole companion – turning, turning, again and again, alone in all that vastness, without the least sign of anything one might call human. Almost as punctually as he leaves in the morning, my cousin is scheduled to come home, his day's work done.

Around the silent farmhouse all was clean and tidy, the yard in perfect order, the machines put away, and the barn doors closed this late autumn day. I meandered around the house. A high sliding door had been installed in one of its walls. By standing on a log I managed to look in through a window. I was thunderstruck by what I discovered. With the ceiling removed and the partition walls demolished, the house was now just a huge shed, almost entirely filled by the Massey-Harris tractor.

The sight might have hurt less if a particularly delightful memory of this house in happier days hadn't superimposed itself on the present. One evening during the year I was a teacher in the neighbouring village of Cardinal, I arrived when I probably wasn't expected. It was mild and snowing abundantly, one of those tranquil, silent snowfalls that come straight down, undeflected by any wind, and as steadily as if to smother all traces of uncleanliness. There must have been some happy gathering, because all the lamps were lit and the house was resplendent, and through this same window I could see silhouettes bustling about cheerfully. But the most beguiling part of the scene was outside, where a delicate stream of light from the brightly lit windows was falling on five or six horse-drawn sleighs lined up by the door. Since there was no real cold in the air, no one had bothered to take the horses to the stable. They'd been left hitched to their sleighs, with blankets thrown over their backs, and more blankets had been spread over the sleighs to keep the snow off the seats. Ever so gently, the snow was piling up like an additional warm, fluffy blanket over the covered seats and over the animals standing there with their heads drooping, asleep on their feet, you'd swear, if you hadn't spied their eyelids blinking now and then.

Just as I'd stood at the end of the little dirt road from where I could see all that boundless space and been certain I'd find happiness some day, when I witnessed the scene on the night I describe my heart was flooded with longing for something still more wonderful, which was peace of mind. But now, standing on a log with my hands cupped around my eyes the better to see through the window, I was discovering something I couldn't believe: the ultimate, un-suspected fate of one of the most-loved houses of my life.

I stopped at my cousin's in the village. He lives in a pleasant, very modern, ranch-style house. The West is covered with them. In a friendly way I took him to task for having turned the house associated with our childhood memories into a tractor shed. He laughed as he defended himself.

"The wood's all rotted," he said. "It may as well at least be used for that."

There was nothing to be done about it. Just as he could justifiably have accused me of having no practical sense, I could have accused him of having nothing else.

Soon after that, I left him and went looking in a rather haphazard way for places and things I kept remembering out of the blue. I hunted for ages for a corner bakery where my grandmother had sent me for a loaf of bread one day when I was very small. I described it as I remembered it to people in the street, who would have liked to help me but didn't remember any bakery answering my description. Perhaps, with time, I'd imagined it to be quite different than it really was. Or else it had long ago ceased to exist. I can't describe the grief I felt at not being able to find that bakery, a grief quite disproportionate to its cause. Yet out there under the high, pure sky, the wind was still dusting up the dirt along the edges of the highway, as it used to when I was a child – except that then the whole highway was dirt. Dust raised by the feet of some invisible walker tramping endlessly along the deserted road, one might imagine.

I found my way to the cemetery on an isolated butte not far from the village, exposed to all the winds and watched over by a few spruce trees, which aren't native here and must have been brought from very far away. Companions in death at last for folk like Grandmother Landry, who'd pined all her life for the dour trees of her childhood that grew on the hillsides at St-Alphonse-de-Rodriguez. Now at least they were reunited, those sombre trees and my grandmother, who was so untalkative and undemonstrative, yet so faithful to her attachments.

I had no difficulty finding her grave and Grandfather Landry's, though I hadn't been to visit them since the distant day when Maman had brought me as a little girl to pray and meditate beside them. I found myself reading aloud what amounted to their abbreviated life stories: that Emilie Jeansonne, born at St-Jacques-l'Achigan in 1831, had died at St-Boniface on March 7, 1917; that her beloved husband, Elie Landry, born in St-Jacques-l'Achigan in 1835, had died at Somerset on August 6, 1912. I noted the fact that my grandfather, though four years younger than Emilie, had died five years before her. How much he'd accomplished in so little time! And besides, having left St-Alphonse-de-Rodriguez almost penniless, he'd managed to put aside a little sum to leave to his children which was quite respectable for those days.

I felt better. Slender and fragile though it was, the bond was still holding fairly well between us, we wanderers across the centuries. I managed to picture their two old faces to some extent, but in that I was probably helped by having seen their photographs.

I moved along a few paces, staying inside the Landry family plot. A few feet away there rose two large monuments, recent ones certainly, in modern style and more ostentatious too: no doubt Luzina's and my uncle Excide's. I took another step and received such a shock I thought I must be seeing things. Two high, matching stones confronted me, standing on end side by side. In characters that leapt out at me, one bore the word "Father" and the other one "Mother". In English! I searched in the back of my memory for Luzina's angular face, already lined by illness in my childhood but glowing with a warmth of heart that the relentless advance of tuberculosis never snuffed out. I saw my uncle with his eyes always in pursuit of some thought, either a jovial or an inconsolably sorrowful one. Those two who had never been called Father and Mother in English by anyone while they were living would be identified that way for ever, here in this little cemetery beneath the unsullied sky in the middle of nowhere. They'd been taken from me more surely that day than on the day they died.

I left the cemetery. High in those imported trees the wind was rising. Its long recitative, murmured in a far-off voice, gripped my heart. A voice retelling a pathetic tale of human lives, lost on the earth's face and in history.

AS MUCH as I'd let myself go during the holidays, with my endless rides on the prairie and the airy castle building they lent themselves to, as soon as school began I'd fling myself into my schoolwork with equal abandon. Having wandered to my heart's content all summer, I now stayed riveted every evening to my little desk in my secluded room, reading and getting as much of the material into my head as possible. I learned by heart with extraordinary ease. Very often I'd read a paragraph attentively but effortlessly and then realize that that was all I'd had to do to remember it word for word. However, I soon forgot a text I'd learned without a lot of effort.

I'd promised Maman I'd apply myself so totally to studying that I'd always come first in future, having resolved to make it up to her that way for all her sacrifices for my benefit. However, I didn't begin to do so in the year following my appendectomy. Before coming to that I had to have more time, and even another illness which kept me at home for several months and made me lose a school year. Now I was a year behind my former classmates and quite crushed by the fact. I also had to see my father, who was very ill now, worrying constantly about my future, to the point of confiding to Maman that he was afraid they'd never be able to get me through my studies. But most of all, I think, I had to realize that my mother was driving herself mercilessly, trying to run the house.

How did she do it? I think it was mostly by taking lodgers and sometimes boarders. It seems to me we always had strangers living with us. Sometimes they were well mannered and pleasant. That kind we treated like family, and some we made friends of and missed long after they left. Others we disliked, finding them coarse or loud, and those we had the greatest difficulty enduring under our roof. In either case, independent as we were by nature, I wonder how we put up with not having our house to ourselves for years. The fact was that the money it brought in was practically all we had, apart from the help Maman got from Rodolphe and Adèle. So, as she'd often remind us, she on whom it was hardest, we just had to swallow our pride and learn that our house wasn't entirely our own. But she promised us it would be one day, once all the strangers had gone. But when all the strangers had gone it was because the house had been sold. Now we ourselves were like the strangers we'd had under our roof all those years, people who had no real home. Now we knew what it was like and felt sorry for them.

From Rodolphe at this time, Maman sometimes received really lavish sums, so big she'd pale and exclaim almost dolefully, "How could he have guessed that today's the day we have to buy coal for the winter?" or "that today's the last day for paying the taxes?"

Alas, the time would come when a crestfallen Rodolphe, the day after one of his shows of largesse, after a poker game with friends and a thousand other foolish things, would ask for it back, and she, with shattered face, would give it to him, saying in his defence, "He isn't obliged to support the family. He isn't at all."

I don't know how we could have carried on for so long with so little if it hadn't been for one of the chimeras the weary soul cherishes so. On our horizon there was always a kindly mirage to bolster our flagging hopes. When I came to read Georges Duhamel's *Le Notaire du Havre* (*Letter from Havre*), how well I recognized us all in the Pasquiers, who were also living on an illusion. Our illusion was "the land" in Saskatchewan. My father had acquired it when he was establishing his settlement at Dollard, along with other acreages he had had to let go one by one as our need for money became urgent. To this piece of land, *the* land, he remained doggedly, unshakeably attached. When things were at their worst, he who was not an optimist by nature was the one to offer encouragement.

"Anyway, Mélina," he'd say, "we've still got our land in Saskatchewan. If we can hold on long enough it'll save us in the end, you'll see."

To which Maman, emboldened by such confidence, would reply, "Yes, thank God, we've still got the land in Saskatchewan. When we absolutely have to, we'll sell it, but we don't have to do it now, the time's not come yet."

That faraway piece of land, transfigured by our fancies, daily given new reality in our imaginations, was for years the invincible refuge that saved us from total demoralization.

Sometimes, when the sun was setting at the end of the lane, spilling its rays into our back yard, we were sure we could also see its golden light filtering through the high, waving wheat on our land in Saskatchewan.

The oddest part of this whole story is that when I finally saw that land with my own eyes, long after it had ceased to belong to us, it looked just the way we'd seen it in our most rapturous daydreams. It really was a vision of intense blue sky, flaxen harvest, and wide-open space to comfort the heart.

V

I MUST HAVE been about fourteen when I began to immerse myself in my schoolwork the way one enters a cloister. I'd been beating around the bush, telling myself over and over that I'd get down to business next month. Then there came a day when I began to suspect that Maman was losing ground, and that she wouldn't be able to hold on if she didn't soon get some encouragement to brace her. The year-end examinations were approaching. I began reviewing my schoolwork in earnest. I'd get up well before the rest of the household and come down to study in the peace and quiet of the kitchen while I had it to myself for an hour or two. When Maman came to put the morning porridge on the stove, she'd find me at the big kitchen table with my books spread around me. So as not to disturb me she'd greet me simply with a nod, as she might one of our boarders, and a look of approval and commendation. Then she'd set to work with as little noise as possible.

At the end of that year I came first in my class for the first time in my life. I even won a medal for some subject or other. But what I'll never forget is Maman's face when I brought home the first instalment of her reward. It was immediately as though I'd lifted the weight of years past from her, and her anxiety about the years to come as well. She didn't pay me any lavish compliments, but she was radiant. Though she didn't know it, two or three times I heard her boasting about me to neighbours, artfully finding an appropriate opening in the conversation for the disclosure that "my daughter won the Bishop's medal this year." Once I appeared on the scene just as she was dropping a reference to that ordinary everyday medal, and I was struck by the expression in her eyes. They were shining as I'd rarely seen them do, like two deep pools of tender radiance from which all the dark, bitter waters of hardship seemed to have been drained.

That was the support I was able to give her. How could I not have wanted to keep on giving it? She'd spared nothing in her support of me. It made me giddy to see myself able to lighten her step at so little cost. Coming first made me giddy, too. I even wonder if this wasn't the beginning of a habit that wasn't altogether good, because I took it very badly when I came second one year, uncovering a weakness in needing to come first that I had to learn to fight.

In any case, coming first wasn't such a remarkable feat as it might seem. What, apart from studying, could I have flung myself into with such abandon at the age of fifteen or sixteen in those days? We didn't engage in any sports to speak of. I did have a pair of skates, a present from my brother Rodolphe, and I learned to skate more or less in time to the lovely *Blue Danube Waltz* they used to play over the loudspeakers at public skating rinks. But that was all. I had to wait till I was earning my own money before I could buy myself a tennis racket, and later a light bicycle which was my pride and joy, and finally second-hand skis which were much too long for me but on which, for lack of hills in those parts, I was a very solitary pioneer of cross-country skiing years before it became the vogue.

But that wasn't until my young adulthood, my early twenties or even a bit older. I was late growing up, as often happened in those days. At fifteen I was a little old woman always buried in my books, with a weak upper back already, and my outlook cluttered by a hodgepodge of useless knowledge.

Even Maman came to think I was overdoing it. To make me leave my books and get to bed at a reasonable hour she'd sometimes cut off my electricity by taking out the fuse for the circuit my room was on. This way she could retire in peace, knowing I wouldn't be putting on my light again that night.

But at last I was keeping the promise I'd made her some years earlier in the hospital; year after year I was bringing home the medal awarded by the Manitoba French Canadian Association for the highest marks in French. Then I won the most coveted of all, the one given by the Quebec Department of Education to the student with the highest year-end marks in French in all Manitoba. If I remember correctly, it bore in effigy the rather Roman head of Cyrille Delage, the noted Quebec writer on wines and gastronomy. My collection of medals was impressive by now, almost filling a drawer. Maman kept them carefully there, where they wouldn't get covered with dust. She who'd attended only a humble little village school and never won anything more than a fifty-cent book, which she still cherished, was quite dazzled by my drawerful of big fat medals; I suspect that when she was alone she often opened that drawer so she could admire them at her leisure.

Later I was to cause her much grief over those medals, and therein lies a tale I may recount if I have time. Now that I've begun to spin out my memories, they're tumbling out so thick and fast it frightens me, like a never-ending thread. It isn't going to stop, I tell myself. I'll never get down more than a particle of it all. Can it be possible to have enough inside you to fill tons of paper, if only you get hold of the right end of the thread?

In grades eleven and twelve, the Manitoba French Canadian Association prizes were fifty and one hundred dollars respectively. These were handsome sums in those days, almost comparable to today's Canada Council and Cultural Affairs grants, and you didn't have to apply for them, which was especially nice. I won both of them, which covered my enrolment at normal school and the purchase of the necessary books, so that I cost my parents practically nothing after I finished school, and that was essential, since by then they'd come to the end of their meagre resources.

When we were so far from Quebec, for those of us who finished school the achievement wasn't so much to have done so but to have done it in French as well as in English. And despite the law that allowed only an hour a day for the teaching of French in public schools in French-speaking neighbourhoods, it seems to me that the French we spoke was every bit as good as in Quebec, in the same period and for similar social strata.

Who or what was responsible for this almost miraculous situation? Certainly our collective fervour, the presence of some outstanding French immigrants among us, too, which brought distinction to our milieu, but most of all the zeal and tenacity of our schoolteachers, mostly nuns but also some lay teachers, who used to give extra, unpaid time to the teaching of French despite already onerous schedules. A few used to take quite brazen liberties with the law; passionate and defiant, some of them drew the ire of the school board; they may have done us more harm than good.

When the provocation was not too visible, the Department of Education closed its eyes. As long as the children were able to show they were learning some English when the inspector came, the rest was more or less accepted. We were always vulnerable, of course, to an upsurge of hostility from small groups of fanatics calling for strict application of the law. For a time there was a rumour that there was an investigator on the warpath. The standing order at the time was that if the investigator or indeed anyone from the school board appeared unexpectedly, all our French textbooks were to be hidden, evidence of lessons in French erased from blackboards, and our English books prominently displayed. No doubt there were tense moments of that kind in some schools and perhaps even in mine before my time, but personally I was never aware of any such dramatic visit. Yet the danger was quite real and it galvanized us. We used to feel it around us; perhaps our teachers had something to do with maintaining the feeling. Then it would fade and our passive resistance would resume, which perhaps wore down the enemy more effectively than an open revolt. Sometimes I wonder if the opposition we were subjected to wasn't a service rather than a disservice to us. There were so few of us that if we'd been left alone the easy route would have been the fastest one to perdition, it seems to me. We were certainly spared the easy route. And we managed to learn and preserve the French language in all its beauty and elegance, but to tell the truth it was for the pride of it, the dignity; it couldn't equip us for everyday life.

In any event, if we were going to pass our exams and get our degrees or certificates, we had to comply with the program laid down by the Department of Education, which meant learning most subjects in English: chemistry, physics, mathematics, and most history. So we were more or less English in algebra, geometry, the sciences, and Canadian history, but French in Quebec history, French literature, and particularly history of religion. This gave us an odd turn of mind, constantly alert to readjusting our focus. It was like being a juggler with all those plates to keep in the air.

Sometimes this was a blessing. I remember the keen interest I took in English literature as soon as I had access to it. And for good

reason. Our French literature textbooks acquainted us with Veuillot
and Montalembert, pages and pages of them, and very little else;
practically nothing of Zola, Flaubert, Maupassant, even Balzac. And
what idea could we have of French poetry when it was reduced
almost exclusively to François Coppée, Sully Prudhomme, and La-
martine's "Le Lac", which we parroted so many times that today,
by some curious reaction – mental block perhaps – I couldn't recite
a single line of it. And yet I remember getting 99% for my essay
on that poem in a competition sponsored by the Manitoba French
Canadian Association.

The doors to English literature, however, were open wide and
gave us access to its greatest minds. I'd soon read Thomas Hardy,
George Eliot, the Brontë sisters, Jane Austen. I knew Keats, Shelley,
Byron, and the Lake poets, and adored them. Fortunately for French
literature, our program of study did include the sparkling Alphonse
Daudet. At fifteen I fell upon his *Lettres de mon moulin* (*Letters
from My Mill*) and learned it by heart from beginning to end.
Sometimes I wonder if the soft spot in my heart for Provence,
which has taken me to every corner of it, isn't partly owing to my
enchantment at my first encounter with graceful French prose when
I was fifteen. Without this, French prose would have seemed very
dreary beside the English. If, at that age, I'd been able to read
Rimbaud, Verlaine, Baudelaire, and Radiguet, I can only imagine
what it would have done to me.

My first literary encounter was with Shakespeare. He profoundly
repelled my classmates and, it seems to me, hardly enthused the
nun who was our literature teacher either. But I was enthralled by
his passionate earthiness, joined sometimes to such sensitivity it
would melt your heart, the expression of the soul's upwelling, with
all its tenderness and turmoil.

I had the good fortune to attend a performance of *The Merchant
of Venice*, presented by a London company that was touring Canada. The magic began for me at the Walker Theatre in Winnipeg
– which in itself predisposed me to the sorcery of the stage, with
its rows and rows of ornate balconies, its immense chandeliers, and
its heavy crimson velvet curtain. All question of French or English
or forbidden or imposed language disappeared. There was only a
language that transcended languages, like that of music. In the
highest balcony, leaning over the rail towards the actors – who

from that height looked very small – I could barely catch the words, which for me were pretty obscure anyway, yet I was spellbound. I've never really been able to fathom the fascination of my very first evening of Shakespeare, a fascination which is as much a mystery to me today as it ever was.

From then on the teacher, who had trouble comprehending the Bard, would rely on my insight, which wasn't all that great, but then I made up for the shortfall with enthusiasm. She maintained that if you were enthusiastic – or seemed enthusiastic – you could make the inspector swallow anything. What it took was memorizing. We were then into *Macbeth*. Since she couldn't help us understand the play, there was another recourse.

"Learn bits of it by heart," she implored us. "Then the inspector won't think about asking questions."

One evening I came upon a "bit" which was just about incomprehensible but which captivated me anyway with the indescribable shade of darkness I was sure I could see in it. The next day, burning with excitement, I recited the whole of Macbeth's great monologue, "Is this a dagger which I see before me...."

The teacher couldn't get over finding me so passionately enamoured of that remote poet of Elizabethan times. She seemed a bit put out, in a way, but was quick to see the benefit she might draw from my aptitude. Subsequently, in fact, whenever we were expecting one of our Visiting Mothers with a particular penchant for English, or some important gentleman from the Department of Education, she would put me on notice.

"Save the class, Gabrielle. Stand up and give him 'Is this a dagger....'"

I was already saving the class through the Manitoba French Canadian Association's year-end competition. I thought it was a lot to be saving it in English too. But I was a bit of a show-off, I think, perhaps owing partly to our collective inferiority complex, which led me to seek approval at every opportunity.

The inspector arrived. He addressed us in English, of course.

"How are you getting along with Shakespeare, Sister? *Macbeth?* Oh, fine, fine! Does anyone remember by which names the witches on the heath hail Macbeth?"

I was like a cat on hot bricks and shot up my hand. I was the sole volunteer. The evening before I'd been turning the pages of my *Macbeth* and by happy coincidence had lighted upon those gloriously resonant salutations.

The inspector smiled as he looked at me. Who else would he have looked at? All the class but me practically had their backs turned to him. I jumped to my feet and pronounced, "Thane of Glamis, Thane of Cawdor."

That I should know those strange-sounding salutations seemed to make him unbelievably happy. It appeared he felt himself to be in enemy territory and was as much afraid of our reactions as we were of his. He asked me if I knew some passage of the play by heart. I lost no time drawing the mask of tragedy over my face and launching full tilt into "Is this a dagger...."

Strangest of all, when I first saw *Macbeth* performed in London many years later I discovered that I hadn't been too bad a Macbeth way back then, in my tone, delivery, in everything but accent, which was straight out of Deschambault Street and must have been excruciatingly funny.

But the inspector didn't laugh. He seemed moved. Perhaps he sensed a significance in that classroom scene which was as strange as that of the witches on the heath. Perhaps he had an inkling of what it was like to be a little French Canadian in those days in Manitoba, and perhaps he felt compassion for us, a secret admiration, even.

"Why do you love Shakespeare so, young lady?" he asked me.

The young lady was hearing herself so addressed for the first time in her life, and was overcome. She replied with something off the top of her head, having no doubt heard it somewhere.

"Because he's the greatest."

"And why is he the greatest?"

That bothered me and I thought a bit before risking a reply.

"Because he knows all about the human soul."

That seemed to make him even happier than my answer about the witches. He studied me with touching benevolence. That was when I first discovered how dearly our English-speaking adversaries can love us, providing we play the game and show what good, obedient children we are.

"Are there any other English poets you like?" he asked me.

I knew Coleridge's "Ancient Mariner" by heart. I'd learned to love it the year before from an elderly nun who adored fine alliteration, and who would recite it to us in a dreamy voice with a faraway look in her eyes.

"We were the first that ever burst into that silent sea...."

I recited the old ballad for him as he'd certainly never heard it before, swaying to the rhythm of the lines, picturing the sailing ship lost in the Sargasso Sea.

The inspector had apparently lost sight of the fact that there were thirty-five pupils in that class, thirty-four of whom were as silent as posts.

When he took his leave, accompanied to the door by the teacher, on whom he was lavishing warm felicitations and much "Madame..., dear Madame...," I told myself, "Soon I'll be the one getting the compliments. Sister must be pleased with me."

At the door he redoubled his effusions. The teacher beamed. I thought I heard snatches that just might have been about me: "brilliant young lady...will go far...."

Ah, far was certainly where I'd decided to go. But in what direction?

At last the teacher came back to her place behind the desk high up there on the platform, up the two steps I so constantly tripped on in my years at school. Her face still bore a hint of triumph. Was it because we'd hoodwinked the inspector, or because she fancied she'd suddenly become a superlative English literature teacher? Who could say? I approached her, a bit too eager to learn what had been said at the door about me.

"Was the inspector pleased with me, Sister?"

She glared at me, suddenly all disapproval. The demon pride was what the nuns used to hunt down in us most diligently, all the while reminding us relentlessly that as French Canadians we must lift our heads and hold them high – so how were we supposed to know when to bow them?

Then she softened a little, proud of me but feeling she shouldn't show it. She shot an almost affectionate rebuke at me which made her the first to recognize my natural inclination, though neither she nor I knew where it would lead me.

"Get out of my sight, you little romancer!"

THAT WAS in my last year at the Académie Saint-Joseph, grade twelve, which I very nearly never took. When I'd finished grade eleven, I overheard my father and mother talking about me. Once again their voices reached me from the little summer kitchen, through the open door on a mild summer evening in late June or early July. I always found it profoundly disconcerting to suddenly hear them talking frankly about me in the belief that they were alone. I was on the point of moving away but curiosity kept me hovering near the door, trembling; a curiosity mixed with much heartache, and fear of learning the worst.

My father was admitting that he had neither strength nor courage left, saying wearily to Maman, "If I'm going to live to see her able to earn her living as a teacher as you've always wanted, Mélina, she'll have to get there soon. I won't be able to wait much longer."

I think by then he'd conveyed the land in Saskatchewan to my sister Adèle in repayment of loans she'd advanced him. So we didn't even have that illusion any more. Papa was therefore arguing that I should go straight into normal school that autumn.

But Maman was being stubborn.

"When she's doing so well at school, getting the highest marks and all, taking her out now would be so unfair! And then, have you considered that without grade twelve she'll only get a school leaving certificate, not matriculation, and that'll make problems for her later when she wants to teach in the city to be near us."

"You talk as if I can choose how long I'm going to live," grumbled my father.

I ached to rush out and tell them I was going to get a job, any job, to relieve them of spending all that money on me. I think I couldn't stand the idea of their being here together again because of me, like refugees from their lovely big house in this kind of shack, even though they felt at home here, perhaps because it was more their style. What held me back was fear, most likely. Fear of life, which so often looked appealing, even exciting, but so often like a dark, tormented landscape ahead of me. And then once again came the thought that if I was going to repay Maman for the endless sacrifices she'd imposed on herself, nothing less than dazzling success on my part would do.

My father heaved a long-suffering sigh.

"Have it the way you want, Maman." He called her that, as we children did, in the last years of his life. "I'd have liked to see her standing on her own feet before I go."

SO I TOOK grade twelve despite all the obstacles – a ridiculous expense, an outrageous luxury for people in almost desperate straits as we were. Fortunately I won the hundred-dollar scholarship given by the Manitoba French Canadian Association. I'd come first in French five years in a row. It occurred to our principal to check my year-end marks in the Department of Education examinations, and she found what she'd expected, that I'd come first in English too in those five years. This was cause for rejoicing at school and among the nuns. But for my part, as I remember, all I felt was a kind of indifference. I must have begun to realize that coming first didn't really mean very much. The honour brought me another trophy, of course, which went to fatten the collection in my medal drawer.

Then there came the long-awaited day of what we called *la graduation*. There were twelve or fifteen of us graduating, I think, a fairly big group in those days when not many girls of our milieu went that far in school, often by choice but mostly for lack of means. The principal, who loved an excuse for holding celebrations and receptions, decided she couldn't let the occasion pass without making a big splash that "would for ever be remembered in the annals of the school."

A large number of both French and English dignitaries were to be invited. The commencement ceremony was to take place in the auditorium, with parents and guests seated in the audience and we, *les graduées*, sitting or standing on the stage where everyone could see us, with all the ferns from the convent arranged behind and around us. It must have given us a sylvan setting indeed, since the big backdrop behind us, I think I recall, was painted with tall interlacing trees as well. We were to be dressed all in white, including our shoes. In the crook of the left arm, near the heart, we were to hold identical bouquets of red roses, bought all together at a small discount and costing us five dollars each. And we were to be photographed up there on the stage in all our glory, holding our bouquets, and it was all to be so beautiful that some of our teachers were already close to tears as they coached us in the bows we were to make, "bending from the waist, but never looking down...."

And so for the day that should have been one of pure delight for her, Maman was obliged to eke even more than usual out of nothing. How she did it I'd rather not know, but I had my two dollars for the photograph. "Smile, you pretty liddel ladies," beseeched the Armenian photographer, for there was always one of us drifting wistfully off as the shutter snapped. He never did get us all smiling together at "the beautiful life waiting for you, just think, liddel ladies, like a morning in June." I had my white shoes. I had my bouquet of roses, the first bought flowers I'd ever held. A florist's delivery still makes my heart skip a beat, and it's probably because of those roses.

And the dress. Where could Maman's thoughts have been when she sat down to make it? I think I recall that Papa's condition worsened about that time, although I myself didn't really notice, I was in such a turmoil over pleasing him by coming first. Increasingly, everything was falling on Maman's shoulders and on hers alone.

From up there on the stage, I searched and searched through the faces in the crowd. Finally I caught sight of her, and she remains for ever in my memory as I saw her then. Her poor face was grey with fatigue – she may have finished my dress only late the night before – but was lifted, straining towards me, smiling at me across the distance. For all its sunken eyelids and drawn cheeks, it shone with pride, and that hurt more than anything I'd seen before because suddenly I knew how much all this had cost. The wave of cruel realization swept over me, gripped me in vice-like anguish, robbed me of all my joy in the day, then faded, leaving me to my insouciant youth up there in my place of honour.

I seem to have forgotten all the rest of that scene. To bring it back I have to look at the photograph. It shows pretty well how things were. My dress isn't very stylish. The hem is rather uneven. The collar's a bit askew as well, as though Maman had cut it wrong and not been able to fix it. But the girl seems not to know she's awkwardly dressed. The large, anxious eyes look far away towards the vast unknown called life, and it's her confidence that overcomes a kind of shadow from the future hanging like a cloud, darkening this, her greatest day.

I can talk about her without embarrassment. The child that I was is as much a stranger to me as I would have been to her if she, at the dawn of life as they say, had been able to see me as I am today. But from birth to death and from death to birth, through remembrance on my part and hopes and dreams on hers, the two of us keep moving closer to a common meeting ground, as the distance between us grows.

VI

I ENTERED the Winnipeg Normal Institute that autumn. It was a big building in barracks or firehall style, on Logan Street as I recall. For a time we'd had a normal school in St-Boniface, where the courses were given in French and the goal was to prepare a body of teachers to teach in French. My elder sisters, Anna and Adèle, had studied there. Now all that was in the past. So from a school run by French-speaking nuns, where despite all the obstacles placed in our path we managed to live pretty well as we did at home, we now passed into an institution which was strictly English. Well, no; we did have one French-speaking instructor. She came a number of times to pronounce three or four laborious sentences reminiscent of Ionesco's comically mechanical verbalizations in *The Bald Soprano*. Perhaps they even originated in the same textbook. Having by mistake posed questions to one or other of our little French-speaking contingent and got real answers in real French, she ceased thenceforth to call on us at all, and the lessons proceeded as previously, between people talking at cross-purposes without understanding a word of what they were saying.

But we weren't just passing from one language to another. We were passing from one climate to another. We were leaving a little world in which the nuns overprotected us perhaps, sheltered us too much from reality, and venturing into the lion's mouth, one might say.

There, the most apprehensive of our teachers had led us to believe, our faith and our fidelity to our past would be sorely tried. We would need to show unshakeable determination. More important, there in the enemy camp we'd be duty bound to do honour to our community by our fineness of character, our exemplary conduct, our excellence in all things. And if confrontation proved inevitable, we'd have to face it courageously.

That was the foolish state of mind I was in when I took the streetcar one fine morning for the long ride, interrupted by an aggravating transfer, to the gloomy building on Logan Street. Though it terrified me at the time, today I really have no clear recollection of the building itself.

Sometimes, when she was not too "hard-up" as she used to say – she knew so little English that it was significant she'd picked up the expression – Maman would give me twenty-five cents for my lunch at the school canteen; the rest of the time she'd make me a sandwich to eat with a piece of cheese and an apple.

In my class of about seventy-five students, only five or six of us were French-speaking. Two were country girls and were so shy they'd shrink into the ground if one of our instructors so much as looked at them. What could be expected of comrades-in-arms like that? I saw from the beginning that if ever I should have to do battle here, I'd have to do it with a very small army. For a time I saw the school as the scene of a battle to be waged, and nothing else. Hitherto, the tactics we'd been taught to use against our English adversaries had been tact, diplomacy, cunning strategy, and polite disobedience. In my imagination, the time had now come to cross swords. I was soon presented with my opportunity.

After perhaps a week of classes, the school's principal, the kindly old Dr. Mackintyre whom I became so fond of later, came to give us his principal's word of welcome. He was a teacher of psychology, and he delivered an hour-long, rambling peroration consisting merely, to me at that time, of an old duffer's well-intentioned maunderings. In fact, long before the notion of self-fulfilment came to be common currency, this man was talking of nothing else, using terms like "an opening out" and "a blossoming of self". Once started on his favourite topic, which was that a child is not made to suit a school and so the school must suit the child, that "those dear young creatures before everything else should be happy in school", he could go on for hours on end.

He had a strong Scottish brogue, a fine head of white hair, and, I was soon to learn, a warm, kind heart.

As he spoke, I was waiting for an opening. Suddenly, there it was. I put up my hand, asking to speak.

Agreeably surprised at such interest in the midst of the prevailing somnolence, he adjusted his spectacles and turned to the seating chart showing each student's name and place in the room.

"Miss Roy," (pronounced the English way in that milieu) "you have a question to ask?"

I stood up. My knees were shaking, only barely holding me up. But there was no turning back. It was now or never for my profession of faith. My voice sounded very weak, as if rising into a vast acoustical void and coming back from afar distorted and quite unrecognizable.

"I agree with you, sir," I said, "that a child's education must first take account of his own personality."

"Well," said he, all smiles, "I see you've been closely following what I've been saying. Have you something to add?"

"Yes, that I see a terrible contradiction between theory and practice. For example, take the case of a little French-speaking child coming to school for the first time in his life, and it's an English school. From the minute he arrives he'll have to be put in the mould designed for little English Canadians. What chance will there ever be for his personality to blossom?"

A deathly silence fell around me. I'd touched the forbidden subject. Woe to the one who lets scandal through the door. I had the impression the whole class was turning away from me. Dr. Mackintyre studied me with a look of surprise, but one in which there was neither animosity nor disapproval.

"Quite so! Quite so!" he said. Then he invited me to consider that the subject hardly lent itself to class discussion and suggested that I stop by his office after four o'clock; we'd talk about it then.

I sat down and the aftershock of my audacity hit me. I was sure I was done for. I'd be expelled from the school, dashing Maman's hopes and proving that my father's gloomy misgivings had been right after all. Ah, how well inspired I'd been to go looking for martyrdom! In my agitation, I even began gathering up my books and notes, getting ready for my inevitable dismissal.

At four o'clock I went to the principal's office. The stoop-shouldered old man with the shock of white hair gave me a weary smile as he waved me to the chair on the other side of the huge desk.

"Brave girl!" he muttered. In my surprise I didn't realize at first that he was speaking of me.

Then he confided that when he was a young man in Scotland

he'd experienced the same racial and linguistic injustices suffered by the French community of Manitoba. And that he'd often been laughed at for his burr, too.

"Language is the vehicle of communication," he observed, "but it's created more misunderstanding in the world than anything else, except perhaps faith."

He then pointed out that since our French contingent was not a large one, it would probably be better not to waken the sleeping hounds of fanaticism on either side; that he could see only one course for us to follow, which was to excel in everything, always to be better than others.

"Work at your French," he said. "Always be faithful to it. Teach it when you get the chance and as much as you can...without getting caught. But don't forget, you'll have to excel in English too. The tragic thing about minorities is that they have to be better, or disappear.... Can you yourself, dear child, see another way out for you?"

I shook my head.

Adroitly, he then questioned me about my family, the position my father had held, my studies with the nuns, all the way down to what we lived on, as I recall. He seemed to be better at patching together my pathetic story than I was myself.

"Poor gerrrl," he was saying now. "Poor young gerrrl."

He shook my hand very warmly. And when I was out in the corridor he called after me in a loud voice, "Never give up!"

I left with much to think about. It hadn't escaped me that the extremists on our side, who were pushing for French teaching exclusively, and for a refusal to learn English, would have us driven to tragic isolation or else, sooner or later, to the point of packing up and leaving. While there were still a few Québécois coming to join our ranks in Manitoba, far more often it was the opposite: our young people, raised in French, leaving to settle in the mother province. I myself dreamed of it. Dr. Mackintyre, it seemed to me, had been talking the language of friendship, and it matched the counsel given us by some of the most astute of our teachers at school.

After that I stopped trying to provoke our teachers, although there was one who seemed determined to provoke me. This teacher's history lectures seemed to be aimed at me from the ill-starred day when, on the strength of what we'd learned from the nuns, I insisted there couldn't have been any bad popes. Thereafter, at every opportunity the teacher would trot out the schemers, the poisoners, the quarrelsome, the fornicators, and the incestuous among the popes. Though I was no papist, I could have become one at the goading of that rabid anti-papist. But I kept choking back my indignation. I was determined to take what was worth taking while I was there and leave the rest. Ruefully, I'd discovered I could be liked, and even considered charming and lovable, as long as I stayed in my place, second place that is, and showed I was content to be there. All I was trying to do after that was get good marks. The hard, solitary path I'd seen ahead of me when I was a child was indeed mine, there was no getting away from it.

My father's health was declining day by day. This had been going on so long that I hadn't yet realized how fast his condition was deteriorating now. But his heavily lined face and his deeply sunken eyes, in which there was only suffering now, used to follow me throughout my morning streetcar ride, when I'd sometimes open my books and try to review my work. They haunted me still at the school during lectures, and I had to summon every ounce of will to rivet my attention on what at the time seemed to be the most important and pressing parts of the course material. I was working hardest on my English accent, having made the class laugh several times at my expense. I finally threw myself totally into my work and lost sight of my father's suffering image.

That's the way it's been too often in my life. In my haste to accomplish and thus bring support, comfort, or reason for pride to those I love, I haven't been attentive enough to see that they couldn't wait.

DURING the second term we were sent out into various schools of the Winnipeg School Commission, where each of us was to take charge of a class under the supervision of the regular teacher, who would evaluate our teaching prowess and ability to keep order. The marks we'd get from the teacher were to count heavily in our final marks for the year. Most of us were terrified by the prospect, because if we happened to get a harpy for a teacher it could be disastrous. Which is what happened to me.

I'd barely opened my mouth to introduce myself when she wanted to know what nationality I was, because of what she called my peculiar accent. And when I spelled my name for her she snorted, "French, eh!" Without further ado she told me to carry on with the lesson where she'd left off; I don't remember what the subject was, geography perhaps. All I recall of that class is the horror of it. The pupils were from a district known to be a rough one. They were fairly big, aged twelve to fourteen, and half boys, half girls. They quickly saw how shy and frightened I was, and went wild. I've never heard such an uproar in a classroom. They slammed the lids of their desks. They slapped the sides of them with their rulers. They made buzzing sounds in unison or whistled. The teacher didn't lift a finger to help me. She stood a little to the side with her arms crossed and a hard little smile on her lips, appearing to enjoy watching me getting deeper and deeper into trouble. Beyond my despair of the moment, another still more devastating was rearing its head: if I have to cope with this to be a teacher I'll never make it, I was telling myself, I'll never be able to stand it. And I saw the door to the only occupation I'd been prepared for closing before me. In truth, I was losing my grip on everything: this classroom full of children making fun of me, my rapidly vanishing future, my confidence in my capabilities, and even my hope of passing my final examinations.

But most devastating of all was the haunting image of my ailing father. His pulmonary edema had suddenly worsened and he'd been hospitalized for several days. On account of his age, he'd refused the operation that had been proposed to him. After receiving treatments merely to give him some relief, he'd been allowed to return home. This had made him so happy that in my youthful obliviousness I thought he had recovered. The improvement lasted a few days and then, two nights previous, he'd stopped pacing the downstairs hallway and come, towards dawn, to the foot of the stairs, calling to Maman in distress. She'd gone to him at once and immediately had a little bed from upstairs brought down for him so he'd be close by and she could care for him while continuing to go about her work. In resisting his illness he'd stayed on his feet so long I was very alarmed to see him take to bed, but I couldn't believe this phase wouldn't last at least a few months. Before leaving the house that morning I'd gone to look at him as he slept, still under the sedation given him during the night. I'd been struck by the change in his face and had asked Maman if I hadn't better stay at home that day, but knowing what a hard day was awaiting me and how nerve-racking it would be to put it off, she took it on herself to reassure me, not realizing herself, perhaps, how close the end really was.

"Go and do your best," she'd told me. "When this day's behind you you'll be happier and in better shape to help me."

Those images and anxious words were large in my mind as I faced that roomful of rebellious children and tried once again to get their attention, to no avail. My voice, weakened by fear and the turmoil inside me, didn't reach them. I wonder if the words I was trying to speak even got past my lips. Perhaps they did, because I seem to recall a boy laughing loudly as he mimicked me.

Then, at the point where I could take no more and was perhaps about to break down in tears, throw in the sponge, turn tail and run, the door opened a crack. The school principal beckoned to the teacher, who went to join him in the hall. She returned with a very different face. First in surprise and then in fright, I thought I saw sympathy for me in her expression now. She bent forward and said softly in my ear:

"Go now. Go quickly. They've just telephoned to say your father...is...very ill...."

VII

I TOOK THE streetcar. It must have been just a thrifty reflex, because I think I remember the principal, or perhaps even the dragon-teacher, offering to lend me the money to go home by taxi.

The trip was slow and the stops at practically every street corner drove me frantic. I was tempted two or three times to get off and walk, I was so sure I'd get there faster.

At the transfer point for St-Boniface, just before the Provencher Bridge, I saw my nephew Fernand, my sister Anna's eldest son who'd just become an office clerk, getting on my streetcar – or perhaps I was getting on his. Our eyes met across the crowd. We realized we'd been called to the house for the same reason. We elbowed our way through the crowd to be together. The closeness of our ages, only three months apart, had earned us a lot of teasing, and consequently we'd felt uncomfortable and tended to avoid each other. He didn't like being called my nephew any more than I liked being called his aunt. But now, though neither of us said a word or even looked at the other, we joined our little fingers on the seat between us and kept them joined.

The room where my father was dying adjoined the living and dining room. At one time he'd used it as an office and we continued to call it *l'office*. I don't know who first used the English term. Perhaps my father himself, since he was accustomed to using English for anything related to his office work in Winnipeg, where it was the only language of work permitted; or my mother, out of a kind of ingenuous respect for the sort of thing he did at work, which was so far removed from her lowly domestic occupations. Now that I've at last come to wonder about it, who is there to tell me? The room was furnished at that time with a big roll-top desk and a safe, and its walls were covered with very detailed maps of

Saskatchewan and Alberta and others of the townships, on which the locations of his settlements were marked with circles. It was here that my father had often worked far into the night, writing reports to the government or lists of supplies of all kinds needed by the next group of settlers who'd be starting out for their new homes under his guardianship. Maman had probably established him there for the sake of convenience, so she could look after him without constantly having to run up and down stairs, but perhaps also having thought it fitting that his life should end here, where he'd known his hours of greatest hope.

When we reached the house, Fernand and I, still with our little fingers joined, it was full of people. I'd be at a loss to recall exactly who was there, for I had eyes only for the head on the pillow. I have never seen such an avowal of pain on a human face. Not physical pain; from that, at least, he'd been delivered by a strong sedative, which was no doubt also affecting the thinking realms of his being since he appeared unconscious, though from time to time he'd still give a little moan as if in recollection of suffering more than from its present effects. But what his face expressed, now that all defences were down, was the incredible accumulation of suffering in a single human life. I was fascinated by that defenceless face; as I looked at it, I was hearing a soul's long, soundless lamentation for the first time in my life. So that's what life is, I said to myself, a torment so frightful one's face can no longer mask it when the end comes. And I think it was that extraordinary, otherworldly openness which must at last have made me see death as something majestic and beautiful.

We had a little tabby cat which had come to adore my father – it's a mystery why cats are instinctively drawn to melancholy souls. He kept jumping up onto the pillow despite my mother's efforts to shoo him away. He'd crouch very close to the dying man's face and watch it intensely. When Maman was out of the room for a minute, he put out his tongue and gently began to lick the fine white fringe of hair on the still temple, remembering, perhaps, all the fondling my father had lavished on him. I left him alone. It seemed to me our little Mephisto was showing the tender familiarity we ourselves shrank from in the face of approaching death, and in his innocence was the only one still treating my father like a friend, the rest of us having more or less abandoned him.

Not far from the bed, some neighbours were kneeling and praying aloud. I watched the little animal stretch out a soft paw and touch my father's forehead, perhaps in his way trying to get him to pay attention. I heard sweet voices asking God to receive my father's soul. Then Maman came back. Scandalized to find Mephisto occupying so prominent a place in such a tragic scene, she picked him up and took him away, and shut him behind some door. Long afterwards, we could still hear him mewing disconsolately through the murmur of prayers.

At last I knelt down with the others, not so much to pray, I think, but to be closer to the event, this end of a life which was so engrossing me. This was the first time I was to witness death and, as happens with everyone, I think, the first feeling it awakened in me was such a burning, infinite, and prodigious curiosity that for the moment it was distracting me from grief. I'd been hauled away from the insignificant tussle we call life and brought face to face with the total mystery of existence, and this death on this day was telling no more about existence than had the first death to come upon humankind.

Scattered among these painful thoughts came all kinds of other ordinary ones, some almost trite. Now that I was closer to my father's face, I observed again how much he looked like photographs I'd seen of Tolstoy in his latter years: the same high forehead and receding hairline, the same furrowed cheeks, the same eyes deeply sunk in their sockets – and, not so long ago, the same piercing gaze which seemed to look deeper into the soul than any other I've known. Naïvely, it also pleased me to liken the love that both of them had for the Doukhobors, for whose settlement in Canada Tolstoy had contributed the royalties from one of his great novels. Despite their fractiousness, my father had always defended them and continued to attend to their needs long after conducting them to the virgin lands on which they were to settle. It occurred to me, too, that in French he and Tolstoy bore the same given name, Léon.

Suddenly my father's death throes became more pronounced. His chest sagged. His mouth opened wide and gasped for air with a rattling sound. His eyes, however, remained closed as if from exhaustion. For several seconds his body remained still, then with a longer rattle the terrible struggle resumed. It was as if someone were trying desperately to tear himself away from life, and when

I thought of it that way, as a struggle to be free, it seemed to me that life had been impossibly cruel to him. At last he lifted his hands limply as if to push everything away. He opened his eyes, not seeing anyone around him, I think. Though unseeing, they seemed to follow a light across the room. Another breath, not as deep or from as far away, more like a sigh this time, came just as far as his lips like a last little ripple fading on a beach. His head fell to the side. There was no sound, no struggle now. Silence at last.

Then Maman approached. She looked at the face of her lifelong companion with a curious fervour that I had never before seen in her, one which saw much more in this dead man than any of us had ever seen in his lifetime. Gently she closed his half-open eyes. Then in the midst of the prayerful silence there rose a high-pitched wail which I didn't realize at first was mine. Astonished to hear me cry out that way, Maman dropped everything and rushed to comfort me. Kneeling beside me, she put an arm around my shoulders and drew me to her, rocking us both as if to lull our pain.

I couldn't yet understand why my grief was so acute. I hadn't thought I'd loved my father so deeply. It was now my turn to have my eyes opened, and I couldn't stand the hard reality that death was teaching me in so short a lesson. Does a man need to die for his life to become important in a way unsuspected mere seconds earlier? And must one's own soul be laid bare, stripped of its cover in relation to that life? In this moment I discovered a thousand and one lost opportunities for showing my father the affection now pouring out of me like a pent-up torrent. Only last week he'd asked Maman why I hadn't been to see him in the hospital. She'd made excuses for me, saying I was very worried about the lesson I had to give in one of the city schools, working every night preparing all kinds of approaches because I didn't really know what would be asked of me, that he'd soon be home in any event. There was truth in all this, but it was also true that I hadn't gone to see him because I didn't know how to behave or what to say to him when he was so sick. We'd never learned to talk to each other, each always hoping the other would start and break the ice. Only now I realized he'd craved affection, wanting it so badly he couldn't ask for it for fear of being rejected. Now I knew it was this fear which used to make him seem so severe. I knew because I could see that I'd always been that way myself. The truth was that we were two of a kind, each living in fear of finding our poor, shy love for each other misunderstood.

I began to cry in great sobs, I was so distraught that life should be such a tissue of misunderstanding. Thinking perhaps that my misery came from feeling my father hadn't loved me, Maman now tried to persuade me otherwise. Still kneeling beside me and rocking me as she held me to her, she whispered that two nights ago when he'd begun to suffer so much he'd told her she could depend on me because I was really a brave, hard-working child; that two or three weeks ago, when I was running a bit of a fever but had gone to the school as usual, he'd been very upset, saying, "She's got my delicate health, poor child. I'm afraid she's going to have a hard life." And so on, not suspecting she was wringing my heart, because my grief lay in seeing no possibility of making amends. My relationship to my father would remain for ever as it was when death separated us. Nothing could ever be added, taken back, corrected, or wiped away.

If only I'd had just one visit with him in the hospital. "One little visit," I told myself pleadingly as if it just might be possible, as if the lost opportunity might miraculously be recaptured. Or perhaps I resented his not waiting, not giving me a little more time to bring him my teacher's certificate. So I wept as I thought about the joy we could have had together.

Now there was no going back. All I had to console me was my memory of that wheelbarrow ride with my old father holding the handles high and me in the box, lifting to him what I really believe was a beaming face.

MY FATHER'S remains were exposed at the house in an open coffin, as was the custom then. In the house on Deschambault Street there had been similar observances for two other members of the family: my much-loved Grandmother Landry, who'd come to die there at the age of eighty-four when I was eight and whom I remembered well, and my sister Marie-Agnès, who'd died as the result of burns when I was a baby. The house was therefore no stranger to the simple yet dignified preparations occasioned by a death in those days.

Maman had removed everything removable from the living room, and the rest, just the piano as I recall, was draped in black, as was the big window looking onto the street. In the middle of the room stood the coffin, surrounded by tapers whose flickering light played night and day on my father's stone-still face, now and then creating a fleeting impression of life. He looked very distinguished in his best navy-blue suit; he'd worn it so little in latter years that it looked brand new, though it was very loose around his wasted shoulders. Although this was no longer the fashion, he had on a hard wing collar which held his neck and head very straight, reminding me of the picture I still had of him wearing a collar like that for some evening event, which would have been a rare occasion indeed. Or perhaps I wasn't really remembering such an occasion, just imagining it from the story Maman had told us a dozen times about the invitation she and my father had received to the lieutenant-governor's ball, and about the extraordinary adventure this had led to.

Yes, some twenty years or more before, when my father was already well on in years and my mother still young, though old enough to have given birth to almost all her children, they really had been invited to a ball for the first and only time in their lives. I loved the story. Maman used to tell it as though it were funny, something to laugh over, but I'd always thought it rather sad. Why did it keep popping into my mind out of the blue at this time, during meals for instance, or now, when the flood of callers was about to begin and I was here alone in the stillness and quiet beside my father's open coffin? Alone, that is, except for the little tabby cat. For he'd been quick to learn to make his visits to his dead master at times when Maman was too busy to see him slip by, and when no one was there but me; he knew I'd never chase him away. He'd jump up on the coffin and crouch on its edge with all four feet together, and stay there motionless, his eyes big and reflecting the light of the tapers, staring at my father's face. He never touched it now. He just watched it intently. I think he and I were equally engrossed in the drama of death, he on one side of the coffin and I on the other.

But what had made me think about the ball just then? Perhaps the big gilt-framed photograph of my father when he was young, which Maman had hung on the living-room wall. It must have been taken about the time they met, or perhaps earlier, because he

74

couldn't have been much more than thirty. He was a stranger to me as he appeared in that picture, a handsome young man with curly hair, a trace of a smile in his eyes, and an honest, open face alive with hope and ideals. The face of a man with a sense of fun and also hope, confidence, and, to a certain extent, ambition: all the things that nourish the soul. I'd have been very surprised if anyone had told me then how much I was like the young man in the heavy gold-leafed frame, especially around the eyes.

On the same wall Maman had also hung photographs of my grandfather Charles Roy and his sad-faced wife, Marcelline. The portraits upset me terribly every time I looked at them, and I resented Maman's having given them that place of honour.

We'd never known those two except through those awful portraits and the occasional disclosure let drop by my father. I felt such an antipathy towards them that I refused to recognize anything about myself in them. I imagined I was descended only from the Landrys, a breed in striking contrast, light-hearted, fun-loving, romantic, even a little fey, as well as gentle, loving, and passionate.

But at this moment, having turned my eyes to the grandmother I'd never known, I found I was suddenly deeply moved by that cheerless face with lips closed tight as though holding back too deep a sorrow to convey in words, a sorrow perhaps never confessed except in this silent photograph. From the frame beside Marcelline's, the face of her husband glared down, Charles Roy, my grandfather, grimly stern and uncompromising. Yet however hard his eyes, they seemed to be brimming with the misty sadness of never having known what it is to love or be loved; a self-appointed judge of morality, he was alone in the world. The little I knew of him, gleaned from scraps my father let fall in emotional moments, was that he was hostile to anything that was joyful or mind-broadening, and particularly to books, which he considered to be the most evil things on earth.

One day something very strange happened between my father and me. I'd escaped to some corner of the house and was reading; I seemed happy, I suppose, as one always is when borne off by the magic of a well-told story, or merely the elation of seeing oneself in words more adroit than one's own. My father appeared and stood looking at me. In a voice that was a bit husky and full of despondency, he asked, "D'you know how lucky you are?"

I looked up at him, astonished. Then he blurted out this extraordinary revelation:

"When I was about the age you are now, I was reading one night in a corner the way you're doing, only by candlelight, and I was happy for a while, when all of a sudden my father was standing over me, shouting, 'There you are again filling your head with lies and bad influence instead of getting on with honest work! Give me that cursèd book! All that's written there is lies!' And he snatched it out of my hands. He lifted a lid from the stove. The flame was high because the night was cold and we'd made the fire roar. My father threw my book in it, the only book I had. I can still see it burn, all my life I've seen it burn."

Now, alone in this room with his remains, I finally grasped all the bitterness of that outpouring so many years before. I began to weep softly, not for me and my omissions and regrets but for a thirteen-year-old's grief borne for a lifetime without real consolation, and now beyond consolation.

Not long after that incident, according to Maman, young Léon left the paternal home and went to Quebec City, where he took employment as a junior salesman in a shop. He was paid so little that he couldn't afford a room in the city and slept on a pallet under the counter on which, by day, he displayed merchandise for sale. This surely must be the story I was told, yet I'm so accustomed to stringing out facts and story-telling that a doubt has crept into my mind, and there are times when I tell myself it just couldn't have been so. Now I have no one left to resolve my hesitation and corroborate the story as I believe I heard it.

In due course my father was taken under the wing of a compassionate and generous priest who bore the cost of two years of study for him in a classical college, though whether in Quebec City or elsewhere I don't know. Then he went to the United States, where for the next few years he was so constantly on the move that who knows where he'd been, as Maman used to say.

Despite my distaste, I returned to the latter-day Savonarola, the burner of books who was at the root of those misfortunes. I began to understand where my father's gloomy side had come from, the side that showed increasingly as he aged. Also his fear of being misunderstood, which made him touchy. As for my book-burning grandfather, to whom could he have owed such bitterness of soul that all he'd ever spread around him was more bitterness? My feeling was that one would have to go back indefinitely, into the far, far distant past, to discover the real source of ill, or of good.

My eye fell again on the portrait of my father as a young man, the one I was comparing with his face in death, and despite myself the story of the lieutenant-governor's ball returned to my thoughts.

The invitation had come to the house. My parents must have been living in the house they rented when they first came to St-Boniface, before the one on Deschambault Street was built. I imagine that house filled with young children, and with tears, laughter, and rumpus. I can see Maman, a bit frazzled, perhaps doing the laundry, wiping her hands hurriedly on her apron before opening the large envelope with the gold crown on the flap. Then a bolt from the blue! "Mr. and Mrs. Léon Roy are requested to attend a ball at...."

Did she begin at once to picture the dress she'd wear, and how she'd make it, and what fabric she'd use? What is certain, because she told us a hundred times, is that her mind was made up immediately: nothing in the world would keep her from going to that ball. My father was away at the time for a week or two, visiting his settlements. He might come back bone-weary, as he often did, and not much interested in getting himself all dandied up for an evening like that, one which would surely intimidate him, unaccustomed as he was to social gatherings. Maman set out to persuade him to accept, and she succeeded. How did she do it? Had she already made her dress of peach-coloured satin? Did she put it on to show him, with her beautiful black hair done up in a chignon? And did his heart melt to see the radiance of the young woman, who'd never in her life known a single hour of social triumph? I had the strongest urge to run to her in the kitchen, where, mastering her grief, she'd be preparing supper for the country relatives who'd come for the funeral and for whom the least she could do was keep them for a meal or two. I could imagine the look she'd give me if, in the midst of her grief and her concern for her guests, I appeared with questions like, "Maman, the night of the ball, how had you done your hair? Surely you had some little bit of jewellery to wear, didn't you?"

At the time it really did seem important to me to get all the details of the story right then, as if this were its last chance, like a dying fire's, to give a final little flare of warmth to our hearts.

In any event, she'd enquired of a number of civil servants' wives who were better versed in the customs of polite society than she was, and had ascertained which of the social graces were important to observe on arrival at Government House and during the course of the evening. She made herself what she called a *sortie de bal* or evening wrap, which was probably a long, voluminous cape to throw on over her dress. For inspiration in her sewing she no doubt went to the evening-wear departments of the fashionable shops in the city, perhaps trying on some dresses, and why not the most expensive while she was at it, just the way she did when she made my jodhpurs. But this time, for once in her life, the place of honour was to be hers.

At last it was the night of the ball. She must have been radiant, with her eyes sparkling, as she still was nowadays when confronted by some happy surprise. Father must have worn his best plain, dark blue suit, like the one he was to be buried in — I couldn't remember ever seeing him wear any other colour. His black tie would have been fastened, as at present, with a tie pin finely set with an opal, a gift from a group of grateful settlers, a possession he cherished beyond any other in his life and which, the day after tomorrow, before the coffin was closed, Maman would take from him to keep in remembrance.

So they left for the ball arm in arm, young again perhaps, both light of step as though released from their constant burdens of duty, cares, and frugality. At the corner they took the streetcar. Maman didn't feel the incongruity of being all dressed up in her ballgown, rubbing shoulders with weary-faced, sleepy labourers in the dimly lit, rattling and lurching little streetcar. It let them off fairly far from Government House. They continued on foot. Only when they reached the gates to the grounds, with the imposing house blazing with lights from every window at the end of the driveway, did they begin to feel intimidated. Carriages were passing to right and left of them, splattering them with mud as they went. They pressed on to the entrance, where an aide-de-camp was opening the carriage door for each arriving couple, who then, the man supporting his lady by the elbow, had only to advance a step or two to find themselves, gay and resplendent, in the shelter of a marquee, with the sound of music issuing in great gusts whenever the door opened on the glittering interior. Father was the first to want to turn back. "Let's go, Mélina, we don't belong here." But she was not to be persuaded, not yet. The vision still shimmered in her head. She dragged my protesting father almost to the bottom step. The only thing that finally won out over her vision was the disdainful gaze the splendidly uniformed usher cast down his nose at them. Maman then looked at her dress and saw the spattered mud, and at her shoes and saw that they were soiled. She whispered to my father, "Léon, let's ignore him. Let's walk by as though we're just looking. After all, this is where the representative of the people lives; anyone can come just to look. We'll walk around, then go out again."

Around the corner she spied a low window looking into the great reception room. She found that by standing on a stone she could get a fine view of the interior. My father, overcome by embarrassment, kept saying, "Come away...," but she remained standing under the window, one hand on the casement to balance her. Later, when she told me the story of that already distant evening, she laughed merrily at herself as she said, "Can't you see me watching through the window as the men in tail coats and the women in dresses with trains came forward, and then the women curtseying to the lieutenant-governor and the men bending their heads a bit haughtily, and all of it in English; you know, I could even hear the aide-de-camp announcing 'Mr. and Mrs. Hugo McFarlane....' Then another couple would come up, the woman covered in pearls and diamonds and the man in decorations.... Can't you see me in my little homemade dress," she said, "can't you see the two of us, your father mortified and me all muddy as though I'd come straight from the fields...." She laughed and laughed and there didn't seem to be a trace of rancour or bitterness, only the natural sense of fun in someone who could look at herself with perfect clarity and humour.

"Your father kept telling me we should leave," she said, "but I wanted to see the ball begin, and the couples dancing."

The orchestra struck up a waltz. The lieutenant-governor bowed to a lady. Then, she holding her train in a gloved hand – "To think," recalled Maman, "that I never knew you had to have long gloves" – and the lieutenant-governor a bit starchily, together they led off the dancing. Then other couples formed and Maman watched them waltzing about beneath the great chandeliers while everything sparkled, the crystal drops of the chandeliers, the diamonds around the necks of the dancing ladies, the medals against the dark suits, the eyes of men in love and of women conscious of being desirable....

I returned from my curious journey into the past hoping to have discovered perhaps an hour or two of happiness in my father's life.

They came home by streetcar; they weren't unhappy, insisted Maman, not at all unhappy; she, indeed, still felt all lit up by the festive spectacle. Even with her hair a bit mussed and her dress a bit muddied she must have been very beautiful that night to my father, who had so seldom seen her dressed up for a party, scintillating with excitement. Who knows, perhaps that night was one of the great nights of their lives. My sister Marie-Agnès was born less than a year after the lieutenant-governor's ball.

I was endlessly amazed, there beside my father's remains, to find myself already so eagerly engrossed in searching back for the smallest scraps I could recall of his life. I didn't know then that death's first effect is to bring the deceased to life in the minds of those who have loved that person, and with a clarity and intensity never again equalled.

I leaned forward and by the flickering light of the candles studied the poignantly fine face my father would present ever after in my memory. Great dignity emanated from it. It had calmed my grief and even my regrets. I was fascinated. This face of death, like many others later in my life, never spoke to me of a void, or of nothingness. Neither did it speak to me of another life, or another world. To me, what was there was total mystery, something never even to be glimpsed, total release at last, darkness intact, and for this reason, perhaps, more beautiful than anything I'd ever seen on earth. When I looked at my father's face I had the impression that life, almost everything about life, was one distraction after another, all meant to conceal the essential truth from us.

ALMOST AS SOON as the funeral was over I had to get back to my studies to prepare for the approaching examinations. To my great surprise, I passed them without difficulty. Perhaps the dragon-teacher had repented at the last minute and given me a good mark.

Or perhaps Dr. Mackintyre had intervened. I'll never know, but I finished not far from the top of the class.

If the news had come in time it would have brightened my father's last days, but now I didn't know what to do with it. I longed to be able to bring him back to life so I could tell him. What was so great about it if it was just for me? Later it was Maman I longed to bring back, so I could tell her about all the wonderful things that were happening with *The Tin Flute*. In my imagination she wouldn't believe me as I told her, and I'd be saying, "Come on now, Maman, I'm almost rich, so you can rest in peace now." And she, back there in the shadows, would be shaking her head sadly, not believing I wasn't still poor and defenceless. Later still it was my sister Anna, who'd always been so worried about what love, marriage, and family ties would do to me; I'd have been able to tell her those shackles had in fact been rather good for me. But she wouldn't have heard and would have kept right on worrying about me as always. Nowadays it's Dédette I keep calling to in vain, wanting so much to tell her it's all right about a particular sorrow in my life, the one she knew about and was so upset by. But however many times I tell her that I've got over it, that it doesn't hurt much any more, she never hears me. I've learned from life that we don't so much want our loved ones back when we're unhappy as to soothe the worries they had for us in life. For it seems to me we can't free them of those worries, even when we've been freed of them ourselves.

Which is probably why I feel so much better if I see Maman or my sisters with happy, untroubled faces in my dreams at night. But no dream has ever let me see my father young again and smiling, as I've seen the others.

VIII

JUST BEFORE the school year finished at the end of May, Dr. Mackintyre called me to his office. When my father died he'd written me a beautiful letter full of affection and comforting thoughts, which I regret not having kept. In those days I was so obsessed with having my hands free that I kept nothing.

I entered and thanked him for his letter. Visibly moved himself, he waved aside my thanks and gestured me to a chair. Quite a few seconds passed before he began telling me almost excitedly that he had news for me, not just good but excellent news.

I must have looked at him unbelievingly because he quickly confirmed it, then explained.

At that time of the year, he told me, a school board without enough substitute teachers sometimes asked the Normal Institute to send them one of its graduating students. He'd just had such a request and had thought of me. The school was in a little village about fifty miles from the city. The trip wouldn't cost much. I'd earn five dollars for each school-day. But the best part of it was that when I applied for a permanent teaching job, which would be soon, I'd be able to show I'd had a little experience, without, he observed artfully, having to specify that it had only been for a month.

As I listened to him I felt that my life had already turned a corner. The ink on my teacher's certificate wasn't yet dry and already I had a school. *My* school! Suddenly I was so overcome with joy I could have flung my arms around his neck. And at the time I didn't even know what a rare piece of luck this was; only three schools had made such a request and there were three hundred students finishing the year at the Normal Institute. In my case, of course, the school and village were French, so I fitted the bill perfectly. All the same, getting my own school when I was barely out of teachers' college, what a stroke of luck!

I literally ran home, and I think I was even skipping when there was nobody ahead on the sidewalk, the way I used to as a little girl.

I came bounding into the kitchen.

"Maman! Maman! Guess what!"

I wonder how many times I'd burst in on her that way, all youth, verve, and excitement, when she was coping with her worries and grief. I think she was making jam. The wood stove had been stoked to the limit and was giving off a searing heat. Her face was almost as cooked as her jam and her cheeks were beet red, which emphasized the joylessness in her eyes, the still-fresh memories of bereavement. There had been no triumph, no achievement since my father's death to help her cope with her grief, it's true. I was rather ashamed of my euphoria but I really couldn't contain it.

"Guess what! A school, Maman! My first school!"

"Stop your babbling about a school!" she retorted, losing patience. "We're still a long way from September. And you're just out of school yourself."

"That's what's so wonderful! I've got one already. For the month of June. I start the day after tomorrow. *My* school, Maman!" And I tried to throw my arms around her, tried to spin her round with me.

It was too much. She shoved me away almost roughly.

"A school? Where?"

"At Marchand."

"Marchand!"

All of a sudden she was bristling and hostile. I was bewildered. Hadn't her life been focused on seeing me get a school at last so I could stand on my own feet? Suddenly, as if to emphasize her disapproval, or revulsion as it seemed, she tore off her apron.

"Not Marchand," she flung at me. "Never! It's a dreadful place! I've heard about it. The boondocks! You're not going there!"

"The boondocks?" I said. "It's only for a month, for goodness' sake, and I've got to start somewhere. You can't expect me to start at the top after all."

"But Marchand! Ugh!" She looked as though she might be sick.

In the end she came and sat down at the kitchen table. She folded her hands and stared in front of her, not believing what was happening, hurting with the pain for which she herself had laid the groundwork. And finding distress when I thought I was bringing her pleasure, I reminded her of this, not thinking I was rubbing salt in her wounds.

"You're the one who's wanted me to be a teacher all your life."

She was weakening, about to give in.

"When is it?" she asked in a small, resigned voice.

"Well, I really have to leave tomorrow."

"Tomorrow!"

A shower of exhortations began to fall on me. With all those uncouth people out there I'd have to be careful to keep my distance. Be polite, yes, but never familiar. Make sure I didn't get put upon, either. "Oh dear," she sighed, "you're too young to start off surrounded by tough, bad-mannered hicks."

"Maman, so what if I have to learn fast?"

In the end she mustered up a smile for me and left everything she'd been doing to come and help me pack.

By the next day she'd found an acquaintance who was going to be driving in the direction of Marchand and had agreed to take me.

Such was her distress over seeing me leave the house that I think she forgot to kiss me. All that mattered was that I should look out for myself, keep my place, stand on my rights, and, if the going got too tough out there, come home.

ONCE THERE, it was abundantly clear that the only place I could stay was the hotel, since there was nothing else except some wretched wooden shacks built right on the sandy ground, scattered among clumps of scrawny spruce trees. Forty years later I would draw on this mournful setting and the sorrowful event that marked my first day of school at Marchand to write "The Dead Girl", the episode that came to light so strangely in *Enchanted Summer*.

But that day when I set foot in Marchand, terrified and homesick already, how far I was from having any sense of the aptitude I had – or would have, like a seed lying dormant in the ground long before germinating – for turning moments of my life into stories that would create a bridge between me and other people. And those moments that have made me feel the most alone have often won me the most hearts among strangers. One knows less about one's own destiny than about anything else on earth.

84

Not until I was halfway up the precipitous stairs on the way to my room, behind the hefty figure of the lady hotel-keeper, who was lugging up my two suitcases, did I suddenly remember one of Maman's most specific enjoinders.

"Before you take a room find out the price," she'd said. "Be very careful they don't take advantage of your inexperience. Considering what you're going to earn, don't let yourself in for more than twenty-five dollars a month, room and board."

Behind the ample back I heard myself pipe up with the question in a voice so faint and shy that scorn was the only reaction it could draw from a person so unmistakably sure of herself.

"Madame, the rent...what will it be? How much will you be asking?"

Perhaps irritated that I should bring it up in the middle of the staircase, and to her back, and in any case being of a nature to want to take me down a peg, she plonked the bags down right there.

"First off you can do yer own fetchin' and carryin'."

Several steps farther up, when it was my turn to be out of breath, she deigned rudely to tell me what I wanted to know.

"Anyway, young miss, you needn't think I'm gonna feed you and give you a bed and light and...and...for less than twenty-five dollars a month."

I heaved a sigh of relief despite her offensive manner. That was the limit Maman had fixed. I could accept it without argument, and Lord knows I had no heart to haggle with that awful woman.

My room was small and almost bare, but clean. A clean little prison cell. My landlady cocked her chin at it and left without a word. I sat down on the foot of the narrow iron cot with its dreary white coverlet just like the ones in convent dormitories. But all I really saw was the window. It looked out on one of the most lifeless vistas I've ever seen. Nothing moved in that landscape. Nothing even stirred. There were trees all over, standing alone or in sparse clumps, and all of them were still, petrified, waiting for something to happen. As though the wind had stopped outside the village, not daring to cross a mysterious, invisible line, while all within lay paralysed, struck with some terrible foreboding.

I went downstairs and, taking a wrong turn, found myself in a big, bright, airy kitchen, certainly the most pleasant room in that whole peculiar hotel, where elsewhere the blinds stayed depressingly drawn, leaving everything in deep gloom. My landlady was getting a snack for the children, five of them, I think, who would be my pupils the following morning. But they paid no more attention to me than to a stranger whose business here was and would remain no concern of theirs.

The mother was cutting thick slices of beautiful white bread which couldn't have looked more appetizing. Since the people who'd brought me were in a hurry to go about their business and get home before dark, we hadn't made any stops where we could get a bite to eat. I was dying of hunger. Next she spread each slice of bread thickly with strawberry jam. My mouth was watering. Each of the children was given one and then ran outside, taking big bites and licking the jam off their lips as they passed me. When they'd all been served I raised my eyes humbly to the provider. The bread was so generously cut and spread and smelled so delicious, I wonder if I've ever wanted a slice of bread and jam so much in my whole life. My landlady looked me straight in the eye. She took the bread and wrapped it in a clean towel to keep it fresh, then put it in its tin box and slammed the lid. She took the pot of jam, screwed the lid back on tight, and put it in the cupboard.

"Mind you don't get yourselves dirty now," she called after the children. Then to me she said crisply, "Supper's at six."

I went outside. I took the path leading to the schoolhouse, which was not far from the houses and, like them, built right on the sandy ground. I went in. I sat down at a desk that was up two steps on a dais if I remember correctly, unless I'm confusing it with the school at the Little Water Hen. The silence around me was oppressive. It weighed heavily on my stomach. It even invaded my thoughts, frightening them and preventing them from taking shape. Through the row of windows in the south wall of the schoolhouse I could see a straggly troop of those puny spruce trees standing as motionless as one could imagine, stuck in their woebegone poses. And sitting there I peered into the obscurity ahead of me, trying to catch a glimpse of the life awaiting me.

IX

THE FOLLOWING September I began teaching at Cardinal, a larger and less indigent village but no livelier, located on the opposite side of the province. I was dreadfully homesick there and uncomfortable besides, for I was boarding in a flimsily built house with the barest suggestion of heating, even when winter set in and its winds blew through the thin walls. If I didn't freeze to death it was because my landlady took pity on me and made me a voluminous feather comforter. Pulled up over me in bed, it felt like a light and marvellously soft mountain. After that I wasn't cold any more, not at night anyway, even when the water in the pitcher beside my bed froze hard.

In the last chapter of *Street of Riches* I think I recreated the atmosphere of that village fairly accurately. It also figures briefly in *Children of My Heart*, the book I'm putting the final touches to at present. Nowhere, however, have I tried to describe it exactly as it was. That's something I don't think I could do any more. Nowadays I need to break up the elements of my own experience, separate them, reassemble them, add to them, leave this or that out and perhaps invent things. That's often the way I manage to convey the most authentic mood, an intangible depending neither on any precise detail nor on the sum of the parts, but somehow on an almost equally intangible and seemingly strange composition. It would bore me to death now to describe a house faithfully just as I see it, or a street or a corner bar, the way I did in *The Tin Flute*. I made myself do it then, partly for the sake of realism, it's true, but also to discipline an overactive imagination, to make myself look carefully at everything and not allow myself to get into sloppy habits of describing things with no roots in reality.

I'm therefore not inclined to dwell further on the village of

Cardinal, though the year I spent there was one of the most important in my life. That year turned a spoiled child into an industrious young teacher, perhaps even a first-rate one, since the inspector's report must have had something to do with my getting a position the following year at the Académie Provencher in St Boniface, just a stone's throw from our house. Now Maman could stop worrying about my living in the boondocks.

One of the good things about Cardinal – the best thing, as I saw it – was that it wasn't very far from my uncle Excide's farm where I'd spent such happy summer holidays and which I loved so much. That year I spent almost every weekend there. I'd take the train on Saturday morning and get off fifteen minutes later at the next station, which was Somerset. From there I'd find some way to get to the farm a few miles away. Or I might just wait, knowing that my cousins hardly ever missed coming to town to shop on Saturdays. We really would have had to try very hard not to run into each other, either at the general store or at the Chinese restaurant, where one of us was always having an ice cream. After sleepy little Cardinal, where the only sound for hours on end was the wind, setting foot in Somerset seemed like coming to a mini-metropolis, and I'd be in a lather of excitement.

Sometimes, when he had business with the blacksmith-cum-garage mechanic in Cardinal whose work he liked best, my uncle would come and get me on Friday evening. Then we'd speed off in the high old Ford, the hard tires pitching us constantly one against the other on the bumpy roads he'd take because they got us there fastest. There'd be total silence during the short trip. Though he could be talkative when he wished, he never spoke to me when he drove, and I learned to leave him to his silent woolgathering, having soon realized that he didn't like it intruded on when driving. At first I found his moodiness disconcerting, but I'd still be happy and excited because I was headed for a little piece of heaven, so to speak. I'd have two whole days at the farm, perhaps a bit more, because occasionally my cousins would take me home very early Monday morning to give me a blissful, unbroken Sunday. All week I'd be obsessed with the thought that a treat like that should be earned, and I'd work twice as hard to deserve it. I would have worked as hard anyway, perhaps, but not as eagerly.

So I spent the weeks working like a Trojan and the weekends laughing, singing, and dancing, and time went by very quickly.

My uncle's house was well heated; I could wash my hair and walk around as it dried without risk of catching cold. My cousin Léa and I would spend hours playing duets over and over on the old piano in the living room, ready at any minute to collapse in paroxysms of laughter when we'd hear a squeak like a mouse's among the high notes. That squeak had been the piano's distinguishing feature ever since a mouse had chewed the felt from one of the strings and made a nest with it in that corner.

On Saturday morning, Léa and I would go out and stroll up one side of the main street and back again, pretending we didn't know that the eyes of the young bucks of the village were on us. If we didn't do that, it was because the young bucks came calling on us. There was a great deal of ceremony involved in these visits, which amused me no end, though I could never be persuaded to play the role expected of me. If a young suitor came calling for the first time and we liked him, we were supposed to let him know without saying so, by handing him his hat with our own hands when he left at the end of the evening. This meant he could come again. Not handing him his hat at the door when he'd sung us a song with his eyes fixed on ours, having sort of dedicated it to us with a bow before beginning, was nothing less than a serious breach of hospitality, of which I was guilty many times. My uncle, who was so freewheeling himself in some ways, scolded me for it, even predicting I'd never find a man to marry me if I kept brushing off honourable intentions so clearly demonstrated. But to me it was all too comical. Whenever a young man stood before me, gazing at me with sheep's eyes as he sang one of those western laments that all seem to have the same tune, it was all I could do to keep from laughing in his face. And it was even harder to contain myself when he stood at the door waiting with his hand out for his hat.

That's the way it was at my uncle's; I'd be light-hearted, playful, and teasing again, disrespectful of customs and no doubt enjoying making myself conspicuous. During the week I'd come back down to earth in the freezing cold house in Cardinal. I'd do my preparation for the next day at the school, where there was a bit of heat at least, and return to the house as late as possible. There were no books or music in that house; the only entertainment the family had was telling each others' fortunes with cards or reading palms or teacups: a distraction common to those in whose lives nothing ever happens — I wrote about it in *Street of Riches* — endlessly asking inanimate objects for promises of a future filled with adventure and fantasy.

THE COMINGS and goings between Cardinal and the farm went on all autumn, and to my immense joy were not interrupted when winter came. By then we'd become too attached to each other, I to my cousins and they to me, to give up our evenings together. But winter soon turned very harsh. One Sunday night I was taken home in a "cabin" sleigh through a raging snowstorm. Years later I used that episode as the basis of "The Storm" in *Street of Riches*. Another time when we made the trip in an open box-sleigh, the cold was so perishing that my cousin and I, sitting side by side on the single seat, pulled the fur robes over our heads and virtually buried ourselves in them, leaving the horses unguided. I was rather worried they might not find their way.

It was Cléophas who was taking me home that night.

"Bah," he retorted, "if we're going to freeze to death, what's the difference whether we know where we are or not? You needn't worry, though. The poor beasts have taken you home so many times they know the road by heart, you can be sure of that. And they're in such a hurry to get back to the stable they'll keep up a good trot, too."

Luckily it was a perfectly clear night. The crusted snow shone almost as brightly as the vast expanse of stars I could see twinkling busily any time I opened our fur tent to get a little air. The night was so resplendent with its crisp, steel-sharp bite and its blazing lights that I felt something like shame to be hiding from it like that. But the cold burned when it reached my lungs and I'd duck back under cover. My cousin, who'd be half asleep, would growl at me for letting in the cold and beg me to keep still. We must both have slept a good part of the trip, partly torpid from the cold and partly asphyxiated, no doubt. A sudden stop jolted us awake. Dazed and alarmed, we sat up, rubbing our eyes. The horses had come to a stop at the door of my boarding house.

I jumped out.

"Bye," I said to Cléophas.

"Bye," he replied.

I could hardly hear him. He'd already pulled the fur robes back over his head. Then, of their own accord, the horses turned the sleigh around and trotted briskly away.

Since one or another of my cousins always had to take me home – though it often seemed to be Cléophas's turn – I should have recognized how much trouble I was giving them and considered not coming so frequently. But the good-hearted fellows never complained. And when Friday came around you'd think I was possessed; I'd hear the irresistible call of the piano and violin in my uncle's house, the chases upstairs and down, the laughter, the singing, the harmless giddiness of our time of life.

IN MARCH the weather became abominable. It poured with rain for two or three days, and when the countryside had become as pitted and potholed as a muddy cattle-pen, the cold returned and froze all the humps and hollows rock-hard. Then again mild weather came and turned all that surface into a huge swamp of wet snow and mud. One Monday morning, Cléophas wondered whether to take a sleigh or the buggy to drive me home. Luckily he decided on the buggy, because there were long stretches of road without a trace of snow, which we never could have navigated with a sleigh. But those were still the most difficult. We would inch ahead through a morass, with each turn of the wheels flinging splatters of mud onto our clothes, down our necks, and into our hair. Soon we couldn't help laughing when we looked at one another, because our faces were black with mud and our eyes showed through as if we had masks on.

My uncle warned me that this was the worst time of the year, that nothing, either sleigh or buggy, could get through, and even less a car, so I should wait a bit; he would come and get me as soon as the roads were passable.

When I wrote *Where Nests the Water Hen*, I gave my stouthearted Luzina that dreadful kind of weather to travel in, and I think I knew what I was talking about when I described the problems she and the unsociable Nick Sluziuk had to face.

I waited two, then three weeks. A bright, unclouded April sky was enough to convince me that the whole countryside should now

91

be dry enough for travel. In the village it was hardly muddy at all any more. In any event, I could go at least four miles of the distance to my uncle's in a nice, dry train. Then, by taking shortcuts, I'd have only about as far again to walk. I told myself there'd be no trouble getting there, even if the ground was still a bit wet. Besides, I'd been planning to do that last leg to the farm on foot one day. That Friday, at five minutes past four, I was lucky enough to catch the hand-car going to Somerset. So there I was with the railway hands on a little mobile platform driven by a lever vigorously pumped up and down by one of them. We bowled along in the warm spring breeze between brimming ditches, accompanied by the song of water freed from the bonds of winter.

Where the railway crossed the little section road which was the shortest route to my uncle's, I said goodbye to the kind and helpful men. In a twinkling they were gone, far away already, and I was alone at the edge of what looked like an endless expanse of mud and puddles of water. It was a lonely spot. There was a house nearby, but it had a forbidding air. I had never seen any signs of life there when I passed. In front of the silent house the road was flooded; a usually docile little brook had swelled to the size of a raging river and was sweeping across with rumbling sounds. I was testing the footing with a toe when a man rushed out of the house.

"The road's blocked. Where d'you think you're going?"

I shouted my reply.

"You won't make it," he shouted back. "Stay here for the night. Tomorrow the water may have gone down."

Nothing in heaven or earth was going to stop me from attempting to cross that watercourse. I advanced a few steps and the water came up to my ankles. A few steps more and it was nearing the tops of my knee-high boots. I felt it on the point of spilling into them. I kept advancing very slowly, bracing myself against the current with a stick I'd picked up at the edge of the swollen brook. By now I was afraid I'd be swept off my feet at any minute. Then suddenly the strength of the current slackened. I'd passed the deepest part. Now with each step the water was getting much shallower. I reached solid ground.

On his veranda, his dog beside him now, the man raised a hand as if calling on heaven to confirm that there'd been magic in the feat. The dog was standing half-upright with his front paws on the veranda rail, watching without a sound through the tangle of long hair over his face, as stupefied as his master. Just a couple of hours before, I was told later, those two had watched from the same veranda as another traveller had been forced to retreat, a tall, husky man who'd had water almost up to his waist at the place I'd victoriously crossed. I turned slightly to wave at my silent audience of two, then continued down that totally deserted road as the daylight began to fade. There was no other house on the road between there and my uncle's.

At first I walked along the edge of the road and hardly sank in at all. Under what was left of the snow, my feet were finding spongy but fairly firm ground, and I kept up a pretty regular pace. I was buoyed by the lingering glow of light in the sky, too.

In fact, despite the dismal sight of fields half-clad in shreds of dirty snow, the ominous woods in the distance, and the uniformly muddy colour of everything except that little band of light in the sky, for no reason that I can comprehend the magic of that mysterious time of day was working on me as it has so often in my life, lifting me on a wave of irrepressible confidence. So I walked along that deserted road with no more fear than if help had been at hand on all sides.

Soon I realized that those forbidding woods, that line of sodden black tree-trunks I'd been seeing for some time at the far edge of fields still covered with snow, must be none other than the woods fringing a dried-up lake on the edge of my uncle's farm. Even in summer we didn't often cross through those woods, though I didn't know why. That's the reason I hadn't recognized them at first. If I cut through there, I thought idiotically, I'd reach the house much sooner, saving myself almost two miles by road. My boots were beginning to be very heavy because I was walking in gumbo now, and at each step I was lifting enormous gobs of it which were very hard to shake off. I was getting tired. The witching hour had yielded to a uniform ashen greyness, darkening minute by minute. The shortcut was looking more and more attractive. Suddenly, without further thought, I left the road and struck off across the field towards the dark woods.

At first the snow carried me reasonably well. Only when I'd walked perhaps half-way across the field did it give way beneath me, suddenly, as if to swallow me up. I was up to my hips in a kind of crack that was very hard to get out of because the sides were as soft as the bottom. I managed to crawl out and get to my feet, but just a few steps farther on I sank in again, this time to my waist. Then I found my feet weren't touching bottom any more. My boots began to fill with ice-cold water. I remembered then having heard my uncle grumble one day about a spot on his land where it was still impossible to grow anything, a kind of rotten swamp that he'd never been able to drain. This was what I must have ventured into. Lying flat on my stomach, I realized I was on a thin, semi-frozen layer of snow, no doubt barely covering a small lake, perhaps a deep one. I looked at the line of trees not far away. My only salvation lay there, I thought. I struck out for it, still on my stomach, inching forward with a kind of swimming motion, now with my arms, now with my legs. Behind me I was leaving a series of large holes like a row of graves for a multiple burial in some weird cemetery. I'd lost my flashlight in one of them. I finally reached the line of trees, but I found no firmer surface there, only shelter, one might say, from the great leaden sky spread across the earth, which was now quite colourless. But there was no shelter from the rain which was beginning to fall, without wind or rumbling thunder but hard and steadily, as if it would go on for ever. The weight of my sodden clothes was dragging me down, closer and closer to the water beneath me – the layer of rain-drenched snow and ice that just barely separated me from it was getting thinner by the minute. Not far away, coyotes hurled their bone-chilling call into the night. It didn't affect me the way it usually did. In a way I think I was already beyond fear. It seems to me the feeling I had was one of waiting for something, or even more, perhaps, an urgent, anxious, and infinite curiosity. So I was mortal! And not just mortal but capable of dying an exceedingly stupid death, just yards from the house I loved so much, so close to people who loved me. I think my most crushing realization was that love gave so little protection. If I had cried out at that time I would have done so in vain. Who in that house with its doors and windows well closed would ever hear me calling for help? At that very moment they were probably gossiping cheerfully in the big, friendly kitchen. Of all that happened that night, what hurt most was probably the thought that they would be blissfully unaware that I was fighting off death; that their deep affection for me wouldn't warn them that I was in danger.

I stayed still, lying flat and on my back now. The softening layer of ice and snow still supported me, provided I hardly moved. I lay and gathered my strength, and after a while regained a modicum of reason. I realized that I wasn't going to get out of there by pushing ahead, but by going back the way I'd come.

It was horrible. I relive it in my dreams at night sometimes. I retraced my route from hole to hole, making each one deeper. I must have left fifty or more almost full-length imprints of my body. I reached the road. It was perhaps there that I had the most trouble forcing myself to keep going, for I was gripped by an almost irresistible longing to stay lying on the icy ground and go to sleep, at least for a moment. But I managed to get up and, staggering, set off down the road. My clothes were beginning to stiffen on my body. The water in my boots was turning to ice. It kept raining. Sometimes I'd begin to shiver, then I'd feel so hot I'd think of getting rid of my coat. My soaking hair was stuck to my face. I don't know how I made it over the last few hundred yards. I seem to remember dozing off now and then; I'm not sure I wasn't asleep a few seconds at a time as I continued to walk. Finally the house appeared, all lit up and cheerful-looking through the trees of the same wood whose other side had been so disastrous for me. How good and how sweet life seemed at that moment! But my last really clear thought was that I mustn't say anything about my adventure to the people there so as not to frighten them about what might have happened.

I reached the door. It must have been at least ten o'clock. I'd never arrived at the farm on my own so late at night. It seemed to me only proper to knock on the door.

Silence fell in the big kitchen. Then the door opened. In the rectangle of light I could see them all for a moment as they really were, so kind and lovable, but at first they didn't recognize me. They honestly thought I was some unfortunate stranger lost or in flight, someone whom pure chance had led to their door seeking shelter from the vile weather.

I heard a few words as though from very far away, and fell into their arms.

95

They took care of me, pampered me, and nursed me back to health. Oddly enough, while I was ill under their care, and even later, we never talked about my adventure. Not even the faintest allusion. Not until years later, in any event.

I would never again come to the farm without being invited and brought, but I hasten to add that I didn't have to sit around waiting. Almost every week one or another of the family would turn up, often just as I was dismissing my pupils, giving me barely enough time to go and gather a few things to take with me. They'd realized how I felt. We'll move heaven and earth to return to where we've been happy, even if it costs us our last breath.

X

MY APPRENTICESHIP in the country was not a long one, and in a way I regret it, for there life taught me its most cogent lessons, administered roughly sometimes, even harshly, lessons I learned well and never forgot.

Immediately after my year at Cardinal I was engaged to teach at the Académie Provencher. This was a rather grand name for what was really a big public school – an elementary and high school combined – under the jurisdiction of the Manitoba Department of Education and located in the heart of French-speaking Manitoba, the old quarter of St-Boniface. I was perhaps jumped over the heads of more seasoned teachers who had applied before I did, but if there was any favouritism I owed it undoubtedly to Brother Joseph Hinks, the school's *principal*, as it pleased us to call him in the English fashion. The residence of the Brothers was on Cathedral Street immediately opposite the girls' school I had attended, and Brother Joseph had been well placed, particularly when working in his garden, to watch us passing on walks in crocodile formation, arriving one by one, or possibly exchanging confidences, in any event paying no attention to the gowned figure ostensibly absorbed only in his roses. It seems that with his natural gift for observation and judgement of character, he would size us up from a host of small details and decide long in advance which of us he would favour if ever we should apply to teach at his school. His opinion carried much weight in the choice of staff; it was even said that no one became part of it against his will. He was an Alsatian by birth, a rather small man who impressed partly with his very elegant cuffed and buttoned black cassock and white bib, but even more with his naturally distinguished bearing and profound humanity. In no one else have I ever seen such goodness of heart combined with such authority. All it took to calm a roomful of obstreperous school-children was for him to appear and stand composed and quiet with his hands behind his back, a knowing little smile on his face. In Manitoba he soon came to be regarded as one of the most re-markable educators of his time; even today I see schools adopting methods which he had already put to the test and sometimes re-jected as detrimental nearly fifty years ago.

The high marks I'd got from the inspector at Cardinal combined with the principal's recommendation were enough: at twenty, there I was on the teaching staff of our city's major school for boys, which must have had nearly a thousand pupils at the time.

Though Brother Joseph made all the decisions himself, he had a clever way of consulting us and letting us think we'd made our own choices. For instance, he asked me if I didn't think I'd be happy and at my best teaching the youngest children, having decided himself that this was where I'd be most effective. He wasn't mis-taken, but how on earth could he have known when he had seen me only three or four times?

At Provencher we had two first-grade classes. One was for French-speaking children who, first and foremost, were taught the rudi-ments of their own language, which meant taking rather broad liberties with the province's education laws. After that they learned a smidgin of English, at least a few nursery rhymes of the Humpty Dumpty kind, which they'd recite with such verve for the inspector that he'd be quite won over. That was an old trick practised back in my own early school-days, which apparently still worked.

The other baby class was open to all non-French-speaking chil-dren, who were considered English-speaking though there weren't really any of English origin, but rather Russian, Polish, Italian, Spanish, Irish, Czech, Dutch, almost everything imaginable; those who mostly gravitated to the English side eventually, except for some Italian and Walloon families. This motley class was assigned to me. So I, a young French-speaking teacher, trained to serve my own language and culture in every way possible, found myself in charge of a class of children representing nearly all the nations on earth, most of whom knew no more English than they did French. At first we communicated through sign language and a lot of smil-ing. I didn't feel there was anything absurd about this; I thought of my class simply as a mirror of our country, which is about as rich as any on earth in ethnic variety. I became very attached to it and very close to those children, and they taught me a great deal about the folklore, songs, and dances of their people, as well as something deeper, something both painful and joyous. So much so that when Brother Joseph suggested I move up to a third- or fourth-year class a few years later, I begged him to leave me with my little immigrants. He needed no persuading. I wonder if he'd perceived that I was born to serve the League of Nations in a sense. Or perhaps it was my little charges from all corners of the earth who inspired in me the dream of universal understanding that has been with me ever since.

So I began adulthood already launched on a career, seemingly for life, in conditions that looked almost unbelievably good to Maman after our years of hardship. In fact, because of the Depression, my starting salary at Cardinal, a hundred and ten dollars a month, was reduced to only ninety-six in St-Boniface. Nevertheless, to Maman the life we led was easy and pleasant in comparison to the way it had been before.

"It's almost too good to be true," she'd say from time to time. "Do you think it'll last?"

She had such confidence that things had finally begun to go right for us that she even thought we might manage to "save" the house, as she used to put it. Yet we'd always known that we'd have to resign ourselves to parting with it one day. The taxes and heating bills alone would have eaten up more than half my salary. So Maman had to keep on renting rooms and scrimping and saving to cover a good proportion of our day-to-day expenses. It didn't work. She kept accumulating small debts without my knowledge, just as she'd done behind my father's back.

In our lucid moments we were almost agreed, for a few hours at a time, that we should put the house up for sale. There were only three of us, Maman, Clémence, and I, living there the year round now. Surely we'd be just as comfortable in a small rented apartment which would cost less and cause less work for Maman.

"Yes," she'd say, seeming to have come around to the idea. "I'll get after it tomorrow. I'll go and see So-and-so, who might be thinking of buying.... You never know."

An hour or two later I'd find her up on a table washing a ceiling because it was "smoky", according to her. Or outside giving directions to a neighbour who'd come to dig over our vegetable garden, which just happened to have got bigger that year.

I have to admit that after we'd been talking about selling it, the house had a way of seeming more attractive than ever before, with its row of white pillars, its crab-apple trees in flower, and the elms my father had planted, now as high as the window of my attic room, where I'd spun so many dreams of marvellous accomplishments as a child. That house was part of us as only a house can be whose inhabitants have experienced everything from birth to death within its walls.

"To think," said Maman, "that when your father brought me to see it before it was quite finished, hoping I'd fall in love with it, I couldn't hide my disappointment. 'But it's much too small, Léon,' I said, 'with all the children we've got! Where are we ever going to put them all?' To think that now we're finding fault with it because it's too big!"

My father had spent almost half his life saving enough to build it, penny by penny, then the rest of his days trying not to lose it. There were times when I felt bitterly resentful towards it, the way you do towards a person you love who can wheedle anything out of you. It used to suck us dry. One year it would have to have a new roof. Next it would need repainting, which would have to wait till one of my brothers was free to do it. Then the heating system would begin to wear out. Above all, the taxes ate away at us endlessly. While our earnings were being cut, the taxes increased year after year, especially the school taxes, which did little to benefit us since we of the French-speaking community had to maintain our own French private schools in the largely English suburbs of St-Boniface. So our determination to preserve our French language also helped ruin us in the end.

"Come on now, Maman, you know perfectly well we'll be beaten one of these days. The house is dragging us under."

"But it's home for us in the meantime," she'd say. "As long as we have it, as long as there's a place to come home to, we'll be a family."

And this was true. Adèle, for instance, who was teaching in increasingly far-off corners of northern Alberta, as though doggedly trying to recapture the pioneering days of her youth, still came back to us often in the summer holidays. Each time she came she'd been converted to a new fad diet; one year it was nothing but spinach, lemons, and apples; another, nothing but prunes and oatmeal. But the year she arrived home with a summer's supply consisting of nothing but oranges, grapefruit, dates, and nuts, it vanished so fast from her cache in the cellar that she had to finish out the season eating at table like the rest of us. I seem to recall this as being one of the rare times she deigned to behave like everybody else. My poor sister! I realize now that she craved affection and longed to be understood and accepted, but everything she did seemed designed to rebuff affection. I've often wondered if people like Adèle are incapable of reaching out to others because there's no love in their lives, or whether their inability to reach out has kept love at bay. I still don't know which it is. It must be the same conundrum I found in my book-burning grandfather's portrait. How far, O Lord, must we go back to find the source of unhappiness in a person? There's a degree of it in all of us, no doubt, but so much more in some than in others.

Rodolphe, who was a telegraphist and then a station-master before having no job at all, like so many others during the Depression, came to visit often, especially when he was posted near St-Boniface. He would arrive in fine fettle, with a song on his lips, just a little tipsy, and his pockets stuffed with bank notes which he'd distribute magnanimously on all sides. "A fifty, Ma, I bet you could use that, got to keep the wolf from the door, you know. No, no, keep it, it's yours, I don't want to hear any more about it!... Clémence dear, how'd you like a nice crisp new ten? Take it, take it.... And Ma, while we're about it, take another fifty, while there's still more where that came from. Need another to fill the gaps, maybe?" And like as not he'd turn out his pockets the next day and take back almost everything he'd given away, and perhaps borrow a little besides so he could get home. But he was always full of devilment, and would play airs from *Rigoletto* by ear, drawing sounds from our old untuned piano that no one else could, or sing a hearty, rollicking toreador song that would have all of us walking or jigging more or less in time to it. When Rodolphe arrived, the whole neighbourhood knew it, and rejoiced.

"Little sister," he'd say to me when I was fifteen or sixteen, stroking my hair, "you've got the most beautiful hair in the world. Who," he'd demand of some unseen audience, "could have more beautiful hair?"

"Clémence," he'd say to my invalid sister, "one day I'm going to take you to see the Rocky Mountains – the greatest wonder of the world!"

He overflowed with affection, and could inspire it with just a smile from his twinkling brown eyes. But as soon as he'd done so he'd be off to light another spark.

We forgave him everything for so long, so long...until he drove us to despair.

He spent the last years of his life in Vancouver, living on his war veteran's pension and writing us letters that were funny in a way uniquely his, I think, constantly laughing at himself, his youth (one day it was there and the next a thousand miles away), his follies, his vanished hopes, the human merry-go-round, people's good intentions unfulfilled, all of which produced a steady stream of mirth, besides something faintly audible in the background, like a stifled sob.

He was found dead one night in his tiny apartment, which he always left unlocked to allow the cronies around him to come quickly to his aid in case of an asthma attack. His pockets had been emptied, perhaps by those same cronies who'd been supplying him with alcohol and sometimes real help, and who sang with such feeling at his funeral. Or perhaps someone had merely recovered a loan.

Our pious little nun, Dédette, our Sister Purity, the spotless lamb in the muddy barnyard, was then on missionary duty, one might say, at a poor convent at Kenora in Ontario near the Manitoba border; later she spent several years at Keewatin in the same region, where she led a life of real poverty with a single companion in a shack that barely kept out the rain. Yet in all her religious life she was happier there than anywhere else, she confided to me when the time came for revelations, shortly before her death. But occasionally she had to emerge from those faraway woods, where she was almost forgotten even by her community, for gatherings of the community or personal retreats in St-Boniface. Then she'd obtain what she considered a very special permission: almost a whole day to spend at home with her family. Now that I know what the brief breath of freedom meant to that loving soul, I don't even feel like smiling any more. As fleeting as it was, it was enough to sustain her passion for life.

She'd come to us early in the morning brimming with joy, convinced she was bringing us happiness and would find only that. But before long there would be some little confession let slip by Maman, some family news long concealed from her, a host of little signs, and she'd begin to see the ugly old face of misfortune and suffering she thought she had banished from the earth by the sheer force of prayer before an altar. Poor little nun! We'd always see her leave like a wounded bird trailing a damaged wing, crushed to have been back and seen what the world was like.

But I'd rather talk about when she'd arrive – a delight to behold! I must say Maman had always done everything possible to make sure it would be a day of charm and light-heartedness, almost of luxury, one that would hide as never before all trace of want in our family life. Once, when we were really at a low ebb, she even went as far as to buy a magnificent damask tablecloth for the occasion. For Dédette never came alone but was always accompanied by "one of our sisters", and while Maman was certainly bent on doing honour to Dédette, she was probably more anxious to enhance her image in the eyes of her companion, who might be from a wealthy family, and for whom, in any event, we had to do things nicely.

So one fine morning a pair of dark figures would take shape at the end of Deschambault Street, dressed in the voluminous black habit of those days, with all-concealing skirts and starched white band across the forehead and veil floating in the wind. Soon one of them would detach herself from the other and run forward, dignity and seemliness flung aside – a little flying nun, a real one. Maman too would take off like an arrow. At the gate, usually, they'd come together and embrace like two souls who'd had to cross the desert – or life itself perhaps – in order to be together. Much later, when nuns were beginning to have a great deal more freedom, I wrote to Dédette's Sister General and obtained permission for her to spend a few weeks with me at Petite-Rivière-Saint-François. When I met her at the station in Quebec City, I watched her run to me with the same eagerness, the same outpouring of joy as when she'd run to Maman on Deschambault Street. I don't think I've ever seen a person run to a loved one the way she used to.

When I was called to her bedside seven years later, as she was dying of cancer, I carefully broached the subject of that deep attachment for her family. Why, I asked her, when she loved life so much, had she become a nun? I'm still haunted by the reply she gave me. When my own time comes, I hope I'll be able to talk about it with as much passionate simplicity as she did.

MAMAN WAS so right when she insisted that as long as we had our house we'd be a family, that happy or unhappy, at least we'd be together.

With the house sold and Maman dead, we did get together a few times more, Adèle, Clémence, Dédette, Anna, and I, at Anna's lovely property in St-Vital, with its house and little outbuildings all white with blue trim, nestled along a lazy loop of the winding Red River. Our old Bell piano had come to rest there. I used to let my fingers wander over its yellowed keys, trying to bring back a tune my father had been particularly fond of. I'd feel a wave of sadness rise up in me, as much for what I sensed I was going to lose as for what I'd already lost. I'd reached an age where one begins to lose much, and being the youngest in the family, I sometimes glimpsed a period in which I'd see all my remaining family depart before my own turn came.

Then Anna died, far away among cactuses and giant saguaros, their arms raised in beseeching gestures to the sky, almost in the desert; she'd fled to Phoenix, where her son Fernand lived, in a last desperate effort to be freed of the cancer that had been eating at her for fifteen years. There it caught up with her, and there under the sunny Arizona skies she was buried. Now our family had no nucleus at all. Clémence, everybody's child, who often saw better and more gravely than we, which was perhaps the source of her trouble, one day in a state of agitation put it another way: "There's no house for us to go to any more."

SO NOW WHEN I go to Winnipeg for my visits to Clémence, who is in a home, I take a room in a hotel. It's a very curious feeling to be in an air-conditioned room a step away from the city where

I was born, grew up, went to school, and earned my living, and suddenly to realize that I'm waiting at least for the phone to ring, though I haven't yet told anyone I've arrived.

I do get invitations and would be received with genuine warmth, but my cousins, my sister-in-law, and various other close or distant relatives, all of whom are getting on in years, live in what amount to tiny cubicles, which serve as living room, dining room, kitchen, and bedroom all in one; when the sofa-bed is folded up and everything is tidily in place, you can move around, but only just. They find it convenient. They say that it's really better that way when you're growing old and can't get help for love or money.

There's no longer really anything to make me feel at home in Manitoba, except the little section roads that stretch away beneath the endless sky, if only I can get to them, and if when I do my friends will just leave me alone for an hour or so to commune with that utterly silent horizon. There are some who understand, who'll take me to the edge of the open prairie and release me as you'd release a bird, then go away pretending they have things to do elsewhere. They know they won't lose me, though many's the time I've longed to go and lose myself for ever out there – that's just a childish fancy; one doesn't put oneself away like that, however strong the urge may be at times.

So I set off, feeling buoyed nevertheless, walking towards the red glow low down in the sky where the prairie ends, because for the magic to work I need not only an illusion of infinite space but also the gentle time of day just before nightfall. Then, for a few moments, my heart may soar once again.

XI

MAMAN WAS HAPPY during the last years we spent together, though less on her own account than because she felt I was content with my lot.

She had seen Adèle, a fine young woman and a striking beauty, enter into the most disastrous marriage; it broke up almost immediately, but the memory – or the shame – drove her all the rest of her life, a hunted creature always on the run to increasingly distant points, the frontiers of civilization, "Adèle's hardship villages" as we called them. She would teach for a year or two, rarely more, and as soon as life began to be a little less harsh, would take off for some other, even more primitive outpost. One would have said she never could punish herself enough for having strayed into love in her tender and vulnerable youth.

Maman had Anna to grieve for as well. Anna had married too young and her husband, though probably a good and affectionate man, was not her equal, in either education or sensitivity; her exceptional gifts were gradually stifled by a dreary, stultifying existence. She always made me think of Chekhov's *Three Sisters*. I often remember seeing her stand motionless at a window, gazing out but seeing nothing, as though knowing she'd been destined for better things and it was now too late. The burden of sorrow in her heart was something I never suspected when I was young. It was a long time before I conceived a great and profound compassion for my sister Anna.

Maman also watched helplessly as our beloved Rodolphe sank into alcoholism, gambling, and all sorts of other folly. Not so long before, he had been the very image of youthful charm: brilliant, funny, irresistible in his exuberance. She died before the worst happened, thank God, though she had seen enough to hasten her end.

I, the youngest, was to all appearances happy with my work, doing the best I could and finding it satisfying. For recreation I took part in group activities, played tennis, went to parish gatherings. A little later I was to join the Cercle Molière, a purely amateur theatrical group which, under the direction of a marvellous couple, Arthur and Pauline Boutal, came to play a major role in our community. I learned a great deal from that group. Even before then, however, it seemed to Maman that of all her children I was the only one to have a flair for happiness. She had suffered so much on account of her children; distressing failures, Clémence's incurable illness, the vagabond existence of her eldest son, Joseph, from whom we'd hear nothing for years on end. She'd admitted to me one particularly depressing day that she was afraid not one of us would ever find happiness. "I think" she told me, "the biggest cross one can bear is knowing that one's children are unhappy." That was the only lifelong sorrow she ever confided to me; others she quickly dismissed, saying, "It's nothing much, it isn't really so bad.... It'll pass...."

So it was no wonder she took new heart, began to hope again, with me and for me. I could be gay and entertaining, I did wicked parodies of local characters, I often made her laugh till she gasped for breath, and as for love, though I seemed to inspire it then as naturally as I breathed, I wasn't yet letting myself be caught.

Only one thing may have worried her somewhat. That was when I'd shut myself up, night after night for over a month at a time, in the little front room on the third floor, the cherished refuge of my childhood rediscovered when I was twenty-two, the little attic room where I'd been visited by my early reveries. Those workings of my imagination, I know now, had been rich and nebulous enough to nourish a whole lifetime. How curious it is that our childhood reveries come to us at an age when we know nothing about ourselves, and yet, like heralds of things to come, they teach us more about our own nature than anything else ever will.

There in my attic I'd scribble page after page. I had stories of a kind crowding into my head, and I kept trying to put that fermentation into words. It all seemed so alive when I started, so how did I end up most of the time with empty and pompous words I'd never used before? I'd plunge this way and that, into humour, realism, mystery, and horror in the manner of Edgar Allan Poe. When the excitement passed, having briefly given me the most extravagant notions about what I was doing, I always saw that I'd written only childish prattle, worthless flashy trivialities. Nothing on which I could build a project, or a life, or from which I could even draw a little hope. I'd tear up what I'd written. After a while I bought myself a small portable typewriter, a very light one which almost jumped off its base when I used it, because I imagined that my style, by the very fact of being typed in unerasable characters, so to speak, would stand out more and have better form. I think all it achieved was to make everything shorter, because I'd avoid words whose spelling I'd have to look up in the dictionary. Which was progress of a sort.

Out of all I wrote, sometimes I'd find one phrase rather pleasing. It would come close to having that mysterious life that can sometimes be infused by a fresh new arrangement of everyday words. But it wouldn't seem to be mine. Had it come back to me from something I'd read? Or did it come from a me that didn't yet exist, someone I wouldn't have access to for quite a while, who, from far in the future, occasionally condescended to point briefly in the direction I should be going? I'd lose patience. I'd come down from my perch. Maman, much relieved, would see me leave with my tennis racket under my arm, or go out to the lane, climb on my bicycle, and pedal away, always – a curious clue in itself – towards those little oak woods to the west, where the sun would be setting.

Maman pointed out one day that when I left the house in late afternoon, I always set off towards the west.

"What's so special about that direction?" she wanted to know.

"It's so beautiful, and it stays beautiful long after sunset because the colours don't go for ages."

"Your father loved it too," she said. "In the worst of our bad years he'd always sit facing the west in the evenings, remember? Then he'd start hoping again that some day we'd be free of our troubles and have a little happiness before we died."

Then, as if she hadn't cherished those illusions as much as the rest of us, she flung me a caveat in a tone approaching bitterness.

"You can see whatever you want when you turn that way!"

LIVELY, exuberant, mischievous though I appeared to be, and probably still was at the time, the worm was already in the apple so to speak; or at least, something was eating away at my merry, carefree nature. Hardly a day went by without the strange thought entering my head that I wasn't really at home here, that I had a life to make for myself elsewhere. I'd been brought up to be French, but what would I find here to nourish and sustain me? Apart from our rehearsals at the Cercle Molière, practically nothing. So I'd hurry to Winnipeg to hear concerts, or to watch entranced as the great dramatic characters I'd discovered in my teen years came to life before my eyes: Lear, Richard, and poor Lady Macbeth forever sniffing her hand, from which all the perfumes of Araby would not wash away the smell of blood. It was always the same hateful dichotomy: in French we'd play Labiche, Brieux, Bernard, even Molière, all rather clumsily, but it was nice, pleasant; in English I'd hear great words that remained in the heart of the listener indefinitely.

It didn't escape me that our life was an inward-looking one, which led almost inescapably to a kind of withering. The watchword was survival, and the principal standing order, though it was never formally pronounced, was not to fraternize with the outside world. I seemed to feel a little more of my lifeblood escaping every day.

I can still recall bits and pieces of the almost constantly carping and negative preachings of those days: the beach was an accursèd place, dancing was an abomination (especially the popular slow waltz of my twenties), going steady was a mortal peril, particularly between "us" and "them" because it led to mixed marriages, the direst of calamities.

Sometimes you'd have thought we were living in some walled enclosure during the wars of religion, Albi withstanding the Saracens, or some other luckless mediaeval city under siege behind a bulwark of prohibitions, portcullises, and interdicts. Where was the Joan-of-Arc fervour of the days of my teens, our loyalty to the best in ourselves and to each other, the spark that fired our enthusiasm and a kind of boldness bordering on open revolt? We were jaded, I suppose. There had already been many defections...or departures. Sooner or later every one of us would face the inevitable temptation, either to cross over to the English side and give in peacefully rather than perpetuate a long, drawn-out death, or to leave and go to breathe the air of our origins.

However, one, two, and then three years of teaching in St-Boniface passed very quickly for me. With an eye to a possible departure, I'd begun to put aside a sum of money each year, a minute one, since the circumstances Maman and I were coping with were as difficult as ever. Where would I go? To Quebec? The previous summer, friends had driven me there during the holidays. One night as we neared our destination we were driving late so that we could sleep that night on Quebec soil. The trip had taken almost a week. I was fighting off sleep in the back of the car. It would be an affront to the revered motherland to come to her the first time fast asleep. In the end I lost the battle and my eyes closed in spite of myself. And when I managed to open them again, all the road signs and advertising were still only in English! So I implored my friends, in case I should really go to sleep, to please, please wake me up the minute we crossed the border.

What was I expecting? That everything would suddenly be different? That the language I'd been told was the most beautiful and charming would flow from every mouth? That friendship would beam at me from all eyes? Surely I'd be instantly recognized and accepted. "Ah," they'd say, "she's one of our own who's returning to us." And they'd rejoice over the lost daughter come home.

Instead of which I found I was that curiosity, a little Franco-Manitoban who still spoke French, bully for her! Or sometimes "the little cousin from the West". In vain I'd explain that both my parents were born in Quebec and that I was returning to my roots. Nobody treated me as though I'd come home. I remained pretty much an outsider, in fact. "Very nice, speaks just like us, but not exactly family." I realized then that we French Canadians don't really have a sense of common blood. Of nationality, yes, but not from the heart like the Jews or other scattered people. Our own, once out of sight, are no longer really our own. I have been deeply hurt by the distance that the Québécois kept at that time and continue to keep between themselves and their brothers in the rest of French Canada. But now that I've lived long and happily in Quebec – more happily, at least, than anywhere else in the world

– and have received its government's highest literary honour and many signs of affection besides in return for my deep love for this land, I almost want to smile at my youthful oversensitivity. One of our common characteristics, something all we French Canadians should be able to recognize in ourselves, is that easily wounded sensitivity. Still, in spite of the admiration I receive (perhaps mostly because of *The Tin Flute*), I sometimes sense a kind of disappointment that this rather widely appreciated author wasn't born in Quebec. And perhaps sometimes a kind of vague resentment or disapproval – what else could I call it? – that my loyalty to Quebec, deep as it is, doesn't shut out the rest of Canada, where we as a people have wandered and suffered, yes, but throughout which we have also left our mark.

So the next time I left I wouldn't be returning to Quebec. Why not Europe? Yes, that was it, I'd go to France. Perhaps France would recognize me as her own.

I must have been mad! Yes, raving mad in my frenzy to be loved, wanted, to feel at home somewhere at last. I must have been really dreaming to imagine I'd be more warmly received in France than in Quebec. The astonishing part is that in fact I did get that warm reception, but much later; such an unbelievably warm reception that I very nearly fainted with emotion. Which goes to show that I may have been mad, but not insane.

FOR THE TIME BEING all was confusion in my head, as in a cloud-filled sky. Deep inside me was something I was carefully hiding from myself, I was so frightened of the stern face it would show me. This was my urge to write, when I still hadn't the least idea how to express myself in a personal or engaging manner. I think it was the Quebec writer Paul Toupin who said that discovering the sound of one's own voice is in itself a very difficult experience. Nothing could be more true. Furthermore, I kept longing for a home and not knowing where it was; perhaps even then I was hoping it was the whole world and all mankind. I'd long for a past, and it would slip away from me. I'd long for a future, and see none on the horizon.

Then suddenly I'd emerge from my doleful soul searching, and having stopped searching I'd find everything, and especially the marvellous current of life and youth that buoys us up and sweeps us along and fills us with joy at every moment, because our hands are free again, ready to take whatever comes our way. When Maman saw me back to my cheerful self, it would make her forget debts, taxes, compound interest, the vicious circle holding us tighter and tighter in its grasp. What can she have been made of? How often I wish I had her capacity to rebound from adversity into the sunlight! One day she'd be overcome by the burden of the bills to be paid, at the end of her tether from "plugging holes", borrowing here to pay there, running hither and thither, a plug here and a patch there, then she'd get up the next morning a different woman, confident we'd get through, she'd seen it in a dream or heard it when she woke, like a great liberating breath. We'd be able to save the house and save us all, the strayed, the lost, the estranged, we'd be together at least once more and be happy together.

And as she used to when I was little, she'd begin to mesmerize me again with her marvellous dreams, in which everyone lived happily ever after. Our rich but hard-nosed uncle, for example, would have a change of heart and leave us part of his fortune in his will. Or Anna, who kept buying Irish Sweepstakes tickets – it was illegal in those days – would win the grand prize and divide it fairly. But I loved her true stories even more. In the ones she made up "for fun" she didn't pay much attention to credibility, but the true stories depended on keen observation and a sense of relevant detail. Where did she find those incomparable little stories she was always telling the moment she had some relief from her worries? She found them everywhere. I never saw her leave the house, if only to pick vegetables in the garden for the soup pot, stopping for a word with the neighbour across the fence, without bringing back some little story, in which each detail had its place and the important thing had the important place, and was always a surprise. So she'd hardly have left before we were watching for her return, knowing she'd bring back some shrewd, very funny, and very true observation, though we could never guess what it would be. Every time she stepped out of the house she was on a kind of adventure that sharpened her perception of life and things around her. She was Scheherazade bringing delight to our captive years in poverty. Now that I think of it, it seems to me that I was rather like her at that time: one day depressed, feeling we'd never be free of our heavy debts of the moment, the next day walking on air because, as I'd worked in my attic room, a sentence had flowed from my pen that seemed to contain a glimmer of what I wanted to say. A miracle! Could pain be avenged by writing about pain? Could capturing something of life in words bring us to terms with life?

Maman was then getting on for sixty-seven or sixty-eight, my age now, when at last I'm taking time to think about all the grief she must have known. It's all very curious. We don't really empathize with our parents, it seems, until later, when we reach their age at the time in question, not having realized how alone they felt when we were there beside them. (An excruciating truth which is the whole underlying theme of *The Road past Altamont*, in which I didn't really try to say much more.) I thought Maman was happy, I wanted to believe she was happy, because she'd often still give way to gales of laughter, particularly if she was laughing at herself.

This woman who had seen her adorable little daughter burn alive before her eyes (Marie-Agnès, my elder sister by three and a half years), who had watched her handsome son – perhaps her favourite child – ravaged by alcohol, and who had seen her husband slowly die a broken man by her side, this woman who'd hardly spent a day without wondering where the next day's money would come from, is the one I picture with her head thrown back and her mouth wide open in laughter, her eyes glistening with tears of merriment. A woman made young again despite her sorrows. Who had lifted her spirits that day, so that a happy memory prevails in my mind over so many gloomy, grey, and oppressive ones? It may have been me, and come to think of it, it must have been me. I was about the only one left who could make her laugh like that with my nonsense.

My older sisters used to resent it. "Maman will give her anything," they used to say. "Maman's soft on her." Yet it wasn't exactly that. The truth is that she was old and I was young; I'd become the sunshine of her old age, so to speak. And the thought that one can be somebody's sunshine is enough to make one glow more brightly still.

It's true, in fact, that I often made my mother laugh. Now, in

113

my late years, if all I have to my credit is those moments of genuine laughter that brightened her anxious old age, I can perhaps forgive myself some of the sorrow I caused her.

XII

AT ABOUT this time a group of St-Boniface boys and girls joined forces to form something like a company of strolling players. All of us had talent: some for music, some for dance, and some, like me, for *déclamation*, as it was then called. We used to tour the French-speaking parishes of Manitoba giving variety shows. One could say we were a modest version of today's summer theatres, except that, far from getting any grants from anyone, we were helping a "good cause". Our cause was the Jesuit college of St-Boniface, which was always more or less on the brink of financial disaster, like almost all our confessional institutions.

There were ten or twelve of us, I don't remember exactly. One, a good pianist, had a repertoire to please almost everyone, from the languorous waltzes of those days to boogie-woogie. He was also a clever cartoonist. (It has only now occurred to me how surprising it was that such remarkable talents flowered in our stony soil.) He would set up his easel at an angle on the stage so that the audience could watch as he drew. Then he'd pick a head from the crowd at random and begin sketching with broad strokes. The subject would begin to be recognized by others in the audience, then by the subject himself, and a murmur of approval would run through the room. We had a kind of clown too, a tall, ungainly fellow with dangling arms, long, spindly legs, a dazed expression, and a silly smile. He just had to stand there and the whole room would laugh with that curious, delighted chuckle of a person who sees a comic image of himself. Then our Gilles would begin his gags and wisecracks, partly improvised and all side-splittingly funny. He deserved the laughter he drew.

For my own act, I would make up and deliver monologues, rather in the style of Yvon Deschamps today but much less polished. Still, they must have had their modest effect if I can judge by the applause. In the days before Culture, Departments of Cultural Affairs, and TV, our public wasn't very demanding, it's true. On the other hand, it wasn't always easy to get a laugh out of those poker-faced little country audiences in their Sunday best.

The rest of our program included skits, songs, accordion music, and dances. In all, an engaging, bubbly product of slightly silly youthful exuberance.

So when our working day was done we'd leave our classrooms, offices, and service counters and take to the highways and byways of Manitoba. In two battered old cars crammed to their roofs with some of our scenery and props, our costumes, our musical instruments, Fernand's easel, and the makeup box, we'd speed off along little secondary roads in the gathering dusk to nearby villages, reserving the more distant locations for the weekends.

In this period I really came to know our little Manitoban French villages, which I realized later were so much like the ones in Quebec, with their invariable focal point of church, presbytery, convent, and cemetery...except that here each village was surrounded by endless space and silence. Fragile and alone beyond an unbroken prairie, they really went to one's heart.

We performed at St-Jean-Baptiste, Letellier, Notre-Dame-de-Lourdes, La Broquerie, Ste-Agathe on the Red River. I think it was at Ste-Agathe that we gave our show in a beautiful hayloft over a brand-new barn on the outskirts of the village. We were christening it, in a sense. There were no cattle yet in the beautiful clean stalls below, in any event. So far only a little hay had been brought in.

When we'd scrambled up the ladder with all our equipment, we found ourselves under a huge arched roof in the biggest, loveliest auditorium imaginable, an uninterrupted vault without windows, openings, or recesses anywhere to break its continuity. We must have been the first to play in a totally modern theatre, like some of the most experimental performances of today. At the same time, the space incorporated one of the older traditions of the theatre, heavy timbers having been laid to form a stage at the front of the hall. On either side we had small areas closed off from view by potato-sack curtains, which served as wings, dressing rooms, loges, whatever. From there, through holes in the potato sacks, we watched the elegant ladies and gentlemen arriving via the ladder, all a bit breathless, the parish priest hitching up his cassock and the ladies their skirts. But they did look distinguished once settled in their chairs, which had been arranged in rows of fifteen, with three substantial armchairs for the dignitaries in the middle of the front row. How those armchairs had been been hauled up the ladder is something we wondered about long afterwards.

I've never spent as fragrant an evening. It seemed to have captured all the balmy smells of summer, brought in, no doubt, on a handful of grass, in a clod of earth stuck to a boot while crossing a field. Together with the distant lowing of a cow tethered to a stake, this made the summer-theatre atmosphere complete.

In very small or isolated villages, we sometimes performed by gaslight. During one of these shows, the lamp had been dimming imperceptibly for some time before any of us realized what was happening. Finally, poor Fernand was on stage trying to draw a face, not understanding why he could barely see any more. Thinking perhaps that his eyes were failing, he suddenly exclaimed loudly and anxiously, "I can't see, I can't see!"

In a twinkling a burly fellow leapt to the stage and then onto the table beside Fernand, reaching up to pull the lamp down on its chain while a companion approached with a small hand-pump. To resuscitate the lamp, they followed the same procedure I'd watched at my uncle Excide's when I was a child. Air was pumped into the mantle, the flame came back to life, and we were bathed in a harsh light, the lamp buzzing like a swarm of angry insects. We realized then that we'd given part of our show in semi-darkness. There were protests from the audience that people had missed things and hadn't got their money's worth, so we started all over again from the beginning and the crowd laughed just as hard the second time as the first. After that, no wonder I thought I was promised a brilliant career on the stage.

At the end of those evenings we were usually thanked by the parish priest. Some priests, it's true, were hidebound, intolerant, and authoritarian, even despotic. Yet recalling these occasions, probably happy ones for them, I seem to remember kindly, jovial old souls who were paternally good-natured and a bit naïve when surrounded by their parishioners in festive circumstances.

One of these elderly priests took it into his head one night to give his parishioners a lecture on the art of succeeding in life, taking us, the performers, as examples, in our presence.

"This fine young dancer, now," he said, referring to one of us who had done a tap-dance number, "this disciple of Terpsichore, do you imagine he rose to the height of his art overnight? No indeed, my friends! He had to spend weeks and months practising all alone in some out-of-the-way corner at home – perhaps in his barn. And there, for hours at a time, it's been step, hop, tap... tap...tap...."

Though addressing a handful of parishioners on a purely friendly occasion about a very nonreligious subject, the old priest assumed his preaching voice, which carried to the farthest corners and brooked no argument. Suddenly he was talking about me, it seemed, and I was trembling in my boots.

"The lovely young person," he thundered, "whom you saw come forward, bow graciously, and then begin, and talk...and talk...and talk...with nothing, not even a scrap of paper to aid her memory.... She had to keep all that in her head, the little rascal! Talk... talk...talk.... We heard every word. We knew exactly what she was saying. Do you think she had all that ready in her head just by getting up one fine morning and saying, 'Today I'm going to see what I can do'? No, no, no! She had to spend hours and hours practising in front of her mirror, saying to herself...now wrinkle your nose...next give your little smile...now that charming little wave.... And that, my brothers, is how you come to succeed in life."

AT LA BROQUERIE, I believe it was, the parish priest was a handsome old man with an opulent, snow-white beard. He spoke in a soft and hesitant voice, pausing in an odd way every few words, as though he'd lost the thread of what he was saying and had to retrieve at least the end of it before he could continue.

"My young and talented friends...," he began and stopped immediately as though puzzled. He bent his head as if perusing his beard. Then, a little smile brightening his gentle face, he looked up, saying, "friends come from so far to be with us...." Again he was lost, looking down into his beard, even pressing it gently here and there with his fingers. At last the words came forth..."to be with us and bring joy to my old heart...."

The pattern continued until the end of the affable little speech. After "my old heart" we heard... "heart which swells with fatherly regard...," then "regard of an old friend in La Broquerie...." Each phrase tailed off in shy little mumbling sounds. Then he'd find the thread of the thought again, apparently somewhere in the silky folds of his beard, as though it were a hiding place filled with wishes, memories, and gentle words.

THOUGH MAMAN generally went to bed early after her well-filled day, she'd try to stay awake until I came in, no matter how late, so she could hear about the events of the evening right away.

Sometimes fatigue overcame her burning curiosity and I'd find her asleep. How could I have had the heart to wake her as often as I did? I didn't know, it's true, that she was sleeping very little then in any case, three or four hours a night at most. But even if I'd known, I don't think I would have understood any better what it is to sleep poorly.

I'd sit on the edge of her bed and give her an impatient little shake.

"Come on, Maman, wake up!"

I think I did this because I couldn't have stood not sharing my story with her right then, when it was ready and fresh and funny. It would have lost some of its flavour by morning. I was convinced this was so, though I didn't understand why. I've learned since that a story won't wait until you've dealt with something you think is more important: a letter to write, an interview to give, a trip to take. A story's time comes when it comes, and if you're not ready then, it will rarely come again. If it's made to wait, most of the mysterious, elusive life it has when it's fresh will be lost.

So I'd wake her up. She'd have a moment of confusion, during which she'd look every minute as old as she was and I'd be briefly afraid. Then she'd recognize me, and propping herself up slightly on the pillow, she'd say, "Tell me about it."

Often by the faint glow of a nightlight, or even just the light of the moon through the window, I'd recognize in her face the same eager expectation of a story that I'd felt myself as a child. Now it was my turn to give her relief from the burdens of life. When the evening had been particularly exciting, I'd sometimes take over an hour from the little time I had left for sleep that night so I could bring her my gift still warm and alive. Often, you're only as good at storytelling as you're allowed to be by having a receptive listener; I think I was never listened to so receptively as in the middle of the night by my poor mother after I'd dragged her out of her scant sleep. She'd laugh, she'd lean forward to hear every word, since I kept my voice low to avoid waking Clémence, she'd nod approval, she'd ask for reruns, like slow-motion movie clips of certain episodes. By the time I left her, my excitement would be soothed and I'd be ready for sleep, but she'd be too wound up to go back to sleep. She probably spent the rest of the night remembering the most amusing parts of my story, because sometimes, if I'd left my door open, I'd hear her chuckling to herself. Or else she'd indulge herself with stories of her own, imagining me, as it pleased her to do even in old age, just the way I was then – young, carefree, congenial, and full of fun, as one generally is while still in the flower of youth.

I LEARNED from Maman that you mustn't hold a story back when it's ready, but you mustn't rush it either; that you have to let it ripen naturally, sometimes for quite a while if it's to have all its own special qualities. I was also to learn that when you try to make it too perfect, fiddling with it constantly, overworking it – or just telling it too often – you sap it of its life and in the end, like any living thing, it may simply die.

That's what happened to my story of the venerable priest who kept losing the end of his sentence in his long white beard.

Maman had liked the story so much, and I suppose had made me tell it so often (or perform it, rather), that I'd been putting less of myself into it each time, leaving it to get across on its own.

One evening when she asked for it again, I told her a bit testily that it wasn't funny any longer and wasn't worth telling. She admitted that in fact the last time I'd told it she'd perhaps laughed a bit less spontaneously. Then she pondered a while.

"After all," she said finally, "it's only natural for stories about life to wear a little thin. Just like life."

That exasperated me.

"Stories wearing thin! What am I supposed to do about it?"

She smiled at me soothingly.

"Make up new stories or combine old ones. Or keep telling an old one but made over so it's new."

I think that was the first time I began to see — fortunately still far away and very vaguely — that the road I'd be taking in life wouldn't ever lead tidily to what writers, when they reach the bottoms of certain pages, naïvely or in self-delusion call "The End".

XIII

WAS IT SPRING or late autumn when we went to Otterburne? We left in such haste at the end of the day, we'd barely had time to swallow a quick bite. Either the evenings hadn't lengthened yet or they'd already shortened, but whichever it was we had to hurry so we wouldn't be overtaken by nightfall on the way.

None of us had ever set foot in Otterburne, though it wasn't far from fine villages like St-Pierre-Jolys and St-Malo, which everyone knew because they were on well-travelled highways. Otterburne, however, because it was badly marked or on some out-of-the-way stretch of secondary road, was considered almost impossible to find. It was so isolated, so shrouded in perpetual loneliness, the saying went, that it was sure to be totally forgotten some day. Yet it had once been the site of one of the most important agricultural colleges in the region; my cousin Cléophas had been a boarder there for several years. It also had a school for Indian children run by a religious order. I don't know whether Otterburne's decline had already begun at the time I'm speaking of, or whether there was just a feeling of decline in the air. In any event we'd been told, "For heaven's sake try to go to Otterburne. They're so lonely out there, it'll be a blessing to have you come and make them laugh a little."

Having missed the main highway almost as soon as we'd left the city, we struck off along some secondary roads rather than turn back. None of them had any signs. Soon dusk was upon us. It rolled in from the depths of the prairie like a light mist. The whole countryside took on the appearance of a dream, clothed in a delicate, semitransparent blue. We weren't paying much attention and we went from a secondary road onto little dirt roads, though apparently still heading in the right direction, judging by the brilliant red streaks left along the horizon by the setting sun. The country around all those little dirt roads was consistently deserted. Gilles, our lovable clown, kept laughing about it and singing one of his crazy, rollicking songs at the top of his lungs. For my part, I recall being stricken with gloom. The same Otterburne which was then so impossible to find was to play a harsh, emotionally charged role in my life one day. Was I foreseeing that, so many years in advance? Probably not. Hindsight is letting me read things into the way I felt on that strange night forty years ago.

At last a light from a lonely farm appeared, seemingly distant but really very near. We knocked at the door. A woman came out.

"Otterburne? It's very close. You're almost there."

She pointed with outstretched arm to a spot in the infinitely deep, blue distance. A faint light seemed suddenly to appear in the spot to which she was pointing.

"There, see it? You can't miss it."

"A thousand thanks, Lady of the Twilight," Gilles carolled in his most ingratiating voice.

We set off again, our eyes glued to that fragile flicker, then we lost it. In those flat surroundings, whatever could have hidden it? A haystack? A wretched little tree? We wandered around for a good half-hour before coming upon another, equally lonely farm.

"Otterburne!" The man stood on his top step and pointed in the direction we'd come from. "You must've gone right through it. It's there, right close. Just gotta folla the light."

The light, the light! We'd no sooner started off again with our eyes fixed on it than we lost it again...and came to yet another farm on the other side of the village. It seems we went through it three or four times before finally stumbling upon it, the way a ball can roll around the rim of a hole before falling in. Three streetlamps unbelievably far apart brought us to a source of information.

"How come you ain't seen us before?"

Two oldtimers were sitting on a wooden bench in front of the station, pipes clenched in their teeth, contemplating the warm evening.

"Where's the hall where the show's being given?"

"The meetin'? You got here too late. Ain't gonna see nothing. She begun two hours ago, maybe more. Reckon she's about over by now."

Gilles put his head out the car window. "It's not finished, it hasn't even started. We're putting it on."

The second oldtimer spat at least three feet.

"You can't be them. Them's actors. They come on time. Must've. They been there in the hall with the people since...since when, Nésime?"

Nésime pulled out his watch and squinted at it in the light of the stars.

"Since half past seven. The time the priest said. There's some got there before so's to get a better place. Must be three hours them's been in there."

"It's my thinkin' them's prob'ly pretty near cooked by now," said the first oldtimer, "what with the heat the way it is, an' all bit by mosquitoes, too. Less'n them's lit their pipes."

"In your thinking, is it worth going?" asked Gilles.

"Depends," replied the younger of the oldtimers. "There's them that says it'll tickle you pretty good, so if you gonna catch a bit you better git over there quick."

"How come you're not there?" demanded Gilles with a frown.

"I ain't got nothing 'gainst playacting," said the older of the oldtimers, "only a night like this'n it's good being outta doors. Better to spend it out with the stars than shut up in some ol' curling rink. Got only me own smoke to bother me here."

We found the old curling rink at last on the other side of the village. People must indeed have been there for a good long time, and been pulling a lot on their pipes, because when we went in all we could see through the dense billows of smoke was a big straw farmer's hat here and there, the same one, it appeared, in every corner of the hall.

The priest stood up at once and addressed his parishioners.

"The performers have arrived at last. They're young people with delicate throats, so everybody stop smoking. Stop right now!"

The smoke diminished infinitesimally.

From the stage we still couldn't see our audience, and they probably couldn't see us either.

"Can you see me?" shouted Gilles, who'd been pulling faces and getting no response.

"Only the nose on your face," shot back a wag.

"We're really sorry we've arrived so late," offered Gilles. "We got lost."

"Ain't the first that's happened to," commented an invisible spectator in the thickest of the smoke at the back of the hall.

Suddenly we heard an anguished cry from Fernand, who'd gone groping around the stage.

"No piano? What am I supposed to do without a piano?"

Usually, as soon as we arrived and while the rest of us were making up, he'd play some rousing marches to put the audience in a good mood, and help us recover from our roadweariness.

Gilles stepped to the edge of the stage. The smoke had begun to lift and the effect was bizarre, no doubt as much so onstage as below, where we could now see nearly whole bodies, but not all with heads yet, or at least not attached to heads.

"Does anyone here have a piano?" asked Gilles.

A lady at the back seemed to feel obliged to speak up.

"I've got one. Last year I lent it when the bishop came. They brought it back all out of tune, so I don't lend my piano any more."

"And quite right, too," said Gilles agreeably.

As the suffocating smoke dispersed, the audience was making a piecemeal discovery of our clown, those long legs and long arms attached to that long body and long sad face, and there was general astonishment. Almost every mouth was open.

"Lend us your piano," Gilles was wheedling, "and if it comes back to you with a single note out of tune, I'll give you a new one."

"Okay then, that's fine," rejoined the lady.

The priest stood up.

Nearly a third of the audience left on the mission. The wait promised to be long, since the lady lived at quite the opposite end of the scattered village. To coax further patience from that most patient of audiences, Fernand began to sketch one of the faces finally emerging in the uncertain light, a strikingly handsome head wearing a tall, wide-brimmed hat. A whisper of amazement swept through the old curling rink.

"It's Ubald!"

Then the piano arrived, borne by eight stalwart men, four on each side, who practically lifted it over the heads of the audience.

It was nearly midnight. Having just finished his sketch, Fernand leapt from his easel to the piano and struck up some introductory chords. A few sleepy people sat bolt upright and rubbed their eyes in surprise to find themselves still there on the hard little wooden chairs. But almost everyone swung into the spirit of the show, as fresh and ready to be entertained as if they'd just arrived. I seem to recall that show as one of the most resoundingly successful we ever gave.

WHY DO I still have such a vivid memory of that evening, with its glimmering lights and shadows, its laughter and sudden silences engraved so deeply in my mind? Perhaps the silent little prairie village of Otterburne was sending me a message that night that I'd be back. That forty years later I'd be driving the same little roads bathed in twilight, hunting once again for a village as impossible to find as ever, chasing after the same light, repeatedly catching sight of it and losing it again, but this time in dread of what was awaiting me. We often do, in fact, return in sadness to places where we've known joy long ago when young.

IT'S SIX YEARS ago now. I'd hurried to Winnipeg on account of Clémence. I was waiting to be picked up at the hotel. The air conditioning filled my ears with a monotonous drone. And big dark shadows were looming in my heart.

Dédette, Sister Léon de la Croix in religion, had died in the spring of that year. She was carried off by a cancer whose first signs were detected too late, when she still seemed young and full of life. As soon as the Mother Superior of her convent telephoned to say that the surgical exploration had revealed an already inoperable cancer, I jumped on the first plane. The medical prognosis gave Dédette only two months to live.

So this was my second trip to Manitoba in less than six months. I had to face up to it. I'd be returning now to the scenes of my childhood only to watch my relatives die, to reap sorrow.

In the spring I'd spent nearly a month at my dying sister's bedside. I saw her every day, often several times a day. All I did, as I recall, was beat a path from Dédette's room to my cousin's, where I was staying, and from my cousin's to the convent. As a result, Dédette and I, who'd never had much chance to get to know each other, became so close we began to feel inseparable. I'm still amazed that her approaching death finally enabled me to feel her presence, to see her – even to the colour of her remarkable eyes which I'd never really seen before – and conceive an affection for her that deepened from day to day the better I knew her. Why, I used to wonder sometimes, do we get to know someone so well when we're about to lose them? Dédette's death would have caused me less grief if I hadn't come to know her so well – yet I wouldn't for the world have been deprived of that grief.

Her room in the convent's infirmary was not much bigger than it needed to be to die in, but the window – a symbol of opening and liberation – was immense, one of those high windows typical of convents of the old days. Whenever Dédette was drowsy after a sedative, or if I couldn't bear to see signs of pain flickering in her face while we were talking, I'd move a step or two closer to the big window, and each time I'd be astonished at how beautiful I would find the sky in the midst of such sorrow.

So to break the appalling awkwardness between the one who's going to die and the one who's going to survive, I began, hesitantly at first, to talk about the sky. The one we know, or think we know, since it's always there before our eyes.

"I think our Manitoba sky's one of the most beautiful in the world," I said to her one day, "and I think at last I've discovered why, just today. That's odd, isn't it?"

"Why is it one of the most beautiful?" she murmured.

"Because it's so high, Dédette. So free of smoke and dirt, not spoiled yet by the foul breath of industry and big cities. Perhaps because the land it's over is so flat, too. Though the Greek sky is also very high and just as blue. Homer talks about it all the time in the *Iliad* and the *Odyssey*. What made me decide to go to Greece was all the nostalgia in his descriptions of the sky."

"I didn't know that. Tell me more."

"In Russia, too," I went on, "there must be something about the sky that gets inside you, because in *War and Peace* Tolstoy speaks of the 'towering sky' through Prince Andrei as he lies gazing up at it, mortally wounded in battle and dreaming of peace and harmony."

My dying sister listened. Only my stories of travel or accounts of happy moments in life seemed to distract her from the sadness of going.

"Tell me some more," she'd plead. "In my convent I haven't seen or known anything of the world. Tell me more."

UNTIL THEN I'd always thought that when there's serious talk between two people, one about to go and another who'll be staying, the conversation ought to turn to the one who's going, who'll soon know everything. It isn't always like that at all. Anna, just before she died, talked to me at length about the drabness of her life and not having had her due from it, as though hoping at least not to be forgotten. All Dédette wanted was to hear about my life, which she imagined to be successful, happy, and filled endlessly with gay, sparkling events.

To bring a smile back to the emaciated little face with its eyes like deep holes full of suffering, and because she wanted me to, I concocted a fairytale life of uncommon friendships, unqualified success, fame unspoiled by envy. I wasn't really making it up, just picking out the high points, the peaks, and leaving the rest untold, and so it was that I knew my cup had been filled. Yes, on the brink of death Dédette helped me discover that life is, despite everything, an imponderably marvellous thing. But that's another story, which I'd very much like to tell if I'm allowed enough time. I think that every day I become more like the dervish in the desert who had more and more stories to tell the older he got, and less time left to tell them.

But I must return briefly to Clémence and the day Dédette seemed to be rebelling against God Himself, as if He had made a serious blunder and mistaken her for someone else.

"I can't die!" she protested. "God can't let it happen. He knows how much Clémence depends on me. I can't leave Clémence alone!"

I went to the big window. I looked up at the towering sky, hoping to find some inkling of the meaning of Clémence's life on this earth. A gifted, wonderfully sensitive child, full of grace and intuition, whose power of vision was perhaps too great, and whose mind was suddenly struck a dark and terrible blow, leaving her to wander like a lost soul on earth. Not totally, though, and that's perhaps the most dreadful part. Her ravaged mind still showed such astonishing flashes of intelligence, such clear signals of distress, that we'd be more upset than ever to see her return to her mysterious corridors of escape. How much Maman had suffered on account of Clémence was something Maman herself never really talked about; the pain was probably beyond words. But often she'd look at each of us in turn, beseechingly, pleading for reassurance.

"Who'll look after Clémence when I'm gone?"

Our Clémence has been an enduring sorrow bequeathed by one sister to another, each one, as she dies, passing on the legacy to a younger sister; strange, priceless legacy.

After Maman's death it was Anna who inherited Clémence. She took good care of her, going often to the little room where Clémence lived alone, taking her home to her lovely property in St-Vital for a few days, trying to entertain her, taking her downtown to buy clothes, when she herself was not too ill. But even so, Clémence would sink into silence and deep gloom. In those days so little was known about her disorder. It would send her into phases of overexcitement and agitation, when anything at all would upset her, then plunge her into sombre withdrawal inside herself, where no help could reach her. At that time I'd thrown myself body and soul into writing and was fighting for my life, in a sense, living alone in Montreal. My conscience was fairly clear about Clémence. "Anna's there for the time being," I'd tell myself. "Anna's keeping an eye on her." And as I'd done with my father, and with Maman, I kept thinking I'd have time when I'd done my writing to come and help Anna help Clémence.

But having floundered right and left, grasping desperately for a little happiness, Anna died. As was perhaps befitting for such a life, the end came in an oasis, in a desert. In Arizona. For Phoenix is surrounded by sand, and none of its royal palms or date or grapefruit trees would be there had water not been brought vast distances at great cost. Otherwise probably nothing would survive there except the strange saguaros, some of them empty cactus shells, through which the trapped wind blows with mournful organ sounds. An image of illusion; there's perhaps none more perfect than Phoenix. Anna spent her last few days of human torture gazing at tall trees with red flowers, poincianas, swaying gently against the bluest sky there ever was. "Is it true," she'd murmur, "am I really seeing that marvellous tree, or am I still only dreaming?" I was at her bedside shortly before her death, staying at a motel not far from the clinic. Her youngest son, Gilles, came to join us and found a room at another motel nearby. Fernand was living with his small family in a trailer park. Paul, the third son, came with his wife and stayed at Fernand's. There we were, a nomadic little group camping on the edge of death, so to speak, not unlike the penniless Mexicans who'd come to a temporary rest around us, not unlike a good many wandering Americans, in fact. I remember feeling that we fitted the situation perfectly.

We had time for only three short bits of conversation, Anna and I, though we'd at last discovered a thousand and one things to tell each other about our lives. Only a brilliant mind, a keen intelligence, a passionate heart could have produced something I heard, bending close one day near the end, when she, groggy with sedatives, an intravenous drip in her heel and a tube somewhere else, fixed her eyes on a patch of blue sky and murmured:

"Everywhere else but here it's winter, it's cold. But here it's spring! Can it be that only here is real?"

"Yes," I said, wanting to comfort her, "it's only here that's real." But she looked at me sharply, the way she used to long ago, when she was letting us know we needn't try to put anything over on her.

"There's something I must tell you," she said to me two or three times, but then she'd fall into a heavy, sedated sleep. I thought, she's going to talk to me about Clémence. She's going to leave her to me. My turn's come.

But no. Not yet. After Anna died I learned that a whole year earlier, knowing she was nearer the end than she'd given us to believe, she had put Clémence in Dédette's hands.

DEDETTE in her convent! How ever could she begin to manage the running around, the shopping, finding clothes for Clémence, bringing them to her, perhaps having to exchange them, all the things Clémence was incapable of doing for herself, or perhaps at some point had simply decided weren't worth the effort.

Those things were on my mind the day we buried Anna. The sky was radiant. Since there were only two of her three sons, one of her daughters-in-law, and myself to attend the ceremony, plus three chance friends of the kind who seem indispensable one day and are nowhere to be found the next, the priest suggested holding it at the graveside in the cemetery. He arrived wearing a surplice, with a choir boy and his aspergillum. Chairs had been arranged on the grass in the semishade of a slender tree with delicate leaves. We sat down. It was the tenth of January, 1964. Everywhere, not so far from this miraculous oasis, it must have been winter. Here it was perpetual spring. The cemetery was a profusion of giant poinsettias, hibiscus, and clusters of vivid red jacaranda. Insects buzzed merrily, flitting from clump to clump. The buzzing mingled with rather sweet lamenting sounds from a Mexican family weeping at the grave of a loved one in the distance. There was something infinitely tender and trusting in their praying voices. On a branch of a paloverde a mockingbird sang as though his heart would burst, the "gentle bird of youth" so beloved of southerners, and no wonder, once you've heard it sing.

At last our hearts were filled with love for Anna, whose frustrated, demanding nature could no longer alienate us. Why, I asked myself, is she only now getting the love that would have made her life? I hadn't yet completely returned to the faith of my youth from which, I believed, a dictatorial, unfair, and narrow-minded Church had driven me. But now a nagging riddle was drawing me back – what is life, and what is death? It seemed to me that Anna's life and death had made God necessary. No life or death until then seemed to me to have made Him so necessary. In one of her very last moments of consciousness, she had murmured so faintly that I'd had to put my ear to her lips to hear her, "I want to believe, but I'm not sure, that there's someone at the end.... Do...you think...?"

I took it on myself to tell her there was, though I wasn't sure either.

"Yes, Anna, someone's waiting for us, someone who loves us as much as we've hoped and longed to be loved all our lives."

I'd laid the trap and now I was caught in it. Now I needed assurance myself. Perhaps it was in that comforting little cemetery in Arizona, where even an inconsolable grief couldn't block out the mockingbird's beautiful song, that I began again to want God, at any cost....

I SHUDDERED suddenly as I stood by the big window in Dédette's little infirmary room, startled, here at the bedside of my dying sister, to find I'd been lost in thought about another sister's death six years before. And I'd forgotten what had made me think of it...ah, yes...Clémence!

Well! Dédette had managed to look after her superbly. Convent rules had already begun to be relaxed at that time, but even if they hadn't, dear Dédette, though she observed rules scrupulously, would have found a way to bend a few for Clémence. But she didn't have to. On the contrary, some of "our sisters" had important connections and hence influence, others had friends with cars, others time to spare, and others frequent reason to be in shops, and all of them were trying to outdo the others in looking after, in fact coddling Clémence. What I hadn't foreseen was that when these women who'd renounced the world were given an opportunity to help someone by returning to it, they became like a swarm of bees, each anxious to do her part and each contributing what she could.

This was how Dédette managed to have Clémence admitted to a very good, brand-new government home for old people still able to walk around. Clémence had a lovely ground-floor room with a little flower garden and all the care that her condition required. It was in the pretty village of Ste-Anne-des-Chênes, which I remembered well since Maman had taken me there on pilgrimages, organized perhaps in competition with Ste-Anne-de-Beaupré in Quebec, or perhaps in spiritual affiliation with it.

It was rather far from the city, about fifty miles. Nevertheless, with the help of all her car-driving acquaintances Dédette managed to go there often, bearing a birthday cake for Clémence, or a pair of stockings, or a nice little pink bathrobe unearthed by "one of our sisters" at the clearance counter in Eaton's basement. And what's more, these visits allowed Dédette to work off a bit of the footloose urge shared by everyone in our family.

This is the place where I should tell the story about Dédette's and Clémence's visit to me at Petite-Rivière-St-François in Quebec's Charlevoix County. I rented a little house for them there, next to the cottage I'd had for several years – three weeks of light, of summer, of incomparable, exhilarating happiness before the dark days that followed almost immediately. That will have to wait till later, though, or else my poor dervish will tangle himself in the threads of his interwoven stories. For the moment we'll stay by the high window in the little infirmary room where I'm looking at the peaceful sky and picturing the ferment, the bustle, the mobilization of kindly zeal that Clémence's humble and apparently pointless existence had guilelessly set in motion.

Before long, all was not well at Ste-Anne-des-Chênes. Despite the activity on her behalf, Clémence was lonely. Then Adèle came on the scene, planting the idea in her head that the two of them would be better off living together in a little apartment in St-Boniface. For the first time in her life, I think, Dédette telephoned me long distance. She was in a frenzy and her voice was high and shrill. "Just imagine! I had all that trouble getting Clémence into Ste-Anne and now Adèle wants to take her out. If she leaves they'll never take her back."

"We can't allow that," said I. "It's madness and we've got to stop it at all costs."

"But how?" pleaded Dédette across the line from Manitoba.

How indeed! We had no power of attorney from Clémence to look after her well-being. For the moment she was free to do anything she chose, however disastrous it might be.

"We'll pray," said Dédette before hanging up. "Who knows, it might work out this time."

It didn't work out, any more than it had before. Those two poor women, for all the love and compassion they really had for one another, were bound to grate on each other's nerves. Feeling that we'd overprotected Clémence, as perhaps we had, Adèle went too far the other way. "You can do that, Clémence," she'd say. "Learn how to do things yourself." Which soon drove Clémence to hysteria, since her nerves invariably went to pieces at the least difficulty. Furthermore, Adèle, taking after Papa, was slow to get moving in the morning but came to life towards evening. Then she'd make strong coffee, go out and come back in, walk around half the night, meditate, bring back the past, write her recollections...while Clémence, having gone to bed "with the chickens", would be trying to sleep. In the early morning Adèle would be tired from her excitement and activity during the night and want to sleep, while Clémence would have had all she could take of staying in bed and want to stir things up a bit. Perhaps the cruellest part was that for too long they were both prepared to suffer each other rather than suffer alone. Dédette tried to spare me and at first didn't tell me what was going on, which I'd been suspecting, in fact. One evening she called me from Manitoba in great agitation and announced:

"I had to put Clémence in hospital. Don't be too worried."

Then she told me, speaking fast because long distance costs money, that it was perhaps a blessing in disguise...because, through the good offices of "one of our sisters", Clémence had been seen by a psychiatrist, and he had said, "You must put her in a good institution." It was already almost done, a place had been found. A home run by some Sisters of Providence, very dedicated..."and our sisters know their sisters...."

"Where?" I finally managed to put in.

There was a silence. The cost of the unused line time was a measure of Dédette's discomfort.

"Otterburne," she said with a sigh that reached me from beyond the Great Lakes and across part of the Manitoba prairie.

"Oh Lord!"

I could see the little village that was so secluded people had always said it was in danger of being forgotten sooner or later. I could see the shadowy little roads and thought I saw a solitary figure wandering aimlessly along them, perhaps a lonely Clémence, she too trying to patch together the threads of her life.

"Is there at least a bus to get there?"

"No...but one of our sisters has her family there. They come and take her back with them quite often. I'll have opportunities to go. And then, if we don't take the place, there won't be another one."

I sensed she'd reached the end of her tether.

"That's fine, Dédette. Do whatever's best. Whatever you think."

IT WASN'T so bad. The Sisters of Providence were perhaps not the most learnèd or cultivated of women, but they knew how to comfort the suffering, and before long they had begun to win Clémence's trust. She was under the care of a Korean doctor, brought there by heaven knows what saga, who looked after her better than she'd ever been cared for, perhaps, calming her with words of wisdom and medicines that were not too harsh. The fresh air helped. I saw her next when Sister Ross, the Mother Superior of the home, brought her to visit Dédette and me at the convent, when Dédette was dying. I was told she was much improved by then. Still, it was a great shock to see the frail little figure, the face sunken and toothless because she wouldn't wear her dentures. Her eyes were huge and searching, a little confused, as if the filmy veil drawn by the drug Largactyl between her and the rest of the world didn't keep her mind from groping for her sufferings of old. I wondered how to tell her that Dédette didn't have long to live, and even whether I had to. We entered Dédette's little room together. Clémence knew at first glance. I saw this in a strangely awakened lucidity in her eyes, which were usually expressionless. But she controlled herself well. She even grumbled to us about the food provided by "those sisters". She'd always grumbled about the food wherever she'd been, and we thought it was just a favourite gripe. One day much later I tasted what she had on her plate at the home and, merciful heaven, it was awful! I think now I realize that people don't get really appetizing meals in any home or hospital where many need to be fed at once.

As soon as we'd left the room, Clémence turned to me and with that seeming indifference induced by sedatives, which is perhaps the most distressing form of pain, she said:

"We're not going to keep our Dédette, eh?"

I put my arms around her. It was like holding a little bundle of clothing wrapped around a feebly struggling mass of suffering.

I took her back to the entrance hall where Sister Ross was waiting.

"I'll bring her back to you next week," said Sister Ross.

"That's very kind, Sister."

"Not at all. We have to come into town every week or so. Clémence may as well take advantage of it."

She had a pleasant face and the pleasant, straightforward manner of a sensible country woman. I didn't in the least expect to become as fond of her as I did, only to lose her too, not many years later. Now when I begin to be fond of someone I'm always terribly afraid, because it seems it will never be for long.

When leaving Clémence I told her I'd try to come and visit her in Otterburne.

"If you can," she said.

In the end I didn't go during that trip. What kept me from going? Something that no doubt seemed important at the time: proofs to correct, the English translation of one of my books to review with the translator. My books have taken a lot of time that I might have given to friendship, love – to obligations of the heart. But friendship, love, personal obligations have also taken a lot of time that I might have given to my books. The result is that neither my books nor my life is well pleased with me these days.

STANDING at the high window, I returned to Dédette's bedside from a memory triggered by another which, though it had lasted perhaps two minutes, had taken me years back over space and time.

"About Clémence," I said to Dédette, "I don't want you to worry. If it...turns out that you can't look after her, I'll do it. It's time I took my turn."

If I'd expected to put her mind at rest with a promise like that, I was sadly mistaken. I still had much to learn about my sister and, through her, about at least one aspect of the eternal enigma, death. In her eyes appeared the intense distress of someone who perceives that she's being abandoned to death, since the living are taking over those of her duties that are still unfulfilled. In that instant I realized that the worst part of dying is feeling abandoned. Though she didn't know it, her eyes were saying: I'm going to die and you're going to live, all of you around me are going to live. So we aren't the same any more, we're separated already, me on one side and you on the other.

It seemed so true I was ashamed to think that I was going to consent to live, while she would be dead; that I'd done so after each of the deaths that had touched me. If we really loved each other, I said to myself, as soon as one of us went, the others would go also. If we really loved each other, we'd all join hands and walk together into the ocean, towards the Creator, saying to Him, "Don't take us one by one, it's gone on so long; take us all at once." God was waiting only for this, I thought, and then would take pity on His creatures and their love for each other.

SUDDENLY the telephone rang at my elbow. I came back with a start to my hotel room in the land of funeral-taper trees and a wind of despair, from the little infirmary room beneath the tall Manitoba sky, and from a time long before that, when my mother's voice was asking, "Who'll look after my sick child?" A glance at the clock told me the journey had taken perhaps fifteen minutes. Yet it had crossed more distance than all my plane trips laid end to end. What an astonishing amount of ground one's memory can cover!

I lifted the receiver. I heard a gentle, loving voice, like cool water taking the sting from a burn. It was Sister Berthe Valcourt. When Dédette died she was Mother Superior of the convent in St-Boniface. My sister had died in her arms early one Monday morning. She'd opened her eyes very wide, Sister Berthe told me, "like someone who's going to cry for help," then she'd recognized the nun and murmured, "It's strange...strange...," and, as though recovering from some infinite surprise, just had time to pronounce Clémence's name. Then she was asleep for ever.

A few days earlier, however, she had been perfectly lucid and had clearly and unmistakably given Clémence into Sister Berthe's care. "Gabrielle's far away," she had said, "and so busy already with all her obligations, her letters, her books, her public, and her health so delicate, too. How's she ever going to run back and forth doing everything Clémence needs?"

Sister Berthe had accepted responsibility for Clémence as though she hadn't needed to be asked.

Now her soothing voice was saying, "I finished my seminar a bit earlier than I expected. We still have nearly two hours of daylight, and I have the community car. How would you like to run out to Otterburne and give Clémence a hug?"

How would I like it!

Three minutes later I was at the hotel entrance, though Berthe had warned me she'd need a good quarter of an hour to get there.

XIV

ISN'T IT CURIOUS how life repeats itself? It's as if there were re-hearsals for some future event. The first time we have a feeling of *déjà vu*, and the second time, much later, we're confused in the strangest way. Is it because I now know what I thought I knew then, we wonder, or did I really know then what I know now?

In any event, as we left the city Berthe missed the main highway and we found ourselves on the little secondary roads I'd been on long before, roads which she, a good deal younger than I and always in a hurry, didn't know at all. She was upset. "In all the time I've been going to see Clémence in Otterburne, I've never missed the right road before." I smiled vaguely, a little guilty. I and my memories must have led her astray, that was all. Or else I'd talked too much and distracted her. Whatever the case, she didn't know where she was but I remembered it well, even the time of year. No mistake, the first time had also been in early autumn, harvest time, when the fields of high, golden wheat wave gently in the west wind, in the shimmering light at close of day. For all the sorrows I'd accumulated since the last time I'd been here, I still felt a surge of joy to see the waving wheat, a little sadly I might say, because my distant youth was lending me a small piece of all its happiness – or rather a memory of this happiness.

Soon Berthe confessed that we were lost.

"These little roads put me off!" she exclaimed.

"I've always loved them," I said. "The devil must have made you do it just to please me."

"The devil, indeed!"

Twilight was advancing rapidly, flooding the prairie with what might have been a deep blue liquid, from which nothing clear emerged.

I could hear Gilles's voice: "Otterburne – can you tell me where it is?" And the answer: "Over there, don't you see the lights?"

"We're very close, though," insisted Berthe. "I have the impression we passed right by and missed the turn."

"Aren't there just three streetlamps in the village?" I asked.

"I think there are five or six now," she replied, "but there's the home too, three storeys high, and it should be all lit up at this hour. Usually you can see it from a distance."

I began to look for it. With three floors lit up, it should be easy to find across the dark, uniform prairie.

Very shortly I spotted a glimmer.

Sister Berthe was impressed.

"You have good eyes."

"It's because I trained myself very young to look out into the prairie at this hour."

"What were you looking for?" she asked, affably but with genuine curiosity too.

With my thoughts far away I replied:

"Happiness. Maman kept saying some day he'd surely come our way. I was afraid he might miss our little Deschambault Street, so I used to go and wait for him at the corner, looking out on a kind of open space that was there in those days. I thought of it as the prairie because you could see a long way. I never thought happiness could possibly come from any other direction, just across that dreamy open prairie."

"On foot?" asked Berthe softly so as not to disturb my memories.

"Oh, yes, on foot. And I'd recognize him when I saw him.... Later, when I was fourteen or fifteen, I used to go and wait for him at the end of a little dirt road at my uncle Excide's farm. It must have been on the edge of a plateau, because when you came out of the bushes you could suddenly see such a vast expanse of sky and land it made me feel the world was mine."

"Did you ever see him?" asked Berthe more softly still.

"Twice there was a tree in the distance that looked like someone walking, and for some time I thought it could be he. Only he always stayed in the same place, as if he'd stopped to think and hadn't made up his mind to start again."

We were arriving at the door of the home, whose façade was almost entirely lit up. It looked like a strange, brilliant constellation at the end of the village, which was half in darkness and about as somnolent as when I'd come there the first time. I could hear our gales of laughter then, but dominant in the foreground were unhappy events of years to come, too numerous to count, it seemed.

How many worn-out bodies and minds were contained in that large establishment on the almost empty prairie, how many lives forsaken, stowed away for ever, locked up, forgotten, I learned only later, fortunately. But fortunately too, I also learned how much unfailing kindness was devoted to relieving all that misery.

Sister Berthe went with me to the second floor, as far as Clémence's door. There she left me. I knocked lightly. I heard a cheerless voice telling me to come in.

CLEMENCE WAS SITTING in semidarkness at the foot of her bed, on a grey blanket neatly folded in four, the way one imagines prisoners in the evening in their cells. She seemed to be part of the vast twilight, now deep night-blue, entering unimpeded through the window, a high one here too. I could barely make out her features but saw very well that she was frighteningly thin, her face terribly small, her body all huddled up as if trying to take as little room as possible in this world, perhaps even to disappear completely. Yet she'd held up well at Dédette's funeral. She'd been dressed appropriately, had received condolences with dignity and a perfectly suitable word of thanks for each person. True, at the time she'd felt like part of the family again…whereas here in this lost village she must have felt we'd abandoned her.

It gave my heart such a wrench I really didn't know how to start a conversation with the poor child. She'd barely turned her head towards me when I entered.

"Would you like me to turn on the light?" I asked gently.

She gave a little shrug.

Did she think she was back in our poorest days, when Maman would ask us not to turn on the lights until we really had to? "As long as there's a little light in the sky we can wait," she used to say. Or did the gentle half-light suit her sadness, the way, in fact, it had always suited me?

"It's still light enough, but turn it on if you like," she said with indifference.

"You're right," I said.

I sat down beside her, tried to put my arms around her and found her stiff, unyielding. She barely let me kiss her on the cheek, and as I did so, kept her eyes on the limitless twilight still sweeping in slow waves into the tiny room. With my arm lightly around her waist, I turned and looked at the sky with her, in silence, and thought how much its colour matched our souls.

I was sitting on a corner of that horrid grey blanket, which had probably come from an army surplus store. I made the blunder of finding fault with it, or rather with whoever had given it to her, either to be rid of it or instead of a better present. People often gave her clothes they didn't want any more, and she, imagining perhaps that they'd been given in generosity, would refuse to part with them. Or perhaps she became attached without illusions to her fusty old things, for some obscure reason we could never understand. I know now that unhappy people take pleasure in surrounding themselves with old, dreary, unattractive objects.

"I'll buy you a much prettier one for the foot of your bed, Clémence," I said. "How about a pink one?"

Her hand clung tight to the ugly blanket as if to a dear and faithful friend.

"It's warm and still good," she said. Then after a silence she added, "What more would pink do for me?"

I felt I had to explain that we weren't poor any more and could allow ourselves some indulgences.

"I've got plenty of money now to buy you nice things, Clémence."

"Money!" she said scornfully, and with the look in her eyes, with her whole wasted face, seemed to be rejecting something that had done nothing for humankind in the depths of misery. Then she asked me — and I still don't know whether it was a childish question or one of great wisdom — "Do you think it helps?"

In her presence that day, I was no longer sure of anything. Certainly nothing shakes our confidence more than being with someone who has none; that's why we can't bear it, perhaps.

"You'll see," I told her, as one always does in such circumstances, "you're going to get better, Clémence. I'm going to help you. You're going to get well again."

I was so shaken to find her in this state. I kept blaming myself for it. But there were others I blamed too. In the city there were still family friends and cousins, male and female, who claimed they cared for me, yet not one of them had taken the trouble to go and see Clémence. "Otterburne's too far," they'd say. "There's no bus to get there." "It's the end of the earth." They treated her as if she were already buried. But had I done any better, always so busy writing my stories, as though this were my most essential duty? How do you know which duty is the most essential? Perhaps each has its turn and you have to keep hurling yourself this way and that, trying to do justice to one at a time, while the rest are screaming all around you for attention.

"You know, I've come from Quebec especially to see you," I said, as if asking to be forgiven.

"You like your Quebec?" she asked without much interest.

"I've made my life there," I said.

"Maman came from there, Papa too," she murmured, as though I didn't know, or perhaps the better to register such an unusual fact in her solitary existence.

"Would you come there to live with me, or near me, if I came and got you?"

She kept gazing at the gradually darkening sky, like someone dreaming of finding a real home at the end of time.

"No," she said. "Papa's here, Maman's here; they're here for ever in the cemetery. I'll stay with them."

Then she reminded me with a degree of defiance:

"There's still a place in our family plot in the old cathedral cemetery. That's where I want you to bury me later."

"I'll do that, Clémence dear."

Then she seemed to feel a little better and I decided to change the subject.

"In the meantime, we have to get you some new clothes. To-morrow morning Sister Berthe and I will come and get you and take you to Eaton's. I'd like to buy you two or three pretty dresses and a coat and some shoes...."

She let me talk on, adrift in a deep sea of indifference. What did she care about shoes, stockings, lovely new handbags, and silk umbrellas? By the last glimmers of daylight, faint rays still filtering through the window, I saw that there was no hope in her eyes. Still beautiful eyes, sombre brown, moist with the tears of life, but empty of the thing that quickens the soul – though who knows what that really is? My heart ached as I looked at her. Without reflecting that every day hope is disappointed in this life, hope was suddenly what I wanted at all costs to bring back to my poor sister's eyes. I didn't know the price I would pay; the many trips from Quebec to this poor, forgotten little village, the countless letters I'd write, the endless encouragement day by day. But most of all, yes, most of all, once hope was restored to her I would be even more committed, for how can we ever abandon someone we've "saved"?

I left her in the blue half-light she didn't want interrupted, even to see me better before I went.

Sister Berthe was waiting for me in the car. She comforted me with kind and soothing words. Being with me again after so many years, Clémence was bound to be very apprehensive at first. She was frightened by any change in her routine, any emotional ripple in her isolated existence upset her. But she'd get used to it gradually. Even tomorrow I'd probably find her a little less difficult. And it wouldn't really be long before she'd begin being affectionate again.

I listened in astonishment. You'd have said she was talking about her own sister as much as mine, that she knew Clémence perhaps better by now than I did myself.

What strange compensation heartache sometimes brings! My most loving sister, Dédette, who was always best at comforting me, had no sooner been taken from me than a substitute was given me, a stranger, but every bit as tender and as close. Had Dédette known, wanted it so, perhaps? I thought I recalled seeing in her eyes, when the end was near, during the most difficult moments of our separation, a mysterious look of relief.

Gently Sister Berthe squeezed my hand. Then we started home. Moments later, turning off the road from the village onto the highway, what should we see, as visible as could be against the deep blue sky, but a sign saying "Otterburne".

We glanced at one another with a furtive little smile.

"So it really is on the map," I said.

"By the highway too, which I'll never miss again," said Sister Berthe, "and only thirty miles from the convent. We'll come often. And soon you'll see Clémence come back to life."

The twilight resembled a great watery deep that made you think it must have crept over the whole earth by now. I slowly began to feel better as it worked its old magic upon me. Perhaps this bewitching time of day was reviving fragments of the old dream of my youth. I peered into the blue of the night that now united earth and sky, and imagined that tomorrow would indeed be better.

XV

NOW, TO PICK UP the threads of my story, I must reach far beyond these sorrowful events to what was probably the most sheltered period of my life. Yet I found reasons not to think I was happy, reasons for preparing to leave, for on my little Deschambault Street I was hearing the call of the far-off lands people used to refer to respectfully as the "old countries", those of our earliest ancestors who had come to North America.

It took me seven years – eight counting Cardinal – to scrape together, penny by penny, the sum of money I felt I had to have to contemplate leaving. I had about eight hundred dollars in the bank. I raised this to almost nine hundred by adding the modest proceeds of selling my bicycle, my fur coat, and a few other objects. Maman was alarmed to see me disposing of things she knew I treasured. It didn't help to tell her I was only going for a year, which I earnestly believed; to her I was behaving like someone burning her bridges, or turning a page in her life.

Precisely how my plan to go to Europe developed and why it took over and ruled my life so utterly, I'd still find it difficult to say. So at the time, I suppose, I didn't understand it at all. It was, it must have been, one of the mysterious calls one hears and obeys blindly, half confident, half confused. I was looking for something, but what? The little things I'd written so far were so worthless. On the strength of those alone I'd never have dared announce I was going to devote myself to writing. No, even in my own eyes, this was not something I was cut out for. And yet I was faintly conscious sometimes of seeing myself in the future, not, indeed, as having become a writer, but as struggling and struggling towards this goal. This was perhaps one of the most accurate premonitions I ever had, concerning either myself or anyone else.

On the other hand, I had had some success on the stage with our amateur theatre groups, Le Cercle Molière, where I played in French in *Blanchette* by Brieux, *Le Gendre de Monsieur Poirier* by Augier and Sandeau, *Le Chant du Berceau* and *Les Soeurs Gué-donnec*, and then with the Winnipeg Little Theatre in English. Naïvely, I believed that I had some talent for the theatre – and perhaps I did. Since one must always have a plausible explanation to offer for what one does, I would say I was going to London and Paris to study drama. People thought I was very daring, very full of myself to be departing into the blue this way. I wonder what they would have thought if I had admitted that my real purpose was to see what the world was like on the other side of the hill I'd been living behind and that I was counting on this to show me what it was I was looking for.

But I had a feeling my urge to leave hadn't begun with me alone. Often I thought it must have come from previous generations, whose yearning for fulfilment had been sapped by undeservedly obscure lives, an urge reborn in me, inspiring me to strive for their ultimate liberation. Perhaps I was still gripped by my old childhood dream of making it up to my people with my own success. I liked to keep telling myself so during these months of torment, for I was often terrified by the uncharted future towards which I kept driving myself. I suddenly grasped how big, how impenetrable my future was, seen from my peaceful, countrified little Deschambault Street: a misty vastness in the distance, pierced but not dispersed by brilliant lights. I wanted to turn back but it was too late. I had put the inevitable between myself and my fear, as I was learning to do to protect myself from perpetual indecision.

It must have been my last year of teaching, or possibly the next to last. I still had my first-grade class. I was comfortable with my little immigrants and they seemed comfortable with me; we were drawn together by a subtle feeling that we were all strangers – at least, strangers to an absurd element in life that was ruining it for humankind.

Surprisingly, after a tenacious fight to keep me at home, Maman suddenly gave in. I told how her resistance ended in *The Road past Altamont*, partly fictionalized, or transcended rather, but contain-ing the essential truth, and I don't want to return ever again to that old wound.

She resigned herself more readily than I expected to selling the house. From lack of experience, I didn't understand at the time that she was tired out from struggling, but only where material possessions were concerned. Later, although more tired than ever, she found enough energy to come and visit me in Montreal. And if her children were unhappy or in danger, she'd run to them still, even just before she died.

It would have been impossible to keep the house. I was the only one in the family to have a steady income in those Depression years, apart from Adèle, and even she, as I recall, didn't always have a school during that dreadful period. After seven years at the Académie Provencher, I was earning ninety-five dollars a month for only ten months of the year, less pension fund deductions in the last three years. At the time I never expected that the little sum I recovered from the fund, two years later when I returned from Europe, would virtually save my life as I faced an agonizing decision in my wretched little room on Stanley Street: whether to go back to Manitoba or stay in Montreal.

For the moment, our unpaid property and school taxes, plus compound interest, amounted to over a thousand dollars. We also owed a great deal to the wood and coal merchant.

My brother Germain had no school, and to avoid being a further burden to us was obliged to accept a temporary post at the College of St-Boniface, which was in such straits it could offer him only bed and board and a little pocket money in return for twenty hours of classes a week. He reduced his tobacco ration to almost nothing and spent the winter in a coat worn to threads. He often held his hand across the front of that coat, I remember, about halfway down, to hide the shabbiest part; at least, this was a mannerism we'd never seen in him before. When he finally obtained a teaching post in Saskatchewan, I had to lend him the price of his railway ticket, nineteen dollars and fifty cents. I remember the sum exactly, I suppose because it seemed so enormous.

In the course of the year he spent in St-Boniface, his wife Antonia found herself a school of several grades in a remote area, but for a salary that no one would have dared offer a man; there was not much compunction about doing such a thing to a woman in those days. Out of her sixty dollars a month she had to house, feed, and clothe herself, bring up their two-year-old daughter whom she kept with her, and, of course, pay the cost of travel and their medical care in case of illness. Germain left for Saskatchewan in high spirits. The school he'd been offered was not far from his wife's. He would be able to visit his little family on weekends. For a reasonable sum, a neighbouring farmer rented him an ancient buggy and an equally ancient mare, which rarely went faster than a walk.

Antonia often told me how, when she'd finished school on Friday evening, she'd take Lucille's little hand and they'd walk quite far down the road to the top of the only rise of land in the flat countryside, a perfect lookout point. They'd finally see the rig appear in the distance, moving far too slowly to suit the two who were waiting, to say nothing of the one approaching. As the distance closed, Antonia sometimes thought she saw the whip rise, impatiently perhaps. But Germain had always loved animals and could never bring himself to be harsh with the old farm horse. The lash would fall rather like a caress on Flossie's broad rump. Slow she may have been, but I think all of them, child, father, and mother, fell in love with Flossie that year. They talked about her long afterwards with curious warmth, as of an old friend in hard times.

Waiting on the high ground, the child would soon begin to jump for joy and wave to her father. Though impatient, Antonia and Germain would just watch the distance between them gradually dwindling.

These two had to wait until half their lives were behind them before realizing their modest ambition of working side by side in the same school, he as principal and she as teacher at the elementary level.

It was during those difficult years, when poverty was so prevalent everywhere it came to seem normal, that I began to think only about taking flight.

MAMAN FINALLY found a buyer and the transaction was quickly concluded, almost without hesitation. All my life, or at least since I'd been able to understand such things, I'd been hearing that selling the house was inevitable. Many times the prospect had come close enough to touch us with its clammy wing, then gone away again and left us in peace a while. Then suddenly it was done and there was no turning back. When Maman told me, pretty calmly, "I've sold the house...," the shock I felt was something I've never really recovered from. For me it's still as though she told me she'd sold a living, breathing part of us that day.

From that point on, Maman seemed to accept the fact with surprising composure. Once liberated from much that she had accumulated in her life, furniture, objects of one kind or another, she perhaps felt for the first time that she could turn to many of the things that she'd been wanting to do. It may have been like casting off a weight. In any event, she seemed to undergo a mysterious and sudden rejuvenation, ready, one might say, for a new, more carefree, airy existence, with no ties but those of the heart.

We didn't get much for the house: once the debts were paid, barely enough to provide Maman with a very small allowance for a year or two – until I came back from Europe, I thought. But we were pleased with an agreement we had made with the new owner. For a modest sum he would rent us three rooms upstairs, made into a convenient little apartment.

Selling the house where I'd been born on March 22, 1909, where I'd first dreamed my most persistent dreams (to which I'm subject even today, tired as I am of pursuing their delusions of beauty), affected me less than I thought it would once the first shock had passed, probably because we were still basically at home. Calmly and without regret it seemed, Maman disposed of our excess furnishings – rugs, lamps, and the big dining-room table. She'd embarked on the course of self-denial that she followed thenceforth until the day she died, when we were stunned to discover that her personal possessions amounted to little more than those of an old nun bound by vows of poverty.

So Maman, Clémence, and I moved into the three upstairs rooms which we ourselves, when we were the owners, had rented so many times to transients for a week or a month, or to people who stayed for years and became friends.

"It's really almost better this way," said Maman. "We still have our trees, our little street, our peace and quiet, without all the worries that go with them." Fortunately, our landlord also loved these things and took good care of them. In short, we were almost happier as tenants in our own house.

THAT YEAR, Maman went as usual to spend the summer with her brother Excide. I went to Camperville, a tiny village of no account on the shores of the marvellous Lake Winnipegosis, one of the most limpid and also most tempestuous lakes in Manitoba. I was to spend over a month with my cousin Eliane, my uncle Excide's eldest daughter, whose husband, Laurent Jubinville, was principal of the farm school attached to the Oblate mission on the Indian reserve. The house stood alone in the middle of a huge meadow full of rocks: a strange, bleak landscape creating an air of desolation. But by the edge of the lake, listening to its tireless voice, I was soothed and happy.

Eliane had six adorable little children, and she herself was slim, blonde, and beautiful, with eyes full of kindness, still very young and, one would say, imbued with the artless dreams of youth. To amuse myself and help out, I gave lessons to the three eldest. I've never seen children want to learn as badly as they did. Years later when I wrote *Where Nests the Water Hen*, I borrowed many of the details and elements of Camperville to mix with those of the Little Water Hen, the two regions having much in common. The child Joséphine in *Where Nests the Water Hen* was inspired by Eliane's little girl Denise, who, at barely five and a half, used to follow me everywhere, upstairs and down, outside, through the stony meadow, with her reader in her hand, begging me at every step, "Cousin, show me another page." Often I can still hear those children asking, in their sweet, musical little voices, "Cousin, show us how to do this. Show us...." I found my real children for *Where Nests the Water Hen* while staying with my cousin at Camperville, that's certain. And I confess I also took Luzina's blue eyes, which were always "warm" or "full of feeling", from Eliane. I spent a sweet, dreamy summer there, at peace with myself and untroubled by my plans for the future, just content with the moment, which hasn't often been the case.

I wasn't idle, however. I kept my mornings for my writing, since I wasn't giving up, and displeased as I might be with what I wrote I'd take it up again next morning. This must be when I tried my hand at Indian legends, gleaned from the nearby reserve. I attempted every imaginable genre before finding my own. I wrote a great many pages but kept very few, tearing most of them up as I went along because, having only one suitcase, how could I have carried all that away with me?

In the afternoon I'd call my pupils to school in the family room of the house, which Eliane had assigned to us. I'd brought a small blackboard, chalk, and some erasers, which delighted the children. The three youngest would stand at the door as if at the gates of Paradise, in tears, begging "to come to school too." On Fridays we would let four-year-old Réal come in and he'd sit quietly in a corner, following the lessons without a sound.

To reward my little people, I'd take them swimming afterwards in the cold, sparkling-clean waters of the lake. The waves were dangerous, even at the shore, and Elaine wouldn't have allowed the children to go without supervision. It was an exciting treat for them to be able to discover their lake at last, less than ten minutes from the house. We'd come back washed and a bit limp, the eldest boy carrying golden-haired Marielle, who was two.

In the evenings I'd ride my bicycle along the Indian trails. They had probably been there for generations and generations, and were always quiet, winding, springy under the wheels or feet, and as enticing as if they'd just been discovered. The rustling of leaves accompanied me as I rode — soft woodland music played every summer since the days of the "savages".

The wonderful summer holidays came to an end. I went back to my class at the Académie Provencher. This would definitely be my last year of teaching.

By the end of September, Maman had still not come home. That year the threshing had been much delayed by torrential rains. She was no doubt loath to leave her brother before the heavy work was finished. But I imagined that she was also finding consolation for the loss of her house in the permanence there, things that never let her down: the farm, the high, clear sky of Pembina Mountain, the seasonal farmwork which never changed from one year to the next.

When October came I began to feel she was overdoing it. Her brother was so much younger than she, I didn't like to think of her, at sixty-nine, working her fingers to the bone for him. I suspected that before coming home she was putting the house in order, inspecting the curtains, mending the ones that were still holding together, making new ones to replace those beyond saving, filling cupboard shelves with jams, jellies, and vegetable preserves of all kinds. I suppose I was a little jealous, but I resented the fact that she should put herself out so much for a brother who at times, I felt, had taken rather too much advantage of her.

At last she came home. It was a late October evening. There was frost already. The first snow was about to fall. She arrived with a fat suitcase bulging with jams, pembina jelly, sweet butter, fresh cream – to us, priceless presents from the farm, which Maman intended to share with others. Some of these good things had been sent with Maman for Rosalie, her only sister living in Winnipeg, whom Uncle Excide hadn't wanted to forget.

The next morning, with a cold coming on and extremely tired, I thought, she was determined to go that very day to take Rosalie her share of presents. I'd found her looking poorly when she returned from the farm. She'd lost weight and seemed to have worked beyond her strength, as if on purpose, to escape some kind of punishment, perhaps. I tried to keep her from going, telling her that the day was cold, the sidewalks icy, and that my aunt could certainly wait another day for her share of gifts from the farm. To which she replied that she had brought some homemade bread that Rosalie was particularly fond of, and she wouldn't dream of not letting her enjoy it right away, poor soul, after all she'd spent the summer glued to her sewing machine. At that I lost my temper and told her it really was ridiculous, a woman of her age slaving all summer at Uncle's, then when she'd barely set foot inside the door going out in the streets again like a beggar woman.... I stopped short. Dumbfounded, Maman and I looked at each other. She'd always been the one who'd talked to me that way. "D'you think, just because you're young, you can go on burning the candle at both ends the way you're doing?" Or, "Go on then, do what you like, waste your strength and don't listen to reason, only one day, my poor girl, you'll have to pay for it...."

There we were all of a sudden, each in the other's shoes. I was the one who was scolding, and Maman, just as I'd done, was shrugging her shoulders, putting her nose in the air and going right ahead with what she intended to do, as if to say, "When are you ever going to leave me alone!" Then I knew how like her I was. Understanding now why she was arguing, always giving me the same backtalk, I felt the deep compassion for her that one can feel only through one's own helplessness.

I WATCHED her waiting for the streetcar at the corner, her arms full of bulky packages, in a coat that wasn't warm enough, perhaps without gloves, and for the first time in my life she looked to me like a poor woman. Her wealth of dreams had always made her seem rich to me, but out there at the streetcar stop, her eyes cast down and her head bent, she seemed to have reached some unaccountable impasse. In the darkest days of our money troubles, and even our family quarrels, I never saw her so afflicted, less by the winter wind than by a wind of defeat.

XVI

I WAS UNEASY all that day, though I couldn't put my finger on the reason why.

"Maman hasn't phoned?" I asked when I came home.

"No," Clémence said, "she must be on her way. Or else Aunt Rosalie has kept her for supper."

At six o'clock I called my aunt. She told me Maman had left two hours before, presumably by streetcar.

It was seven o'clock when a policeman rang at the door. He was bringing me the news that Maman had had an accident in the street and had been taken to Misericordia Hospital, which was not far from my aunt's. She had been crossing the icy pavement to reach her streetcar and had fallen and broken her hip. The driver of a car had picked her up.

I left immediately for the hospital, which was at the other end of the city, in an English neighbourhood, of course. Riding in the streetcar, I wondered how Maman had managed, since she knew so little English and probably had no money with her. In those days you practically had to have money in your hand to be admitted to hospital, or at least have a guarantor present.

She was in a four-bed ward and there was a French-speaking woman in one of the other beds. They had already been talking, and I think were helping each other to communicate with the nurse.

As soon as she saw me in the doorway, though in pain (and I learned later she was suffering horribly), her face lit up with joy. Yes, it shone with real happiness, all the more visible for having to overcome her concern and remorse for the commotion she was causing, not to mention her physical pain. She had so seldom inconvenienced anyone, asked so little for herself all her life, that the way I ran across the room to her bedside, instead of seeming natural, was to her perhaps the first real proof that I loved her. It gave her such joy despite her discomfort that my heart ached at the sight. I think she cherished the memory all the rest of her life. And then, she'd arrived in a poor woman's clothes – who cares about underwear when the clothes on top aren't much to look at? – and she must have felt vindicated, comforted to see me appear in my nice little rust-coloured fall suit. She introduced me to the other occupants of the room rather elatedly, partly because of a rising fever but also with a note of pride, the strange, almost painful pride she felt in recognizing her children as unquestionably superior to herself. But in spite of the sedative she'd been given, I sensed she was suffering considerably, which she certainly wouldn't admit. Only later, when the room had been invaded by visitors, first for the Ukrainian, then for the French Canadian from Ile des Chênes, then for the Mennonite, and they were all talking loudly in their several languages, the men even smoking pipes, only then did she give me a message with a look in her eyes that said, "Get me out of here if you can."

"Tomorrow," I said aloud, "I promise I'll see about it. Right now, do try and get some sleep."

At the door I turned to give her a smile. I could see myself, lying as she was now, in another four-bed ward, watching miserably as she left so she could get down to work and save me. And everything today seemed so identical to yesterday, with the roles reversed, that I felt as though it would never be possible to change our lives, and almost all hope abandoned me.

Riding home on the streetcar through the darkness, heaven forgive me, I foresaw that Maman might remain a permanent invalid, or at the very least considerably handicapped, that at best her accident would consume most of the money left from the sale of the house, that I wouldn't be able to leave her under the circumstances, meaning I wouldn't be leaving at all. I saw my dream being snuffed out, like the dreams of many of my forebears no doubt, the curious dreams that had driven me for years to achieve something I couldn't identify, that would allow me to be myself. And I grieved for the part of me that now would never come to life, would remain hidden from me. But I also felt a cowardly kind of relief at being spared that lonely, hazy, difficult road, at being allowed to walk down the comfortable beaten path where I'd have company and support on every side. In the darkened window of the streetcar, I could see myself far in the future, gazing out a window, docile and resigned, contemplating what I imagined I might have been.

The next morning I sought the advice of the school board nurse who regularly made the rounds of our classes. I asked her who was the best orthopaedist in town. "No question about it," she told me, "it's Dr. Mackinnon."

I went upstairs to the principal's office and asked permission to use the telephone. He waved me benignly to his own big comfortable chair and the telephone on the desk. Then to put me more at ease, he even found a pretext to leave me alone. Soon I heard a thick Scottish brogue at the other end of the line. It reminded me of kindly old Dr. Mackintyre and I was encouraged. I had no difficulty obtaining an appointment for late the same day. Meanwhile, Dr. Mackinnon assured me, he would go and see Maman at the hospital.

Brother Joseph let me leave my classroom an hour early. And there I was again, riding a streetcar through parts of Winnipeg I didn't know – how could anyone know all of that big, sprawling city? If I look back on those years, I very often see myself travelling about the city on a streetcar, by day or in a kind of darkness, but always obsessed by some problem, worry, remorse, or unexplained haste. At a later stage, I see myself on the train, crossing breathtaking reaches of the country, travelling towards a promising future, or returning to watch one of my family die and leaving again with a heavy heart. I sometimes think I've most intensely felt life's great emotions, even the feeling of being alive, vibrantly alive, while travelling somewhere in lurching little streetcars or long, wailing trains. Or walking through unfamiliar streets in cities where I don't know a soul. So the characters in my books move, travel, walk endlessly, which isn't so surprising when I myself have sat still so little, have been on the move virtually all my life. Yet I admit to having been surprised when this was pointed out to me, because I hadn't realized I'd created characters who were like myself in some ways.

I arrived late at Dr. Mackinnon's office, having made the wrong transfer on the way. I was taken aback to see a man who was old and ill-looking, with a crimson face and great bags under his eyes.

In fact, he was to die before Maman. I've rarely seen a man so unmindful of his own ills, thinking only of those of others. I'd hardly sat down facing him in the light of a heavy-shaded lamp when he leaned his big white head towards me.

"Don't worry. Your mother's not in danger."

"Oh! Good! What needs to be done, then?"

"Operate. Reduce the fracture. Then immobilize her in a body cast that will cover her trunk, both arms and one leg."

"Oh, how awful!"

"It is indeed. Especially for an energetic woman like your mother. She's wonderful," he volunteered. "I've met two or three people in my life, not many more, who've given me the impression of loving life as passionately as she does."

So he'd already sized her up. But how?

"She hardly speaks a word of English," I said. "How did you understand each other?"

"The way she can mime with her face and hands, she could make the densest lout understand. I also remembered a few words of French I learned when I was young. And your mother can find the words too, when she really has to."

I was amazed at the picture he was describing. It was so accurate I began to feel great confidence in the old doctor.

"Will she at least walk again?"

"It's not certain," he said, "but I think so."

A decision about Maman had to be mine alone. Anna was already suffering the long, drawn-out illness that eventually led to cancer, and had lengthy periods of apathy and extreme fatigue. Dédette was far away and restricted by the rules of her community, and could really help only through her prayers – and how hard she prayed, poor soul! Adèle was even farther afield, teaching school to settlers' children in an outpost in northern Alberta, so she couldn't help me much more than they could. As for Rodolphe, we hadn't had any word from him for some time. No question about it: Maman's fate rested in my hands alone. It frightened me.

"How much will it be for the operation?" I remembered to ask at last.

Instantly I imagined I'd been whisked back to the doctor's office Maman had taken me to, when I was the one to be cured and Maman was asking the fateful question: "How much, Doctor?"

"Ordinarily," said Dr. Mackinnon, "it's two hundred and fifty dollars, but I see little signs I recognize because my people weren't rich and I can tell you aren't either. How about a hundred dollars?"

I shuddered, not because of the sum but because the past was so vivid in my mind I'd lost sight of where I was for a moment.

"A hundred dollars!"

And suddenly, buoyed by the confidence the doctor had inspired in me, I found myself opening my heart to him as I'd never done to anyone before. I told him I had enough money in the bank to pay for everything if necessary, the hospital, the anaesthesia, the operation too, but it was money I'd scraped together bit by bit over eight years so I could go and spend a year in Europe, I couldn't really say why, even to myself. Perhaps it was to test myself, to see if I had the stuff to become someone or something, though I had only a muddled idea what, and it wasn't certain I even had any talent, but that was the way it was and I couldn't help it, it was like a mania driving me to find a place for myself. And it was now or never because soon I wouldn't have the strength to leave, I had only just enough now; I could feel the bonds of routine, security – and love – closing tighter around me every day, the better to hold me back.

He'd pushed aside the desk lamp a little, in case it was bothering me no doubt, and the soft half-light encouraged me as I talked.

Suddenly he stood up, and with feeling and determination that took me by surprise told me:

"Go! Go before life swallows you the way it's swallowed so many of your people. Mine too," he added sadly. Then his tone brightened as he continued. "Do we have a bargain? I'll cure your mother. I'll put her back on her feet. And you'll leave.... Sometime in the future, if you can and if I'm still in this world, you can repay me whatever you think's right. I'll leave that to your conscience."

I left his office, in one way relieved and in another feeling worse than ever. In the streetcar, rattling through yet another part of the city, since I was going straight from Dr. Mackinnon's to the hospital, tears kept welling up and I could barely hold them back. What was making me want to cry was a measure of human kindness I didn't think I deserved. Had my own operation ever been paid for? I wasn't sure. Would Maman's ever be paid for if I didn't have the talent I wanted so much to uncover? I was more tortured by self-doubt than ever before during that interminable ride through a part of town I kept trying to identify; when I wiped a patch of the misted window every so often, I'd see mostly my own anxious face, which seemed to say, "All your life you've received love, devotion, and kindness beyond price. Haven't you something to give in return?"

I found Maman less dispirited than the night before, almost cheerful in fact, chatting with the Ukrainian. Her new friend didn't really speak any more English than she did, so how the two of them communicated I've never figured out. Nevertheless, years later Maman still mentioned her often, telling me hundreds of details about her life, which she could only have learned in those few days in the hospital.

As soon as I began to tell her about my visit to the doctor and the decision to immobilize her in a cast, her cheerfulness vanished. For a moment she was dumbfounded, then she rebelled.

"Never! Never!"

At her age, she argued, it would be madness to let herself be shut up that way. She'd never live through it. Better she accept being crippled and in time be able to move around a bit, and, who knows, perhaps it wouldn't turn out to be as serious as all that.

"And make sure you keep me shut up with you," I said cruelly. I'd suddenly realized that this was the only weapon I had against that iron will of hers.

She blanched. The wound in her eyes told me how surely the blow had struck. She looked down.

"Well, if you think I should go through with it...," she said.

But next morning the principal came to my classroom door to tell me Dr. Mackinnon wanted me on the telephone.

"Your mother refuses to have the operation," the kind, gravelly voice told me.

"Oh, dear heaven! Can it wait? Long enough for me to...?"

"One or two days, not much more. I'm afraid of infection. And her heart's showing some signs of fatigue."

"I'll go to the hospital as soon as possible."

That day Brother Joseph had overheard part of what I'd been saying. He suggested I leave at once.

"But...," I said.

159

In those days I would have had to pay the cost of a replacement from my own pocket, unless there were a death in the family or I were seriously ill myself.

"Go on," said Brother Joseph. "I'll have some of your colleagues take turns keeping an eye on your class. Give them plenty of work to do. I'll spend some time with them myself. It'll be good for me."

Once again I was in a jolting, jarring streetcar. At this time of day it stopped at every corner and seemed to take hours to reach the hospital.

From the corridor I could hear Maman and the Ukrainian telling each other the names of their children: "Irena, Olga, Ivan, Anna, Adèle, Bernadette...."

I brought the exchange to a quick end. I was very angry.

"For three days I've been running myself ragged," I told Maman. "I've found you the best orthopaedist in the city. This morning he put himself out. He came very early from the other end of town just for you. And what did he find? An obstinate old woman who said yes yesterday and who's saying no today."

Maman looked away. She mightn't have felt guilty about saying yes and then no, but she did about making the old Scottish doctor come for nothing; she'd begun to think highly of him.

"I've been told bones sometimes mend very well on their own," she said, "that they join by themselves when they're broken and after a month or two you can start walking again, even with a break like mine. A woman in the next room who had it happen came and told me. And it won't cost as much...."

"And supposing what your woman says is true," I retorted derisively, "what are you going to look like when you walk?"

Thereupon, calling up all my powers of mimicry, I turned myself into an old relic; with one hip protruding, my neck twisted, my face contorted, and one leg dragging pathetically, I staggered across the room, clutching, leaning on anything within reach, moaning, and making enough heavy weather to melt the hardest heart.

The Ukrainian guffawed, even the gentle, sad-faced Mennonite laughed a little, and finally Maman laughed too, won over by the others.

"All right," she said, giving in as easily as a child, "but...."

I knew at once what she wanted. I should have thought of it

before. We had a friend who was a nurse, who was very dear to Maman.

"Clérina's free," I said. "I'll go and see her tonight. I'll ask her to be with you tomorrow when they put you to sleep and when you wake up."

She'd never been anaesthetized, not even when her children were born, and I should have realized that what she was most afraid of was perhaps being put to sleep by force.

She woke up as though enclosed in a sarcophagus, totally dependent on others, even for eating; she who'd never depended on anyone had to be spoonfed at first. For several days nothing was more pathetic than to see her following us about with her eyes, as helpless as a prisoner under life sentence. From the moment she found herself in that dependent state until the day she was released from it, in spite of what she said, I don't believe she slept a single whole night, just in snatches now and then. Yet she adamantly refused to take sleeping pills, even the mildest, even after being lectured by Dr. Mackinnon. In the end he gave up, telling me, "I've often seen that kind of woman, in her generation, absolutely dead set against artificial sleep, even sedatives sometimes, and I've wondered if it isn't because of some deep-down pride."

After two weeks he let us take her home. I'll never forget how we had to struggle to get the stretcher up the stairs with Maman strapped to it, and the anxiety in her eyes as she followed the attendants' efforts to get her past the difficult point. But once in her own bed she regained the courage she'd almost lost for good. She learned to manage quite well with her left hand, the free one. But mostly she spent hours with her face turned towards the window, watching the sky which had always been there, endlessly amazed at how much it had to say to her. Like Anna before she died, like Dédette too, whom I saw turn her eyes to the sky so many times, Maman, always too busy before, was now discovering the depth of the Manitoba sky and marvelling at it, marvelling that you can often see better when in prison than when free. One evening I came home from school and found her contemplating that huge empty sky, and she expressed a thought that haunts me still: "Though the sky sees all and knows all it never says anything, but comforts us anyway. Why, do you suppose?"

We had a practical nurse come in the morning to wash her,

freshen her bed, and roll her onto her stomach like a block of cement to give her a few minutes' change of position. One of our neighbours hardly let a day pass without bringing her a cup of hot chicken broth or vegetable soup. Clémence and I managed everything else ourselves, since Maman really asked so little of us, I realize now at last.

Clémence was a treasure. The minute she was really needed, was asked to help, the poor sick child we'd always tried not to burden with responsibility proved to be a hundred times more effective than we'd thought possible. She cooked adequately the minute Maman wasn't hovering over her, ready to do everything so easily. She brought Maman her small tray, helped her eat, kept the apartment reasonably clean. Best of all, throughout the months that might have been exceedingly difficult, she was less nervous and apprehensive, happier, in short, than we'd seen her for years. All because Maman wasn't at her elbow saying, "Here, I'll do it for you." Since I didn't have much time to help, I depended on Clémence too, leaving her little tasks which she managed to do better and better. One day, almost in secret, she tried her hand at making a johnny cake, the cornmeal bread I used to love as a child. It was light and good. Maman, who hadn't much appetite, made herself eat a piece. Clémence was pleased. When she'd gone back to the kitchen with the tray, Maman, who hated letting emotion show, turned to me, her eyes all wet.

"Don't you think it would have been better for Clémence, really, if I'd been an invalid all my life?"

"Maman, what nonsense you get into your head! Too much responsibility for too long would have been just as bad as none at all for someone like her, you know that."

"You're probably right," she sighed. "It's so hard to know how to handle some sick people. A doctor who took care of her a long time ago did suggest I start her doing things, but then if I asked her to do something, or tried to redo something with her, even patiently, she'd get cranky and ready for one of those awful tantrums when she'd throw things around.... And remember the time she ran out of the house and we had to go looking for her, street by street, one district after another, like a poor little lost dog?"

She put her hand over her eyes, as though seeing this again was too much. I calmed her gently, reminding her that such things were over and done with, the doctor had told us there wouldn't be any more of those crises. She listened, was comforted and, much truer to her nature, was soon pretending she'd quite recovered from the memory and hadn't been nearly as upset as in fact she had.

The only other complaint she made during this time was about her cast. It was much too big and heavy, she said; the doctor had overdone it and he'd have to take some of it off or she'd suffocate.

I telephoned Dr. Mackinnon. To my great surprise he told me he'd come. Even in those days a specialist didn't go out of his way for such small things. He arrived with an impressive array of instruments including long scissors, pliers, and a kind of small hammer. As he laid out his paraphernalia Maman watched, anticipating great relief, it seemed.

Sitting on the edge of her bed, he promised her she'd feel very much better once he'd relieved her of a good piece of her "straitjacket". Privately, he told me that all he could really do was pretend to cut away part of her cast, but that was often enough to make the patient feel better.

It was astonishing how well the two of them had come to understand each other, she speaking in her language and he in his. I'd see them together, he bending his great head towards her, holding her hand, she looking up at him, her eyes shining with confidence and gratitude. I'd say to myself, am I dreaming, or is there something like affection between this elderly patient and her elderly doctor, who's not in much better health than she? Mightn't they have become lovers when they were young? And I thought I could see what an attractive woman my mother must have been.

Dr. Mackinnon took his big scissors and proceeded to cut away a very narrow strip of plaster from around Maman's neck, handing it to me at once with a clear indication that I must dispose of it before Maman saw it.

"I took off *un grand morceau*," he said, "*et vous allez voir* a great improvement."

Maman ran her free hand around her neck.

"Oh, yes," she declared, "it isn't nearly as high. It's really a lot better!"

She liked the feeling so much that a week later she asked, "Would you telephone Dr. Mackinnon? If he could just take off a little bit more...," so humbly I didn't have the heart to refuse.

He came three times from the other end of town, each time to trim off a "chunk" no wider in reality than half an inch. Everything was going to be fine, he told her. She'd soon be let out of that thing. "And then you'll be full of beans, like a young gerrrl again."

At last the day of her deliverance came. Her eyes showed almost uncontainable impatience for the relief to come, and I realized she must have been near the limit of endurance. Without jostling her too much, Dr. Mackinnon, short-winded and crimson-faced, cut into the tough carapace in earnest this time. You'd have said he was freeing a delicate butterfly from its chrysalis with the exquisite pleasure of seeing something born. But he'd warned me that the coming weeks would be among the hardest for Maman, and indeed she could find no rest either in bed or in the comfortable chair we'd carry her to when someone was there to help. Several times I found her sitting on the edge of the bed with her legs dangling, discouraged, not by the severe pain but by still not being able to move around. Once she flung at me as if in accusation, "My legs are dead, you know. They're no good for anything." I didn't see her make any effort to stand up with the crutches we'd got for her. A kind of despair overtook me; it was my fault that she might never walk again, because I'd made her have the operation. Perhaps she was the one who'd known best and I the one who had been blind, wanting to have her cured so I'd be free to leave.

Then one evening I came home to find her walking a few steps with the crutches, followed by Clémence who was biting her lip for fear Maman would fall. The few seconds' effort left Maman exhausted, at the end of her strength. But she had such courage. When she'd recovered a little in her comfortable chair, she looked lovingly and defiantly at the magnificent setting sun whose fiery glow filled the window that evening, as if telling it, "I'll be back, you'll see."

The next day she took three or four steps around the table, holding on for support. Then she began to make rapid progress. One evening she came into the room I was in, walking with mechanical little steps, without support though not too far from the wall. Her face shone with the surprise and delight of a tiny child standing up and taking her first steps all on her own.

From then on, her recovery was unbelievably fast, and when her strength returned it did so almost to excess. Since she'd given so much of herself all her life, we might have expected her to overdo it out of gratitude when it appeared she'd be allowed a few good years yet. As she sat in her comfortable chair between periods of exercise, she began spending countless hours sewing for her grandchildren. She sent little patchwork quilts to far corners of the country. She knitted layettes for expected grandchildren. She wrote letters to distant cousins with whom we'd lost touch since goodness knows when. When I was at school she'd venture down the winding stairs and back up, which I had forbidden her to do. Before I knew it she'd been over to visit the kind neighbour who'd brought her chicken broth and vegetable soup. Shortly after, I found her kneading piecrust dough. She told me calmly, "Madame Gauthier makes pretty good soup. Now I'm going to show her what a good pie's like." She was beaming.

"We really ought to try and make her do things a bit more reasonably," I said to Clémence.

"I suppose you think that's easy."

Clémence was already being a mite grumpy again.

Early one brisk spring morning, I spied a little figure in a familiar dark coat, rather huddled up but standing fairly straight, apparently waiting for a streetcar at the corner.

"I don't believe it! I never thought she'd try to go downtown by herself at this point."

"You'd better believe it," said Clémence. "Her mind was made up yesterday."

Under Maman's arm was a fat, rather lumpy package which reminded me oddly of the one she'd set out with that ill-starred day the previous autumn.

"What's she got under her arm?"

"A loaf of homemade bread," said Clémence sourly, "and you can be sure she's taking it to Rosalie."

XVII

SUMMER CAME. Maman had always greeted it with a delightful array of flowers attractively planted around the white-columned veranda and in borders and circular beds in the lawn. This year we didn't have even a square foot of ground in which to plant the few bright red geraniums from the apartment, but Maman didn't seem to miss the garden as much as I'd expected. As her possessions dwindled, she had more love and attention to give to those she had left. She took to her freedom far better than I thought she would, in fact; it allowed her to concentrate on inalienable possessions. I only came to understand this when I myself stopped wanting possessions of any other kind.

Maman was to spend the summer at her brother Excide's again. Suspecting she'd be so grateful to be cured she'd fling herself more ardently than ever into serving others, I lectured her about her tendency to overdo whatever she undertook.

"At least," I said to her, "when they're shorthanded don't go and offer to milk the cows."

She gave me that too-ready smile of assent which generally meant she'd do exactly as she liked. She'd become as impossible as Grandmother Landry used to be when anyone tried to keep her from overtaxing herself for others.

I myself was going to a curious region some three hundred miles north of Winnipeg, a low plain consisting mostly of muskeg, a mixture of earth and water; a region covered with rushes, lakes, and rivers, and inhabited by countless birds. That's what I'd been told, at least, and that's what drew me to it. I was the one, I think, who first called it the Little Water Hen country. I'd obtained one of the few schools in Manitoba that the Department of Education kept open only in summertime, owing to the region's remoteness, poor communications, and harsh climate. I was to be boarded by the local people at their expense, and so would pocket my full five dollars a day from the Department. I hoped thus to repair a large part of the dent in my savings made by the unexpected expenses of the winter. For the moment this was all I was counting on, but in fact the Little Water Hen cast an indescribable spell over me which left a lasting imprint. The rest came as a bonus: my discovery of one of the most delightful places in the world; the longing it left with me for a fresh start in human experience on earth; the book which, much later, grew out of my own time there (a novel about a tiny school at the end of the earth, the first on earth in a sense); the book's good fortune in being chosen for study in many schools in Canada and elsewhere. When I left for the Little Water Hen, all these extraordinary developments were as unsuspected on my part as, indeed, are almost all the essential landmarks in our lives to come.

And just as well! If I had had some premonition of what was in store for me, the experience would probably have done me less good. No, I needed to be totally at the mercy of the harsh solitude; it forced me to turn to my seven little pupils, the few adults in the vicinity, the birds, the wind, the island's vast silence, needing companionship so urgently that it was granted me. From this moment, everything changed between me and the remote land I'd thought completely without interest when I arrived. Solitude has so often brought me to a better understanding of people and things.

Maman was worried at first. When I'd had such a good position in the city, I was behaving like Adèle, she said, running off to the most God-forsaken places.

"When are you leaving for the other side?" she wanted to know. That's what we'd acquired the habit of calling the countries of Europe when the two of us talked, and the term suited Maman's feeling about them perfectly.

I was to return to St-Boniface at the beginning of September, leaving shortly after for Montreal, where I would board ship for London and Paris. My passport was applied for and my passage booked.

"Well then," she said, "I'll come back from Excide's in time to...."

I knew the word "goodbye" had stuck in her throat.

She was no longer fighting my decision. She still didn't understand why I'd want to leave my enviable job, my dear little pupils who loved me so, and a life that must have seemed close to heaven in her eyes. But if she didn't understand what was driving me, she'd begun to sense it, I think, to sympathize, without reflecting that she herself had been subject to some hidden imperative all her life. From that point on, if she'd had the means she might have gone so far as to help me leave.

She would have been the only one. No one else gave me any support. Our little French, Catholic city hadn't put such sacrifice, self-denial, and discipline into raising us only to let us leave without raising barriers. There are times when I'm convinced the community would have kept us at home by force if it could have. We were so few that anyone who left was considered to be deserting, abandoning the cause. My sister Adèle, who was inclined to go to extremes and use theatrical language, accused me of betraying my people. Anna was more restrained but thought I was being headstrong and was certainly in for some bitter disappointment. You'd have said they resented my doing what they hadn't dared do when they were young, which they probably regretted now. I can't really blame them. Almost certainly, I'd been held back less than my older sisters.

But it was our poor defenceless Clémence who made things hardest for me. Maman had often kept her home from school in the early stages of her illness, so it was often she who looked after me when I was very young. She used to take me on walks which were much too long for my small legs, but from which I'd come home happy, convinced I'd seen exotic, new, and exciting things. As I recounted in *Street of Riches*, she often took me to the wild side of our little street. Her talk, which upset people because it was full of strange, poetic digressions and weird references to the family dead as though they were living, didn't bother my childhood logic in the least. The two of us were very close when I was small, and I think I recall running to her quite naturally for assurance if I was frightened. Later, when the dreadful illness had left some invisible part of her permanently crippled, it was she who would cling to me, drawing a kind of confidence from my youth and initiative.

She observed my preparations for departure with a peevishness which in her was a sign of confusion and fear. One evening she stopped at the door of my room and watched as I was putting things in order.

"So it's true you're going?"

She looked at me steadily with those huge, dark-circled eyes which were always so quick to see pain in the offing, far down the road perhaps, in a sense never mistakenly. I didn't fully understand their distress until years later, when in my hour of greatest need I felt the hand I'd most counted on withdraw from mine.

"Come on, Clémence, I'm not going for ever!"

She kept looking at me unbelievingly, having now lost all confidence in me, perhaps, so hurt that she suddenly blurted out her perception of the truth.

"You're leaving us!"

THINGS LIKE THAT come out sometimes, and once they're out you hear them as long as you live. They stick in a corner of your memory and you can't get rid of them. They lie in wait at some turn in your thinking, often at night when you can't get back to sleep, when the old wounds always find you first. Perhaps even when you're only ashes and dust, or an immortal soul, you'll still remember them. And if these words prey on you all your life and perhaps beyond, there surely must be some truth in them.

DEDETTE WAS BACK from Kenora for a brief period about this time. She had come to take over a grade seven or grade eight class at the Académie Saint-Joseph where I had been to school. She still loved especially to teach teenagers, as I loved to teach the youngest children. She used to say, "It's the age when the flesh is wakening, yes, but ideals too." Removed as we might have presumed she was from our preoccupations and anxieties, she was the one who encouraged me. One day when I couldn't cope any longer with my doubts and indecision, I found myself at the big front door of the Académie asking for Sister Léon de la Croix. I always felt peculiar calling her that.

I waited for her in one of the two identical little parlours, each containing a piano, to one or other of which I'd so often been sent to practise my scales and sonatas when I'd been a pupil there. I heard her bell ringing in the distance: three short and one long ring, or perhaps the reverse. Soon after, I heard her footsteps hurrying down the main hallway.

Dédette's footsteps! In the family we used to say we could have recognized them among thousands. I sometimes imagine that even in the Valley of Jehoshaphat, if things are really as they're said to be, I could pick out Dédette's footsteps from all the others. They weren't the footsteps of a nun at all. Doubtless her community had tried to make her conform in her walk as in many other respects, but luckily it hadn't succeeded in this, at least. Brisk, hurrying, impetuous, sometimes hardly seeming to touch the ground, at intervals heavy on the heel, her footsteps told everything about her nature: her strong will, her diligence at controlling herself, and her perpetual failure to keep the loving, childlike extrovert in her from running passionately towards the world she'd renounced long ago.

Far down the corridor her footsteps would already be hurried, would quicken on the stairs leading down to the parlours and again in the remaining few feet of corridor, then fly irrepressibly as soon as she saw the face of whoever was waiting for her. There'd be a whirlwind with flying skirt and veil, you'd be caught up, spun round joyfully as though you'd had to come a vast distance to be reunited with her, not just across the street. Perhaps she was right. Perhaps there ought to be a whirlwind and spin-around at every meeting of two people who love each other, even if they've been living next door. At the time I didn't realize how surprising it was that Dédette, the most exuberant, most passionate of us all, had been the one to enter religion. Dédette was Dédette, a real phenomenon – pious, boisterous, demonstrative, meditative – I could see no further than this.

She arrived all out of breath and threw her arms around me, crooning, "My little Gabrielle! My little Gabrielle!" rather plaintively as if I'd been restored to her after a long captivity.

Then she became very calm and made me sit down, drawing her chair as close as possible. She had the rare gift of being able to switch instantly from great excitement to seriousness, the most attentive, observant silence. This was probably something she'd learned through constant effort, but deep down it must also have been related to her tendency to foresee the sorrows of this world more readily than the joys. And to tell the truth, once or twice I saw the ardour, animation, sparkle fall suddenly from her face, to my great surprise leaving instead a sombre, desolate, lightless, and tormented landscape, an ashen waste; then the ardour, animation, and sparkle would return and I'd think my imagination had been playing tricks on me.

At present she was searching my anxious eyes.

"Dédette," I said, as if calling from a distance, "I really don't know what to do any more. Everybody's mad at me for wanting to go.... But...I feel as if my life depends on it."

She took my hand, made me stand up, and led me to the daylight under the high window. In the clear light of the sky, my sister and I really saw each other for the first time in our lives perhaps, for both of us seemed astonished, I to discover the misty grey of her eyes brimming with a wistfulness I'd never noticed before, she to find heaven knows what, for she kept turning my face gently to the light. In order to see what is, do we really need more than the clear, unobstructed light of the sky? Suddenly she clasped me in her arms, drew my head against her shoulder, and as though she had her Lord's assurance of help for me, in whispers as impassioned as if she were putting her eternal salvation at stake, she told me:

"Go! Go! Go!"

SEVEN YEARS AGO, when she was on the point of death and I had come to be with her and was sitting by her bed in the little infirmary room one evening, I asked her if she remembered the scene in the parlour.

She opened her eyes but didn't give me the smile I'd hoped for. Since the moment her physician had told her she had a cancer that was already well advanced, there had been no smile in her eyes. They still showed love, and her deep concern for others, but not the light that only a smile can bring. Of all the relatives I've watched die it was she, the fervent believer, who seemed to put up the most resistance. She gave her last smile soon after her operation, when she thought she was going to live and was contemplating the things in life that are good, tender, sweet, fragrant, delicious, all at once; there was so much beauty in that smile that she made me see them too. Since then I'd been using all my wiles in the hope of bringing a smile to her face once more at least. To no avail. Only gravity

171

ever showed there now, which was strange in one who had been so animated. She just nodded in reply to my question, then added in the same grave voice as always now, "You don't forget things of the heart. Perhaps that's all we have left in the end. And there aren't a lot of them."

I asked her again if, when she'd urged me with such feeling to go my own way, she'd seen some favourable sign for me. She gave a little frown. From Providence, I added.

She told me no. It was just that when she'd seen so much worry in my face – so young and already so worried – she'd remembered a moment in her life when, at the age of eleven, she'd awakened in the country to a crisp summer morning filled with lovely house smells, toast, coffee, jam, mingled with the smells entering through the wide-open window, new-cut hay, phlox in bloom, dew-soaked earth, and she'd felt so heady with life, and so grateful to the Creator for all the joy He'd given His creatures, that of her own free will she decided there and then to give up part of it and enter religion.

"Do I understand," said I quite incredulously, "that you renounced the world because you loved it too much?"

With the grave manner I still found so disturbing, she bent her head in what might have been a nod.

"I was eleven...," she said again with a kind of remote compassion for the child she had been.

Though she wouldn't have admitted it, a sad little quiver in her lip told me she felt she'd been deprived of her share of earthly happiness for having been so trusting as a child.

"You always said that only God could give us total happiness," I protested, trying to comfort her.

"Maybe He wants us to taste happiness on earth too," she said, "or He would have made all those wonderful things for nothing!"

"But who's seen them better than you, Dédette? You've seen more out of the corner of your eye than those of us who've been free but busy with other things...so many distractions."

I saw that I had indeed comforted her a little. After I left, during the weeks she had remaining, I wrote her a letter every day, sometimes twice a day, always trying to persuade her that she'd felt the splendours of life more vibrantly than anyone else. And after she died I kept on trying to talk to her, to find her at least in the wind,

172

the trees, the world's beautiful things.... From this came *Enchanted Summer*, a strange book, I'll admit, which has an appearance of humour but underneath is deeply serious. Whatever its failings, I think it does capture the essence of Dédette, her open, childlike spirit, her lifetime of yearning so determinedly repressed.

With the long letters she wrote in her few moments of free time, or on her pauper's holidays at the Sisters' little summer camp on Lake Winnipeg, Dédette taught me, in the glow of fireflies, the cry of a bird somewhere in the sky, the song of rippling water or of leaves on the trees, such humble but beautiful things, to see something of God's grand design at work. I have only tried to pass on what her perceptive eyes illuminated for me.

XVIII

I LEFT FOR the Little Water Hen at the end of June, as soon as the school year at Provencher was over. I took the night train to the little town of Dauphin, where I was to change to another bound for Rorketon. It was appallingly hot. I arrived at Dauphin early next morning not having been able to sleep a wink all night, aching with fatigue. For this journey into the wilds, I had rather foolishly put on a white linen suit, which became horribly rumpled from tossing and turning on the seat of the train. I think my face was smeared with coal dust too. But the worst was still to come. I would have a long wait for my train to Rorketon, the station master told me. How long? He couldn't say exactly. It could be two hours or half the day, maybe more. There was no saying with that train. It came when it could and left when it was ready. That was the kind of thing everybody had to put up with here, he said gently, suggesting that I try to do the same.

I didn't know anyone in Dauphin. Besides, since the train could arrive in three hours or at any minute, it would be best not to leave the station. It was stifling inside. Outside, however, there was a wooden bench under the station master's office window. It was short and narrow, but I wrapped myself in my coat and tried to find a position that wasn't too uncomfortable. I was so tired that with my head on the hard armrest, slipping half off the seat at times, I think I did sleep for brief spells. I'd wake, curl myself up some other way, and sleep a minute or two more.

The station master must have been observing me through his window for some time, feeling sorry for me as I tried to get some sleep under the sky like a derelict, in my beautiful little linen suit. I imagine he was really rather shy and hesitated for some time before coming out to give me a startling invitation.

174

"Listen, Miss. I'm alone at the station because my wife's away on holiday. She put clean sheets on our bed before she left. I haven't had time to go and sleep in it yet. If you'd like to sleep in a good bed, it's yours; lying on that bench, your neck and shoulders and back are going to be sore pretty soon."

As sleepy as I was, I managed to sit up and open my eyes fully so I could look at the man who was saying these things. He was fairly young, nice-looking, with blue eyes showing a kind of warm concern to see someone in discomfort; he seemed like the Good Samaritan in person. All the same, I had wits enough to remember that he'd said his wife had just left so that he had the place to himself. He must have read my thoughts because he told me he had a pile of reports to finish before the train came. And there was the bed doing nothing, he said, while I needed it so.

Besides feeling some shame at the thought of rebuffing a good intention, I wanted that bed so badly I followed him without further hesitation. He led me to the bedroom, took off the counterpane, folded it neatly and put it on a chair, turned down the bed, which had indeed been freshly changed, put the two pillows one on top of the other, plumped them, and said, "There now...." He promised he'd come and wake me before the train arrived and promptly left, closing the door behind him. I took off my suit and slipped between the clean sheets. I think I was asleep the minute my head touched the pillow. Only seconds later, it seemed, I felt the gentle touch of a hand and heard an unfamiliar voice saying:

"Miss, your train will be here in ten minutes."

I dressed hurriedly. I arrived on the little station platform in the middle of a beautiful, warm, fragrant summer day. I'd gone to bed at six in the morning; it was now two in the afternoon. I was well rested, my face was fresh, my eyes bright. I was ready and eager for the remainder of the journey.

The station master beamed.

"You look altogether different than you did this morning," he said. "I was up twice to see how you were doing, and I've never seen anyone sleep so soundly."

I studied him in silence and saw nothing but pleasure in return for the confidence I'd put in him, and something like gratitude for my having let him show me such kindness.

I had this man rather in mind when I had Luzina say, in *Where*

175

Nests the Water Hen, that you need only place yourself under another human being's protection for him to behave towards you as you would wish.

So years before I wrote that book, I'd already unconsciously stored away some scattered, unconnected elements of it. You could say I had them close to my heart, but wouldn't have access to them for years to come. At times I used to feel I was becoming a huge reservoir of almost inexhaustible impressions, emotions, and observations, if only I could have access to them. But though you'd expect having access to what's inside you to be the most natural thing in the world, it's often the most difficult.

From the train I saw the station master standing in the middle of the platform, watching me go, sadly, like a relative – or rather, like one of those strangers who are so unlike strangers, with whom you cross paths and whom you never forget. I gave him a little wave. He lifted his hand to his green visor and smiled slowly, shyly. Sometimes I wonder if, when my first books appeared – particularly *Where Nests the Water Hen* – he made the connection between the author and the young woman to whom he'd given a bed one summer morning, and if he said to himself, "I thought I might hear more of her some day."

Finally the long-awaited little train began to move, and at once I had the impression it was blazing a trail through hitherto virgin Nature.

THAT RORKETON train! My friend Jean-Paul Lemieux has understood and portrayed it superbly in his series of engravings that illustrate the Gilles Corbeil edition of *La Petite Poule d'Eau*, the French text of *Where Nests the Water Hen*. No doubt to emphasize the feeling of isolation – but also of rescue, for the train is the only lifeline men have in those deserted wastes – he's shown it in winter, coming across the low, snow-covered plain, from the ends of the earth it seems. But I made its acquaintance in the season when its lonely path is dotted with countless delicate flowers.

I'll never forget that journey. Like a journey through summer itself, heady with wild smells, fragrant ones, with Nature's warm breath, and some of her most endearing sounds. Sometimes we'd hear the piercing trill of a bird, sometimes a sudden rustling of leaves or a strident signal from some insect.

The big engine, built for pulling a whole convoy, had only one passenger car coupled directly to it, with a caboose right behind that. The caboose was a kind of cookhouse-cum-dormitory for the train crew, who had to shuttle back and forth between Dauphin and Rorketon at constantly changing hours, without a stop between the two; a moving home away from home where the men could eat, sleep, and rest. Sometimes they simply stopped for the night beside a field or a small lake.

Passengers and mail weren't all the train carried. It was a mixed train, as it was called then, and also carried freight. The day I was travelling, a car behind the caboose was loaded with a big pile of railroad ties, replacements for the rotted ones on the line. We went at about the speed of a farm horse because the men were throwing off ties as needed, judging by eye, two or three here, three or four a bit farther on.

When we were on a section of track that was in good repair, the brakeman would go to the caboose and cast an eye at his stew, lifting the lid of a great black pot on the little stove. A mouth-watering smell would waft forward to the passengers. There were four of us in all: myself, the Department of Health nurse, a cattle dealer, who to my great surprise came back to life as Isaac Boussorvsky in *Where Nests the Water Hen*, and an individual with his nose in reports and papers who declined to help us identify him.

The irresistible smell brought me to the door of the caboose. The brakeman looked up from his steaming pot.

"Smells good," I said.

"Hungry?" he asked.

I must have given him a panhandler's smile. Incredibly, I'd embarked on this journey back through time and civilization without bringing anything to eat.

I received a good heaping bowlful, and the brakeman brought similar helpings to the nurse and the cattle merchant. The nurse passed around some homemade cookies, still warm, out of a big bag which she'd put inside a bigger one to keep them fresh. The brakeman came back shortly with cups of scalding-hot tea.

When the cooking smells had disappeared through the wide-open windows and doors of the train, the smells of Nature entered.

It was the season of wild roses. With their bright colour, they were spread over the countryside like a setting for a never-ending banquet. Their perfume was intoxicating. Above them, insects of every description darted and hovered, buzzing covetously. Then, after the panorama of roses, among the tall grasses there appeared masses of such pretty little blue flowers nodding on their long, delicate stems that I longed to see them more closely. We were going so slowly I decided I'd have time to jump off, run and pick some, then run back and get on again. The engineer was leaning out of his cab enjoying the sights and fresh air of our surroundings. When he saw me scurry into the field, snatching up a flower here and there, he called to me not to be in such a hurry, we had lots of time, and without further ado applied the brakes. The train waited nearly ten minutes while I picked a bouquet.

When I climbed back on with my arms full of flowers, everyone, including the cattle man, smiled at me kindly, as if at some vision of youth, wish-fulfilment, or childhood reverie. The warmth of those smiles made me so happy I've never forgotten it. I sometimes think of my companions that day as a group of new-found friends who are still waiting for me somewhere, on a little train that doesn't exist any more.

The train arrived in Rorketon shortly before suppertime. I hurried to a boarding house kept by a Mrs. O'Rorke, if I remember correctly, where I was to meet Mr. Jos Vermander, formerly the postmaster in St-Boniface, who some years earlier had been promoted to post office inspector for northern Manitoba. Lacking information, I'd telephoned him to ask how to get to the Little Water Hen. He told me to meet him in Rorketon and we would leave together for Portage-des-Près, the last hamlet on the final leg of the journey, and also the site of the last branch post office.

Very early next morning, we left in an ancient Ford driven by a Ukrainian, a Métis guide riding with us. I was getting to know my country in a totally new light. I related some of this journey in my introduction to the George G. Harrap school edition of *La Petite Poule d'Eau* (this introduction has been reproduced as "Memory and Creation" in *Fragile Lights of Earth*). But I'll never really be able to convey how awestruck I was to be travelling deeper and deeper into the wild, the distant, the inaccessible.

At last, among some scrawny little trees along the rutted dirt road, we came to a few mournful wooden houses, a chapel, and a school made of rough planking; a village of a kind, it seemed. This was Portage-des-Près. My heart sank at the thought of spending the summer here. But I was deluding myself. My place of employment was even farther still, some thirty miles away, on an island separated from the mainland by two rivers. People called it Jeannotte's Ranch. There was only one way to get there and that was by the postman's battered old truck, which had just left and wouldn't be back for another week. I didn't know what to do.

Jos Vermander just laughed. He was used to such difficulties.

"Give me time to look at the postmaster's books," he said (the postmaster was also the general storekeeper), "and I'll drive you to your island on the Little Water Hen myself. You don't think I'd go away and leave you here, do you?"

So it was thanks to him that I reached the Little Water Hen. I imagine that if I'd stayed at some point on the way all summer the Department of Education wouldn't have been any the wiser, and would have paid my salary anyway, just in case.

After adventures far too numerous to recount, we reached the island on the Little Water Hen shortly before nightfall.

Under an already dark sky, I found my destination: a huge, low-lying island, almost indistinguishable from the gurgling rivers full of eerily whispering rushes, and upon it a single house flanked by small outbuildings. I looked at my destination with dismay close to panic.

I'm particularly fond of one of Jean-Paul Lemieux's engravings. Almost negligible at the very bottom of the picture are the three small buildings that show a human presence, the house, the sheepcote, and the tiny, rough cabin that served as a school. Hanging over this frail cluster is an immense, very black sky that takes up two-thirds of the little picture: a primaeval sky. It might be hostile. It might be overpowering. But there are one or two faint stars, even farther from Earth than stars usually appear, and with them hope glimmers, seeks to pierce the great night of the ages.

When I look at this engraving I'm always amazed at how well the artist has conveyed both my feeling of desolation upon arriving at night in a corner of the world that seemed so totally cut off, and the vague hope I was still to discover.

AS AT CAMPERVILLE, I organized myself in a very few days so I'd have something to do every minute of the day, the only way I could cope with my overwhelming loneliness.

I would wake early – the lambs bleating around the house took care of that – and scribble in my little bedroom with its low window just above floor level, or in the six-by-seven-foot schoolhouse, sitting at my rustic desk carved from wood that still smelled of sprucegum.

Then my pupils would arrive, seven in all. Four came from the house nearby and the three others from beyond the rivers, sometimes brought by their father, sometimes guiding their fragile craft over the rough, fast-running water alone, poor little souls. I taught them reading, writing, arithmetic, and, rather like Mademoiselle Côté in the book, a reawakening to their French ancestry. I could have taught only this for all the Department of Education would have known, being on another planet so to speak. But wanting to be conscientious, I did try to teach a few subjects in English. To tell the truth, it didn't much matter here. The hard, isolated life, the urgent necessities, the ever-present sky, all taught me that school should be a place of coming together and not of division.

Because of the appalling heat that would build up in the schoolhouse, around three o'clock I'd end the lessons and we'd all go swimming together in the Big Water Hen. A more beautiful river I've never seen. It flowed between flat banks covered with succulent grasses, wide and peaceful, but with a restless current one had to be wary of. The water was always crystal clear, sometimes the dark foliage-green of the reeds growing on either side, as Lemieux paints it, sometimes a soft blue blending with the sky, a reflection that made you think there was another river flowing by, bearing an endless flotilla of white clouds. All the time, night and day, you could hear its deep, rich song, which must have remained unchanged since the beginning of time. Its water was good to drink, so transparent you could see yourself in it, so clean you'd come out of it washed as nowhere else. I realized then what a pure river was, and that was before the atrocious things man has done to water, when it was still like the innocent eyes of the earth.

When supper was over and the dishes were done, Madame Côté, my landlady, having nothing now to occupy her thoughts, would sit by a low-silled window and gaze at the beautiful but empty countryside, letting a deep sadness show. She seemed so forlorn, poor woman, that one evening I made a suggestion, for want of something better:

"Would you like it if we walked a little way by the river together?"

Even today I'm still astonished when I remember the pleasure brought to her face by such a simple invitation. It was as if I'd said, "Let's go downtown. There's a movie...." She went to her room and returned wearing her hat, which I hadn't ever seen before. For a walk on a rough path by a river in the wilds, this was so unexpected that I was speechless for a good long minute. I can see us still, walking one behind the other because of the narrowness of the path, I in my jodhpurs, which I'd taken such care of that they were still perfectly presentable, and Madame Côté ahead in her incongruous velvet hat, telling me all about herself in fragments, pausing often to catch her breath. Furthermore, the walk I'd so innocently proposed seemed to have created a stir in the tranquil atmosphere of our existence: it brought running, to fall into step behind us in single file, four hens, three cats, the dog, a piglet, the rooster, and, inevitably, a good number of the lambs and ewes that roamed free on the island. Our little procession made its way beside the river as though along a village sidewalk. Perhaps this was the fancy that so delighted Madame Côté and roused the envy of the rest of the household, those I hadn't invited, who watched through the windows as if to say, "How lucky you are and why didn't you take us too?"

I WAS BEGINNING to be happy. I was settling down on the island I'd come to in such a frenzy of anxiety. The weather, which can demoralize us more than anything else perhaps, ceased to bother me. It was as though I were shorn of my past and to all intents and purposes had no future. I hardly gave a thought even to my plans for leaving. I'd been set free. Like my island, borne on its waters from one day to the next, I was living in the present. This was one of three or four wonderful pauses in my life when I've had time to rebuild my physical strength and state of mind. Without them my health, always more or less fragile, would perhaps have failed. In any event, this was certainly what I needed before confronting the emotional turmoil awaiting me. I withstood it only because I'd had this period of calm, silence, and concentration on what I was discovering.

But I hadn't yet written a single line from which I could draw the least satisfaction. How long it takes to get where you ought to be going! Then as soon as you arrive it's time to move on.

Still, without realizing it, when I left the Little Water Hen at the very end of August I had almost everything I needed for the novel I wouldn't begin to write until 1948, some of it found here and some at Camperville. Almost everything, that is, except the kind of life I would be leading in the meantime, which would also colour the book. The intriguing thing about the life of a book and that of its author is this: as soon as the book exists even vaguely in the far corners of the unconscious, everything that happens to the author, every emotion, practically every feeling and experience contributes to the book, enters and becomes part of it, like the water from a river's tributaries throughout the river's length. So a book really is a part of its author's life, provided that it's a purely creative work, of course, not built from other elements.

XIX

AT THE BEGINNING of September I was back in St-Boniface, where I had a room with board at the Misses Muller's for a few days while I waited for Maman, who was to join me there. This, of course, was when I fully realized how badly I missed our house and formed some idea of how much Maman must feel its loss.

I didn't go back to see Deschambault Street, thinking it would be too painful. Nowadays when I go to Manitoba, thoughtful friends will drive me there. We slow down, then stop in front of the house that was ours. It's changed somewhat but it's been kept in good condition and I always feel grateful to its buyer, who has obviously taken great care of it. I look up in silence at the little third-floor window, at which I used to listen on spring evenings to the mating songs of frogs from the ponds at the bottom of the street. And I feel compassion, not for the adult I've become, knowing well that the future is only really glorious long before you reach it, but for the child up there who was so dazzled by its glory.

Maman arrived from Somerset. She was to return there after I'd gone and would come back to St-Boniface with Clémence in the autumn, when they would take an apartment in town. Again I found her thinner, her face drawn, as though a little shrunk. I was annoyed to find her looking so tired and chastised her, no doubt rather bitterly, for tending to overdo things at her brother's. She told me it wasn't the little chores at the farm that had tired her; on the contrary, they'd diverted and relaxed her. She'd just recovered from a bad cold she'd caught one evening in a sudden rain while picking wild berries. What she didn't say was that she'd worn herself out defending me against Anna and Adèle, who'd both been nagging at her constantly for having spoiled me, pampered me too much, reaping only my ingratitude, for there I was going off and leaving her without support when she needed it most. Now, in answer to a rather sharp comment of my own, she defended them against me, begging me not to be cross over the way they felt because they hadn't been as lucky as I had and were a bit envious.... Wasn't it that way in almost all families?

At which I lost my temper, retorting that I'd had enough of families with their everlasting squabbles, that all most of them wanted was to smother the ones who seemed to be trying to break away. Maman looked wounded, and her eyes turned wearily to the big brass bed.

It was the only one in the room. I was going to sleep in the same bed as Maman for the first time in my life, I think, unless I'd done so when I was very young, which is likely, though if I did I don't remember. I'd always been an independent child, insisting on keeping rather to myself, my own bed, my own little place to study, away from everyone else. Maman had understood this need and respected it, perhaps having wanted privacy for herself.

Lying side by side, neither of us could sleep. Fears for the future; sorrows of the past; insecurity, life's constant companion. Being side by side and defenceless in the dark made these things weigh all the more heavily on us, perhaps. Ever since that night I've felt that unless you've lain in the same bed beside someone, even one of those closest to you, you can't know much about that person, and you'll probably know even less about yourself.

I sensed Maman near me, tense, not allowing herself to move for fear she'd keep me awake. I was doing the same for her.

"You're not asleep yet?" I said finally.

Then she admitted to not having slept more than two or three hours a night for a good many years, and some nights not even one hour. She had a little chuckle at her own expense, part grief, part irony. "Life plays some mean tricks, you know," she said, "waiting for us at turning points we've looked forward to for ages, just so it can tell us it's too late now.... When I was a young woman with babies crying at night, I'd have to get up and I'd be just about asleep on my feet, nursing this one, changing that one, and I'd promise myself, 'When the children are grown I'll make up for all this. I'll sleep and sleep at last as much as I want....' "

"Poor Maman! What then?"

"Then by the time the children were grown and I might have

slept through the night, sleep had turned its back on me, caring no more about me than water does about the driftwood it leaves on a lonely beach."

When my turn came to lose my ability to sleep, when I was so ill with a toxic goitre, I kept remembering what Maman had whispered that night in the big brass bed at the Misses Muller's, and I thought it more heartbreaking than anything else she'd ever confided. All those years without ever getting enough sleep, counting on having it later, wanting it, craving it increasingly, then at last when you're free to give in to it, finding it isn't there any more; it's gone and won't be back. It really is like being left behind on an empty beach, with no protection from your racing thoughts. On the other hand, if I hadn't known insomnia, would I have known what it's like for someone who suffers from it? I might never even have been able to imagine Alexandre Chênevert in *The Cashier*, let alone create the tortured soul who never slept and so had no relief from his vision of human suffering. You might say that every sorrow brings enlightenment and each enlightenment reveals more suffering.

We both pretended to be on the verge of sleep a few seconds longer, then abruptly I put an end to the silliness and spoke up about what was bothering me.

"Those two little rooms you've taken for yourself and Clémence – it seems to me you'll be cramped and have no view. I'm afraid it's going to be very depressing for you."

No, she assured me, and tried to convince me that once the house had been sold, the sacrifice made, she'd felt liberated, and perhaps this was true. She didn't much mind now where she lived. There was a lot to be said for getting rid of things. When you can lose nothing more, you can finally relax. She'd taken far too long, she said, to realize that furniture, rugs, and that kind of thing just tied you down as you aged.

I listened, almost more grieved at this detachment than I'd been at her still recent determination to cling to every reminder of the past.

"Don't worry about me," she continued in a semi-whisper. "If it weren't for not knowing what's going to happen to Clémence, I'd be quite content."

She moved closer and whispered more softly as if the walls might have ears.

"She's been cranky all summer at Excide's. Or else she'd go on long walks by herself. I don't know how to handle her any more."

There was a moment of silence, then she continued with almost childlike candour.

"D'you think when people suffer it might be because their parents won't face up to something, and sort of pass it on to their children so they don't have to think about it any longer?"

"What are you trying to say?" I asked.

"Perhaps Clémence was always prone to mental illness," she said, "but something awful must have happened to bring it on so suddenly. The doctor thought at first there'd been some kind of religious trauma. We never knew for sure. Clémence wouldn't ever say a word to give us any idea what might have happened – and that says a lot in itself. But words I heard her say when she had bad dreams, and the look in her eyes sometimes, and the peculiar way she'd refuse to do certain things, made me suspicious that perhaps...one day...at confession.... She was such a pious little girl, so conscientious...she was only fourteen then...maybe...you know...."

"Oh, Lord above, Maman, that's enough!" I exclaimed, wanting more to spare her than to spare myself, as I recall. But I felt deeply for her, having to live with such an idea and keep it to herself, even if, as she hastened to add, it might never have been anything but a figment of her imagination.

"How could you go on praying...and believing...after having an idea like that!" I scolded.

"Turn against the truth of the Church, just because of one priest...one poor, tortured creature, for goodness' sake?" she retorted. "You can't understand much about life to talk that way!"

A few minutes later, wearily and sadly, she asked me to forgive her for letting herself talk about this just before I was to go away. It was just that she was so worried about Clémence.

"Who'll take care of her when I'm gone?" she said. "Sometimes I'm afraid, very afraid, there won't be a soul in the world who'll look after her."

She'd said it, it was over, but the words kept ringing in my ears, and they'd ring at intervals for the rest of my days, like mournful bell-buoys tossing on the waves at sea.

Then, surprisingly, I saw the procession of lambs and ewes I'd seen a hundred times ambling beside the Big Water Hen, so long a line it must surely have passed the same spot again and again. To me, this scene was all the peacefulness of evening drifting over the sleepy countryside. There was the river in its inexhaustible splendour, its cool green waters flowing ever more extravagantly but always as abundantly, wending through a thousand open pathways in a sea of reeds to the river's mouth, great Lake Winnipegosis. Among the slender stems, the surface splashed with diving waterfowl. Little water hens bobbed for food, heads down, rumps up. Here and there ducks rose in close formation, necks outstretched. And I wondered how life could contain such beauty and also such tragedy as I thought I saw ahead for Clémence. It seemed to me that I could see her lonely figure against the dusky sky, wandering endlessly along unfamiliar little roads bathed in shadow. I had no idea that when I went searching on the darkened prairie for Otterburne again years later, I'd find those little roads just as I saw them that night.

What upset me most, I think, was feeling that the world was too beautiful to allow her tragedy. I lost hope. Lost hope that I'd been born to be happy. There must have been days when Maman also lost hope for me.

"I'm not going," I said. "There are too many obstacles."

Maman sat bolt upright. She reached over my head to turn on the light. It was dim, but her eyes, though still weary and sad with worry over Clémence, burned with renewed energy.

"That's all we need!" she declared. "Your ticket's bought, your passport's ready, everyone's been told, your replacement at school's been found, and now you go and change your mind. You'll have everybody laughing at you, and so they should!"

"Have everybody laughing at me? I'm used to that!"

"You're going," she said emphatically. "Otherwise you'll never forgive yourself, and you'll have me never forgiving myself either."

Now that I was beginning to waver, she found the only argument that could comfort me and raise my hopes again.

"Pay no attention to what people say. The truth is, you're the only one of my children who's stayed as long with me. Whatever they say, the others all left the first chance they had. Joseph first at barely fifteen, he was a wanderer if ever there was one. Then Rodolphe not much older, though at least he came back once in a while. Anna married when she was nineteen. Adèle left young too. And to answer the call of God, as she put it, Dédette left us at twenty-two. In a way the first Agnès also left us for God; He took her so young, a dear little girl of fourteen. Then Marie-Agnès, lost when she was only four. You can't remember, you were just nine months old when she died, and it's a shame because she was crazy about you. She wanted to carry you around in her arms all the time. I often wouldn't let her. I was afraid she'd drop you. Sometimes she'd come and take you out of your crib thinking I didn't know, and try to hide you somewhere. I let her do it sometimes; she was only three and a half and it was so sweet to see her carrying you with a hand supporting your back as I'd shown her, trembling with the effort because you were already a fat baby."

I think we both smiled through our tears at the picture that Maman had described so often I used to imagine I remembered it myself. Though I hadn't really known her, I'd always thought of Marie-Agnès as the closest to me of all my sisters, and perhaps the most dear to me.

"You're the only one I kept. Till now." Maman's voice was firmer. "Do you think I could forget you've stayed with me till the age of twenty-eight?"

I didn't tell her it wasn't just because of her that I'd stayed, though she probably knew this as well as I did. It was good I didn't say it. From that night of whisperings we needed to be left with a feeling of lasting closeness, unshakeable tenderness towards each other.

"Go to sleep now," I told her.

"You too," she replied.

Neither of us went right to sleep even then, each still hearing echoes of the things that had passed between us that night, echoes we'd hear ever after. What a little thing it takes sometimes to unite people, or estrange them! If we hadn't lain in that big strange bed together, Maman and I, we might never have known many things about one another.

A moment later Maman spoke again. Once more her voice was a little strained.

"Tomorrow morning, or this morning rather, how about going to mass together, to pray for your plans to work out?"

I was silent. I should have expected this. For some years, though we'd never really talked about it, I'd been avoiding religious observance in what amounted to revolt against a dogmatic attitude that saw evil in everything, laid claim to sole possession of the truth, and, if it could, would have denied us any communication whatever with a generous human disparity. Not wanting to hurt Maman's feelings, though, I'd managed not to lock horns with her over this, and when possible had avoided letting her know I hardly ever went to church now. Nevertheless, she couldn't have failed to see that I'd lost the fervent faith of my early youth that she'd so loved in me. Her own faith, I suppose, was so strong, so thoroughly tested – or else so ingenuous still – that she wasn't distracted by the Church's very human aberrations, but kept her eyes fixed on the bright light at its centre.

Could I refuse her the comfort she was asking? I told myself that it wouldn't be such a crime to go through the motions, and that if I could borrow a bit of her faith to lift me briefly in unison with her, I might not even need to pretend.

I agreed to go, immediately sensed enormous relief on her part, and must have promptly gone to sleep. Minutes later, it seemed, she was shaking me gently, considerately, as she used to when she woke me to go to mass with her when I was a child. But then it might have been winter, still dark outside with a howling wind, and she must have hated to drag me from my nice warm bed out into the cold air with a few stars still twinkling above. What urgent need she must have felt to make herself do it! This same need must be dictating to her now.

We dressed back to back as we used to, and set off in the crisp morning air for the cathedral.

I'd walked this way beside Maman almost since I took my first steps. Suddenly I was imagining what all our walks placed end to end would add up to: the walks to Eaton's on bargain hunts; to church on Sundays of course; to the forty hours' devotion and to gain indulgences; sometimes, at the peak of a torrid summer, to

189

Assiniboine Park, though it took hours to get there, to enjoy the cool shade of the trees and admire the fountains and perpetually green lawns; to River Park also, where I loved to look at the animals gazing out with captives' eyes from behind their bars; and often, just because we enjoyed it, up and down our own little Deschambault Street when the heat of the day was past.

On one of these pleasant summer evenings, since I was now "a big girl" as she put it, she decided to enlighten me on the facts, or as I think she said, much more appropriately, the "mysteries" of life. She was so ill at ease I could hardly understand a word of what she was trying to tell me, except that being a woman was so humiliating it made you want to die. We shouldn't really blame the women of those days for not knowing how to talk about love and the body; they were very inhibited about such things, and so considerate of their daughters that they thought they were doing us a favour by leaving us as long as possible in ignorance of what was awaiting us. It's taken a long time for the light to reach us women, centuries of obscurity and silence. Our mothers put such toil and determination into achieving a better life, and along the way, I sometimes think, not an ounce of it has been wasted.

I thought about all this as I walked beside Maman, and my heart was full to bursting with memories I hadn't realized I possessed. Going away does so much – almost as much as death – to open our eyes to the people we're about to leave.

Once again we went to a pew at the front of the long nave to be as close to the sanctuary as possible, among the elderly women in black who were counting their beads and saying Hail Marys under their breath in the dim, warm glow of the tapers.

We knelt side by side as we'd done on the day we'd come to pray before my operation. With feelings as confused as they had been then, I watched Maman pray. Today too, she was undoubtedly praying that I be spared suffering. Yet only suffering really teaches us to love.

THAT MASS must have been my last for a long time. Many years later, God's presence throughout this world seemed very clear to me, leading me to consider the Church's practices not so puerile after all, since they had helped keep the light at its nucleus alive for me. I won't deny that when I returned it was partly from a nostalgic desire to be kneeling again beside my dead mother, and how could I do this except through God? Sometimes I admit to myself that what I like best about the idea of eternity is the chance for me to unburden myself to my loved ones, and them to me, so that all the misunderstandings in life may finally cease.

IT HAD HURT to think that my friends and school colleagues were letting me leave without having a little goodbye party. This was always done when one of us got married. I didn't mind not getting presents. What grieved me was that they should let me go as if I didn't matter any more, the ultimate sign of what I took to be a kind of disapproval.

But when the evening of my departure came and I arrived with Maman at the old Canadian Pacific station, to my surprise there were friends in every corner of the concourse. I was positively jumping with joy, running from one group to another, suddenly overcome with dizzying tenderness for these young men and women of my own age who I hadn't believed were so close to me, but who suddenly were. I was encouraged by their presence to do my utmost to be a credit to them, like others of our little community whose success, we considered, reflected on us all. There were even some friends from the days of our touring shows. Fernand, the pianist-cartoonist, had brought me a little jewel box which, though I had practically nothing to put in it, I would cherish with special fondness, because Fernand lived very meagrely and I was well aware that his gift could represent piano lessons given all over the city.

They all came with me to the platform. I saw with pride that they made quite a little crowd, just for me. The long train gave a shudder from end to end and emitted little bursts of steam, the voice of elation, I thought.

My friends crowded around for a goodbye hug, some bearing little ribboned packages, others slipping into my coat pocket or handbag an envelope in which I'd find a bank note with a few words like "For a pair of stockings..." or "For a square meal some hungry day...." Dear, kind friends. How grateful I was, in the moments of need that inevitably came, to have an essential pair of shoes or solitary meal, thinking, "He doesn't know, but this is Hector's or Valen's present today."

The conductor shouted his "All aboard!" I jumped onto the step of the train. The little crowd of friends waved and blew kisses, calling out goodbyes and good wishes. I was giddy with joy at the unexpected demonstration of friendship. Then, in the midst of my euphoria, beyond the sea of young, smiling faces, my mother's distraught little countenance caught my eye, suddenly old and creased with the grief she could no longer hide. I'd been so carried away by the affection being shown me I'd forgotten to kiss her goodbye, and with the look in her tired eyes she was allowing herself just barely to remind me of this. I remembered the look we'd exchanged on the day of my graduation, when I searched for her from the stage and our eyes met, hers shining with so much pride that they lit up my whole being. Today the light seemed on the point of going out. I jumped off the train. I ran to her. I put my arms around her. Why hadn't I noticed before how tiny she was? Her body was like a child's. I hugged her as tight as I could. I whispered goodness knows what silly exhortation to take care of herself, which she hadn't ever done, even when life was being relatively kind.

It was she who first loosened our embrace, saying, "Your train...your train!" because it had slowly begun to move. I jumped back onto the step of my car. I clung to the handrail. I looked at but didn't see the young faces, the smiling faces. I could see nothing but the lonely little figure in the midst of happy people. I watched her pull her rather skimpy coat around her, something I realized only now I'd seen her do at least a hundred times. It revealed so well the way she was, proud and diffident at once. Her sorrowful eyes were fixed on me as though they'd never lose me wherever I went. It became unbearable. I saw too well that she knew I wouldn't be coming back, that destiny was taking me away to another life. My courage failed. It was clear now that I wasn't leaving so I could make good for her, as it had pleased me to believe. Dear heaven, it was really so I'd be free of her, wasn't it? Free of her and the family woes clustered about her, in her keeping.

On the platform now I was seeing only people not really there: Anna with the dejected face of a woman of many gifts who'd never used any of them to advantage and would blame herself to the end of her days; Clémence with her brooding eyes dark-ringed by illness; Rodolphe, his face ravaged already; even Dédette in her nun's habit, showing in her saddened face that she was sorry not to have known a bit more of the world before she renounced it. They all seemed to be reproaching me for their failed or unfulfilled lives. "Why is it only happening to you? Why not us? Mightn't we have found happiness too?"

I was even being condemned, I thought, for putting myself beyond the reach of sorrows still years away, waiting here.

Then, at the end of the platform, there appeared a little crowd from the past, dressed in black. There were my forebears, the Landrys and the Roys too, the Connecticut expatriates, their ancestors who'd been deported from Acadia, their descendants repatriated to St-Jacques l'Achigan, my St-Alphonse-de-Rodriguez relatives and those at Beaumont, even my Savonarola grandfather whom I had time to recognize beside Marcelline, his eyes dark and smouldering as in his photograph...the terrible exodus my mother had introduced me to one day....

Can I deny finding in my heart that perhaps I'd always wanted to break the chain, escape from my poor dispossessed people? Who among us hasn't wanted this at some point? Loyalty is so difficult.

Next I think I shed some tears. Of shame? Compassion? I'll never know. Perhaps it was the bitter taste of desertion that made me cry.

Now, with the rhythmic sound of the train as it travelled through open countryside, the great, comforting dream of my youth, beguiling as ever, took hold of me again. It was showing me a future in which I'd have time for everything. Time first to save myself. If you drown, what use are you to anyone else? Then time to return and save the others. My dream was telling me I'd be allowed plenty of time.

II

A BIRD KNOWS
ITS SONG

I

OF ALL THE foreigners who stream into Paris every day there was surely never one more bewildered than I in the autumn of 1937. I knew absolutely no one. However, a letter had been sent from my faraway Manitoba to prepare the way for me. Meredith Jones, who taught French at the University of Manitoba, had asked one of her former students who was living as an *au pair* in Paris to help me out a bit, find me a boarding house, meet me at the station. We were to recognize each other by a book she was to have in her hand and a Canadian magazine I was to carry under my arm. But I'd lost my magazine. The strangest part is that today I can't remember the name of the young woman with the book whom I sought so frantically, and who helped me so much when I finally found her.

I stepped out into the terrifying horde that gets off a train arriving at the Gare Saint-Lazare from the coast. In the sea of constantly changing faces, I kept trying to recognize one I'd never seen before. I was caught up by the shouts, the hustle and bustle, the powerful surges of movement, at times finding myself somehow going against the current of humanity and being taken to task with "Hey you, can't you watch where you're going!" I recall this as being one of the first things I heard said to me in Paris. I also made the blunder of trying to ask someone in a hurry for information, and was put firmly in my place. "For information, there's Information," snapped the man, then, perhaps feeling a mite remorseful, as he moved on he tipped his chin to indicate a direction. Next I spied a kind of uniform. I had a fleeting moment of hope for rescue, but I'd hardly begun my tale of woe when its wearer sent me packing. So I was looking for someone, was I! Well, the station was full of people looking for each other. Then, obviously hoping for a more open-handed client, he shouted over my head, "Porter! Porter!" though people on all sides were trying to catch his attention, also calling "Porter! Porter!"

In the end I let myself move with the crowd and before I realized it I was swept past the turnstiles and into the swarming concourse. I lost all hope of finding my compatriot. I went to a wicket, from which I was sent to another, where I was scolded for not knowing enough to read the signs on which, I was told, everything was indicated. And indeed it must have been so, for looking up I was confronted by a forest of symbols, words, and abbreviations that made my head spin.

Eventually I came to my senses and told myself that if my compatriot was still waiting it surely wouldn't be in this enormous concourse but most likely on the platform. I went back. At the turnstile the ticket checker stopped me.

"Where d'you think you're going, little lady?" he demanded.

"The other side."

"What side? The seaside?"

I pointed.

"In that case, little lady, your ticket!"

"My ticket!" I wailed in exasperation. "I gave it to the conductor of the train. The one I just arrived on."

"And you want to get back on already?"

In time I became accustomed to these sparring matches which so many Parisians seem to relish. Eventually I even came to enjoy them myself, but for the moment I was in the depths of despair. It seemed as impossible to get anyone to listen to me as if I'd been whisked to the heart of China. I tried to persuade the man at the turnstile, telling him how I'd lost the magazine that would have allowed my friend to identify me, and finished by begging him at least to let me go and make sure she wasn't still looking for me on the platform.

Perhaps because he considered I'd already taken up too much of his time with my muddled story, during which he'd done nothing but study his fingernails, he thenceforth addressed me in non-sentences.

"Platform ticket...."

"Where?"

"Machine...." He pointed.

I found it. As I approached, it looked well disposed, unlike the impatient people I'd encountered, and thus inspired me with confidence. Above a slot it told me it was a platform ticket distributor. I pulled the lever.

Nothing happened.

An elegant gentleman was passing. Though he seemed in a great hurry he stopped to watch what I was doing.

"It might work better if you put in a franc," he said.

I reddened to the roots of my hair and opened my purse. Alas, I had no French money yet.

The elegant gentleman put his hand in his pocket. He took out a franc and put it in my hand, then was on his way, his face closed over other thoughts, it seemed.

I ran after him crying, "Monsieur, Monsieur, please, your name, your address, so I can repay you!"

Without exactly slowing his pace he turned partway around and gave me the first smile I'd received in Paris.

"Really, Mademoiselle, such a to-do over a franc!"

So the first handout of my life is still a bit on my conscience. My benefactor might have been a Rothschild; sometimes I think I recall a scarf and a pair of gloves of a quality I've rarely seen since.

I went back to the turnstile with my platform ticket. I didn't realize I was approaching a new ticket checker, who'd perhaps only just arrived to relieve the first.

"Where d'you think you're going, little lady?" I heard myself asked again.

Dumbfounded, I looked up at him. Though I myself couldn't tell one face from another any more, I reproached him for not recognizing me.

"I told you before. I'm looking for another Canadian who was supposed to meet me, and you sent me to get a platform ticket."

"But there's nobody left on the platform," said the new ticket checker. "Look, don't you see?" He was nicer than the first, which was why I finally realized I was talking to a different one.

He was quite right. There wasn't a soul in sight all the way down the platform. I came back to the middle of the noisy concourse. I didn't dare approach the wicket I'd been sent from to look at the signs. For a while I wandered around aimlessly in the crowd just trying to catch someone's eye, for what purpose I'm not sure, but nobody looked my way. In my frustration I took this as evidence that no one wanted anything to do with me. With no local money, not even knowing the address where a room had been reserved for me, faced with the most callous indifference, I was doomed to go around in circles indefinitely, it seemed. In the vast concourse of the Gare Saint-Lazare I was so discouraged that I formed a very black picture of myself leading a most wretched life in Paris.

Then suddenly the crowd began to thin. It happened so quickly that I was surprised and even more distraught. Soon there were only a dozen or so lost-looking souls still wandering about, making the huge space look ten times bigger than before. Finally there were only two little figures left at opposite ends of all that emptiness. Each of us began a hesitant approach towards the other. I didn't have my magazine and she didn't have her book. She'd left it on the Métro, I learned later. We exchanged beseeching looks. She was the first to speak.

"Are you Gabrielle?"

I flung my arms around her neck as if she were suddenly the dearest soul in the world. Yet I'm still trying to find her name. I seem to have had it on the tip of my tongue for years. Perfidious memory! Will it ever give me back that precious name?

As we went to claim my baggage from the checkroom, she was already doing her best to encourage me.

"Don't be upset by the way strangers treat you here. It's always that way in Paris. You think you've come to a city where they're permanently at war with each other. They quarrel and bicker about everything. It's really just a game, though, and you'll find it's almost always in the cause of justice and logic. Logic's a passion with them, they've got it in their blood like a virus. We all get used to it, you'll see. You even start enjoying it, and when you can beat the Parisians at their own game they surrender in a way that's downright disconcerting. Anyway, what you mustn't ever do at any cost is let on you're afraid of them. Got that?"

These astonishing words came piecemeal to my ears, because my companion had outstripped me and I was scurrying to keep up, often separated from her by a pillar or simply by considerable distance.

At the checkroom I retrieved my two heavy suitcases and my

wardrobe trunk, which must have weighed a good two hundred pounds. However, the porters whose offers of service had rung in every corner of the station shortly before were now nowhere to be seen. When we called for their help our voices went unanswered, piping and pathetic in the cavernous silence.

So my compatriot and I lugged the two suitcases a good distance, though not so far that we'd lose sight of them. Then we tackled the trunk, pivoting it on its corners, watched appreciatively by at least half a dozen sweepers, all leaning on their brooms. They'd have liked to help us, they said, but that wasn't their job. With my baggage all together again, we each sat on a suitcase for a minute to catch our breath. At last we reached the sidewalk and heaved the baggage into a tall taxi while the driver calmly kept reading his *Paris-Soir*. One of us climbed in beside him and tugged while the other pushed strenuously from below. At the last minute he deigned to rise briefly from his posterior and give us a hand with the trunk, for which there was only barely room inside the vehicle.

As we drove into the City of Light at last, along street after street I saw nothing but tall façades severely shrouded in darkness. Even the streetlamps yielded no more than a paltry glow.

"I've found you a suitable *pension*, Madame Jouve's," my compatriot told me, "one they'd say here is *tout ce qu'il y a de bien*, all you could ask for. But tonight for sure Madame Jouve will come down on you like a ton of bricks for arriving so late. After midnight, everything's barricaded like a mediaeval fortress there. Have you seen Carcassone?" she asked, then returned to my landlady. "If she attacks, you counterattack. If she snarls, snarl louder. That's the way to get along in Paris."

"How awful!"

"No, because then you're respected."

Something else I've totally forgotten, perhaps significantly, is my first address in Paris, though I could probably find my way there with my eyes closed. The building was impressive for the period, six storeys and U-shaped, with its front gate and the watchman's cubicle on the Rue de la Santé – my memory can be depended upon for the name of the street.

At this late hour, of course, we found the tall iron gate locked and the watchman's cubicle as dark as a hut in a forest. My compatriot groped until she found a bell near the gate to wake the watchman. I'd never before had to disturb so many people just to get inside and into bed shortly after midnight. I was astounded that a city supposedly dedicated to nocturnal pleasures could also be so early to bed. All I'd seen from the taxi was a succession of huge buildings fast asleep, blocks of solid shadow without light in a single window.

The watchman appeared, still pulling on his clothes but not grumbling too much.

He opened the gate for us. We were in a murky courtyard now, with all six storeys around us in almost total darkness from top to bottom, showing only a feeble glimmer from a nightlight here and there. Then I saw a young crescent moon rising over the dark building, its golden cusps every bit as pure and brilliant as they were in the deep empty spaces of Canada.

Our taxi-driver's heart was perhaps softened by the absence of witnesses. He hoisted himself from his seat and unloaded my baggage onto the sidewalk. Then, one good deed leading to another, he helped us put it all inside the entrance to the building, having made the door open for us by pressing a button or shouting "Door! Door!" I don't remember which. This done, he left with all possible speed, wishing us, " 'Soir, 'sieur-dame."

Immediately the electricity went off. Tripping over my scattered belongings, my compatriot groped for the light button. Just as she announced she'd found it the light went on again. "It's timed," she explained, running over to the button to show me what I'd have to do if I was caught alone in a dark entrance. I'd barely grasped what she was teaching me when she urged, "Come on, get ready to move fast...." The elevator, having been summoned, was descending towards us with creaks and groans, rocking like the basket on an early aeronautical contraption. It opened and revealed an interior that was so tiny I couldn't believe my eyes. I just stood there in astonishment, wasting precious time.

My compatriot had blocked the door open with a suitcase and was straining to wrestle my trunk into the elevator cage, because, she said breathlessly, if it didn't go in first it wouldn't go in at all. Finally it was in, filling the space almost totally.

"We'll come back for the rest?" I asked.

"And leave things down here to get pinched? Never! We'll get it all in."

"But there's no one around."

"That's what you think! Climb up on the trunk and I'll hand you one of the suitcases."

Standing on end, the trunk was already pretty high, and when I was perched on top of it I touched the ceiling of the cage. I succeeded in stowing a suitcase beside me.

Thereupon the light went off. My compatriot ran to put it on again. We managed finally to get both suitcases standing precariously on top of the trunk, on end and side by side. Then, flattening ourselves to the limit between the closed cage door and the mountain of baggage which we held steady with outstretched arms, we began to rise gently towards the sixth floor. Then the light went out again.

I began to laugh uncontrollably, certainly one of the least mirthful laughs I've ever experienced. Nevertheless, it echoed upward and downward with singular insolence, amplified by the funnel effect of the elevator shaft. "Not so loud...not so loud!" my compatriot begged me. She was English-speaking, and though she'd made enormous progress with her French in the year she'd been in Paris she would sometimes lapse into her mother tongue when excited. "You'll wake everybody...," she warned, but to no avail, for the fear of doing just that was making my awful paroxysms worse. But they stopped as abruptly as they'd begun.

The elevator came to a halt. "Hold the lift," my compatriot whispered quickly as she stepped out to find the light button. Though dim, the light blinded me when it came on, I'd become so accustomed to moving around in the dark.

"No noise," warned my compatriot, and we began to drag the baggage out into the hall and pile it beside Madame Jouve's door, making as little noise as a pair of thieves. I'll soon have more to say about thieves as it happens, but not until their turn comes. When the baggage was arranged to our satisfaction, not blocking the passageway too much, I put my finger on the bell, above which a fearsomely distinguished card announced, "Madame Jean-Pierre Jouve."

Almost immediately the self-same Madame Jean-Pierre Jouve

opened the door, wearing a dressing gown, her eyes heavy with sleep and a reproach on her lips, although a polite one.

"This is some hour to be arriving! You could at least have let me know you'd be late, sent me a wire...telephoned...."

Now her eyes were suddenly open wider, for what she perceived first was neither my anxious face so earnestly hoping for sympathy, nor my compatriot's pleasant round one still flushed from battle; not, in short, two plucky young women and their heroic achievement in getting themselves to her door, just the mountain of baggage piled beside it. She gave a cry of dismay.

"That's not all yours...? All that...?"

"I've come for a year, Madame," I ventured.

"And you think you need all that...for just one miserable little year?"

I wanted to tell her a year in Paris couldn't be a "miserable little year", but I didn't have time.

"You're all the same, you Americans, with your tons of baggage!"

"I'm Canadian."

"Same thing, you and your enormous wardrobe trunks," she continued. "Don't you know what a Parisian apartment is like? We haven't got all the room in the world the way you do in Canada, you know."

Yet my trunk was the most compact I could find at Eaton's in Winnipeg, designed especially for going to Paris according to the advertisement, since it asked (in English, of course), "Are you going abroad?" and urged, "Take me with you," promising to make itself small, to fit flat under a bed or stand on end in a corner, to serve as the least cumbersome wardrobe ever with its hanger compartment for suits and dresses and drawers for shoes and underwear. My friends had chipped in to help me pay for it. I'd packed everything I valued in it. And attached to it as I may have been when I left home, how could I measure my fondness for it now that we'd been through so much together? Apprehensively, I looked at Madame Jouve who was looking with distaste at the trunk.

"Listen, my child," she whispered, for the whole conversation of reproach and feeble excuse was taking place under our breath so as not to wake the neighbours, "we'll try to put the suitcases somewhere in the apartment for tonight at least, though I don't see how we're going to get them into your room, but the trunk..."

Her voice, though exceedingly well bred, none the less indicated she would not be crossed.

"…has to go to the basement tonight."

So we put it back in the elevator cage, three of us this time, though Madame Jouve hindered more than she helped because her voluminous shaggy dressing gown kept getting caught in the grille-work of the cage. We descended into the bowels of the earth. Here as upstairs, electricity was apparently dispensed in brief periods, and all we had to see by were feeble little lights spaced along a narrow dirt-floored passageway leading away into utter darkness. At the side was a row of small iron-grilled storage lockers that looked like dungeons in this dismal setting. We manoeuvred the trunk along the passageway, pivoting it on its corners, I with the feeling that having barely arrived I was already reliving one of those stories of the murky side of Paris that I recalled having read with such pleasure when I was safe and sound. I said so to Madame Jouve, who chided me amiably for having too much imagination and letting it run away with me. This, she said, was plainly and simply a safe, clean, and very accessible basement. She was beginning to be pleasant in her own way. She predicted that I'd soon find it a thousand times more convenient to have my trunk down here, where I could come and get what I needed at any time and without causing the least trouble, than in my room, which really was very small. How I agreed with her once I'd seen the room!

At last we arrived at a locker with a number above the door that matched the one on Madame Jouve's apartment. She fiddled briefly with the padlock.

"Well!" she said. "It looks as if it's been forced. It'll have to be changed tomorrow without fail."

This should have put me on my guard, but suddenly, as has happened so often in the midst of difficulties over which I have no control, I was only half there; part of me was revisiting books I'd read that this Paris basement reminded me of. When caught in ridiculous or uncontrollable situations I've often found refuge in memories left by books; they seem so much more comfortable than the reality I'm involved in.

As we moved away I glanced back sadly at the trunk. It looked so lonesome standing on its end in the middle of its dungeon. I had a feeling I might never see it again. But the feeling vanished in the face of a new problem: the electricity in the bowels of Paris had failed. Happily, Madame Jouve had a cigarette lighter in the pocket of her bulky dressing gown. By the light of the tiny flame, for some reason each of us holding the next by an arm like disaster survivors, we returned to the surface.

We let my friend off the elevator at the ground floor and she fled in great haste. She had a long way to go and would only just catch the last bus. As she left she called over her shoulder that she'd be around to pick me up early next morning and we'd go to the police station. On the way we'd have to get me photographed full-face and profile, with my ears showing, and I mustn't forget to bring a residence certificate. If we had time we'd stop and sign the Canadian visitors' book at the embassy.... "Bye-bye till tomorrow...."

At last I was safe and sound in the sixth-floor apartment. Madame Jouve, having made me sit down for a moment, finally took the time to look at me and became almost maternal.

"My poor child, you look all upset. Would you like something to drink to pick you up?"

I think I pictured a lovely steaming hot chocolate, the kind Mother used to bring me, a big brimming cupful, when she too found I looked peaked after a long hard day. I accepted with a smile, I imagine, thinking of the rich, smooth, delicious-smelling drink I could count on when I came in after our evening shows in little Manitoba villages or even in town. And I must have kept smiling a little, because on the heels of this memory came a succession of others which, if I hadn't been woolgathering about finally being in Paris, I would probably never have known were so pleasant or even that they existed.

"I'll make you a lemonade," said Madame Jouve.

A lemonade just before going to bed has always done me more harm than good, since its effect is to make me get up every fifteen minutes. But I didn't have the strength to refuse. Madame Jouve went to the kitchen to squeeze a lemon. She brought me a bitter drink softened just barely with a few grains of sugar. I drank it, managing with difficulty not to grit my teeth.

"Come along now, you must get to bed."

She led me down a corridor to a door at the end, which she opened cautiously, revealing a room faintly and indirectly lit by the new moon I'd seen rising over the fortifications. I still don't know why I kept thinking of fortifications. Perhaps I felt I'd strayed so far off the course of my life that I'd for ever be prevented from returning to it. I entered the small room without seeing a thing.

"Take the bed on the right," instructed Madame Jouve. "If you can, leave the light off so as not to wake your roommate. She has to get up early in the morning."

"But I said in my letter I had to have a room to myself," I found the courage to remind her.

"And you shall have it, my child. I've been caught short because a Swedish girl came earlier than expected."

She closed the door behind her.

I groped my way to the head of the bed, deposited my clothes around me on what might have been a chair and a night-table, though I wasn't sure, then lay down, my nerves beginning to relax at last. But I'd barely begun to drift off to some peace and quiet when my lemonade made itself felt. I got out of bed, found my way to the door, opened it, closed it noiselessly, and guided by a kind of instinct followed a corridor and found the facilities, where I still didn't put on the light, identifying everything just by touch. All without a sound. Until, having found and firmly grasped the chain, I gave it a good pull. You'd think I'd opened a floodgate and loosed a cataract. Not until broad daylight, when I found the flush tank attached almost at ceiling height, giving the water three metres to fall, did I realize how I had set off such a din.

I retraced my steps, dived back into what my fingers told me was my bed, and heard a grumbling sound from the other bed, caused by ill humour or a disturbed dream, I couldn't tell which. I began to doze off. But the lemonade hadn't done with me yet. It even seemed to be waiting until I was back in bed before giving me its message. Off I went along the unfamiliar route through the unfamiliar apartment. I returned. I went back again. According to what I was soon to be told, the deafening cataract sound reverberated twice more through the apartment. Each time I returned on tiptoe, though the impressive gurgling of the tank, filling almost as noisily as it emptied, was certainly loud enough to cover the sound of my steps. What drove me to cause such expenditure of water for the expulsion of so little? No doubt my fear of not doing, when in Paris, as civilized Parisians do, while in fact doing the reverse.

Exhausted, I finally fell asleep. But not restfully. I dreamed I was trudging across Paris with my trunk on my back, having become a street porter, one of those poor wretches of days long past whose picture had sprung from the memory of books I'd read. Next I was tripping on the king's cobblestones at Versailles, fleeing from ruffians who'd been set at my heels. Then I was Jean Valjean of Hugo's *Les Misérables* in the sewers of Paris, clinging to my trunk and being swept along on the evil-smelling waters. The flushing water, the basement at Madame Jouve's, and memories of books from my childhood had joined forces to produce one of the most vivid dreams I've ever had. Suddenly I was attending a *bal musette* with accordions playing and my trunk in my arms, trying to make it dance to a rollicking air. I opened my eyes. It was broad daylight. There was a piano a few feet away taking up two-thirds of the room. My roommate was sitting at it playing with gusto, washed and dressed and hair combed, her bed already made.

"Bonjour, vous, la Canadienne!" she called through her chords and arpeggios.

She made not the slightest attempt to excuse herself for waking me so rudely. On the contrary, she took me to task, though good-naturedly, for having kept her awake with my comings and goings and "that infernal flushing you were doing all night as if you wanted to drain the Seine.... Are you on the trot like that every night?" She warned me that for her part she liked to go to bed early so she could get up and be at her piano bright and early, practising for her admission to the Conservatory.

So began my life with Charlotte, a young musician from Alsace who used to spend eight hours a day at her piano, whom even so I was to miss when Madame Jouve gave in to my repeated pleas and put me in a little cell by myself at the other end of the apartment.

For the moment I'd have given anything for another hour of sleep, but Charlotte struck up a triumphal march. The wretched girl played well, too. My half-dead nerve-ends quivered, tempted by the music. Besides, my compatriot was arriving.

"What!" I heard her say in a loud voice as soon as she was inside the door, "Gabrielle's not up and ready yet? We've got a lot to do today."

To my surprise, when Charlotte paused briefly I heard Madame Jouve rise to my defence.

"Give the poor child time to pull herself together at least. And first you're going to let her have her breakfast in peace."

I appeared in the dining room barely awake. My place was still set, the only one left, at a long oval table. A dainty bouquet of flowers at its centre immediately caught my eye.

"What are they?" I asked, never having seen flowers like these before.

"Anemones, my child," said Madame Jouve, apparently pleased I'd asked.

She was dressed in black, relieved only by a white edging high on the neck, and her chignon was impeccable. I'd defy anyone to recognize the frowsy lady of our basement prowls.

"Marie," she called towards the kitchen, "Mademoiselle's breakfast. And good and hot, eh!"

I lifted the steaming bowl, half fragrant coffee and half scalded milk, and found its taste exquisite. Then I took a croissant still hot from the oven and, since my compatriot had been served coffee too, followed her example and dipped it in my coffee. It was delicious. A warming sun flooded through the window from which I'd seen the moon as if it were rising over battlements. The anemones I've loved so much ever since kept drawing my eye and I longed to touch them. Though my throat was burning, which meant I was probably in for a cold, this morning I felt myself timidly beginning to find my feet in Paris, like a bruised plant in a protective layer of compost. I would willingly have stayed a while at this table; later I would realize that in a way breakfast in Paris is the pleasantest moment of the day, a time of peace and serenity, a time for reverie almost, a pause at the start of the day before you're caught up in the hustle and bustle of life. Many is the time it would help me take new heart, set me back on my feet when I thought I couldn't cope with Paris any longer.

I had no sooner meticulously gathered together the crumbs from my croissant on the tablecloth, as I'd watched my compatriot do, than she was hurrying me away.

"Come on," she said, "we're going to the police station."

Poor girl, she couldn't help hurrying me. She was always being hurried herself by her mistress, who didn't give her much time off, wanting her around all the time to speak English to the children in return for meals and a roof over her head.

So there I was, fresh from the tribulations of the night before, running, stumbling after her across Paris. When she had enough breath left, she lost no opportunity to educate me as we went. "See, at bus stops, if you don't want to be at the back of the line all day you pull this lever on the machine and take a number. It's like the days of Frontenac and Bishop Laval. When the bus comes and the conductor shouts, 'Number, number!' everybody shouts their number and you shout yours too. Only war veterans and pregnant women can get on ahead, but look sharp because I've seen cheating.... Get on now, it's our turn.... Look, over here! That's the famous Café du Dôme where the artists and writers meet. Madame Jouve doesn't even suspect but her precious, much too beautiful Swede (the one who took your room), whose parents asked her to keep a close eye on her, spends whole evenings there with strange men.... We get off here.... Watch it!... Silly girl!... You don't cross streets in Paris except at the crossings between the *clous*, those metal disks in the road. Otherwise if you get run over it's your fault. Did you see the Eiffel Tower just then? It's monstrously beautiful, as they say. Here's the Métro.... We go down this way. Look, here's the *maquette*, the map of the Métro. If you don't know how to transfer to go, say, from the Porte des Lilas to Passy, you press this button and this one. See? Those little lights go on to show which trains to take. It's easy. You're in Paris. Everything's uncompromisingly clear." She added that everyone would keep telling me, "You can't go wrong." All of which gave me plenty to dream about for many nights to come.

II

WE'D SPENT two days under and above ground, running, hurrying, riding, and coughing (my cold had ripened), and my compatriot still losing no opportunity to teach me about Paris. "The Sainte Chapelle? No, we've passed it. The most graceful architecture in the world.... There's Notre Dame on the right. Look! The Arc de Triomphe ahead. Over there...that's the dome of Les Invalides. Napoleon's tomb's there, Egyptian red porphyry. What a dreadful man he was! *Un monstre!*... Downright shameful! How about getting off at the Louvre for a few minutes? Just long enough to take a look at the Winged Victory. *Une merveille, n'est-ce pas?* It's got no head and it's more eloquent than any head.... Come on!... That's our bus just leaving.... Jump!" If she couldn't find the right French word she'd often use an English one.

Near the end of the day my wonderful little guide stopped short and turned to me with a suggestion.

"I put a *bourguignon* on the stove early this morning. It should be cooked by now. Would you like to come and share it with me? I have to warn you, though; you'll have to walk up six floors. My place isn't grand like Madame Jouve's."

I was so enchanted at her invitation to have a quiet meal in what she called her own little corner in Paris, just the two of us, that she could have said two hundred floors and I'd have been just as ready to go. I expected to find the kind of respite which to tell the truth only humble places have ever given me. But I was far from expecting it to captivate me as it did. I felt as though I'd been deprived for centuries of the contemplation, the silence, the un-hurried, dreamy communion with myself that I've never been able to do without for long.

I took her arm. She smiled at me. We stopped running. We

reverted to what we really were, two little Canadians, both rather slow to come to decisions and act accordingly. We could do as we liked again and we wanted to feel at home. And this, I was to learn, Paris can also provide.

We walked on, no longer hurrying. Dusk was falling when we came to a narrow, shadowy street lined with tall, solemn, centuries-old houses. It must have been very near the Seine, for besides our footsteps I remember hearing soft lapping sounds, and at a corner perhaps even dimly seeing an expanse of water, deep green, a little dirty and sad, like an old face in which a long, long story is reflected. How I've loved Paris whenever it has shown me a face that's the opposite of what is called the gay, carefree Paris!

On the way we stopped once for a loaf of bread that was longer and thinner than any I'd seen before, again for a head of lettuce beaded with great cool drops of water, somewhere else for a bottle of red wine so we could drink to my arrival, and finally for a cheese that was so ripe it oozed into my sleeve as I carried it in my open palm. We also bought a little bunch of daisies of a kind the French call *paquerettes*, they too the first I'd ever seen. I couldn't stop looking at their tiny, perfect faces and saying, "So those are *paquerettes*!..." I was almost as happy to become acquainted with these flowers as I was to have found a friend I could depend on. Nostalgically, I tried for years to grow this kind of daisy in my small garden in Charlevoix County from the many packets of seeds I brought back from my visits to France. They flowered, making an even-surfaced, ravishing carpet of many colours at the foot of a gnarled old apple tree, but our country wasn't meant for them and they all very quickly died. I'd wanted to delight our vast Canadian sky with their delicate faces at any cost, but I finally stopped trying.

Before we started up the stairs to the sixth floor, my compatriot asked if I thought I could help with the wood we'd have to take up with us. We went to a dark little courtyard containing several stacks of firewood, one of them hers. We each took a good armful, and with wood piled up to our chins, the bags we were carrying filled to overflowing with bottles, bread, and lettuce, and the bright daisy faces lighting our way, we climbed the spiral staircase up the middle of the big old house. The worn steps and graffiti and other marks on the walls gave evidence of the thousands of pilgrims who, like us, had trudged wearily up to their own little corners. I didn't feel my cold, fatigue, or anxiety any longer. My heart became lighter step by step, as happened in those years whenever I was approaching a moment of unexpected happiness.

At the top of the stairs, gripping one of her packages in her teeth, my compatriot drew a massive key from her pocket and slipped it into the keyhole of a shadowy door which was barely visible in the half-light of the landing. To this day I still picture every detail of the little room inside as I first saw it, the sofa-bed pushed against the wall, books all over, a round table with a cover hanging to the floor on which our two places were already set, and in the middle of the room a real little stove which I fell instantly in love with, it so made me think of good company in dreary hours, even with the fire out. I probably hadn't realized how homesick I must have been since leaving my country, for I went to the stove at once and touched it the way one does a living thing.

But the bewitchment of the place came less from anything of this kind in particular than from the way it was lit, small though it was, by a huge skylight in the roof. The room seemed to be in the sky itself, bathed in a soft, peaceful light that was softening further from minute to minute with the end of day. Never had I seen a room as open to the sky. I entered it as if I were entering a dream, one I'd had all my life: the dream of a haven from human malice, from myself and from others. It's surprising how often I've found such a haven...always very briefly. But the real miracle was that I found it this time in the heart of Paris, and it answered both of my irreconcilable needs, for solitude and warm companionship. All the beauty of the little room must have shown in my face, for my compatriot, who was sitting on the floor blowing on an ember in the ashes, stopped and looked at me open-mouthed.

"What's the matter? You look as if you're in a trance!"

What was the matter? The matter was that my heart was full to bursting and at peace both at once, that I had a feeling of belonging here, of unbelievable well-being. All of which I'd experienced only fleetingly before, like anyone else, of course. No, on second thought better than most, for not many people have ever truly had such a feeling, so indescribable yet so real. At the time I thought it came from outside of me, that the feeling belonged to the place it occurred in. I thought you could possess the feeling by possessing the place, either by staying there or by trying to take it with you – absurd as this may be. My compatriot laughed when I told her I wanted her room so badly I'd exchange it for my all-you-could-ask-for room and board at Madame Jouve's. Otherwise we'd have to find me a room just like it in every way. Then, I thought, I'd be content for the rest of my days.

When she had got the fire going and was preparing the salad, my compatriot gave me her own view of the piece of heaven I thought I had within reach.

"You get all the way up, loaded with as much as you and I brought up together, then you have to go back down to get coal oil for the lamp. You get all the way back up, but you've forgotten to pick up your mail. You go back down. This time you get almost all the way up and have to go half-way back down to find out what the concierge is yapping at you up the stairs. In the end you go all the way down because she's got a registered letter for you. Next you go down to the fourth floor to get water. You make the same trip to throw out the dirty water. Sooner or later you go back down again to the w.c. It's often ten o'clock before you can open your books and start preparing for your next day's classes. You're half asleep over your notes and you'll be half asleep at the Sorbonne while your eminent professor dispenses his wisdom in droning little sentences."

I listened, moved by the pluck she was laughingly revealing, as though poking fun at an absurd quirk in her character. I could now understand how difficult her life was in Paris, but I envied her no less fervently.

We sat down to dine directly under the skylight. To me we seemed to be sitting at table suspended in the sky, as in a surrealist painting. Later, when we were finishing our meal and the last glow of twilight was filtering over us through the opening in the roof, she agreed that when the chores were done a mysterious kind of peacefulness permeated her "little room in the sky", sometimes making her feel it was captured here for ever. Then she told me she had a surprise for me. She made me climb onto a chair beside her and opened the skylight on its hinges. Standing with our heads outside, we could see Paris all around, spread as far as the horizon like a great drowsy monster, sweet and lovable now it had calmed a little, when in any event none of its fretfulness and hurly-burly could reach us up here. I stood on tiptoe on my chair for a long time, gazing at the city the way a child of the woods might gaze at faraway vistas from the branch of a tree. I still wonder if even from the top of Notre Dame I've ever had a more enchanting view of Paris.

My compatriot gently brought me back to reality, reminding me that the time had passed quickly and if we didn't leave soon we'd find the door tight at Madame Jouve's. I sighed as I tore myself away from the sky.

Early next morning, she told me, she'd be caught up again with her lectures and running from the Sorbonne to her mistress's house in time for meals so she could make the children say, "Pass me the salt if you please…. Thank you so very much…." And perhaps to stay with them in the evening if her mistress decided to go to the theatre, which wasn't part of the agreement, but an agreement was hardly ever respected when you were an *au pair*.

I could see increasingly how difficult a life she led and was embarrassed to realize what a priceless gift I'd received from her with all the time she'd given me, undoubtedly time that would cost her dearly to make up. It was comforting to know she'd take me home once again, for Paris at night frightened me, but I owed her so much already I didn't want to abuse her kindness and assured her I thought I could get home by myself.

She burst out laughing.

"Never!" she said. "Muddlehead that you are, you could just as well end up at La Villette…," and I was relieved that the time hadn't yet come when I'd be turned loose alone in Paris at night.

At the door I turned for a last fond look at the little room, which we were leaving in some disorder. It wasn't my intense longing to curl myself up and stay for ever that made me linger; this, I knew by now, just couldn't be. I was obeying a kind of command, one reaching me from the future, from years I hadn't yet lived, urging me to take what was important from this little room and keep it for later when I'd be able to use it. I'd been getting this curious command for some time and with increasing frequency whenever I said goodbye to places and things, since the Little Water Hen perhaps or even before, making me retain as much as possible of whatever I was leaving, so as to take it away with me in a sense.

It was a long time before I realized what those vague imperatives were leading to.

We hurried down the flights of stairs, ran through silent streets where the echo of our footsteps suddenly became the sound of pursuers, jumped onto a bus as it pulled away. Over the weeks and months that followed I didn't have much occasion to bring back the picture of the little room up there among the high rooftops of Paris. It used to come to my mind as a lovely, fragile memory, the kind one tells oneself is worth nurturing; then, finding me un- available, it would retreat again. After a while I lost sight of it. I think I even ceased to have any conscious recollection of it.

So why did it come back to life twenty years later, exactly as I'd stored it away in my last look from the door, with its footed salamander stove, squat and green, its round table littered with the remains of our meal, everything bathed in a soft twilight glow? For what reason other than to bring Pierre of *The Hidden Mountain* here when his wanderings ceased? To the haven I myself had longed for, I brought this exhausted soul to live his last torments and ecstasies. Or perhaps for the illusion of seeing, through the opening in the roof, the vast Canadian sky that's so often the colour of twilight in the North, as he'd seen it from his trapper's cabin long before.

III

SOON MADAME JOUVE, having my introduction to life in Paris at heart, began to take a hand in it herself. For she not only lodged and fed us. She guided us, counselled us, gave lessons in French to some and in deportment to others, discreetly observed the comings and goings of the youngest, perhaps reporting to their parents, and generally kept watch over us with a certain affection which, if not demonstrative, was well-meaning and sincere.

After a week or two of running hither and thither in Paris, I'd had more than I could stand of everything new. I shut myself in my room and stayed there, which I'm much inclined to do whenever I get beyond my depth. Madame Jouve, worried to see me living a hermit's existence now, came one evening to badger me out of it, bearing a book in her hand.

"My child, since you've come to Paris, the most exciting city in the world, and then chosen to shut yourself up like this, at least read. Here, I've brought you a book. All Paris is talking about it. All Paris adores it."

If I were given Alain-Fournier's *Le Grand Meaulnes* (*The Wanderer*) to read for the first time today I might be ecstatic, but to tell the truth I was then far too much like the hero of the book to have any taste for the sad tale of escape through imagination. I myself was escaping this way, the only escape from life we really have, but my own private door led to the riverbanks of the Little Water Hen; to me at the time, everything there seemed to have been ineffably peaceful and harmonious. So I paid only token attention to the book's fantasizing, which seemed pretty tame stuff compared to my own. If the conversation at table among the dozen boarders from almost as many countries turned to the book, I would feign enthusiasm. But Madame Jouve had a way of putting questions that soon exposed such deception. She was almost beside herself with indignation that a young Canadian just off the boat from her native wilds should dare to be lukewarm about a novel that all Paris adored.

She was even more scandalized to hear my reaction the evening she took some of her brood to a performance of Giraudoux's *Electra*. Was the leap from Deschambault Street to the Athénée in Paris simply too great? Was I so truly lost here that I'd ceased turning a receptive ear to the voices of others? Or was the play too erudite, too boring? I shall never know because I've not been much inclined to expose myself to Giraudoux again. It took me longer to admit that the great Louis Jouvet himself aggravated me with his dry delivery, his little disconnected phrases coming out cold and flat, his mannerisms, and what to me was merely face-pulling. On the way through London I'd been to the Old Vic and also to a little theatre in Shaftesbury Street whose name I've forgotten, where I saw acting that was restrained, understated, one might even say untheatrical, a style that was discreet, all shades and halftones and vastly superior to what I was seeing in Paris, I felt. Yet in due course I found this kind of theatre in Paris too, the kind which is so close to reality that it's almost banal, but which enthralls.

On my own, when I finally found the courage to come out of my room, I hurried to the Théâtre Français. At home we'd always called it the Comédie Française, and we'd held it in such veneration that we looked with awe on anyone who'd crossed its threshold. I think I recall that we knew exactly how many such privileged individuals there were in our community and could name them and even remember which play each had seen.

I was all excited as I queued up behind the people waiting at the ticket office for the cheap seats. Gone was my fear of Paris and of doing the wrong thing, which Paris inspired in me at every turn. I became communicative, even talkative, and informed my neighbours to right and left that this was my first time at the Théâtre Français. Some said politely, "Oh yes?" and others asked where I was from and seemed interested in me, and I in return glowed with a kind of spontaneous friendship towards them. I was discovering the magical thread of brotherhood that unites these little clutches of strangers at the doors of theatres (elsewhere too, sometimes, but especially around theatres), which was to teach me so much about others and about myself.

What exactly was I anticipating that evening that I should be in such an effervescent state? I don't remember, of course. I recall, however, that I found as much as I'd expected, perhaps more, in the little church of Saint-Julien-le-Pauvre and in Notre Dame, both of which I'd known first of all through great writers; perhaps this is the case with everyone.

My impatience as I sat waiting was almost painful. The curtain rose. Another shameful confession I'm about to make is that I don't recall what play I saw this first time at the Théâtre Français. I remember other plays I saw there, particularly Racine's *Athalie* with Vera Korène, which I saw on another trip to Paris and which enchanted me. But I've retained nothing of what passed on the stage on my first evening at the Théâtre Français except the sight of an old, fat, pot-bellied little actor lending his ridiculous proportions to the young hero of the play. He had a voice that could shake the whole building, however. He used it without the least variation, beginning each alexandrine as deep as a voice can descend and rising from one pitch to the next till he reached such a shrill note it made you imagine he was hurling it at you from the top of a tower. Up...down...up...down. Up and down the scale he went, over and over, trembling on his little old legs. His phrasing would start with a kind of subterranean rumble and end with clarion calls from the ramparts. I really couldn't follow the play at all, I was so preoccupied with the elderly young star's antics. In Winnipeg I'd known a French lady, formerly with the Comédie Française, she said, who used to declaim La Fontaine's simple, homespun fables in the same way.

I cast a shy smile around me, looking for smiles of complicity to reinforce my impression that I was watching something ludicrous, but saw only solemn and respectful faces. Dear heaven, was I the only one in the world to see things as I saw them? If so, my solitude was worse than I'd sometimes suspected. I even suppressed my silly urge to laugh, an urge which rather frightened me since it had almost turned to hysteria in the elevator.

All the same, a few days later I hurried back to see Rostand's *Cyrano*. I knew long passages by heart, which I must have recited myself with a certain grandiloquence, perhaps at the time thinking them noble and uplifting. But it left me very ill at ease to see Cyrano mortally wounded, yet hours later still standing, still thrusting out his sword and long nose and speechifying. If this was drama, I thought, I'd never believe in it. It was too contrived. Too over-done. Or else I was wrong for it. Little by little this was becoming evident. What was difficult was admitting it. For I was here in Paris to study drama, or so I tried to make myself believe. What other reason could I have to stay?

To make matters worse, Madame Jouve, to whom I'd confided something of my plans to study drama, kept needling me. "You won't get anywhere just dragging your feet around Paris," she scolded me. I had finally emerged from my room and was now tramping endlessly about the city, venting my indecision and doubts about myself. "Come now, child, you're not going to settle your mind that way." In which she was mistaken, for it's often while wandering alone in strange cities that I've best been able to settle my mind, though along lines other than those I had thought I should follow, almost always better ones.

"It's just struck me," she said one day, "why shouldn't you go and make enquiries at the Atelier? They say that Charles Dullin takes students and that he's absolutely extraordinary."

I was caught in my own trap and I'd have to go through with it if I was going to keep a shred of self-respect.

Was it she or I who made the appointment? In any event, the fateful afternoon arrived and I went to Dullin's theatre. There was a rehearsal of *Volpone* by Ben Jonson going on, Jules Romains's adaptation as I recall. On the stage amid the dust and ropes and trappings that lie about at rehearsal time was a curtained four-poster bed. Its drawn curtains were flapping furiously as though in a windstorm, or from a struggle going on inside. I didn't know the play. I had no idea what could be shaking the bed that way. Uncomfortably, I watched the curtains billow, rise almost to the ceiling, then fall back all limp and quivering. Someone called from the stage as I stood in the semi-darkness:

"You're looking for someone?"

I mumbled a frightened reply about an appointment.

"Who with?"

"Monsieur Dullin."

Out of the bed popped a short man, crippled it seemed to me, and rather ugly. He scowled at me from under heavy, dishevelled eyebrows. I've never seen Charles Dullin anywhere else so I can't say whether it was he or Volpone I met face to face.

He spoke to me from the stage, his voice reaching me as though from a world incredibly far off and very different from real life.

"You're the young Canadian who asked to see me? Where are you from? Have you done any theatre?"

I thought about our innocent little tours to tiny villages in Manitoba at twilight time, seeing in particular the lonely country roads around Otterburne, though why these I don't know. At this moment I'd have given anything to be back there out of sight, back in the state I'd been in before having the ridiculous temerity to approach the great Charles Dullin, to what end, dear Lord, I no longer had any idea.

"A little, in St-Boniface in Manitoba," I ventured at the back of the empty hall, which made my voice sound very hollow.

At this point someone onstage laughed, probably an extra. At me or perhaps my accent, I had the impression. Or perhaps at "St-Boniface in Manitoba," which may have sounded as comical as "Timbuctu in Mauretania" to Parisian ears.

"Come on then! Come up here!" Dullin-Volpone called. "You're going to do a little mime for us to show us what you can do, using your imagination. Anything at all. Whatever you like. Come along now!"

I would have chosen death at that moment, or at least torture on the rack, rather than go up there on the stage and do a pantomime. My throat was tight and there wasn't a drop of saliva in my mouth, yet I didn't dare cross the old tyrant who, I learned later, was in fact the most kind-hearted of men.

I might well have mounted to the stage even so. But then luckily – or unluckily, depending on one's point of view – the telephone rang offstage. Someone shouted, "Dullin, it's for you!" Dullin shouted to me, "Just a minute! I'll be back." Onstage, two other actors found some reason to turn their backs. Apparently there was still someone in the bed, a woman as far as I could tell, but for the time being she was quiet, now and then saying only, "*Oh la la! Oh la la!*" I threw a glance behind me. There was no one to block my way. The door was even open still. It made an embrasure framed in darkness, a little rectangle of tranquil street, almost pastoral, with a plane tree so close it seemed to be half inside the theatre. If I've retained such a sharp picture of this view of the street, it must be because I wanted so badly to be at liberty out there. I began with great caution to back away towards it. Then, hearing Dullin-Volpone raise his voice saying, "Ah yes, that's the way it goes. We'll talk again...," I moved more quickly. I reached the door. I stepped outside. In fact, I must confess, I fled.

I think I even ran for a bit as though in danger of being caught. At last I calmed down, only to realize that if I'd escaped by the skin of my teeth I couldn't escape my own self-judgement, which was savage. Now I was fleeing in earnest, walking and walking for hours without really knowing where I was going, just straight ahead. Madame Jouve was worried to see me come in so late. When she asked me where I could have got to I didn't know what to say.

The state of mind I'd been in would recur fairly frequently in my life. You run, either to lose yourself or to find yourself. It becomes so unbearable, I suppose, that it numbs your mind and leaves you only half aware of what's around you. I came home from Dullin's theatre in this condition. I didn't breathe a word of my adventure, and seeing my face no one dared ask me about it. And for a long time I tried to make myself believe it hadn't happened.

THE NEXT DAY I resumed my long walks through Paris, still with no plan in mind. A fact I had to face up to was that I hadn't fled the Atelier merely because I was terrified of getting up on the stage and giving a pantomime. Something bigger had taken me by the shoulders and pushed me out of there to save me from a destiny I wasn't suited for...a course that wasn't right for me. But then, if the theatre wasn't right for me, what was I doing in Paris? I think I learned then that a certain kind of lonesomeness is better left to itself than surrounded with advice and consolation. In the mass of strangers in the streets I disappeared with my misery about what I ought to be accomplishing in life, whatever that was. I tramped through whole districts of Paris feeling that I'd seen and heard absolutely nothing, enclosed in a kind of vacuum that I kept as tightly sealed as I could from the humanity pressing around me. The anguish I'd be exposed to otherwise would be just too great.

Years later, however, speech intonations, sounds, smells by the thousand would come back to me from these long walks. I'd see in precise detail a sign at a certain street corner, or the form of a taverner standing in the door of his bistro, beret pulled down over his brow. I had a faculty for storing away details that would be useful to me later, doing it unconsciously, blindly, one might say, thinking all the while that I'd come to Paris just to waste my time. In the long run wasting time has often proved to be its most profitable use for me, but I wasn't conscious of this either yet and kept berating myself bitterly.

BUT THERE were moments. One of those long walks took me to a street whose name I forget, where I looked up at the playbills outside a small theatre and met the beautiful, compassionate eyes of Ludmilla Pitoëff. I stopped to look longer. They were a little sad, the eyes of someone who knows about life, and as they returned my gaze I thought I saw the same warmth towards me that I instinctively felt towards her. Suddenly my indecision, my beating around the bush, my lack of clearheadedness about myself and my inability to get a grip on what I wanted seemed less ridiculous. Ludmilla Pitoëff's big, rather sorrowful eyes were telling me that she herself had known this kind of confusion, that none of us can ever be sure we won't find ourselves in such a state.

The playbill was announcing *The Seagull* by Chekhov. I knew Chekhov through his fine short stories, particularly "The Steppe". But I'd never heard of Georges and Ludmilla Pitoëff.

I'm not sure whether it was evening or still daylight. I seem to remember some bright foliage stirring gently near the beautiful face on the playbill, but I may only be associating a rustling sound with colour. In any event, as though someone had led me by the hand to this friendly little theatre, it was play time when I arrived. I went in. I bought my ticket. I sat down, part of a small, scattered audience. I was as much at ease in this theatre as I'd been apprehensive in Dullin's. The curtain rose. And I was enthralled.

To me this woman, this Ludmilla, wasn't an actress playing a role on a stage, interpreting a character. She *was* the Seagull, come to endure her lot in life before our eyes. Georges Pitoëff, his voice breaking and his face a weary mask, was simply a man, Russian or of any nationality, selected by chance from the overcrowded ranks of day-to-day monotony. Day-to-day existence lived and breathed here as never before, in fact, showing itself to be more powerful than the tumult of high drama, no doubt because it's so much closer to us. The words that gave it life were neither over-blown nor insignificant; they didn't even seem studied, though they must have been carefully chosen to sound so genuinely usual. You'd have said they were words any of us might say on any ordinary day, interspersed with sighs and silences just as in life, where a faraway look through a window suddenly says more than words. As soon as I've heard this ring of truth, how beautiful I've found it, whether in real life or in the theatre. Perhaps most of all in the theatre, which teaches us to look more perceptively at life, to see it laid bare before our eyes in clear daylight. Better than I could have done myself, I felt this performance expressing my own loneliness, my almost constant bewilderment wherever I was, our inability to understand ourselves, all seen through a fine mist of tears, not really bitter ones, almost sweet. Tears welled in my own eyes. I suppose they came from the curious happiness we feel at hearing ourselves expressed so perfectly.

At one point, as we often do when moved, instinctively trying to catch another eye in order to share an impression, I half turned towards a shy-looking young man beside me. Our eyes met and his were wet like mine. "Isn't it beautiful!" we both observed. And the joy that perhaps had brought as large a lump to his throat as to mine in the darkness and silence seemed now to set us free, to lift us in a kind of radiance.

Several times during the play we shared our feelings about it with a whispered word or simply a glance.

"That's what life is like for most people," he breathed in an undertone, simply, quietly, succinctly. "Chekhov's great talent is that he gives life to characters who don't stand out much in a crowd."

At intermission we went outside and walked a little together in front of the theatre. Recalling this, I know beyond possible doubt that it was afternoon, because at the end of the short street I can suddenly and quite distinctly see the tree whose rustling I've been hearing all this time. Still, there are extraordinary blanks in my memory. For example, I really can't picture the young man's face but I can hear him very clearly, always close, speaking in a voice that matched our rather hesitant steps.

He'd come from a village in the Ardèche to study literature at the Sorbonne. He wasn't adapting well to Paris. Until now he'd been feeling absolutely alone here, but he'd recognized himself in Chekhov's world almost as if he were at home.

Then I told him a bit about St-Boniface and how I had dreamed for so long while there of coming to Paris but now had no idea why, which made me hate it.

"That happens to everybody, though," he said.

A bell rang calling us back to our places. The lights went out. Once again we were caught up in the sweet magic of what was really most ordinary. We looked at each other in the darkness several times again, our eyes sometimes moist, sometimes shining with the beautiful things we were hearing. In two and a half hours the stranger beside me became closer to me than almost anyone I'd known before. Did he in his loneliness find me as miraculously close to him?

There was another brief pause in the performance, during which we resumed our conversation.

"How is it," I said, "that a voice that's really as tragic as Chekhov's is so comforting?"

"Because it tells the truth," he replied softly, "and the truth, even if it's tragic, even if it's cruel, is always more comforting than illusions or lies."

When we left we walked a little more together, along with a small crowd of playgoers which quickly dispersed.

With his head on one side he said, "That's the way writing should be, neither louder nor softer. Chekhov found just the note to touch the soul. All his words have their source in a human being's sensitivity. There isn't one that's pretentious. Not one that's false."

"It can't be easy to do," I said. "Why is saying what's true the hardest thing in the world?"

"It is indeed," he replied. "When we start writing we all tend to inflate our voices, try to impress, make ourselves something we aren't. The right note...perhaps one has to have searched all one's life only to find it in the end...."

At this point our hands moved shyly, perhaps as if to join, but a passerby brushed between us, thrusting us apart.

We came to my bus stop. He was going to continue on foot, back to his "hole in the wall" nearby. When I stopped he hesitated

a moment, seeming to be on the point of suggesting something...perhaps just that I might walk a bit farther with him in the
softly approaching darkness. I wanted this more than anything
else, but he lifted his hat and wished me good luck in Paris and in
life...then drew away as if reluctantly. A little farther on, however,
he stopped and turned. I was still waiting in line to get on the bus.
Our eyes met one last time. No doubt too shy to come back, he
raised his hand in a kind of wave and I replied with an equally
mournful gesture. He walked on and soon disappeared among the
other people in the street. One would have said that Chekhov,
having brought us together, had doomed us to the fate of so many
of his characters, vacillating, lost in indecision, incapable of reaching
out unreservedly to one another with a spontaneity that would set
them free.

IV

I NEVER KNEW where I stood with Paris, the cat-city, as Ionesco so aptly called it. One day for no reason at all it would bare its claws and scratch me, and the next it would touch me with a kittenish paw, equally without reason, just because summer was lingering or the sky was kind. I might be rankling from some rebuff when it would disarm me with a toothless smile from an old crone in carpet slippers or the sight of so many flowers on display. I might be warming to it and beginning to think I was happy when I'd get one of those rebukes that so many Parisians use so devastatingly.

Even so, I can't ever forget that I made my first important discovery about myself in Paris; I've never totally lost sight of this.

That day there had been nothing to prepare me for it. I was coming home joylessly in a crowded bus. It was rush hour. Exhausted, the little people of Paris were congregating in weary columns or tight little clusters at almost every bus stop. I followed my compatriot's advice and took a number from the machine. I still don't know if the right it gave was "priority" or "precedence", but "precedence" fits the situation so well I can't help liking it better. I'd no sooner taken my ticket than I realized I was on the wrong side of the street – my bus was just then drawing up on the opposite side. A dense crowd milled about, the conductor standing on the bus platform shouting "Number?" and everybody shouting a number in answer. Each time I saw this incredible scene replayed I was stupefied, but also filled with a kind of admiration to think that every day in Paris little courts of justice held sway in hundreds of places at once, the conductor filling the role of referee, dispenser of justice, and sermonizer, and the injured parties consisting of pregnant women, wounded war veterans, mothers with babes in arms, unaccompanied old folk, and a few malingerers. All of which, of course, did nothing to improve the bus service.

Without a second thought I bounded across the street and joined the harassed little crowd. The conductor called, "Sixty-eight.... Is there anyone before that?" To which a weak voice replied, straining to be heard from the back, "Sixty-five." "Sixty-five...," bawled the conductor. Then came my call, triumphant in the certainty that for once I was a winner: "Seventeen!" "Seventeen!" exclaimed the conductor. "Make way, *m'sieurs-dames*. Come forward, seventeen." The crowd, suitably impressed, parted as it might have for the maimed and halt. Mine was the last available place, standing shoulder to shoulder with others on the bus platform. The conductor fastened a light rope across the rear entrance, which I imagine was supposed to keep us from tipping off at corners. Suddenly intrigued, he held out his hand and took my number.

"Well I never!" he cried, choking with indignation. "I should have thought as much!" he turned to my fellow passengers, saying, "Some people think they're clever. They go and take a number on the other side of the street, then come and get in the crowd on this side. Is that right now?" The passengers he was addressing gave me a vaguely disapproving look, then left me to my fate. He continued, addressing me directly: "You deserve to be put off, little lady. If you ever do that again you won't get off so lightly, make sure you get that into your head!" I did my best to shrink out of sight in the mass of humanity, but he kept his eyes on me and persisted, "They begin one day by taking a place from some poor mother who's hurrying home to put on the soup, then the next...." As I raised my eyes to him in supplication, to my astonishment he winked at me and carried right on in the same indignant tone, "then the next, it's from one of our country's war heroes...." Backs weary, shoulders jostling other shoulders, faces vacant, the passengers paid no more heed to his harangue than to the buzzing of a fly. Finally he wearied of it himself and seemed to drift away in reverie for a while, gazing at a patch of sky far behind the bus.

From the moment I ran across the street the entire little scene had taken perhaps three or four minutes, but to me it had seemed interminable and it had left my nerves tied in a large knot. Little by little, however, I began to feel better, lulled by the rocking of the bus and perhaps yielding to the contagion of my neighbours' drowsiness. You'd swear some were asleep on their feet, eyes open but heads empty of thought.

We were arriving at the Place de la Concorde. I craned my neck, trying to catch at least a glimpse between the close-packed heads and shoulders. The stately square had come to represent what I valued most about Paris. It was like a piece of my native prairie, for which my soul yearned deeply here. Its broad expanse in the heart of the cramped city always brought me peace. I would suddenly have a feeling of relief. And the stone statuary enclosing the space perhaps made it seem even bigger and more open. I had never crossed it without beginning to picture what it would be like in a driving, swirling Canadian snowstorm. I used to imagine how beautiful it would be to watch the progress of the white furor.

Peering between the close-packed heads, I'd caught my glimpse of this marvellous space. Then while the bus took a sharp turn which would have flung us on top of each other if we hadn't been packed so tightly, I had a fleeting view of the Tuileries Gardens. As brief as it was, it showed me the pond with children playing around it, the impeccable rows of round-headed chestnut trees, and down at the far, far end, a fiery red sky, extending the space to infinity. It was just like the flaming sunsets at the end of the lane behind the house on Deschambault Street when I was a child, which opened a path I was sure must reach the edge of the world. An incandescent ray from the far horizon even touched my face. It moved me so deeply I turned to see its reflection on the faces around me, forgetting I'd been an object of scorn in their midst only minutes before. Weariness and gloom were all I saw, preoccupation with cares or the bad news in an open newspaper. Apparently no one else had seen the glorious display of sunset at its most intense. In that instant the city had revealed itself to me, the eager stranger, not to its own with their jaded eyes. And I, marvel as I might, didn't know what to do with it. I would need to marvel many more times yet, uselessly one could say, before learning how to share my wonder with others.

What I can't forget is that seeing the beautiful garden of Paris illuminated by a sun straight from my prairies made me realize I had a faculty for observation I hadn't really been aware of before, together with an infinite longing to know what to do with it.

AFTER MY misadventure at Dullin's Atelier, I can hardly believe I could still have imagined I was cut out for the theatre and kept trying to involve myself in it. I must have been very hard of hearing. Or else I was obeying some vague directive to make sure that all doors were closed to me in this direction, thus forcing me to turn finally to the right one. Whichever it was, shortly after my heady afternoon of Chekhov I wrote a long, rather overwrought letter to Ludmilla Pitoëff, like the ones I quite often get nowadays from bewildered young people who don't really know what to expect of themselves or of life. Into it I poured my admiration for her talent, my own disarray, and the doubts and indecision I was living with; a kind of plea for help, in fact. The effort I put into it no doubt cured me for ever of writing this kind of letter, for I don't remember ever again writing to a stranger in the hope of receiving my salvation.

When I'd finished my letter I hurried to the theatre and left it with the cashier, terrified I'd tear it up if I allowed myself a moment of reflection, I suppose. When the cashier asked if I'd like to wait for a reply, since Madame Pitoëff happened to be inside just then, I shook my head in alarm and fled with almost as much haste as I had from Dullin's.

What was I most afraid of, a rebuff or an invitation? Now that I understand myself better I think I was really hoping for a rebuff – or silence – which would have protected me from trying anything else of the kind, letting me believe that I'd done everything possible and that if I'd failed it wasn't my doing but because of adverse circumstances. In short, I was letting my fate be decided by events, a weakness in my nature which has shown itself too often in the course of my life.

When I'd deposited my letter and scurried away, I wandered this way and that once again, still wallowing in my uncertainties. As I had so many times before, I came finally to the Luxembourg Gardens, not far from Madame Jouve's. Near exhaustion, I would often sit down among the old women who used to come there with their knitting, occupying the same chairs day after day. I would also see the same children day after day, engrossed in sailing their frail little paper boats. This tranquil pause in the heart of the high-strung city used to soothe me almost without fail. But this time nothing could soothe me.

THE MINUTE I set foot in the apartment Madame Jouve rushed to meet me in great excitement.

"Where were you? We've been looking for you for hours! Madame Pitoëff's personal secretary has called twice. She finally left a message and I wrote it down. Here, on this piece of paper.... Tomorrow at rehearsal time you're to come to this theatre. Madame Pitoëff will see you."

Was I happy? Or apprehensive? I don't really know any more.

The next day I arrived at the Pitoëffs' theatre in a very odd frame of mind, ecstatic that Madame Ludmilla was willing to see me but also worried sick over what I was going to have to confess to her.

She was in the middle of rehearsing *La Sauvage* by Anouilh, another author she played a great deal, I believe. As soon as she'd been told I was there she broke off the rehearsal and came down from the stage to where I was sitting in the empty theatre. She smiled as she sat down in the next seat. In the half-darkness I saw her small, delicate face searching mine. She told me she'd been very moved by my letter. So had Georges. When they'd read it again last evening they'd both felt very warmly towards the little French-speaking provinces in the heart of faraway Canada, where the people were still struggling so hard not to lose their fragile bond with France. They'd like to help me, give me guidance if I wanted, but they didn't take students. However, they were prepared to let me attend rehearsals as often as I liked, so that I'd gradually learn at least how a play is produced. Would this be of some use? Did I think I'd benefit from it?

Disconcerted, I remained silent. She asked me then what exactly it was I wanted.

What exactly I wanted. That was the trouble! The further I went the less I seemed to know. Even now when Madame Ludmilla was being so kind, offering me a rare opportunity in the theatre, I was racked with anxiety, still not knowing whether I should or should not accept. In the half-darkness she must have seen signs in my face of the torment you feel when you can't see any way clear ahead of you – in contrast to the courage you have when your course is visible, however difficult it looks. Impulsively she put her hand on mine and gave it a sympathetic squeeze.

"Poor child! Of course you don't know! How could you when you've just arrived in this big seething city from your faraway

St-Boniface! I felt lost here myself for such a long time. Lost...
lost...," she repeated plaintively as if she'd never forgotten the
horror. "Even now, if it weren't for Georges and the children...."

She paused, remembering some difficult hurdles she'd crossed,
I think, then came back to her suggestion.

"Come to rehearsals anyway in the meantime. Even if you don't
yet know what you want, they might help you find out. You'll see
your way come clear little by little, believe me."

WITH THE HOPE she'd inspired in me that I really would see my
way clear eventually, I came to rehearsals...eight, ten, a dozen
times. I don't know how many. I was faithful at first in any case.

I always sat more or less in the same place in the middle of the
empty hall. I'd see the actors moving about the stage reading their
cues and probably their movements from little notebooks each held.
Now and then I'd hear Georges admonishing Ludmilla, "No, no,
love, not like that. Listen, you have to get more inside the character...." Try as I might to follow it all and take an interest, I
became depressed. Nearly deserted theatres have always depressed
me with their actors in street clothes groping earnestly for their
characters, and ropes, pulleys, and all the paraphernalia of a play
in plain view. Never would even a very clumsy attempt at writing
bring me such a desolate feeling, perhaps basically because there's
so much less paraphernalia involved in writing than in the theatre,
or else it's a different, subtler kind you hardly notice. But most
distressing of all was discovering such a contrived reverse side, so
to speak, of what I'd found so convincing and wondrous. I might
even like Chekhov less, I thought, if I saw him taken apart and
slowed down this way.

One day I skipped the rehearsal and two days later I skipped it
again and spent the time instead with my old women in the Luxembourg Gardens. With great relief I sat listening to them talking
about everyday things among themselves over their knitting. The
more I saw of the theatre, the more I was drawn by people's simple,
everyday lives and their everyday language; it was so full of rich
discoveries, all so alive and real. Though I didn't realize it, I was
approaching what would prove to be the right, the only school for
me.

I skipped another rehearsal. After that I was afraid to come face

231

to face with Ludmilla. To escape Madame Jouve's remonstrances I'd go out at the same hours to make it look as though I were going to my rehearsals, but what I was doing was wandering aimlessly about the city. Aimlessly? Not entirely, perhaps, for without conscious effort but with increasing attention I was eavesdropping from door to door, from chair to chair, listening to the voices that tell us about life. But I still couldn't see the way ahead of me any more clearly.

V

AUTUMN IN PARIS was radiant. At least I had mild weather, a kindly sky, and warm rays of sunshine wherever I went. My little beige suit of warm wool with a matching cape to throw around my shoulders in the cooler hours had so far been adequate for my daytime and evening rambles. It became cold late in October, however, and I went to the basement to get my three-quarter-length coat of rabbit fur dyed to look like otter from my trunk. Remembering the problems with the timed lights on my first descent below ground, I borrowed a flashlight from Madame Jouve. It may seem strange that I'd left my trunk alone in its dungeon with such misgiving and then let six weeks go by without going to make sure it was still there. But this was the way it was. Learning to cope with Paris, my persistent uncertainty over what I should be studying, my recurrent, agonizing suspicion that I had no talent and had been deceiving myself with hopes of expanded horizons, all this had so obsessed me that I was spared all other worries.

I walked along the earth-floored corridor with my flashlight beam reaching only a short way ahead of me. This time it was the silence of these cellars which most unnerved me; it was so total I could hear myself breathe. I came to Madame Jouve's locker. Immediately the catastrophe was apparent. The padlock was partly torn off and the iron-barred door was wide open. And my trunk wasn't there! I drew back in dismay. I made sure the number was the right one. No doubt about it, my trunk had been stolen!

I ran back upstairs, raised Madame Jouve, who was perhaps in the middle of a French lesson, and told her the news in a panic-stricken voice which probably everyone in the apartment could hear. Madame Jouve took me aside, begging me to lower my voice so as not to alarm the other boarders and to try to calm down.

Nevertheless, she went at once to get her coat and set off with me for the police station.

As we rode on the bus, Madame Jouve asked me over and over, "You're quite sure you found the door open? You're sure it was your trunk that was missing?"

The constable who interviewed us listened to Madame Jouve explain why we'd come. Then he handed me a long sheet of paper and an old-fashioned pen and sat me down at a bare table.

"Mademoiselle," he instructed me, "write on this paper the entire list of contents of the trunk you declare to have been stolen."

"The list of all there was in my trunk?" I cried in extreme dismay. "That's impossible! It'll take me hours and hours, just trying to remember!"

"To whatever extent possible," he insisted severely.

I sat down, like a suspect about to be interrogated, under a bare, weak lightbulb hanging by its wire from the ceiling. At the long prisoners' table, my bad pen-nib tearing at the paper, I began to write: one coat, rabbit fur dyed dark brown, one navy-blue suit with silver buttons, two pairs of shoes, one brown, one blue to go with the suit.... As the list lengthened, I felt myself sinking into a depression which this time seemed bottomless. I think the reason was less that my clothes had been stolen than discovering suddenly that things I'd paid dearly for, considering my means, weren't really worth much, a pauper's frippery, but they were all I possessed.

As I sat writing, an argument of some kind arose between the constable and Madame Jouve. He was inscribing her replies to his questions and when he'd come to my address Madame Jouve had replied, "With me, at number...."

"So," he concluded, "I'll put you down as landlady."

"Not at all!" protested Madame Jouve. "I'm not a landlady."

At first I didn't pay much attention. I'd just remembered a beautiful little pale ivory satin collar. I'd bought it to brighten up a dark dress one day when I needed to restore my spirits by splurging a bit. Maman, as soon as she examined it, knew it was expensive and demanded almost angrily, "How much did you pay for this? Too much, I'm sure." I was ashamed of being extravagant when she had so little for running the house and I didn't dare tell her. "How much?" she insisted. In the end I told her, shrinking the figure a mite, "Three dollars." She turned pale. "Three dollars!

When I could have made you one just as lovely for less than half the price!''

The incident was one I would have liked to blot out of my life. The reproach, forgotten then brought so vividly to life again, was holding me motionless, pen poised, gazing gloomily into the distance, when I became aware that the constable and Madame Jouve were still arguing.

"You take in boarders and you're not a landlady?"

"I have guests...."

They now had my attention. I turned my head to them. Madame Jouve so detested the taint of commercialism that she used to ask us to have our correspondents address their letters "care of Madame Jouve."

"I am not a landlady, Monsieur!" I heard her say with some heat.

"Yet you've just told me the young lady boards with you. Does she board with you or doesn't she?"

"In a sense, if you like," Madame Jouve allowed, "but I'm not her landlady. I'm responsible for these young ladies. I give them guidance in their studies...."

"And you're going to tell me you do all that for nothing?"

Absorbed though I was with my own distress, I almost pitied Madame Jouve as she fought tooth and nail not to have the abhorrent word appear in the record as her occupation. I felt for her. She had pride. She was making a living in a courageous way, giving a great deal of herself, and she really was far more to us than merely our landlady. But she was trapped, as I had also been so many times, by the merciless logic of the French.

"My young ladies give me something for their meals and their share of the rent, of course, but I don't so much give them board and lodging as...."

"Mademoiselle," the constable said to me, "do you board at Madame Jouve's?"

"I live at Madame Jouve's."

"For nothing? The way you would at your aunt's?"

"Not for nothing...exactly...."

"So you pay for your room and board, you board at Madame Jouve's, therefore Madame Jouve is your landlady, there are no two ways about it. What are you then, Madame, if not a landlady?"

"Oh, for heaven's sake!" exclaimed Madame Jouve with a contained kind of disgust, "You can put me down as former teacher, Lycée..., titular professor of French at the University of...."

She stopped, too aggrieved to keep up the fight.

"All right then, Monsieur, put down 'landlady' if you don't know any better."

"The question is not what you have been or could be, Madame, if you'll forgive me, but what your present occupation is for the record."

I left them to their argument, which didn't seem about to end, and turned back to my list. Now I wasn't sure I'd brought the little ivory satin collar after all. Perhaps I'd forgotten it or decided to leave it at home. At home? Somewhere behind, that meant. Then suddenly I remembered my medals. I'd brought all of them with me in the trunk.

Walls and passage of time at once disappeared. I was far away from Paris. The journey hadn't taken place. I was still safe and sound in St-Boniface. I hadn't yet caused any grief for anyone. It was months before I was due to leave but I already had my trunk and was so delighted I couldn't resist putting some of my things in it already. Maman must have looked now and then when I wasn't there to see what I'd packed. One day she confronted me, very agitated, her finger raised in accusation.

"You're going to take your medals over there! Why? What good are they going to do you in Paris? You'll have them stolen!"

I held my ground.

"But why? Why?"

I couldn't tell her what I had in mind, of course: the medals were gold and if I fell on really hard times in Paris I could always sell them to keep body and sold together for a while, until....

She raised the subject a hundred times over.

"Leave them with me so I can take care of them."

I was just as obstinate, not even trying to understand why she was so determined to keep them.

"What good will they be to you?" I always retorted.

Now, at the other side of the world, I had the answer to this silly question and was filled with remorse for being so stupid. With the medals lost Maman's reward was lost and also, in a way, the special joy I'd been to her.

"Why, oh why didn't I leave my medals at home!" I groaned aloud, forgetting for the moment where I was.

The argument between the constable and Madame Jouve came abruptly to an end. They both looked at me in consternation, their faces keenly sympathetic.

"Your medals! Lost! Oh my poor child!" Madame Jouve cried with feeling.

The constable's manner was now fatherly and he studied me with a kind of friendly but sorrowful expression. Perhaps he had a daughter who'd also won medals, who was his pride and joy....

"Medals meaning prizes for achievement, for good conduct...?" he asked in a solicitous, almost familiar tone.

"Yes, and for history and literature and French...."

"For French! In a country that's all English! Just think of that! Mademoiselle must have been quite a student!"

"Mademoiselle," put in Madame Jouve, "has remained faithful to the language of France in faraway America with a perseverance that deserves our admiration." Afflicted as I already was with remorse, her pride in me left me more disconsolate than ever.

The constable approached and put his hand on my shoulder.

"We'll find your medals for you, Mademoiselle," he said. "Just let me get my hands on whoever took them and he'll pay for it!"

The most extraordinary part of the story is that he did indeed get his hands on the thief, a boy of fifteen who, when he saw he was caught, panicked and tried to dispose of the medals by throwing them through a sewer grate. So their fate was to travel the same course I'd seen in my crazy nightmares of subterranean adventure on my first night in Paris, perhaps stirred up partly because I had left my trunk all alone in its dungeon.

I learned the epilogue only a year later when I was passing through Paris on my return from London.

AFTER I'D REFLECTED on the matter, it occurred to me that the trunk couldn't have been taken out of the building without the watchman's knowledge. By day, when the iron gate was open, he watched constantly from his cubicle beside it. At night he had to come from his room to open it. So I went down and asked him whether he'd seen anyone going out with my trunk.

"Your beautiful trunk from America? Never! I'd have known

it! There isn't another one like it in the whole neighbourhood. It can't have left here, Mademoiselle."

So it was just as I'd thought since I'd decided to do my own investigation. I borrowed Madame Jouve's flashlight and went to the basement. Perhaps a hundred feet beyond our own locker, inside another with its door open, I discovered my trunk, lying on its side, the lock broken, the drawers pulled out, and my belongings strewn about the floor. They were all there too, except my medals and the little jewel box Fernand had given me. In a way losing this hurt almost as much as losing my medals. I went back upstairs, feeling a little better to have recovered my fur coat and some other badly needed clothes and probably pleased besides to have been more expeditious than the police – which wasn't so hard in cases of petty thievery like this.

Madame Jouve, however, was disturbed by my sleuthing. It was her understanding that having signed a complaint at the police station I had no right to retake possession of my things, even though I'd recovered them myself. I groused but eventually had to go back to the police station and cross virtually everything off my patiently detailed list except item: gold medals and item: jewel box.

The poor little jewel box thus achieved a kind of immortality because as far as I know it's still recorded on some slip in the records of the Paris police. I was sharply reprimanded by the constable on duty that day moreover for having regained possession of my goods without police authorization, which made me liable to a fine, but more particularly, I think, for having been ahead of the police with my investigation below ground.

Perhaps I'd become thick-skinned or was too preoccupied with my self-reproach, but in any case the constable's reproofs hardly bothered me at all. I suppose I was insulated from minor hurts by a deepening state of depression.

The real cause of my melancholy wasn't losing my medals; this episode merely made me conscious of being increasingly discontented since my flight from Dullin's theatre. Despite moments of elation such as I'd felt at seeing the transfiguration of the Tuileries Gardens, I was feeling more ill at ease in Paris all the time. It was becoming too much for me. I was sure I wouldn't achieve anything worthwhile here. I began to tell myself I'd probably come to the wrong place. London would perhaps be better.

I had spent a few days in London on my way to Paris in September, the loveliest time of the year, and now it seemed to me that those days had been sheer delight. I'd been shown around by a friend, a young and very talented violinist who'd come from Winnipeg to study at the Royal Academy of Music. This glimpse gave me enough to dream about for a long time. We saw Hyde Park, the lions in Trafalgar Square, Kew Gardens; we poled in a punt on the Thames to Hampton Court; in short, nothing outside the usual tourist circuit, at first anyway. Yet our recollections and persistent dreams are so dependent on first impressions that although the city rarely saw the light of a clear sky at the time, the London I remembered was tenderly sunny, everything bathed in the rosy colour of enchantment. The sun even seemed to be shining on the metopes and ancient Assyrian statues in the British Museum which my friend Bohdan took me to see.

Afterwards, it's true, we did find more of the really entrancing side of London. One evening we went to see *Tobias and the Angel* at the open-air theatre in Regent's Park, with accompaniment provided by the big cats in the zoo next door roaring in their cages, made nervous by an approaching storm. The minute a few drops of rain began to fall a hawker appeared, renting out sturdy woollen blankets at a shilling apiece. Bohdan took one, with which we made a kind of tent, sitting with our heads close and the blanket draped over them. Soon, with almost the whole audience sheltered similarly, the place looked like an encampment. Toby and his dog continued their peregrinations with the rain now falling heavily, seeming to be part of the production.

I felt that everything about my short sojourn in London had been charming and delightful. I told myself that if I was going to return to Manitoba later, as seemed inevitable, I'd do better to study in London than in Paris. Bohdan thought so. He had been writing me saying that I could enroll in a school of drama while taking private lessons in French from an excellent coach he'd been enquiring about for me. Good friend that he was, having read between the lines that I was getting discouraged, he was doing his best to help me with sensible advice. I think this influenced my decision, if one could call it a decision, for I was as restless as the waves of the ocean at the time.

In any event I made up my mind to return to London. Madame

Jouve did all she could to dissuade me. According to her, I was leaving just as I was beginning to settle in. It was pure madness. I was losing everything I'd gained. I was giving up just as my efforts were beginning to bear fruit. If I kept drifting about the world, as I seemed resigned to doing, I'd never amount to anything.

In one sense she was probably right, but not in another. From my gropings, my comings and goings, my aimless wanderings, I learned as I never would have from any straight line I might have followed through pure tenacity.

In November when it was cold, wet, and gloomy, as no doubt my whole life was going to be through my own fault, I embarked on the Calais-to-Dover ferry. The sky was thick with cloud and fog. As the small ship's propeller churned the dark water, gulls cried overhead, close but invisible, expressing so well the pain of departures, and of arrivals. In no time I lost sight of the coast of France. I thought I'd never return and it made me infinitely sadder than I could have imagined.

I would in fact return to France many times. Some of these occasions were the happiest in my life outside Canada; one, probably the best of all, has left me with a glowing memory – of receiving the major literary prize awarded less than ten years later for my first novel. Of these future occasions and the many dear and faithful friends I would make in France, I had no more premonition than I had had of what was awaiting me at the Little Water Hen.

I journeyed for a long time without a compass, but when life itself is the journey, what use is a compass?

VI

STILL WEAK from a devastating case of seasickness, I set foot in London in the worst fog the city had seen for years. Bohdan had found me a room on Wickendon Street in the working-class district of Fulham.

Again I headed towards the unknown with my belongings piled inside a taxi, including my trunk whose lock I'd had repaired after a fashion. We drove through what seemed to be an opaque, unyielding, dirt-coloured cloud. The city was identifiable only through sounds, so deafening in some districts you couldn't tell one from another, so furtive in others they made you think of a blind man feeling his way. The headlights of all the cars and buses were on, but they hardly penetrated the grimy atmosphere at all and looked far away when in fact you were already on top of them. The taxi-driver must have seen many other fogs like this but still took an hour to find Wickendon Street. Oddly, just as we were arriving the dense cloud thinned a little, even formed a kind of clearing around us for a few seconds. As if in a dream, I briefly saw a street of identical two-storey houses, all built of pinkish stone, all surrounded by what looked like reproductions of the same hedge of clipped holly, and in each bay window, identical to the one next door, the same green succulent plant. Then the fog closed again like a curtain across a stage. The street vanished. I wouldn't see it again for more than a week.

With some help from my landlady, Bohdan took my belongings to my room upstairs. He lit my gas heater to show me how it worked. You put a shilling in the slot in the meter, turned the key, and put a lighted match to the jet. This gave enough gas for several hours, after which you had to put another coin in the shilling-hungry slot. He thoughtfully left me a dozen shillings in case I might run out and suffer from the damp cold which, he said, I should beware of with my susceptible throat. Then he was already leaving, my arrival having come at the worst possible time for him. He'd just been asked to play at the Royal Albert Hall as guest soloist with the London Symphony Orchestra. His future depended on this concert and even if he worked night and day to prepare himself it wouldn't be enough.

"Cheerio! Everything's going to be fine here, you'll see. Poor beginnings always have fine endings."

He was courage itself. He'd left Winnipeg carrying his violin as his only possession. He worked his way over on a cattle boat, tending the animals, shut up with them in the hold in return for his passage. As soon as he reached London he'd found a job with a gypsy orchestra playing for diners in one of the big Lyon's restaurants. He spent his nights cheering the hearts of lonely people and his days practising Bach. When he had twenty-five dollars in his pocket, this being the price of a lesson, he'd seek out what he considered the best violin teacher in London. "Here I am," he would say, "I can pay you for an hour. God knows when I'll be able to afford another." Now, less than a year later, he was on the point of signing a contract with the BBC for a weekly hour-long program.

Yet it seems to me I'd always perceived a foreboding shadow over this frail but remarkably strong young man, this prodigious and tireless worker, who at times could be merrier than anyone else. But perhaps I'm just letting my memories of him be coloured by his tragic death during the war when a bomb burst over the house he was living in, killing all its occupants.

Since he was worried about me though I tried to appear calm and content, before leaving he hurriedly wrote down two or three telephone numbers where I might reach him in case I needed anything. He told me not to hesitate to call if I had the least problem.

I managed to pretend I was sure of myself until he left. But as soon as the door closed I felt as though I were shut away here, through my own fault. I went to the only window in the room which might, I thought, overlook a little garden. I wiped away the condensation but the abominable fog pressed close against the other side of the glass, blocking the view completely. I was perishing with cold only a few steps away from the gas fire. Before I could feel any heat on my legs I had to get almost close enough to burn myself, and then my back was freezing.

The silence around me was frightful. Apparently I was alone in this strange house except for the landlady, who'd gone back to her kitchen, and she never made the slightest sound to indicate her presence anyway, not even footsteps since she walked around in felt-soled slippers. Have I ever known a more appallingly silent house? No sound outside. No sound inside. Towards evening I heard someone come in very quietly, then perhaps someone else. Footsteps glided towards neighbouring rooms. Water ran. After this I heard nothing more.

I spotted a little teapot in its tea-cosy near the gas fire. On the mantelpiece there was some tea in a tin box, sugar in another, and of course the inevitable dry biscuits in a tin with a rose-covered, thatched Tudor cottage on the lid.

I lit a gas hot-plate beside the fireplace. A short flame sprang up. I put on the kettle. In answer to the sputtering of the gas there was soon a hum from the kettle as the water began to heat. I began to hope the kettle would whistle, in this country a sign of pleasure to come. It didn't whistle. I drank the first of those countless cups of insipid tea that I would make for myself at all hours of the day for weeks on end, perhaps in an effort to warm my body, or my soul.

I sat on the floor as close as I could to the meagre flame in the fireplace, taking what little help it offered. I felt like a lonely castaway on a desert island in the middle of a white sea which had itself lost all memory of familiar shores. My thoughts went no further than this. I think I soon stopped having thoughts at all. At times, when I've been too completely isolated, hemmed in by too much silence, I've lost even the sense of thinking, as though the frail mechanism of thought — surely always an appeal to others — had jammed somewhere inside me.

HOW LONG WAS I absent this time? A week? Ten days? Two weeks? I lived in a kind of lethargy which I was careful not to break, in terror of letting in some waiting torment. But if I huddled close to my wretched little fire, which I fed with shillings to keep it going, my curious, nameless state of misery was almost bearable. I saw no one and spoke to no one except my landlady.

Early in the morning, an hour when I've never in my life had much appetite, she would enter bringing an unbelievable breakfast consisting of a mountain of pieces of toast – plus the rest of the loaf to slice myself in case I didn't have enough – a pot of marmalade and another of gooseberry jam, butter, cheese, and either eggs and bacon with fried potatoes, or an omelette, boiled eggs, or a fried herring, whose smell alone turned my stomach. The tray was laden further with an enormous pot of tea big enough for at least six cups and a large jug of hot water. She would put it on a small table near the bed, go to the window and open the curtains a little, give a perfunctory glance outside and say, "Foggy again today," then leave. She'd return to get the tray an hour later and finding it almost invariably untouched would comment briefly, neither sympathetically nor disapprovingly, "You don't eat much." At the time of day when I was hungry, she'd return again with a thin slice of ham, a small slice of bread, and nothing else and tell me, always in the same flat, expressionless voice, "You should learn to eat a good breakfast, for in London we don't serve much lunch. But have it your own way."

So in the end I learned to hide some of the excess breakfast to keep for later when I felt like eating. I had caches in the cupboard among my shoes, behind the gas fire, even in my bed, and soon I observed I'd collected enough to eat for the whole day. My landlady, seeing the bread, cheese, and some of the jam and butter gone from the tray, expressed approval with as little feeling as she'd reproached me.

"I see you're eating a sensible breakfast at last."

The next day she added a bowl of porridge and jug of milk to the tray.

I would look at this woman in her drab-coloured clothes, her hair in a hairnet, listen to her saying the same dull things in the same dispassionate voice day after day, and wonder if she was a real person with emotions, senses, hopes, and fears, or if I had an automaton for a landlady.

The rooms around mine really were inhabited, at least in the evening when their occupants came in. I'd listen for sounds that would tell me of human activity. I'd faintly hear a key turning in the front doorlock, almost inaudible footsteps coming up the stairs, another, lighter key-in-lock sound at the door of a room, and this was all. In their slippers with their tea made, for the rest of the evening the people around me must all have been warming themselves alone at their own miserable little fires, just as I was. I didn't see any of them for nearly a whole week.

It took nothing less than finding myself with my fire out and no shillings left to give me the energy to leave my room at last and go looking for my landlady.

Then, in this house which I'd thought must be half dead, I came to a room that was warm and inviting. A stove was purring. From its oven there rose a delectable smell of roast beef with a pan of Yorkshire pudding, though my landlady had said she made only one meal a day and that was breakfast. There was a man ensconced near the stove, the husband probably, which surprised me because I'd never heard a man's voice in this house. She didn't introduce us. He lowered the paper he was reading just a little and said in the same tone of voice as his wife's, neither warm nor cold, just totally impersonal:

"Evening, Miss," then turned back to his paper.

"How many shillings do you want?" asked the woman.

I'd come downstairs with a one-pound note.

Her only comment was, "That should last you a good long time."

Not as long as all that, I thought, looking enviously at the friendly little stove with its firebox filled with coke. But since neither of them invited me to sit down even for a moment, I went back up to my room. In a city where I'd soon find the most naturally warm, friendly, and talkative people in the world, I had to fall first upon this dour couple and London's most silent house. How often in my life I've first encountered the repellent side of cities, situations, and people! This has been an advantage in a sense because then I could only find things getting better, not worse. Keeping what's good until last has often meant that this is the only memory I'm left with.

One evening I made myself go out. The fog was still as dense as ever. However, I told myself that if I followed the low holly hedges by the sidewalk I could reach the end of the street without getting lost. When I arrived I'd seen a cluster of small shops there, even an Underground station. A glow of illuminated shopfronts, diluting the fog to a slightly thinner consistency, told me I had arrived. I pushed open a fairly well-lit door and found myself in one of the ABC chain of tea and pastry shops. I didn't have much desire for more tea but I ordered some anyway, with a sticky bun. Here, at least I was eating in the company of a scattering of customers talking among themselves at their tables, and I still remember the comfort I felt in this little bit of human warmth. The sound of voices and the sight of pleasant-looking faces made me feel so much better that I hated to leave.

Finally I was the only customer left and thought I should go. I set off in the direction I'd come from. After a few steps there was no longer any light to guide me and I realized it was going to be impossible to find "my" house. They were already so alike by day, even down to their identical little gardens, how was one to know which was which at night in dense fog except by their numbers? But the numbers were over the doors and I couldn't see them. I'd go up to a door and look carefully, then stand on tiptoe and strike a match. All I could ever see, if anything, was part of a number.

I wandered from door to door, feeling the way I'd felt in the Gare Saint-Lazare, that I'd never find my way out of this impasse. Once again my weary spirit formed a picture of what life was going to be like for me in Paris, London, or anywhere else.

Suddenly I heard a man's footsteps. Danger? Salvation? One of those muggers I'd been warned about so often who prey on women alone in the fog? But perhaps a Good Samaritan! "Help!" I called. A voice replied, "Coming!" and almost immediately a ruddy-faced bobby appeared, identifying himself with his powerful flashlight.

"Lost, Miss? And a mean night 'tis to be lost in!"

He had a pleasant, open face as far as I could see, but what struck me instantly and forcefully was his speech: old world, colourful, and extremely literary. Time and again in England I would be surprised how often I'd hear such speech from the lips of people who were most unlikely to be avid readers or literary buffs. Where could they have found these uncommon words, these metaphoric terms, this almost Shakespearean cadence?

I can still hear this bobby's "mean night" through the foggy darkness, as if resonating under a low ceiling in some make-believe theatre.

"A mean night to be in. And all the houses being practically the same, 'tis hard indeed to find one's own. And what would your number be, would you know that much, Miss?"

Yes, happily I knew that much. Number 72. I've never forgotten it.

We walked along, the bobby aiming his flashlight beam at the numbers from time to time.

Finally he announced, "Here we are, Miss, safe and sound at your very door! May you have a fine sleep. And pleasant dreams as well."

Such was the first friend I made in London. Often still on a foggy night wherever I am, in a far corner of my memory I see a face in a halo of light and hear a solemn voice wishing me a fine sleep and pleasant dreams.

FOR A FEW DAYS more, however, I nurtured my homesickness, my bewilderment, my fear of the great city, and probably my shame at having given in so completely. Fortunately I've always had another self to tell me off, laugh at me if need be. One evening it spoke to me over my shoulder.

"This is the limit!" I can hear it saying. "Here you are in one of the most exciting cities in the world. At this very moment the curtain is about to rise on hundreds of stages; audiences will be enthralled by the words of great playwrights, lifted on the wings of music, and here you are squatting by your silly little fire feeling sorry for yourself. Really worth all the effort to chuck what you thought was such an insignificant existence in Manitoba, isn't it?"

It was as though I'd been slapped. I looked at my watch. It was only seven-thirty. I grabbed my coat. I clattered down the stairs I'd undoubtedly crept down like everyone else until then. I think I even slammed the door. I tied a white handkerchief firmly to a shrub just behind the holly hedge to serve as a marker when I came home. To make sure, I counted the number of doors from Number 72 to the cluster of small shops. There were twenty-eight. The fog seemed thinner, too, as if about to lift.

I took the Underground and was glad to be with some fellow humans, even the most total strangers. I must have come out at Piccadilly Circus because I remember the signs of theatres and movie houses, the garlands of twinkling lights, all the light on every side overcoming the fog so completely that you saw only wisps of it here and there. In those days it was said that Piccadilly Circus was the crossroads of the world. It must have been true because in the few minutes I stayed at the exit from the Underground, rooted in surprise, I saw a beggar in unspeakable rags straight out of Dickens, a man of rank with a gold-headed cane and black cape lined with white satin, an eccentric lady, probably from Park Lane, clad all in feathers like an exotic bird, a ferocious-looking Sikh, a tattooed sailor, a Highlander in a kilt, some Arabs in turbans, and what I imagine was an Indian princess with a star – or was it a circle? – painted on her forehead. Such an array of faces and forms that I stood transfixed on those steps as though at the edge of Plato's cave watching chimeras come to life before my very eyes. Even today I have trouble separating later impressions of this city I was to grow to love so much from the rich, crazy, sumptuous sight it offered me that night as I emerged from below ground. In London, and in Paris too for that matter, the most marvellous show of all to me was always the one presented by the city itself, on its terraces, strolling its boulevards, or circulating round and round as here, like some unbelievable carousel of improbable humanity in every shape and form.

WHAT PLAY did I see that night? Not *A Midsummer Night's Dream* because that was with Vivien Leigh, still very young, at the Old Vic, which is in quite another part of London. *The Three Sisters* perhaps, or Stravinsky's ballet *The Firebird*. It doesn't matter. I didn't really see anything mediocre in London. I found what was best, instinctively no doubt, and also wisely counselled by Bohdan, who sometimes left a note on his way by and occasionally some tickets he'd been given.

I came back from Piccadilly Circus my head abuzz with images and sounds, though this didn't for a minute hide the fact that I was alone with a wealth of impressions that I would have loved to share with someone. I found my little marker tied to its shrub, dripping with water from the fog. I went up to my room without a single door opening as I passed. I might have not gone out or not come back and no one would have known the difference.

The next day I told myself I'd fiddled enough and while I still had momentum I went at once to enrol at the Guildhall School of Music and Drama; Bohdan had obtained all the information I needed and had been urging me to make a decision. I was obliged to take the complete course in drama from makeup lessons to fencing and tap dancing as well as the actual study of plays. I had to pay cash in the first term, which made an enormous dent in the small balance I had in the bank. It didn't matter. I'd come to a point where I felt I had to launch myself in some direction at all costs, even a wrong one, in order to find out at last what I needed to know about myself.

I CAN'T RECALL exactly where the school was. Another blank in my memory! It couldn't have been far from the Thames because I remember finding myself beside the river every time I had a moment of freedom after or between classes.

I can picture myself walking endlessly along the embankments on days when I had nothing special to do. I walked from Blackfriars all the way to Big Ben more than once. Several times I even ventured farther east, towards the docks and the bustling seagoing life of the Thames, which fascinated me. I went by river launch to Greenwich and down to the estuary. I became attached to that river as I've been to very few people in this world. I loved it when it shimmered in the sun, as on one of the times I punted upstream with friends as far as Hampton Court, Cardinal Wolsey's palace until he was forced to give it up to Henry VIII – Hampton Court of such terrible memory, today a destination for picnickers with its black swans and thick green lawns. Little floating shops went back and forth constantly on the river. If we waved they'd come alongside and we'd buy tea or sandwiches before continuing on our course. I loved the Thames of these cheery, simple-hearted outings but even more I loved the Thames of misty nights with muffled cries of gulls, faint lappings of water against ancient stonework, and the muted bleat of foghorns barely reaching the embankment. Often I'd stay for hours, leaning on the parapet, trying to guess from the sounds what was going on behind the pall of fog. Or simply lost in some reverie, swept along with the soothing flow of the unseen water.

THEN I BEGAN to look for a more cheerful room. I found one through the classified columns. I was now buying the evening paper from an old cockney who had his stock-in-trade on the sidewalk where I emerged from the Underground. One evening I read a description that sounded like just what I wanted. "Sunny third-floor room with small coke fireplace," it said. The address was still in Fulham, not very far from dreary Wickendon Street. I hurried over.

After my street of gloom, the heart of old Fulham was such a busy, lively neighbourhood! My room was on the third floor of a high, narrow building which grew narrower from the ground floor up, with space only for my room at the top. The middle floor was occupied by the owners and the ground floor was entirely filled by a repair shop with a single window on the street side, a chaotic scene of inoperative bicycles hanging by the dozen from the ceiling, leaving room below for hundreds of old phonographs and disassembled radios waiting to be repaired some day. I was to see some of these stay over four months in their blanket of rarely disturbed dust. A crudely lettered sign announced "Geoffrey Price's Bicycle and Radio Repair Shop".

The ground floor was on a level with the sidewalk, onto which the repair shop was partially emptied each morning to give Geoffrey Price room to move around inside amid his jumble of old odds and ends. It was also on the bus route and was one of its stops, in fact. You'd hear a rumble like thunder. Around the corner would come a double-decker bus almost as high as the building. Sharp application of the brakes would loose a soul-searing shriek, then the monster would pull up with its back door opening directly in front of the door of Geoffrey Price's Bicycle and Radio Repair Shop. On a rainy day, people of the neighbourhood said, you could get from Geoffrey Price's to Earls Court or Knightsbridge without risk of having a single drop of rain fall on you.

Across the street was another shop which was just as useful to bus passengers going in the other direction. This was the ironmonger's, which I'd learned to call the paint merchant's in Paris, though at the paint merchant's I recall seeing mostly coal and bottles of coarse red wine. On the third corner of the little square was the greengrocer's, the equivalent of the *verdurier* in Paris. The neighbourhood also included a chemist, a physician with office hours posted at his door, and a dentist whose sign was a huge hinged jaw as tall as a man, which kept opening and closing day and night as if in hope of gobbling up some unwary passerby. Just beyond was an open-air market. From there, early each morning, came the rattle of wooden-wheeled carts bringing vegetables to the stalls.

There was a codfish monger's at its edge. The rankest odours mingled in the air with the most delicate.

You couldn't be in the neighbourhood five minutes without hearing a sound such as the tinkling bell of the flower vendor pushing his little cart full of bright-coloured blossoms or the cry of the glazier, tinsmith, or rag-and-bottle man. Along with the street cries you'd often hear the doleful music of a barrel-organ and sometimes, through the din of all the rest, a pious bell from a little church behind high stone walls somewhere in the vicinity. I finally found this little church one day, hidden by stone and ivy, and a cemetery, the most peaceful in the world with its thick walls and shady trees full of birds – death's tranquil place of rest amid all the bustling humanity. I was to go there often seeking silence when there was too little in the noisy house.

My new landlady was like her neighbourhood, an irrepressible Welshwoman full of jokes, pranks, and mischief and always in a hurry. She showed me the room and I loved it immediately. It was high enough to reduce the noise and had a window overlooking the back, which was surprisingly quiet, a hodge-podge of small yards used for storage or junk, a scene as still as the street was busy on the other side. The fireplace was minute but delighted me because it was made to burn something real. Gladys told me she would light me a fire in the morning when she brought my breakfast, then if I stayed during the day it would be up to me to keep it going. I'd have to buy my own coke and a little kindling for starting it sometimes. Well no, she decided, she'd let me have the kindling. For the room, breakfast, and a bit of lunch – just scraps – it would be a guinea a week.

"A guinea?" I said, puzzled, not having heard the term before.

Gladys explained that a guinea meant a pound plus a shilling. I made her scream with laughter when at the end of the week I brought her a cheque for a guinea.

"There's no such thing really," she told me. "We haven't got any note or coin that's worth a guinea. It's just an expression."

"Well, why do you talk about guineas then?" I wanted to know.

She shrugged. I was stuck with the English lack of logic just as I'd been with the unerring logic of the French and I'd just have to adapt to it. I adapted to it more quickly, in fact, than to the endless reasoned arguments of the French.

This first day when we talked business I almost stooped to beggary.

"For a whole guinea, instead of scraps for lunch since I'll often be out at lunchtime," I said, "wouldn't you give me the same scraps for supper instead?"

Gladys laughed loud enough for the whole neighbourhood to hear, she found it all so funny, my accent, my expressions, my little rabbit coat and my beret which was "so Frenchy". In the end she told me that for a guinea a week, because she liked me so much, she'd "throw in supper and even a bite later on in the evening if you're still hungry, dearie." This was how I got myself a place to live for the best price going in all of London.

There was only one drawback to my new arrangement and that was my address: Lillie Road. "I know it smacks of perdition," agreed my landlady, and having roared another of her window-rattling laughs, concluded that I was getting it at a pretty good price at that.

Though I didn't really think the name smacked of perdition, I was shy about giving my address aloud and avoided it, saying, "I live too far to invite people there," or "It's terribly out of the way." I simply had to put up with it since Lillie Road was close to Paradise for me. Laughing, Gladys tried to make me feel better by telling me it would have been even more compromising if I'd taken a room in Petticoat Lane not far away.

Bohdan came and helped me move. He'd been able to unearth a kind of pushcart on his street. We moved everything I had in one load with a great deal of noise, the rubberless wheels clattering loudly over the cobblestones.

"It's a good thing you're staying so close," said Bohdan. "It won't be long now before my concert's over and then we'll catch up on each other."

He helped me put my clothes on hangers in the wardrobe. I tried to boil water for tea, squatting by the fire. One of the things I liked about it here was being able to have visitors, since with the sofa-bed made up the room became a sitting room.

Bohdan was amused and a bit shocked to see me transplanted to this very working-class neighbourhood. He'd have thought, he said, that for my writing I would have been better off in the quiet of the place he'd found for me. He'd been predicting that I'd become a famous writer ever since we'd first known each other.

While I was still trying to make some tea, Gladys arrived with a tray loaded with buttered scones and cakes and little pots of jam.

"As soon as I saw that young man pushing your things in his barrow I liked him," she confided to me later. "There's not another one like him in all England, you can take my word for it, and you'd better get your hands on him while you've got the chance. Cheerio!"

While Bohdan drank his tea, I observed him in silence. There were dark rings under his eyes and he looked tired, thin, and rather older, though he was really so young.

"Bohdan," I said, "if you're going to go as far as you've made up your mind to, you're going to have to learn to look after yourself."

"Am I going very far?" he shot back, trying to make it sound flippant.

It occurred to me then that despite his frequent cheerfulness I'd always sensed a kind of anxiety in him, as though he had a feeling he was going to run out of time.

"I've got a pretty clear picture," he said, still as though poking fun at himself, "of a stretch of road ahead of me, a few years' worth perhaps, then everything stops, disappears, just drops away suddenly."

"But I can't even see a single day ahead of me and every day I change direction," I said lightly, trying to bring him back to his cheerful self.

He turned strangely serious. "Nevertheless," he said, "your future's certain. I only have to close my eyes and I can see your name in big bold letters. I don't seem to see it on the front of a theatre, though I still believe you've done the right thing signing up for drama. But as I foresee, that's not where you're going to shine. So where will it be? I think I can see your name on the cover of a book, quite clearly in big letters."

"A book!" I retorted. "I haven't even written a half-decent simple little story yet."

In the five or six years I'd known him, ever since we'd first met in Winnipeg, he'd been talking this way, rather like a psychic, and I often laughed heartily at his supposed foresight. This time, however, he seemed so sure of himself it gave me the shivers.

"Let's talk about something else," I said, "you frighten me with your prophecies."

What frightened me most was the intense sadness I'd glimpsed in his blue-grey eyes, a look I never saw again except in the eyes of people destined to die young.

Our tea-time ended cheerfully for all that, with Bohdan pretending to read from the tea-leaves in the bottom of my cup that I was going to write an earthy, populist novel, which wouldn't really be surprising, since I felt so much at home with working people.

Having retrieved this scene in all its detail from the back of my memory, I've come to wonder now why we weren't lovers, Bohdan and I. He was direct, energetic, the soul of loyalty, and sweet, gentle, and charming. I don't know what he saw in me but I think it must have been rather the same things I valued in him, which made me admire him, trust him implicitly, look for his support, want his approval, and cherish him deeply. Perhaps the bond between us was too honest, too limpid, too uncomplicated to lead to love. It may have lacked a weakness or the grain of uncertainty or worry present in almost every love. Bohdan and I never caused each other the least worry except about each other's health. We were just meant to be friends, as they say unfairly. Curious, isn't it, that we place love, which is so fickle, on a higher plane than friendship, which is almost always so faithful.

Faith in each other. It was probably this that basically sustained our affection yet prevented it from turning into love. But in truth I don't understand it any better today than I did then.

Bohdan was more clairvoyant that day than he had ever been, as though he had the answers to my questions of the moment and for some time to come. Just before he left, he leaned against the doorframe and said in his affectionately bantering manner, "By the way, I want very much to introduce you to a young man I met a few days ago. You'll like him as surely as God made little apples. And as soon as he sets eyes on you he'll be forevermore bewitched."

"Another of your predictions!" I bantered back.

"It'll come true in less than three months. Want to bet on it?"

"What's this irresistible young man's name?" I asked, still not taking him seriously.

Halfway down the stairs he called back a name — was I mistaken? — with a tinge of resentment.

I only caught the first name, Stephen.

"Stephen who?" I shouted.

Either Bohdan didn't hear my question or I didn't hear his reply. I wouldn't learn any more about the young man that day, but Bohdan had succeeded in arousing my curiosity.

VII

MY NEW LIFE began, with a scattering of classes here and there over the week. This time I went at it with a stout heart and persistence, though never with enthusiasm. I forced myself.

The times I liked best were still my free days, when I'd escape and go adventuring on the upper deck of a bus. I developed a real passion for these cross-London tours, west to east, north to south. They could take as long as three or four hours and never cost more than a shilling. Invariably, I climbed the little spiral staircase, and if it was free settled myself in the first row at the very front, from where I'd have a commanding view of the sights. The conductor would arrive, find me pretty well alone up there, and ask, "Where to, ma'am?" I nearly always replied, "As far as you go." Often I returned by the same bus without even getting off. Once settled in my seat and in motion I was happy, it seems to me. I came to know a great deal of London this way, as later I would come to know Montreal by riding the streetcars when I arrived there in 1939.

Except for the City and certain hubs like Charing Cross, Trafalgar Square, Chelsea, and perhaps Soho, London was really just a succession of boroughs, each a kind of small town with its own High Street, each joined to the next, an endless procession. I used to love to watch these peaceful-looking towns go by one after the other, their houses attached one to another for whole streets without a break, their flower markets, their everlasting tea shops, and the never-changing vista of chimney pots as far as the eye could see; in the whole city there must have been a staggering number of these small chimneys in the shape of flower pots, because you could often count a dozen on a single roof, or however many little fireplaces like mine there were inside the house. What a curious city, each person alone by his own feeble little fire instead of together with others around a nice fat stove! So much soot had fallen from all these chimney pots and nearby factory smokestacks that you often couldn't see the colour of the brick the houses were built of.

Sometimes I'd come to a miraculous pink brick square around a small park enclosed in a quickset hedge or low walls. Only the occupants of the sparkling-clean surrounding houses could use the park, since only they had keys for opening the gate. Inside one might see a nanny in a shoulder-length veil pushing a perambulator or an old man walking slowly, leaning on a cane.

Not one of these outings failed to uncover something new for me. Sometimes I'd get off the bus and go exploring on foot in a neighbourhood far from where I lived, feeling so much at home I would have liked to stay. Often I made the round trip without a stop, and was always surprised at how different everything seemed on the way back. At times, looking down as though from a chariot, I'd find myself observing all the things that were intriguing and sad both at once, as one finds in any big city. At other times, lulled by the rocking of the bus, I'd lose all contact with the reality of the moment and drift away in reveries, which were almost always happy ones as soon as the rocking matched the rhythm of my thoughts, like a kind of ocean roll.

I WENT TO my classes at the Guildhall, of course, and made heroic efforts to benefit from these as well. Classes in diction, for example, during which the teacher tried one day for three-quarters of an hour to make me say "little" the way it ought to be said, showing me where to place my tongue, finally in exasperation asking, "Where on earth did you learn your English?" Exhausted by trying, I replied listlessly, "Where I ought to have learned French instead." There were makeup lessons to teach me how to disguise myself as a Sioux or Nipponese, for all the good it would ever do me. Fencing lessons. Readings of texts by the great English playwrights. All this part of my life, the part inside the walls of the school, seems today like merely something I dreamed. The dreaming I did on the Thames embankments, the upper decks of the huge London buses, and even on weekends at Gladys's cabin opposite Hampton Court – the poor people's side of the river giving the finest view of the palace – this to me was the only real and lasting part of the life I led in these three or four months.

YET THERE are episodes from these days in London that stand out sharply in my memory.

There was the day when I was attending a class conducted by a Miss Rorke, whom we called "the dragon". She used to rail at us without letup, calling us "snails" because we were slow, I suppose, and zombies and phantoms incapable of making ourselves understood. She wasn't alone; a good many other teachers also habitually insulted and ridiculed us. Why was it necessary to treat us like this when we were already trembling in our boots? It seems, I was told later, that by goading us as a picador goads a bull they were supposed to draw reactions full of pain and fire from us.

It was generally accepted that as a teacher of the English classics Miss Rorke was unsurpassable. Nobody taught Shakespeare and especially George Bernard Shaw better than she. She had played Shaw a great deal in her youth and his acerbic humour had certainly left its mark on her character. She never stopped reminding us of our incompetence. "You want to be actors and actresses, hold audiences spellbound, see your names in lights on theatre marquees...yet you can't do anything properly! You can't walk or sit down or even shake hands, let alone speak lines!"

She was right, too. As I watched my fellow students I could see that, indeed, they were unable to walk or sit down or do anything on stage in a way that seemed in the least natural. I was learning that everything has to be recreated on the stage if it's to seem real, that nothing, even blowing your nose, can be done the way you do it in real life.

I hadn't myself been a target for Miss Rorke's attacks. Then one day I suddenly heard myself being summoned.

"You there! Come and read us a passage." We were doing *The Merchant of Venice*. "Hmm.... Ah yes, Portia's plea to the judge."

This time I couldn't escape as I had from Dullin's. I climbed the steps to the stage. I found the passage. I began to read in a voice that seemed to come from another world, faint, far-off, and frail. I didn't recognize myself at all; someone else was reading, gesturing, while I myself was watching from terribly far away, feeling

258

rather sorry for the poor girl in such a predicament. Then my voice firmed, came to my ears perhaps the way others heard it. I can still hear it even now and probably always will, though I don't remember the words. Life has robbed me of them. As Rutebeuf would say, it robs us of everything with advancing age except the memory of having been young, bold, and foolhardy.

Then all became muddled and blurred. I was no longer two people, one reading and the other watching; I'd escaped from everyone present and myself as well. My shyness and anxiety retreated to the periphery. I was back in my childhood, still in class at the Académie Saint-Joseph. The inspector had come to see what we were doing. Sister Agathe had implored me, "Get up and save the class." And at the Guildhall or in St-Boniface, I was doing my utmost to save heaven knows what.

Gradually my voice became more confident. Around me there was total silence. Something was showing at last through the gaiety I was known for at the Guildhall, surely the old, persistent strain of sadness in me. Were the old woes of Deschambault Street revisiting me, emerging so astonishingly in the words of Shakespeare? The class was dumbfounded perhaps. Who in London had ever heard or would ever again hear Shakespeare recited like this, the Bard in a guise never before seen by his countrymen?

When I'd finished my speech the silence persisted for a good few seconds. Then Miss Rorke said rather gruffly:

"It's a pity you've got such a barbaric accent because at times I actually felt something come to life. But child, I could hardly make out a single word with that horrendous accent of yours!"

Aside she told me, "If you want to come to me in the evening I'll give you some tutoring, without a penny of cost to you, of course."

I went two or three times, I think. After making me rhyme off "which, whichever, witches, whence, where, wherever, either, neither, however, beneath, whole, whatever" and an appalling number of others, she plied me with humbugs, bonbons, scones, hot tea, biscuits, and crumpets. At home, the dragon was just a lovable little old lady nestled in a Victorian armchair, her tiny feet propped on a pouf, her dark skirt draped over them, making me repeat between mouthfuls, "witch, which, wither, whither, wisht, whished,

259

whim, whichever..." or "throne, throw, thorough, through...,"
which I still can't say properly for all the pains she and many others
have taken with me.

I ALSO ENROLLED in a drama course in French with a Madame Gachet
who made me hold a pencil between my teeth while saying, "*Je
veux et je l'exige,*" to loosen up my tongue. She was another dragon
who kept castigating me for "using your face to speak with instead
of your throat, like all you Canadians."

With her I studied Shaw's *Saint Joan* in French translation, which
was ironic in the extreme since Shaw was far more Miss Rorke's
domain. However, Madame Gachet insisted that the shape of my
face and my features and manner were right for it and therefore
Joan was a good role for me. I'd long known Joan's most brilliant
retorts to the Inquisitor by heart but one morning I tried to produce
them and couldn't find anything there any more.

Madame Gachet's interpretation of Saint Joan was like Ludmilla
Pitoëff's, with the delicate features of a little stained-glass-window
saint. It's said that when Shaw went to Paris for the première of
Madame Pitoëff's production he was so enraged that all through a
dinner given in his honour he wouldn't speak a word to her, though
she was sitting beside him. At the Malvern Festival, which I attended
that year, Elizabeth Bergner's Joan was also a little stained-glass
saint and displeased Shaw so thoroughly that he stamped out to
the garden in fury at intermission and went to walk in the maze
in the centre of which this delightful little summer theatre is located.
I had come to Malvern for the day and was in the maze at the
time. Walking along the twists and turns between the high hedges,
every so often I heard angry grumbling sounds and fragments of
sentences through the foliage. At one point I turned a corner and
came face to face with a white-bearded old man who glared at me
for a moment, then continued his tortuous way, muttering angrily.
I stood stock still, overcome with surprise. "That was George Bernard Shaw I just passed!" I said to myself. "And furious too, as
usual."

Each anecdote keeps reminding me of another I'd like to tell, but
my dervish is increasingly aware that he hasn't time to collect
everything coming to him from the past if he's going to finish all

he has begun. What I do want to add is that the only Joan that Shaw ever approved of was Dame Sybil Thorndike's and later Miss Rorke's: a sturdy, rosy-cheeked country girl who was totally rational, reasonable, and realistic: the Catholics' first Protestant saint, as Shaw himself called her.

More sensibly, I also studied Racine with Madame Gachet, until the day she hurled the book at my head in a rage, declaring I didn't understand a thing about this type of drama – which was the very truth.

Madame Gachet had had as pupils such distinguished actors as Vivien Leigh and Charles Laughton. They still quite frequently came to work on their roles with her, of which she made sure her ordinary pupils were aware. In her better moments we were treated to gossip and juicy anecdotes about the great figures of the movie and theatre world, whom she knew and, it must be said, whom she saw with revealing and often merciless clarity.

LOOKING BACK, how hard I tried during this period of my life! Once the weather was milder, I would sometimes go and recite lines from Racine, even after he'd been hurled at my head, in the only place I was sure of neither disturbing anyone nor being laughed at, behind the thick walls of the little Fulham cemetery, so full of dense shady trees and ancient graves. Even here I sometimes had a pang of guilt to be disturbing such long and sacred rest, and stopped to read a few epitaphs here and there instead. They were so plaintive and sweet. Having my Racine interlarded with the echo of these humble, long-forgotten English lives suddenly made me feel that my own story was a thousand times stranger than those I was studying in books. For a little while it would fascinate me more than any mystery.

THIS WAS the pattern of my life during these months in London. I would be lonely and depressed, pushing myself to do things that seemed to be taking me nowhere; then suddenly my youth and the cheerful side of my nature would take over and I'd be finding the humour in things, laughing and making people around me laugh as in the days of our touring shows in Manitoba, as later too, when I was in Provence.

The day I read Portia's great plea, I came down from the stage and was still trembling, the students present gaping oddly, when a tall, handsome young man came forward, clapping approval.

"Let them think what they want," he said, "and even laugh if they like. You have everyone's attention right now."

Naïvely, I took the remark as a compliment. Perhaps it was.

"How about a cup of tea?" he suggested after we'd talked for a minute.

Around eleven in the morning and in mid-afternoon, almost everyone at the Guildhall stopped fencing, dancing, or delivering lines and gathered around small four-place tables in the school restaurant to drink endless cups of tea.

Soon nearly all my class was there in little groups. I noticed that most of them were staring at the tall, handsome young man and me as we sat together, separated slightly from the rest. I could hardly believe the new respect, even envy, in their expressions.

He told me his name and that he was Welsh, but his being Welsh is the only way I can remember him today. While we drank our tea, no doubt he told me he'd studied at the Guildhall and since he was making his career in London he returned to his old teachers from time to time for "refresher courses". Today, though he couldn't explain why, he'd dropped in on the dramatic interpretation class in progress and had at once been captivated by this unusual little creature with eyes so full of a different vision of English drama.

What I didn't yet know was that he was one of England's finest baritones, had sung many times at Covent Garden, and was well launched on the royal road to success. There wasn't a girl present who wouldn't gladly have scratched my eyes out, seeing him court me. Several of them had probably been in my shoes; I soon learned that I was far from the first he'd wooed with the same kind of line.

He lost no time taking out his little black book and asking for my address. Grandly, he informed me he'd be in touch one of these days to take me to one of the evening musicals that were given in the most fashionable salons of London in those days; it would round out my artistic training and give me a unique vantage point for observation.

Alas, rather than own up to living on Lillie Road I was vague, evasive, saying, "I'm on the point of moving.... I don't really know where to...or where I'll be tomorrow." Then, not knowing how to escape from such a fix, I held out my hand, thanked him for the tea, and left almost at a run.

When I recounted the scene to Gladys she told me I was a crazy little nincompoop. The tall, handsome Welshman was well known in London, she said, you could often hear his superb voice on the BBC, and besides, all Welshmen were musically gifted and most attractive. So it would serve me right if I never set eyes on him again.

We hadn't reckoned on our Welshman's determination. He had little trouble obtaining my address and even my telephone number from the registrar of the school. Two or three days later I got off the bus straight into the bicycle shop as always, and almost straight into the arms of Gladys, who'd been waiting for me in a dither of excitement. My Welshman had telephoned. He'd left a message. He really was the one she'd thought, a celebrity! She'd taken down the number. I had to call back as soon as possible from Geoffrey's office.

What she called Geoffrey's office was an ancient roll-top desk ensconced in a corner of the bicycle shop, littered with nuts, bolts, screws, bits of tubing, and an old maul for keeping the pile of unpaid bills in place. Since he knew where I lived and so the harm was done, I called the handsome Welshman.

"Why didn't you want to give me your address?" he asked.

"Because I didn't want people to know I live on Lillie Road."

I heard a hearty laugh that seemed it would never stop, full, deep, and rolling, drowning the traffic sounds from the street.

"Silly little girl!" he said. "Do you know where I come from? The bottom of a coal mine! My father's still an underground miner. I was one myself till I was sixteen. Will you come with me to the Austrian embassy this evening? Watch out though, the ambassador's name is Baron Frankenstein, I'm not pulling your leg."

Without reflecting that he couldn't see me I nodded, but he must have read my silence correctly.

"I'll pick you up at eight o'clock sharp," he said.

We had found a place for my wardrobe trunk on the landing beside the door to my room. I took out my long, bright-red taffeta dress, which Gladys insisted on pressing for me. I found my matching shoes. Gladys did my hair in a bundle of ringlets on top of my head, which made me look like a Reynolds portrait. She had a reproduction of one on her sitting-room wall. To complete my evening finery I had white gloves and a kind of little cape of black velvet. I was ready long in advance and came down to await my prince in the middle of the bicycle shop, sitting on a chair which Geoffrey had hastened to wipe off with a rag. Dressed as always for work in a grey smock that made him look like a jailbird, Geoffrey sat near the wide-open door and waited with me, too much on edge to do any work at a time of such great excitement.

How the news had spread I really don't know, but the whole neighbourhood knew that "the nice little French lady at Gladys's is going out tonight with that marvellous Welsh singer you hear over the wireless." But the neighbours' imaginations had turned the evening's event into a ball, perhaps even at Buckingham Palace for all they knew, which from minute to minute acquired such grandiose proportions that not a soul among them wasn't on the doorstep watching for the Prince to appear. They must have expected him to draw up in a carriage, or at least a splendid chauffeured limousine. I'd become their fairy-tale, the Cinderella so beloved of ordinary folk because she takes them with her to the ball.

The hour was approaching. From their doorsteps, people kept looking up at the big clock over Smith's Watch Repair.

At eight o'clock precisely, with a rumble like thunder as always, came the bus from Knightsbridge. Windows rattled. The monster pulled up with its open door facing the welcoming portal of Geoffrey Price's Bicycle and Radio Repair Shop. Out stepped my Welshman, straight into the shop among the bicycles hanging from the ceiling, in evening dress with immaculate boiled shirtfront, top hat slightly tilted on his head, gold-headed cane in his hand, and – caught at the neck with a clasp and flipped nonchalantly back from his shoulders – a huge, magnificent black velvet cape that swept all the dust off the floor in one pass.

The bus driver, intrigued with the distinguished figure he must have seen alight out of the corner of his eye, rolled down his window and put out his head to watch him enter the bicycle shop, and waited. My tall Welshman held out his hand, drew me out of my little straw-bottomed chair, and led me up the steps of the waiting vehicle. The driver stepped on the gas and we drove away in the same bus in which the Prince had arrived.

The ironmonger, the flower vendor, the fishmonger, the chemist, and the greengrocer, wide-eyed and open-mouthed, watched us leave as if we were the most ordinary of mortals, and couldn't, perhaps would never, get over their disappointment.

AROUND THIS TIME I made other much dearer friends than the tall, handsome Welshman who entered my life in such spectacular fashion, and who faded from it no doubt just as quickly, for rack my brain as I may I can find no further trace of him after the evening at Frankenstein's.

A little later I became very fond of a sweet girl whose parents were paying her way through the Guildhall course in drama, though they themselves had never set foot in a theatre. One day she invited me home for Sunday dinner with her family in the South End across the Thames, a rather distant part of the city where, curiously, my excursions by bus had never taken me. No doubt like every other household in London on Sunday at the same hour, we ate roast rib of beef and Yorkshire pudding.

Phyllis and I went to see a great many plays together. We used to buy cheap seats in what Phyllis called "the gods", a term acknowledging that the section known in Paris as the *poulailler* or "hen roost" was a very high perch indeed. In some theatres we might hang so precipitously over the stage that all we could see of the actors far below was the tops of their heads, often bald. We had little chance of seeing their faces unless, said Phyllis, they suddenly began to "play to the gods", as did the late illustrious Henry Irving one night when, probably remembering his penniless youth, he threw back his head and looking towards the ceiling spoke directly to the impoverished souls peering down from above.

Personally, I don't think I ever saw an actor look up towards us until the time came for applause, and then it was rather pleadingly.

The cheap seats – a shilling each – couldn't be reserved, of course, and were in great demand, so we had to arrive a good hour ahead of time. Even then, there was often already a long queue outside the theatre. We would take our places in line and in no time the queue would have lengthened so much that it disappeared around the corner into an adjacent sidestreet. I've seen it grow so long that depending on the space or the whims of those involved it might loop twice around the theatre, making a kind of lasso. The two loops, one of which seemed to be coming and the other going, would often be very close together and people would converse from one group to the other as they passed. On occasion someone turned up to rent out folding chairs. You could have one for sixpence and sit very comfortably two by two by the wall. Or you could write your name on a piece of paper and pin it to your chair, and without danger of having your place stolen go and have a leisurely bite to eat nearby, or just take a walk.

I liked best to stay in my place with the cluster of people in the queue, an instant family of friends on the sidewalk. If it rained, umbrellas would open wide enough to shelter less prudent neighbours. I often slipped under someone else's umbrella, having asked permission with a glance and a smile or having been invited, and almost invariably I'd engage in conversation with the obliging neighbour. There'd be people reading quietly, holding an umbrella in one hand and turning pages with the other. There'd be women knitting scarves already long enough to reach the ground. "Your lovely scarf's dragging in the dirt," we'd warn them. If the evening was mild and without rain, which was the case fairly often in the course of the winter, street performers would appear. They'd do little dances, sing songs in old, cracked voices, or draw pictures on the sidewalk, then pass the hat and we'd give them a penny for their trouble. Phyllis almost always brought something to eat like buttered rolls and sticky buns, and would insist that we share them equally.

From some of those hours of waiting at the doors of theatres, particularly on pleasant evenings, I have memories of such delight that even the plays for which they should have been merely prologue are pale by comparison in my mind. On these occasions the people of London were the kindest, most considerate, most natural companions one could wish for. I still reflect sometimes that the best play in London's repertory was the one being played on the sidewalk about people ready to share everything, their sandwich with whoever seemed hungry, a flap of their coat with the ill-clad when the wind blew cold, a column of their paper with someone who had nothing to read – I can't count the times a neighbour consented with an amused smile to let me read over his shoulder.

Among these fondly remembered evenings, I spent several with

Phyllis, some with friends of the moment as my only companions, and some with Bohdan.

Bohdan's concert took place and was hailed as a triumph. The Royal Albert Hall audience applauded him at great length. So calm and reserved in appearance, that evening he threw himself into his playing like a kind of Paganini finally unleashing his passionate soul. I was astounded by the intensity I saw in him that night and I understood why we could never be lovers, he and I; he was already totally possessed by his music, and though I couldn't yet make out what it was, I too was driven by some burning imperative.

After the concert he was in great demand, with invitations to play in London and on tour. Anxious to live up to expectations, he worked harder than ever now. He became increasingly gaunt, and to me his eyes often had a feverish look, as though focusing on something which must have been unbearable, for he would murmur, half-seriously, half-facetiously as always:

"The gods don't wait. They don't wait."

I MYSELF would be in the depths of gloom one day and as gay as a lark the next. It was the sunny side of my nature that won me such affection from Phyllis and would win me affection from many others over the years. Left to herself, Phyllis would never have found anything to laugh at in the myriad comical little scenes to be found any day of the week in London, but when she heard me laugh she'd look again and suddenly begin also to see the comical side. She was very grateful to me for showing her this side of things practically every time we went out together.

Often a play we wanted to see took us to a part of the city that was difficult to reach, and once there we might have to hunt through narrow, poorly lit streets for a tiny, secluded theatre. This was the case when we went to see Eugene O'Neill's *Mourning Becomes Electra*, which was showing somewhere in Westminster, as I recall, at the end of a little-known street off a cul-de-sac with the Thames lapping gently at its foot. Since the play is very long, the performance was given in two parts, the first beginning at seven-thirty, followed by a half-hour intermission to allow people to go and have something to eat; the performance resumed at about ten-thirty and ended only around midnight.

At intermission there were already signs of fog, and by the end of the play a real pea-soup had descended on the deserted streets around the theatre. When we came out, a small audience of about fifty, we couldn't see two steps before us and could barely see each other or the streetlight on the square in front of the theatre. Instinctively, all fifty stayed together, walking step by step, elbow to elbow. Apparently no one was really familiar with the area or knew how to find the nearest Underground station. How did I come to be the one leading the group, marching boldly towards a sound I thought I heard ahead of me, which was in fact no more than the fog-projected echo of the steps behind? More to the point, how did the whole troop of Londoners come to be following me as one man, knowing how treacherous a fog can be?

Soon I thought I heard another sound, one not quite masked by the footsteps behind me. Was it ahead? Was it behind? I couldn't tell, but something about it worried me. Suddenly, with all those people behind me, I came to a tall iron grille beyond which a steep slope led straight into the Thames. We'd arrived at one of the low-tide landings for the launches that ply the river. If the watchman had forgotten to close the gate, we could all have marched laughing into the murky water before we realized what was happening. Only when I turned around did I see, by a feeble light reflected off the water, the trusting little band that had followed me all this way, blindly to say the least.

I began to laugh, infecting Phyllis, who began to laugh too. And when Phyllis, in her lovely trained voice, told all those people in the darkness that they'd been letting themselves be led by a Canadian girl who'd never set foot in the district before, everyone else laughed too. Instead of being angry they all crowded around to see what I looked like and wish me well for the future. Then a seasoned Londoner took the lead. We all joined hands and made a chain and, like a band of merry wraiths dancing a farandole, followed him out of the thick of the fog towards the lights of the Underground.

Dear Londoners! Dear isle! How I loved them at this time in my life and at this time in theirs. The English are so warm-hearted, need so urgently to love; on later visits I didn't find the same degree of free-and-easy charm and readiness to laugh at themselves that I remembered, perhaps because I had become too solemn myself, perhaps because they, after the trials and hardships of the war, had lost some of their gentle sense of absurdity.

THE TIME passed quickly despite my ups and downs. I persevered along the course I had set for myself, though I kept announcing I was going to give it all up. One day I'd be at peace with the world and the next the old depression would be back and I'd feel I was wasting my life, and time flew by and winter came to an end without my noticing. In the three months I'd been in London, had I ever really seen the sky, the Thames and the embankments, except in short, fleeting glimpses? Perhaps this was really what made them so unforgettable.

One morning on my way to the school I passed beneath an old linden tree as I did almost every day, and through a break in the fog saw that the branches above my head were still bare. Only the dryish creak of its branches told me for certain where I was, but I'd swear my old friend the linden was bare that morning when the breeze was still on the nippy side.

Halfway through the morning, while I was attending my classes, the air suddenly warmed and the sun came out, even shone brightly for a few hours.

When I came out and walked alone to the Underground it was dark. It must have been the fifteenth or perhaps sixteenth of February. The hour did nothing to spoil my surprise and delight as I passed under my linden tree and, suddenly hearing a new, softer sound, slowed my pace and looked up. I thought I was dreaming. The old linden was covered with leaves! Oh, very tiny still, barely open, newly come into the world, but fragile as they were, rustling in the balmy night air, doing their best to warm the heart. I think I was entranced by the coming of spring in a way I'd never known before. What struck me most was its suddenness no doubt. Just a few hours earlier the old tree at the edge of the sidewalk might have been dead, from its appearance, and now I was seeing the shimmer of its young leaves as they turned towards the feeble light of a nearby streetlamp. The joy that swept over me was itself a rebirth, my own, telling me just how dead I myself had been in many ways.

Years later, when I was writing *The Hidden Mountain*, this joy in the coming of spring would return one day and guide me in

269

conveying Pierre Cadorai's indefinable happiness one evening in the forest at winter's end, when he hears a drop of water fall from a branch to the ground, its tinkling through the silence and darkness seeming to go on for ever.

But for the moment, since there wasn't a soul to share it with, my joy was almost unbearable. I've often enough found suffering difficult to bear by myself, but perhaps solitary joy even more. "I have Gladys, though," I remembered after a moment or two, and I hurried home.

There were two entrances, one through the bicycle shop where Geoffrey, in his eternal iron-grey smock, was working late, and the other by a little side door at the foot of the stairs that led to the kitchen door of Gladys's apartment. From downstairs I could hear Gladys rattling pots.

"Gladys, it's spring, it's spring!" I called.

She appeared at the top of the stairs in her apron, her hands all white with dough.

"So it is, so it is! And I'm throwing in a fine steak and kidney pie for supper besides."

But then she became serious and told me to come up. She whispered that tomorrow was Geoffrey's birthday and she always sent him a birthday card by the post. He liked to get it on the breakfast tray on his birthday with his morning paper and a daffodil. She'd already addressed the card and she asked me, since the weather was so nice, if I wouldn't go back out and put it in a corner letter-box.

I replied that I certainly would if she really wanted me to, but why bother posting it at all? Wouldn't it be simpler just to put it on the tray with the daffodil the next morning without making it do the tour of the district first?

At this she was very put out. Generally such a good-natured soul, she could become cranky for no reason at all. "Because... because...," she almost shouted, then probably against her better judgement blurted, "Because Geoffrey likes it that way, don't ask me why. Half his pleasure's gone if he doesn't get his card with the Fulham Post Office cancellation on it."

"I'll go and post it if you want," I said, "but I confess I find it odd for two people living in the same house to send each other things by the post, unless they're not on speaking terms."

"The envelope's got a stamp," she snapped, to put an end to it. "All I'm asking you to do is pop out and drop it in a letter-box. There's one just two blocks from here."

Even in Fulham, which was all cement, stone, and barred windows with hardly any trees except those in the cemetery, the gentle English spring was in progress. It was showing in almost imperceptible little ways, keeping me in an extraordinary state of exhilaration as though life were new, pulsating, bursting with hope. From the occasional tree along my way came the same tender, caressing murmurs I'd heard from my linden. I was so intoxicated with the spring evening I could have kept walking for ever. I must have passed two or three letter-boxes before realizing I wasn't far now from Fulham Post Office. For the benefit of Gladys's card, to make absolutely sure it would arrive by the first delivery the following morning, I'd best go and post it there, I thought.

Afterwards, still unable to resign myself to going indoors on such a delicious evening, I took a lengthy detour through the cemetery and then along a street where several little gardens were already in bloom. It was a good hour before I arrived home.

Still light of heart, in the best of humour, I opened the little side door and hearing Gladys's voice humming called, " 'Tis done!"

Gladys appeared on the landing above. She seemed happy. Then we both looked down at the doormat at the bottom of the stairs. There under the letter slot in the door lay the birthday card I'd just posted. I bent down and picked it up. It bore the post office cancellation. Had it been delivered by the postman I'd just passed going the other way? I was bewildered.

"I told you to put it in the post," Gladys scolded. "Why did you bring it back yourself?"

"I did put it in the post," I said. "So as to be sure it would arrive in time I even posted it at the main post office."

"You shouldn't have!" groaned Gladys. "They've got a special fast service there. You must have arrived just in time for it to go straight out. Oh, how awful!"

She was inconsolable. Geoffrey's birthday was ruined, his pleasure spoiled, and it was my fault. Or rather, the fault of His Majesty's fearsomely efficient post office.

Sometimes when I wait three or four days for a letter to come from a part of Quebec City right next to mine, or when the single daily delivery is suspended by ice, snow, "study session", or rotating strike...I find myself thinking fondly of that lightning-fast Fulham postal service which so totally foiled Gladys and me.

VIII

was it this magical springtime that brought love to my life? Perhaps. Although the sudden burgeoning of life exhilarated me beyond words that February evening, it also made me aware of how alone I was in London. I had some friends, yes, but only friends of the moment, a very short moment. I had no one I could really count on in a pinch except perhaps Bohdan. And so the intensity of my exhilaration had a bitter side too, for it showed me how desolate it was to be far from home without anyone to love or give me love. Again I was asking myself some hard questions: why I had come to London, what I was doing here, why I was studying drama, and where it was going to lead me. Again everything I'd undertaken seemed worthless and futile beside what I ought to be undertaking. There was also a listlessness, persistent, corrosive, that prevented me from taking an interest in any effort I made to escape from the mood I was in. When you're listless, nothing is worth the effort. I practically stopped going to the theatre, on bus rides, even reading. I think I sank into the waiting state I've often experienced, during which I do nothing but wait for something unidentified to come and deliver me.

This was my state of mind when I set out one day to meet, if you will, my destiny. For all my inactivity I hadn't stopped going once a week, more or less, to Lady Frances Ryder's on Cadogan Gardens in South Kensington. This generous lady used to open her London apartment every day at tea-time to students, regardless of colour, from every corner of the Empire. Bohdan had taken me there and introduced me to Lady Frances. After this formality I was free to come again whenever I wished.

The copious fare served us at tea was for many students by far the best meal of the week, and many would tuck away quantities of butter-soaked crumpets, cheese petits fours, and little tarts smothered in Devonshire cream. The spacious drawing rooms also featured a luxury that most of us had learned to do without: warmth, maintained by central heating. So we'd shed the heavy sweaters we wore almost constantly in winter and move around more at ease, both minds and bodies less constrained, ready for friendly conversation.

Lady Frances would preside over these gatherings herself or would delegate other ladies to do so. They always had theatre, ballet, or concert tickets to distribute, having pried them free of charge out of impresarios and theatre owners by playing on their pride of empire. Fairly often they also had an invitation for one of us to dine with a distinguished Harley Street doctor, or spend a weekend as guest of a great landowner in Ireland or a week at some stately home in Shropshire or Monmouthshire. The great dream of unity among brothers within the Empire was so deeply instilled, on the eve of its disappearance, that we only needed to be students from South Africa, New Zealand, Canada, Australia for the doors of noble residences and simple cottages alike to open wide for us.

In the group called, I think, Overseas British Empire Students, I was the only French Canadian. As such, though I don't know why, I received particular consideration. Lady Frances pressed me many times to accept coveted invitations to Wales, the Midlands, and elsewhere, but the idea of tackling life among the English landed gentry filled me with such paralysing shyness that I always shrank from it. In the end, though, I did accept an invitation to spend a week in Monmouthshire near the marvellous ruins of the old Cistercian abbey celebrated by Wordsworth. Perhaps it was my desire to see these ruins that overcame my hesitation. As Lady Curre's guest I was introduced to fox hunting, black-tie dinners, and some famous personalities, all of which in retrospect make my most fantastic dreams at night seem pale by comparison.

For the moment my feeling towards some of the young men I was meeting at Lady Frances's were no more than comradely. Among them was a giant of an Australian with a heart of gold but an appalling cockney accent and a habit of ending every sentence with "You see?" when you didn't see at all because you hadn't understood a word of what he'd been saying.

Another of what one might call my beaux in this circle was a

New Zealander who was in sharp contrast to the Australian, a tall, reserved, polite young man whose voice was impeccably British and who tried so terribly hard to be British with his bowler hat, his trench coat, and his oh-so-tightly-rolled umbrella that we all thought he was laying it on a bit too thick. He had an important position at the Admiralty. When his mother came from New Zealand to visit him, he invited me to join the two of them on a ten-day tour, which enabled me to become acquainted with the south of England: the splendid red-soiled Devon, Cornwall with its ancient shale castles, the moors, the New Forest, Gloucestershire, and everywhere such wonderful little villages that I sometimes think I must have dreamed them, they were so perfectly nestled in silence and verdure with their old arched bridges, rose-covered roofs, and a peacefulness probably unequalled anywhere in the world. David also used to invite me to dine in fashionable restaurants where I felt uncomfortable. Furthermore, he always seemed to be examining, evaluating me, perhaps considering whether I'd do. When his mother came she was even more obviously looking me over. After a while I began to wonder if David, in his strange, cold way, wasn't in fact courting me with honourable intentions as the saying goes, and mightn't solemnly propose marriage some fine day providing his mother pronounced me suitable. But apparently she didn't, for she went back to New Zealand and David began to space out his invitations, sent me roses, then fell silent, and all was well that ended well. Later, however, I would see him again fairly frequently.

A Lady Wells, who was often our hostess in place of Lady Frances, had introduced David to me, but a month later, having twice seen us leave together, she had a warning for me. "Don't get too attached to that boy," she said. "He's very refined, but underneath the polish he's not very good value. Wait. Some day I'll surely have someone better for you to meet."

One day I entered the big drawing room filled with the hum of conversation to find Lady Wells hurrying to meet me, holding out both hands.

"Dear," she said, "I've someone really special for you to meet. Come."

She kept talking but I no longer heard her. My eyes had turned to a little table in the middle of the room. Of the hundred faces present I was seeing only one – or rather, one pair of dark, burning eyes that were drawing me irresistibly. And perhaps without my realizing, my eyes were drawing him too, this young man I'd never seen before, because once our eyes had met, his never left mine.

I crossed the room with Lady Wells, she holding my hand and I fervidly praying, "If only he's the one she wants me to meet!" As we approached he rose from the table.

Lady Wells said simply, "Stephen, this is Gabrielle whom I told you about...," and probably something else which I didn't register.

He took the hand I held out and the light in his dark eyes shone brighter. He pulled up another chair for me and we sat five at the table. The others began to talk again among themselves. The two of us said nothing. We kept gazing at each other as though too surprised to talk, too astonished at finding each other after coming so far across the globe and through life.

I don't remember anything about the next hour except that soon almost everyone around was looking at us in surprise to see us just sit and gaze at each other endlessly, as if magnetized.

We left together, having agreed with no more than a glance towards the door.

Outside we cast the same wonderstruck gaze on all we saw, as if expecting everything to be different because we ourselves were changed. Stephen laced his fingers with mine and it felt as though our two hands with the fingers joined this way were just one. We walked, swinging our linked hands in time with our steps, not knowing in what direction.

He didn't ask me any of the questions you usually ask people you've just met and who interest you, like where I was from, what I was doing in London, what my full name was, nothing like that. I didn't ask him any of these questions either. It was some time before I learned from piecing together fragments here and there that he was studying political science at the University of London, that he'd been born in Canada of Ukrainian parents and was still a Canadian citizen though he'd lived in New York for years after studying at Columbia. Much of his life remained totally hidden from me for weeks before I began to wonder about it, and then it was very late to turn back and begin over.

For the moment, our fingers interlaced, we were just at the stage of elation at being together. All that mattered was that we'd found each other. Both of us were trembling, I think. With fear? Anxiety? Joy? Perhaps I'll never know. Through my trembling fingers I could feel his tremble too.

We had covered a great deal of ground walking aimlessly as we'd been doing and at last he said, "Where do you live, dear? I'm going to have to face up to taking you home, though that's the last thing I want to do."

"In Fulham. Lillie Road."

"Well, I never!" he exclaimed. "I live near there and I have a very dear friend who lives in the neighbourhood too, Bohdan Hubicki."

So it was he whom Bohdan had been so keen for me to meet! Yet just a few days before, Bohdan had confided, "He's a funny fellow, fascinating in a way that bothers me a bit because you'd say he's trying to make you forget you know practically nothing about him. I don't really know what to think of him. He could be a very fine person, however.... And yet...."

Clairvoyant Bohdan. Remembering these words, I felt a strange foreboding. I withdrew my fingers from Stephen's. I think I tried to put some distance between us but it was like trying to hold back the wind and the tide. Stephen interlaced his fingers with mine again. Just having mine interlaced with his was enough to send waves through me, destroying me one minute and elating me the next.

Softly, close to my ear, he said, "Will you come with me tomorrow to hear Boris Godunov?" He hummed a few bars of the monk Pimen's great Song of Destiny.

I was going to accept at once. I wanted nothing as much, but I caught myself in time. How would I look, what would he think of me if I leapt at his first invitation?

"Tomorrow.... I don't know."

"The day after tomorrow, then?"

"The day after tomorrow, perhaps...yes."

Already I was bitterly regretting having put it off so long and was ready to retreat if he gave the least sign of pressing me, but he said nothing, as though he too was sad at the thought of more than a day passing before we'd see each other again.

After many zigzags we finally came to an Underground station.

The train started up. I watched the names of the stations parade by in big letters on the wall of the tunnel, noticing how we passed gradually from darkness to light as we approached each stop. And like someone in a trance, at almost every one I'd stare at the big Guinness poster showing two huge frothy glasses of beer side by side. A face peered out of the froth on each glass, one serious and the other beaming. Under the first it said, "Sometime I sits and thinks...," and under the second it said, "Sometimes I just sits...." I saw serious-looking people getting in and out carrying long furled umbrellas and briefcases. I wondered who were really living, these people with their haste and importance or Stephen and I on our floating island, from where other people's lives looked appallingly grey and humdrum.

When we came to the little side door at the foot of the stairs leading to Gladys's apartment and on up to my room, Stephen's mood seemed to become thoughtful.

"So this is where you live," he said. "It really doesn't surprise me at all. I couldn't imagine you anywhere else."

He looked at the drab walls, the graceless street in a loving kind of way that made me cherish them.

He didn't try to kiss me or even put my fingers to his lips, just kept them interlaced with his. I didn't know, I still don't know whether he held back because the wisdom of experience was telling him that love is most unforgettable when it's just beginning or whether he was already fulfilled, overjoyed. I think it was this because he suddenly, silently laid his forehead on my shoulder, a gesture of submission, like a plea for refuge. And I, who all my life had so often sought refuge, was so overwhelmed that someone should seek it in me that I could have wept as though just discovering that the whole world longs to rest on a loving shoulder. I wanted terribly to stroke this head, the brown hair with its golden sheen so close to my face, but I didn't dare. I hardly dared breathe. At last he stood straight, whispered a hurried "Adieu...till tomorrow!", then had turned the corner and was gone.

The next day I ran home from an errand I couldn't postpone and called from the bottom of the stairs, "Has anyone phoned for me?"

Stephen had scarcely left when I began to hope he'd call next day to see if I wasn't free after all. And in the scenario I imagined I was saying yes, and he was hurrying over and we were leaving the minute he arrived, with our fingers interlaced as they'd been the night before and our ears still ringing with the least little words we'd exchanged.

But he didn't call either that day or the next. Then I began to be afraid. Afraid he'd been only a figment of my imagination, that he didn't really exist. I'd dreamt him, that was all, and dreaming wouldn't ever bring him back. Or afraid he'd just been trifling with me and had no intention of seeing me again.

But at eight o'clock, all the way from the top of the house, I heard the bell at the little side door. I'd been ready for hours, just in case he did come back into my life, I kept telling myself. I was downstairs in five seconds. I opened the door. There he was, exactly as he'd been when he left two nights before, except that when he saw me his dark eyes seemed to fill with a bright, caressing light.

"So you weren't a dream, thank God! I was horribly afraid, you don't know how afraid I was that you were just someone I'd imagined."

He laced his fingers between mine. We hurried away. We watched the Guinness ads go by at the Underground stations…"Sometimes I sits and thinks…. Sometimes I just sits…." Why is it I still see them so clearly, while so many other details about my dates with Stephen have vanished for ever? Perhaps because Stephen thought them funny and read them aloud so we could laugh together.

All through the opera he kept my fingers interlaced with his and would lift them to his lips and lightly kiss each one. I scarcely knew where I was. I think it must have been the Sadler's Wells Theatre, though I'm not absolutely certain. When Varlaam was singing his song about Kazan and the strings, brasses, woodwinds, and singer were all fortissimo, Stephen softly sang a few bars with them in my ear. I couldn't tell which was the voice from the stage and which was Stephen's, and when I remember sometimes, his is the only one I hear. The opera was being sung in Russian and he was singing the Russian words.

"So you speak Russian too?" I said afterwards.

"A bit of several Eastern European languages," he replied briefly as if he didn't want to pursue the subject.

When he took me home he said at the foot of the stairs, "Don't let's ever stay two days again without seeing each other. It's like an eternity. Promise me we'll see each other every day."

I wanted nothing less myself. At this point I barely glimpsed to what a submissive, dependent state I was being led by my feeling for this young man I hardly knew. Still, that night I did have an inkling and made an effort to regain control and put off our next meeting at least a little while, but Stephen made a suggestion that was just too appealing. We would go to an ancient dockland pub, the Prospect of Whitby, on the other side of the city in the heart of a large working-class district. The dandies and eccentrics of Park Lane had made it fashionable by going there to drink draft beer and lean on the bar, elbow to elbow with cloth-capped labourers and picturesque wastrels. The spectacle was really worth seeing, said Stephen; nothing more typified a certain stratum of English society than its efforts to mix with the common herd in order to appear sympathetic to the people and their hardships.

The Underground was almost always a magic carpet for me, but never more than on this particular evening. We came out deep in the Port of London, almost down to the Thames Estuary, and made our way through dark streets peopled with shadowy, disconcerting figures to the little old pub built on piles over the grey waters of the river. You could hear the Thames lapping at its base. The pub was filled with acrid pipe smoke, the stench of beer, hysterical laughter, and cockney oaths. If I turned one way I might have been in a Hogarth painting with its ale-drinking working-class faces; if I turned the other I saw Pygmalion in reverse, high society with caps pulled over one ear and cigarette butts dangling from lips, playing at being the proletariat. I remember this evening with Stephen very well indeed; as dotty as certain dreams, no doubt perfectly in tune with my state of almost constant wide-eyed wonder at the time.

On the other hand, I remember very little about going with him to the National Gallery. My most lasting memories of a visit there are of a time when I went alone during my second trip to England. I remember particularly, though I don't know why, the portrait of "Giovanni Arnolfini and His Bride" by Jan van Eyck, which comes to my mind almost every day of my life. When I was there with Stephen I didn't see the works of art very well; we were holding hands all the time, that electric current kept passing between us, Stephen was whispering tender things to me, and all I really heard, all my ears retained, was the tumult of my emotion.

NOW WE WOULD linger at the little side door in the peaceful street. Our lips would meet. It was harder and harder to tear ourselves away from each other. Sometimes it was he who wouldn't let me go, often I was the one who couldn't bear to see him leave.

Were we happy? I don't think so. Our love was too feverish, too tumultuous, too possessive to allow us any rest, and when there are no islands of calm at which to pause, love soon reaches a point of exhaustion. My feeling for Stephen destroyed almost all power of reflection in me. He made me think I was living with great intensity, but in reality he was keeping me away from practically everything beyond his control. I was no longer seeing anything but brief glimpses of the world around us, which seemed more and more distant, strange, and out of reach, though it was we who were cut off, wrapped up in our passion, isolated as if for ever. Later, when I tried to analyse what had happened to us, it seemed to me that Stephen and I had been like butterflies or night-flying moths, those myriad creatures of the air drawn helplessly by some ruse of Nature like wavelengths or a certain smell. I wonder if the electrifying attraction we were subject to isn't one of the cruelest of all life's pitfalls and misconceptions. Because of him, once free of this subjugation I was long in mortal fear of the thing called love; perhaps I always shall be.

At the little side door, soon we couldn't bear to separate our hands, our lips. A storm would break, keeping us clinging to one another like two souls swept away in a raging tempest.

One night I leaned against the door and it gave way, carelessly latched no doubt. It swung open by itself. Stephen looked at me, a question in his eyes. We started up the stairs, still clinging to one another. At the first landing we stayed motionless for a while, our heads pressed together, engulfed in a silent turmoil beyond all rational thought, I suppose. We climbed the last flight of stairs holding each other up as though neither would be able to stand alone.

When he saw my room, Stephen seemed deeply moved. "A little room filled with the dreams of youth," he said pensively.

It was true, not only of this room but of all the others I'd occupied alone for a number of years. All must have been imbued with the universal dream inhabiting the human heart, which asks, what will love be like? Will it be kind? Will it hurt me?

Only then did Stephen realize that he was going to be my first lover. He became quiet and thoughtful, perhaps rather afraid. Holding me gently against his chest, he whispered that I mustn't hold it against him if he disappointed me a little, that love rarely gave as much as it led one to expect.

Then, holding me away slightly, he looked at me with a solemn expression of wonder and tenderness.

"Dear heart," he said, "how is it that you've waited for me? Surely you've been loved many times, and you must have been in love. What made you wait for me?"

We sat at the foot of my sofa-bed with our fingers interlaced, both looking straight ahead, into our own lives, neither seeing what the other was seeing. The thought passed through my mind that two people couldn't be more total strangers than were Stephen and I, brought together against prodigious odds in this almost transiently occupied little room. Now I could see that I'd been kept from love by my fear of it, I thought, the certainty that it was almost never happy; but it hadn't kept me from hoping for someone, some day, to fulfil my yearning for this utter unknown.

I put my head on his shoulder and told him that I was probably old-fashioned, but for me love was always a very serious thing, never frivolous or passing. That I'd always considered it to be irreversible in a way. That you really couldn't recover from love, any more than you can from death. And this was probably why it had made me so afraid while attracting me so irresistibly.

Putting a finger under my chin, Stephen lifted my face and studied it at length. There was concern in his eyes.

"You really believe that love's so serious you can't ever completely recover from it?"

"It seems to me it can't be something you simply forget."

"In that case," he said gently, "we'd better just stay friends a while longer till we can see more clearly inside ourselves. And especially, don't you think, we'd better avoid being in this room alone together, it feels so good to a weary pilgrim like me, or you, or anyone on this earth...."

But as he spoke he held me very close and I heard the throbbing of his heart, and the fervid, dancing flame in our eyes gave each of us a delicate, ethereal image of the other. We left the world behind, to overturn and sink…rapturously perhaps…but at least there were two of us to sink together.

OUR HAPPIEST DAYS were in the next few weeks perhaps; we were unaware that they were the last we'd be granted of this period of confidence. Stephen rented two bicycles so we could explore large sections of London together. I'd never ventured anywhere more daunting than country paths or peaceful little sidestreets in St-Boniface on a bicycle, and the thought of braving the heavy traffic of London filled me with terror. I'd never be able to do it, I said. But Stephen kept giving me patient reassurance. He'd be the leader; any time there might be a problem he'd go first and make a path for me; I was to keep my eyes glued to his back and not let myself look elsewhere, follow him without thinking of anything else.

We set out one mildly warm day in May. At first all went well. Stephen had plotted a route through a series of sidestreets, avoiding most of the busy thoroughfares. But we had to confront a few. Before we plunged into one, Stephen would give me encouraging words and signs. Trembling, I'd pedal beside the tall buses which used to delight me so when I was riding all over the city on the upper deck. Perched on my flimsy wheels, almost brushing their sides, I discovered they were four times bigger than I'd thought.

Once, one of the monsters slipped between Stephen and me, separating us. I was so frightened I thought of getting off and just staying where I was, but this was impossible. Ahead there was a monster blocking my way and behind was another which seemed determined to run me over. I simply had to move along with the merciless flow of the traffic. Then, a bit to the right of the bus separating us, Stephen appeared, signalling that the way was clear for me there. I screwed up my courage and rode, looking only at Stephen's beckoning hand. The monster was moving pretty fast but I pedalled by, caught up with Stephen, fell in behind him, and followed as he turned into a quiet street where I could stop and catch my breath. I really thought I'd triumphed that day. I still think so and I've been grateful to Stephen ever since. He had the rare gift of putting confidence in people in order to help them find confidence in themselves. I was still shaking from the fright I'd had, but he told me I'd conquered fear that day and I'd never again feel it as before.

283

In stages, stopping fairly often to give me a chance to rest, we rode to Richmond Park in less than two hours. It was a weekday and there weren't many people there. We had the whole magnificent park almost to ourselves, we and the free-roaming deer, hinds, and fawns. We fed them pieces of bread, which several came and ate out of Stephen's hand. As I watched, I suddenly thought how naturally tender and kind he seemed. It must have surprised me because I found myself saying, as if I'd had reason to doubt it, "You seem so gentle, really. Are you?"

He seemed a bit put out by the question.

"Not very," he said. "In this world you can't allow yourself to be gentle. It makes you too vulnerable."

As we turned away he took my hand and slipped his fingers between mine, rather by habit than with warmth this time, I thought.

"You see...," he began, then broke off, as if he realized he was about to make himself vulnerable. He changed the subject. "Let's go and sit up there on the bank," he suggested.

We pushed our bicycles up a grassy slope. There was a huge tree at the top whose spreading branches were like an umbrella, blocking the heat of the sun. We leaned the bicycles against its sturdy trunk and stretched out on the grass, half in the sun and half in the shade. We lay on our backs with Stephen's head in my lap, forming a kind of cross.

He gazed up at the sky. It was clean and pure above the great island of verdure formed by Richmond Park in the London of those days.

We stayed this way for a quarter of an hour, perhaps more. For the moment we didn't need to look at each other or caress. We were content to lie in a cross and gaze at the tranquil sky, finding such happiness in this that we needed nothing else.

With his eyes still fixed on the clear blue sky, as if the admission were extracted by a kind of infinite goodness in everything around us, or perhaps his own staggering realization, he said:

"I think I love you."

Years, thousands of years it seems sometimes, have passed since that peaceful interlude under the big tree in Richmond Park. Of everything in our relationship, so full of frenzied sensory excitement and its tyrannical power over our lives, two things still stir my heart more than any others. One is the memory of Stephen softly singing me that aria from Boris Godunov, and the other, which moves me perhaps even more, is this confession made in full view of the sky.

IX

HE LEFT ME at the bottom of the stairs that night. I was so tired I could hardly stand. He seemed very weary also, and still had to return the two bicycles. He left without calling back, "See you tomorrow," as he usually did, and didn't turn to give me a last little wave. For a moment, in the harsh light of the streetlamp near the door, his face seemed preoccupied, I thought, though in view of what followed perhaps hindsight made me imagine this.

The next day I didn't hear from him, though ordinarily not a day went by without Geoffrey calling up the stairs, "Your friend's on the phone...." I used to run down the stairs four at a time, and when I took the receiver all I'd hear at first was the thump of my own pulse, then at the sound of Stephen's voice my heart would calm and beat less frantically. Each time it was as though I were afraid the miracle wouldn't happen again – the proof that Stephen was real – and once it had happened I could relax and breathe normally again.

The day after, still no word. On the third day I had to go out and imagined that Stephen had chosen this very time to telephone, so I ran home in great haste to ask if there hadn't been a call for me.

Geoffrey looked at me with such obvious compassion I was humiliated. I stopped going to the bicycle shop to see if there'd been a call. I stayed in my room and waited, and the hours passed the way they must pass for prisoners in solitary confinement. The simmering anger I feel whenever someone keeps me waiting goes back to this – though I suspect I was no stranger to it even then. Anger at being forced to do nothing but wait, wasting my time, wasting my life.

I hardly even read any more. My ear was constantly listening for the phone downstairs to ring. Time and again I would think I had heard it, mingled with the sounds of the street, and I'd run to the door of my room holding my breath, waiting for Geoffrey's voice to call, "Your friend...." I would have been downstairs before he'd even finished, and the sky would have cleared for me once more.

At last I decided to call a number Stephen had given me, rather reluctantly I thought, after I told him I'd never be able to reach him in case there had to be a change in our arrangements for going out. It was the number of the people with whom he boarded, a house I'd never set foot in. A woman's voice answered. Stephen was away, she told me. For how long? She had no idea. Where had he gone? She didn't know. Why did he have to leave so suddenly? With a hint of irritation this time, she told me she didn't think she ought to answer that question.

Totally undone, I went back up to my room. A gaping chasm was opening under my feet. Worse than discovering the mystery surrounding Stephen was discovering how I felt about him. In the centre of the thing that had held me captive for over two months, which I'd thought must be love, something ugly and destructive was now growing, like resentment. Inside of me, distrust had declared war on love and I would never totally recover from this. What I was feeling was a thousand times worse than my long-standing fear of loving: the hostility one feels when caught in a trap after being honest and sincere. Yet I realized that I had been much to blame, for even now I knew practically nothing about Stephen except that he attended the University of London, not very regularly, that he was fluent in seven or eight languages, and that he knew a lot about music. When I searched my memory I also discovered a good many allusions to cities he apparently knew, like Paris, Prague, Munich, Vienna, Budapest, Zagreb, though he had never in so many words told me he'd stayed in any of them.

I resigned myself to telephoning again to the lady whose house Stephen lived in, who could have been a friend, an acquaintance, or simply his landlady for all I knew. This time a man answered. No, Stephen hadn't left any message but he'd certainly be back before long and then would no doubt give me an explanation that would set my mind at rest.

This man had a trace of Stephen's slight Slavic accent. I asked him if he wasn't Ukrainian too. He told me that he and his wife were indeed of Ukrainian origin, though they'd lived in England since the Russian Revolution. Then he urged me not to worry. Stephen would be back any day now and would call me at once.

I was naïve enough to be a mite reassured by all this. I even decided to go out and get some air and was stunned to realize that while I'd been shut up waiting for word from Stephen, summer had arrived and any number of chances for contact with life and Nature had passed me by. Thereupon my feeling towards him turned to something I had never before felt for anyone – active dislike, I think – perhaps even an urge to retaliate, make him suffer even more than he'd hurt me.

But suddenly I imagined him dead as the result of an accident or dying alone in some foreign country, and I gave him back all the love that swelled my heart. Not long after this I imagined the opposite, that he was alive and well and enjoying himself, holidaying beside the sea or in the mountains, and my bitterness towards him returned in full force, more bristling than ever. I wore myself out, by turns loving and hating the same man.

He was away nearly a month. Then one night Geoffrey called up the stairs, "Your friend's on the phone...." I came downstairs, my heart trembling as it had when I felt his eyes pulling me across Lady Frances's drawing room. But this time my trembling emotion was mixed with an indescribably bleak, painful awareness of what a slave I'd become to his phone call.

I heard him speak in his usual voice, the one he used in our daily conversations when nothing special had happened since the night before. He told me the time had seemed long, that it had been hot, that he really wanted to see me. Would it be tomorrow? Or tonight if I didn't think it was too late?

"I've missed you, you know," he added.

I stayed silent so long he asked, "Are you still there?"

Where was I, indeed? Very far away and very much alone in any case, on the kind of barren shore where love leaves you when it ebbs after its floods have sweetly sung, promising happiness. He had only needed to say, "I've missed you...," and I could see the desolation to which this dearest love of my life had led me by the hand and heart. But I didn't want to admit it. I wouldn't want to admit it for a long time yet. Seeing clearly into one's heart is the last thing love wants.

"All right," I said. "I'll leave right now. You leave right now too. That way we'll meet half-way unless you walk very fast."

He seemed disappointed that I didn't want to have him come to my room, but said he would leave immediately and follow an agreed route so we wouldn't miss each other on the way.

When he came into view he was still quite far away and in the light of a streetlamp I thought his face looked thin and drawn, prematurely showing the wear and tear age would bring, he who was still so young and vigorous. This distressed me so that I ran to clasp him in my arms as if to keep him young for ever. We stood holding each other, cheek to cheek, rocking together almost in dance, murmuring endearments..."Dear heart!..." "Stephen dear!"

The spell was taking hold of me again. The flood was trying to rise once more and I would have quickly yielded if Stephen hadn't slipped his fingers between mine as we turned to walk; it was so mechanical that I suddenly realized it was a habit, acquired for others, not just me, perhaps practised at length before becoming so endearingly natural. I withdrew my hand because it hurt, because to my eyes skill and finesse in love suddenly betrayed experience...perhaps a certain inconstancy. But he took it again and began to question me about what I'd been doing the last few weeks. Had I been to the theatre? To Gladys's cabin? Had I at least been outdoors taking advantage of the beautiful weather? Never a word about what had happened in his life all this time.

Suddenly I heard myself asking in a strained voice why he had left me so long without word.

At this he dropped his pretence of light-heartedness and seemed exceedingly nervous and tired. From the warm brown eyes I loved so much, so dependably twinkling and beguiling, the sparkle vanished.

"I thought sooner or later I'd have to talk to you seriously," he said.

We had come to a kind of little square with a bench, some trees, perhaps a fountain. We sat on the bench. Stephen looked straight ahead. He seemed so miserable, so much at a loss that I felt for him, thinking he was about to give me a plausible and convincing explanation for his behaviour and I was going to be ashamed of my suspicions. Already eager to make up, I reached out and smoothed a wayward lock of hair from his brow. He took a deep breath and began to tell me a story which even today I wonder if I really heard from his lips.

Well, he said, since I was so insistent, he was going to reveal a secret part of his life, though it would be better for me not to know anything about it. I'd have to keep what he was going to tell me strictly to myself, and it would still be only part of what he considered he had a right to tell me. As for the rest, I'd have to trust him.

I already felt as though I were involved in some far-fetched novel, and now here he was delivering a warning in an impassioned voice I didn't recognize as his.

"It would be best, of course," he said, "if you didn't expect too much of me, and I should have warned you before, because in a way I'm not free and won't be for some years to come. I've committed my life – part of my life – to the cause of my persecuted country, and there'll be no rest or personal life for me till I've avenged the Soviet Union's crimes against my unfortunate brothers."

I listened, thinking, he's making this up, he can't be a secret agent; but I saw in his face that he was serious. I challenged him.

"What's this unfortunate country you're talking about? Weren't you born in Canada? Isn't that your country? Or even the United States since you consider that your second country?"

"I'm talking about the Ukraine," he replied, "which Stalin reduced to one of the worst famines in history because she resisted Bolshevism. Do you know how many of my people died of hunger in a single year just in Kiev?"

"Your people, if you like," I retorted, "but at that rate all suffering people are yours, and mine too, ours. Why the Ukraine any more than any other country? You don't even know it yourself."

From the look on his face I could see I was wasting my breath trying to reason with him. A fierce exaltation was closing his mind to any other voice.

He told me his recent journey had taken him to a Soviet-dominated country to make contact with an agent of the London Ukrainian Association. He'd been tailed by the KGB, which had been after him for some time, and had had to stay hidden in a peasant's barn for nearly a week, almost without food. It was a miracle he'd escaped alive. This was why he hadn't been able to get in touch with me. Anyway, couriers were forbidden to communicate with anyone outside the network when they were abroad, to avoid endangering lives. He was putting me at peril just talking to me as he was now. He therefore begged me earnestly to keep what I'd learned tonight strictly to myself.

I listened, still thinking it was just a bad dream.

Little by little he revealed fragments of his other life. I learned that he belonged to a group of Ukrainian militants financed by Ukrainian-American patriots, and its cause was nothing less than the overthrow of Soviet power in the Ukraine and the restoration of the independence it had enjoyed for a single day during the First World War.

I had already had a premonition that his dreams, aspirations, and secretiveness made Stephen profoundly alien to me. That night, sitting on the bench in the little square, I was convinced that in all essentials we had nothing in common.

It wasn't simply discovering that I didn't come first in his life that hurt me so. After suffering so much on his account I was wounded even further to learn what kind of passion was standing between us. If I had been able to share it I might have felt less betrayed, but the whole thing seemed totally absurd, unreasonable, particularly when he admitted that his studies at the University of London were partly a cover, since without an ostensible occupation in London he'd be even more suspect in the eyes of the KGB, which had agents in the city.

I said no more that night about my thoughts, however. I couldn't, I'd received such a blow. For sitting on the bench with the leaves rustling softly overhead as in Richmond Park not so long before, as in Rutebeuf's poem, my love had died. There was no mistake; I knew it instantly. What I didn't know was how long after the mortal blow love keeps trying to come back to life, begging to be allowed to live. One of the most terrifying and unfathomable experiences of all to come our way is this stubborn fight, one's poor deluded soul wanting to be rid of what one's body wants to keep.

We began to walk again. What a lovely summer evening it was! The beginning and the end of a love affair...two immortal moments, one might say, which remain for ever in one's memory, while much of what has occurred between is erased. I still breathe the scent of flowers as we walked beside the old Fulham cemetery. I remember the smell of freshly watered lawns. I hear the sound of our footsteps in the still night. All of this reached me from a world I had lost, as if with love I had lost all that makes the world warm and wonderful.

No doubt relieved to have unburdened himself, Stephen was talking about things we would do together. In his happiness to find everything back as he imagined it would remain, he even whistled a cheerful tune for a few minutes. Then he talked about Cambridge, which we'd have to go and see some day, but especially, no doubt, the famous Magdalen College at Oxford. He had a friend there who would show us around. And we mustn't fail to go to Canterbury, the heart of old England in Chaucer's time. He was even making long-range plans for much later when he'd regain his freedom after three, four, or at most five years devoted to the Cause. He would return to teaching, perhaps in New York. Then, he led me to understand, if I wished we might unite our destinies.

I no longer believed him. I would never believe him now. That night he had shown me a heart far too full of political passion to leave room for a love that was warm and alive.

And yet, at the little side door, when he looked at me with those magnetic eyes and opened his arms, I went to them, taking refuge from the heartache and pain he'd brought me. And in a kind of love which now could only increase the distance between us, we sought the cure for our need for love.

I despised myself for this. I began to struggle with all my strength to detach myself from him. If it was he who telephoned, I wasn't in. I'd be out at times when he might come. I'd return very late, sometimes to find him waiting for me at the little side door, and wearily, yearning to bring back what once had been, I would go to him. And then I'd hate myself more than ever.

Meanwhile I was doing nothing, and seeing with increasing clarity the destructiveness of a love such as mine had been. I had virtually abandoned my studies. I saw no one. Once again I became a solitary creature, but now my disgust with myself nagged me constantly besides.

Worst of all, for a long time I too had to leave someone who loved me almost totally in the dark. During this time I think I remember receiving anguished letters from my mother, reproaching me either for not writing at all or for sending meagre little letters that weren't much better. Since I couldn't or wouldn't tell her things she would disapprove of, I'd no doubt been writing platitudes which made her suspect I was hiding what was important.

Towards the end of June Stephen had to leave hurriedly on another of his dangerous secret missions. I learned later that this time he'd been to one of the Balkan countries to deliver some tracts to an intermediary. There were no telephone calls or letters, only a note slipped under my door apologizing for not being able to give me any news; the less I knew about his activities, the better for my own safety. Perhaps he was right.

There was total silence for a while, but this time I was gradually becoming used to it, even began to relax a little. I was desperately lonely, however. Phyllis had gone to Dorset. Gladys was almost always at her cabin across from Hampton Court and I didn't feel like going there any more. Even Bohdan was away on a concert tour in the north of England. Affectionate, honest, courageous Bohdan; if only it were he I loved, I kept thinking, how different things would be! But would they really? In Bohdan's life music had always and would always come first. Even in my own life I often sensed that I must keep room for something other than love, something perhaps even more demanding, and so I would be torn just as Stephen was torn. Yet I wanted to be loved exclusively, with an undivided love.

Living longer doesn't teach you much about love. Still, by now I think I understand that if I demanded so much of Stephen and couldn't abide his having another and equally important interest, in a way this was to get even for the bondage imposed on me by my feeling for him. Sooner or later I was bound to rebel against such total domination over my life. Undoubtedly I was already hoping for a tender, dreamy love; a haven and refuge. But can love ever be peace?

X

IN THE END I came to hate the little room I'd thought was so calming at a time when I was more or less calm already. In July under a white-hot roof, it was stifling. It's strange how often I've had little rooms that are made unbearable by the summer sun at times when I've been most alone. Scarcely a year later I would have another room very like this one at the far end of Dorchester Street in Montreal; early in the morning I used to escape from it and go down to the river where it was cool.

There were so few trees and green spaces in Fulham, and its working-class hustle and bustle, its cries, its smells, the incessant growl of lumbering buses arriving or departing at the door and shaking the whole building from top to bottom – in short almost everything I'd rather enjoyed not so long before – came to be more than I could stand now that the heat of summer had settled in.

I fell into the habit of slipping away to Trafalgar Square, where I'd spend whole days. The water from the fountains filled the pools beneath and the pools overflowed, keeping the huge square relatively cool. Like innumerable passing tourists, like a great many poor people of London who had nowhere else to go to taste the pleasure of water, I used to plunge my hands into the overflowing pools, sometimes my arms all the way up to the armpits. I remember how good the water was. I remember it better than the many times I've bathed in the sea in the course of summers filled with the play and pleasure of water.

I would buy something to eat at one of the little mobile canteens that appeared wherever there was a crowd and eat it right there. I'd read, or pretend to. I'd watch clouds of pigeons fluttering around Nelson's Column. I don't think these parasites are as fat anywhere else as they are in Trafalgar Square, where they're fed the best of everything. In return they never stop cooing. I'd see couples go by with their fingers interlaced. Sometimes I shut my eyes so as not to see them and sometimes I watched with pity. Didn't they know what misery they were courting? I was sure any love was doomed to die of disappointment, heartache, and exhaustion. At least I had escaped, I thought, well armed never to let myself be caught again.

Day after day I'd come back to sit in the square. In the ever-present throngs there were as many Londoners, residents of the neighbourhood and workers from nearby offices, as tourists with guidebooks in their hands and cameras slung over their shoulders. I was soothed by their company, always changing but always the same, like the waves of the sea. Strange how often in my life I've had crowds of strangers as substitutes for friends and family.

In fact I'd begun to yearn for another kind of company, without yet being fully aware of it. Here in this teeming city square, re-freshing visions of whole forests of trees, secluded pathways, and water flowing through river grasses were beginning to stir in me. But I'd been deprived of the pleasures of Nature for so long that they might have been coming from a world and time I'd lost for ever.

Eventually, one day when my mind could focus a little better on my surroundings, I noticed small forest-green buses arriving every half-hour from one direction or another. They would drive around the square and come to a stop beside a marker that was also forest green. After letting off passengers and taking on others they would depart again, cheerfully I thought, for a destination which for some reason I took to be a happy one. I had ridden around so much on London buses, how had I failed to discover these before?

This Green Line went close to forty miles into the country, so you could go out and come back in a day, perhaps even half a day. I learned this from an old cockney who came and sat on the bench beside me. The Green Line couldn't be better named, he told me, for its buses travelled only verdant lesser roads around London to enchanting half-forgotten villages, olden-day places, "the lovely old England", leaving speed and thundering traffic to the Great West Road, the Great East Road, and all the evil-smelling major arteries.

295

Moments later, one of the sprightly little forest-green buses appeared and drew up at the Green Line sign. From where I sat I could easily read the tall letters on the front that announced its destination. "Epping Forest", they read. Why did it make my heart leap, as if this were the place of healing for me and I shouldn't lose a minute getting there? All I remember of this moment which had such a momentous repercussion on my life is an irresistible urge to drive away in that bus. It gave a gentle roar. It would be leaving any minute. Suddenly I raced across the square. The bus was already in motion when I jumped onto its step. The driver took one hand from the wheel, held it out to me, and drew me inside. As he manoeuvred into a free lane, he chided me gently for giving him such a turn, nearly running under his wheels like that.

"This isn't the forest yet, so you can't go running round like a hare without looking right or left."

We left the noisy square behind. Without realizing, I was on my way to one of those blessed havens to which life has steered me over the years, each a place in which to pause and gather strength and momentum before moving on.

"WHERE TO, MA'AM?" asked the driver-cum-conductor with the affable manner so many Londoners used to have with foreigners, as though sensing their vulnerability better than anyone.

"Epping Forest," I said naïvely, clutching the handrail with both hands.

"Epping Forest's a big place," he observed. "Isn't there a special part where you'd like to get off?"

"I don't know the forest," I said. "Could you show me a pretty place where I could walk a while without getting too far from the bus route, so I can catch the bus back after a few hours?"

"So it's just to go walking you want?" He smiled at me approvingly.

We'd been talking loudly enough for several other passengers to have heard. They weren't your usual city bus riders who, though often helpful, are generally people with things on their minds, in a hurry. These were people relieved to be going home to the country after a tiring day in the city, or city folk whose modest means permitted only outings to the country not far from London. To my great surprise, almost all took pains to help the driver and me decide where I should best get off.

"Beechwood's a pretty spot," said an elderly lady sitting three or four rows behind the driver. "Did you know," she added for everyone's edification, "Tennyson used to go there for peace and inspiration."

"Beechwood is a pretty spot, it's true," said another lady who'd stopped her knitting to join the discussion, "but it isn't on this route. The young miss might run into trouble making the transfer and get lost and all worn out when it's peace and quiet she wants."

"That's what we all do," said a man's voice quietly somewhere down the bus.

Someone else was determined to send me to the town of Epping where I could have tea at a reasonably priced inn beside a forest path. There I'd have plenty of time to cool off and recover from the awful city air.

I listened to these kind souls taking such pains for me and wished I could please every one of them by going to all the places they were suggesting.

The lady who was backing Beechwood pressed her point. "Some of the beeches were already big when the village of Beechwood was named for them three hundred years ago," she said.

This wasn't the first time I'd found instant friends in a group of total strangers and it wouldn't be the last. It's like getting a present, and of all the presents I've ever received, probably none has brought me more pleasure. Yet I've never imagined I could make strangers want to help me this way at will. I've always had to have a genuine need for help, which I suppose in some way becomes apparent. My need that day, my unconscious appeal to others, was perhaps apparent the minute I stepped aboard the bus.

An elderly man sitting halfway down the bus, his knobbly hands propped on the crook of his walking stick, suggested I transfer and go to Waltham Abbey, "the oldest church in England, y'know, started by Harold, the last king of the Saxons...a rare gem, y'know...." He kept on in the loud, strangely metallic voice of people who are a little deaf.

"Here now," an ironic voice protested, "when she don't even know the forest yet, what's the sense of sending the poor young foreign miss chasing all over the place after the oldest church in England?... If it really is the oldest."

We passed King's Cross and my fellow passengers still hadn't decided where they should send me. The driver finally settled the matter in favour of Wake Arms.

"There's only an inn," he told me, "but it's a friendly place. You can stay there if you like till I come back in two hours' time, or you can go for a walk. On the left there's a quiet path mostly in the forest but not too lonely. Sometimes it comes out in the open and there are farms in the distance now and again…oh yes, and a beautiful moor full of red heather. It's a lovely little path that I'm going to come and explore some more soon myself when I've got a day off."

This was how I came to buy a ticket to Wake Arms. I've never been the same since and I still marvel that such a small decision, just agreeing to go to Wake Arms and not Epping or Beechwood, had so many extraordinary consequences that today I get lost when I try to retrace them all.

I sat behind the driver and made a nuisance of myself, I'm sure, asking him over and over not to forget me when we reached Wake Arms. I was suddenly so enamoured of this unknown place that I didn't want to go anywhere else.

The driver kept reassuring me with a friendly glance in the little mirror in front of him, and finally I calmed down. At least, though a twinge of anxiety lingered, I began to feel soothed, an effect that steady motion has always had on me. Now we weren't picking up many people and the bus moved along at a good pace.

The lady sitting beside me asked me what country I was from.

"From Canada," I told her.

"From Canada!" she exclaimed in a tone of real affection, whether for me or my country I didn't know, but I soon found out. "It's one of our countries, Canada is," she concluded.

I returned her smile with what was probably a rather peculiar one of my own, trying to show gratitude for her warmth but also disapproval of her assumption that I and my country were hers. Then I settled down to enjoy the ride.

Curiously enough, after discussing my case so thoroughly the other passengers left me to my thoughts, no doubt returning to the peace and quiet of their own. We rode along in almost total silence, a busful of people freed of each other yet united, all absorbed in nostalgic musings.

The city took a long time to release us, let us escape from it. It kept catching up. I had never come this way on my long upper-deck bus rides. The endless city suburbs I was discovering sprawled even farther than I had imagined. Each time I thought they were giving way to an unkempt countryside with billboards sprouting in the fields, they would begin again, with the same High Street, the same little huddle of commerce, the same ABC tea-shop. This was the first time London had ever looked to me like life imprisonment for millions of human beings. The faces I saw as we passed were dejected, burdened, blank. But I confess I'd never before been in any of the city's grimiest, most depressing boroughs.

My relief was all the greater when at last we were bowling along roads with little gardens full of tall flowers and half-timbered cottages often half-hidden under masses of climbing clematis. I'd never seen anything like this before except in pictures and I kept turning my head to keep each one in view as long as possible.

Today when I remember so many unexpectedly pretty country scenes, often in the most surprising places, it makes me think that with their thousands of different little pastoral jewels the English must have invented country scenery – though they have undoubtedly also invented the filthiest and most inhuman of cities. For having done such harm to Nature, have they tried to make amends by nurturing and preserving it?

Suddenly we were in the forest. For some time it had looked cool and inviting but rather distant, still inaccessible. Then all at once it came close. Now it was really all around us, branches from either side joining overhead to make a marvellous continuing archway filled with millions of sparkling, winking specks of sunlight. The great trees, the mossy trunks, the deep rich green must all have come down to us from some long-past age. Probably nothing much had changed since the days when Robin Hood and his Merry Men used to leap out to plunder the coaches of the rich to help the poor, as the legend goes.

The driver must have recognized my delight as he watched me watching the forest through his rearview mirror, for when I glanced in it I saw him smile with the genuine pleasure you feel when you find someone enjoying what you enjoy yourself.

"Marvellous, isn't it?" he commented when I turned my eyes gratefully back to the great, serene archway overhead, all my weariness and heartache banished for the moment.

The bus slowed.

"Wake Arms," announced the driver.

The inn was all alone in a small forest clearing by the road. For the time being, with its pub closed and the upstairs windows shuttered, it looked either deserted for the day or abandoned to a deep torpor. It had a very beautiful sign, as did all English inns in those days, which hung well out from the front of the building on a wrought-iron frame. What was on it? I must have known but, alas, I can't remember.

The driver handed me a timetable. He'd marked the return times with a wax crayon and he made sure I noted that after seven o'clock the buses were less frequent.

I don't think I paid very much attention. Perhaps I already had a feeling I wouldn't be going back that night.

He raised his hand in goodbye. He wished me a nice walk and a pleasant day. He closed the door and the bus pulled away. Through its windows I could see hands waving. Perhaps even the elderly man with the walking stick was waving, or was it his raised walking stick that I saw? Sometimes when my thoughts wander, for no reason at all I see that bus disappearing for ever, leaving me at the side of an unfamiliar road. And through the dappled green reflections in its windows I see hands, a little blurred, waving to me still after all these years.

IT NEVER even crossed my mind to disturb the sleepy inn for information or any other reason. I set off at once down the narrow track leading from the bus stop into the forest. It was just a cycle and walking path, in fact, and I didn't meet a soul. At first I enjoyed being completely surrounded by nothing but Nature. I kept seeing swarms of bees, wasps, and butterflies pass by. I walked on and on, loath to turn back, drawn farther and farther down what I would call a trail, at least around the next curve, for it kept bending one way or the other, always in full sunlight, however, since at this hour the sun was directly overhead and the shadows no longer reached me. Soon I felt very tired from the heat and fresh air, and probably from relaxation of nerves long under tension. I was also thinking that I was foolish to venture so far into the deserted forest and that soon I wouldn't have the strength to return to the bus stop in case this path didn't really lead anywhere, as I was beginning to suspect.

But I couldn't resist walking a little farther, then a little farther still, driven by the excitement, the anticipation of happy surprise that I've always experienced on unknown roads. This couldn't be the path the driver had talked about in any event. I'd seen neither farms in the distance nor heather-covered moors. Either he'd been mistaken or I'd misinterpreted what he'd said. Small bushy trees grew thick and tangled, pressing close on either side, really very wild, and never an opening to any horizon. This appeared to be a part of the forest left to regrow after some blight or other calamity, for it was clear no cutting had been done for some years. I could just as well have been in the bushlands of my own Manitoba as in one of the most populous countries in the world. But my surroundings pleased me greatly because I could imagine I'd never left home, hadn't flung myself so recklessly down the highways of the world and so still had all my opportunities in life and love ahead, undiminished.

I kept on for some time without thinking, so tired that I was dragging my feet, barely conscious of the time and what country I was in. Eventually, however, frightened by the persistent silence and near the end of my strength, I was about to turn back when I saw signs of habitation just ahead, half hidden in the trees. A minute more and I would have turned away from one of the most extraordinary encounters fate ever brought my way – unless the events of that day were all pure chance. But it's even more difficult for me to believe in chance, all things considered, than in the intrusion of the marvellous into my life.

THE LITTLE HOUSE was very low to the ground and surrounded by trees and flowers, the hollyhocks and tall, pale blue delphiniums reaching almost to its thatched roof. It couldn't be made for living in, I thought, just for playing at living in; the humble little Tudor cottage of Old England on the tins of fine biscuits my mother used to buy when I was a child, mostly for the tin I'm sure, because we treasured those tins and kept them for years to hold batch after batch of other, less expensive biscuits.

The minute I saw it I felt as if I'd returned to the safety and peace of my early childhood. There was a sign nailed to a tree, which I can see in every detail, though I've forgotten many more important things. In crude, hand-painted letters it read, "Fresh-cut flowers, tea, scones, crumpets...1 s." Under an arbour at one side there was a rustic wood table with chairs to match. All around, the air was full of the ecstatic humming of bees, wasps, and hornets, drawn undoubtedly by the flower garden from miles around. Perhaps the swarms I'd seen go by were coming here and had arrived not long before me.

I knocked at the squat little door under the low-hanging eaves. It was opened by a young hunchback with the pleading eyes one often sees in the disabled. I asked her if it was too early for tea and she said no, she was just about to put the kettle on, in fact. Barely fifteen minutes later she re-emerged bearing such a heavy tray for her frail arms that I hurried to help her. When I saw all the food on it for such a small price I couldn't help asking if enough people came this far to make so much preparation worthwhile. She told me it was surprising how many came.

"When they get away from London they're keen for fresh air and freedom, I suppose," she said, "but they're not always sure where to get off the bus. A driver I don't know seems to suggest Wake Arms quite often. Perhaps he came himself one day and keeps hoping he'll come by again. People are like that, aren't they, wanting to go places they know about but haven't been to? I'm that way, all my life I've wanted to go to the seaside. In any case, they take the same path as you. Some take it by mistake, I imagine, but the good Lord sends me quite a few customers, whatever it is."

With obvious pleasure she lingered a few minutes more, watching me enjoy my tea, then went back inside the house.

In no time I'd devoured just about everything on the tray, including a little pot of black-currant jam that the wasps descended upon, competing frantically with me until I thought of putting a spoonful aside for them, which they went to and ate delicately, leaving the pot for me. Since then I've known that wasps and humans can eat together peacefully in a garden if one is generous enough to provide a little share just for the wasps.

Made drowsy by the heat and all the food I'd eaten, I had dozed off when the young woman came back with a big pot of hot water for stretching out my tea.

"Sleep, sleep, " she told me with gentle insistence. "I'll just take the tray away so the flies won't bother you."

My eyes were so heavy with sleep I could hardly keep them open, but I still knew vaguely where I was. Would I ever have the strength to stand up, set off, and walk all the way back to Wake Arms? It didn't seem possible. But most of all I simply didn't want to leave. I felt as though no harm could reach me here; the peace of this place would be mine as long as I stayed. I called the young woman back.

"I walked much too far getting here to go all the way back today," I said. "Couldn't you make some room for me for the night?"

"I would with pleasure, but it's a wee place as you can see," she said with a sad little gesture towards the house. "There's hardly room already for my father and my mother, been paralysed for years, she has, and it's me as does for her, then there's my brother, he's a bit simple, poor lad, he comes home late sometimes when they don't keep him the night at a farm where he's worked all day in return for supper and a bit of kindness."

Suddenly I was wide awake and listening with excitement. It was as if an enchanting page from one of the English novels I'd adored were reaching my ears straight from the very person who'd been its source and inspiration. Just twenty miles from London, guided only by my lucky star, could I really have stumbled upon exactly the old-world atmosphere and surroundings described in the works of George Eliot and Thomas Hardy? So thatched cottages weren't the only things surviving from a time I'd thought long past, recorded only in books.

The young woman was worrying about me. "An idea's just come to me, you know," she said. "If you think you can walk a bit more, not far, scarcely a mile by this same path, you'll come to a wee village called Upshire. Don't stop at the inn, it's not much of a place. Look for Century Cottage. Knock and ask for Esther. Esther Perfect. Tell her Felicity sent you. I'll be a deal surprised if she doesn't welcome you with open arms. She's got room. It's big, Century Cottage is."

I was already on my feet, needing no more to make me find fresh new energy. I left a shilling and a few pence on the table and set off. The heat of the day was still heavy, as were my feet, but I was buoyed by the same curious anticipation that had flagged only briefly all day. Felicity showed me the direction of the village and several times I heard her rather thin little voice calling encouragement after me, saying, "You won't regret it, oh, you surely won't regret it!"

XI

FOR SOMEONE approaching from the south as I did, the village was set on a gentle upward slope tapering away into a beautiful clear sky. Behind, the forest pressed close, a constant companion, but the vista ahead was boundless and the unexpected sight of so much space was probably what made me take an instant liking to Upshire.

It was all on one side of the single street, which must be rather rare in England – old stone cottages, dear little old church and churchyard surrounded by yews, some less ancient cottages, post office, pub, and vicarage standing in endless contemplation of a huge open plain much like the horizon of the Canadian West that I described in "Where Will You Go, Sam Lee Wong?" in *Garden in the Wind*. The sight of this plain rolling away in magnificently broad, fluid waves lifted my spirits with the same kind of magical lift I saw in those waves, perhaps because I came upon it from the forest as I used to come to the open prairie when emerging from the woods on my uncle's farm. Nothing is quite like the downs of Essex, this is certain, their strong earth swell rolling on and on, driven by the same wind since time began.

The forest, patiently beaten back on the near side, dwindled to a slender, dark line in the far distance, blending with the horizon. Between this and the village, as if barely sketched, you could just see some solitary farm buildings with herds in the fields moving so slightly you could mistake them for big rocks at times. In a hollow much closer I saw what looked like a small manor house with a Georgian façade, and on the top of a mound a curious, intriguingly ancient-looking stone slab. I marvelled to think I had found so much of England's long past so unspoiled barely more than an hour from London.

The reason, I was soon to learn, was that everything here – the fields and pastures and farm buildings, the village, the forest game preserve, the small manor house, even to a point the church and churchyard – belonged to the squire of the manor, who so far had prevented the metropolitan sprawl of London a few short miles away from expanding towards Upshire. With the metropolis chafing to come and spawn more of its narrow building-lots, High Streets like all the others, rows and rows of identical little houses, and of course ABC tea-shops by the dozen, how much longer would he succeed? But for a time at any rate, the powerful swell of the downs would roll on undisturbed, on some days beneath big masses of white cloud scudding to or from the Channel.

I found Century Cottage without difficulty. Though with its second floor it stood much taller than Felicity's little house, it seemed to be no less buried in a tangled profusion of flowers. I walked up a path winding this way and that, perhaps as dictated by the flowers themselves in their determination to grow and spread where it suited them. I must have disappeared, I thought, among the tall delphiniums, giant hollyhocks, and Canterbury bells bearing more big sumptuous bells than I've ever seen anywhere else. I thought it strange that among these tall, haughty flowers were others, tiny and dainty, which seemed perfectly at home growing at their feet. A scent of mint kept wafting my way from some corner of the garden, mingled with rosemary perhaps. As at Felicity's, the air positively vibrated with the buzzing of insects, like the clamour of voices around a banquet table.

I came to a door of dark wood. I reached out for the knocker, but as if I'd had enough strength only to bring me as far as this doorstep, I suddenly drooped against the doorframe. I think I was so tired that tears came to my eyes, so exhausted I felt I was arriving not just from Wake Arms or Fulham, or from a love that had left me more alone than it found me, or from the agonizing uncertainties I'd been living with so long, or from a thousand mistakes on my part, not just from these but from much farther, the very beginning of my life perhaps. This was my last thought before letting my head fall against the door, no longer able to keep my eyes open. This was how Esther must have found me, almost asleep on her doorstep.

CAN I REMEMBER exactly how I saw her for the first time once the weary haze over my eyes had gone? I don't know. Throughout the twenty-five years I knew her she never seemed to age; her face remained almost unchanged, as if she were made of something that time cannot disfigure.

Her face was rather long and thin as in many Englishwomen, often giving them a pensive air, and was always framed by a bandeau tied at the back of her neck. The effect would have been severe if not for the countless wisps of hair escaping to dance about her brow, cheeks, and slender neck, a kind of halo, a flowering as wayward as her tousled little garden.

But what struck me most from the first were her magnificent hazel eyes. Though warm and gracious, they seemed to look into the depths of one's soul. Wiser and more discerning eyes I've rarely seen, yet they probed with kindness, and I thought that what they must unfailingly discover was the hurt inside one that cries out for help without one's knowing.

I had barely begun to explain how I'd left London on a whim and ventured too far to go back tonight – a tale muddled with odds and ends about Canada and why I'd come to England – when she put out both her hands and drew me inside.

"There I was just a minute ago," she said, "complaining to God that He hadn't sent me any of His creatures to save for so long, and now look, here you are, like a bird that's flown so far and fallen right on my doorstep! Come in, come in! Of course there's room for you here."

A very few minutes later, as if I were a guest she'd been expecting, she said, "Would you like to see your room?"

I followed her up a rather steep staircase. She opened a door. The most inviting country bedroom met my eyes, with a big brass bed, a washstand complete with water jug and soap dish, and a fireplace with a mantel holding a cluster of small old photographs in frames, and other keepsakes. "This is my mother, she's been gone so many years...and this is my brother John who died in the War, gassed, so his lungs burned slowly away...." Then a sprig of Scotch heather, "the brightest colour of any in the world...," a pebble from the shore of the Irish Sea, dried flowers under glass. But best of all were the two big, high windows on the front side overlooking the downs. They were framed, not the least obstructed, by airy white tulle curtains drawn to either side. To me, the great

307

waves of the downs were even more delightful from this modest height than from ground level. I could see them far into the distance, an endlessly repeating swell of silent stillness flowing to the far horizon. And from here I could also see the intriguing stone slab more clearly.

"What is that, Miss Perfect?"

"A monument to the memory of Boadicea."

"Boadicea?"

"Our dear queen of the ancient Britons. She was fleeing from the Romans in her chariot but they were about to overtake her, and rather than fall into their hands alive she swallowed a mortal draught of poison. They say she gave up her soul about where that stone is standing."

In everything I was discovering this day I didn't know which was more delightful, finding the past so very present or finding a present so steeped in the past. But even the rarest delight couldn't keep me awake, any more than the most nightmarish memory. I was practically asleep on my feet.

Esther pulled down the counterpane, folded it, and draped it over the foot of the bed.

"To look at you I'd say you'd run all the way from your faraway Canada without a single stop for breath," she said. "Come on then, lie down. Rest a while. I'll come and tell you when tea's ready."

My protest was feeble, sleep gaining the upper hand.

"But I've just had an enormous tea at Boadicea's...no, Felicity's."

"I've heard that before," she said, "but I make nice hot scones, and when you've smelt them you'll be like everybody else...you'll eat them by the dozen. Anyway, tea won't be ready for a good hour. Father likes to go to bed early so we usually have what's called high tea. It's later and we eat more than at ordinary tea, more like early supper, really, a bit earlier than supper and a bit later than tea."

"I thought," I said sleepily, "it was only the Anglican Church that was divided into high and low."

For the first time I saw the gentle, reproachful smile I came to love so much, the only expression of censure she ever allowed herself, I think.

"Don't laugh," she said. "The High Church certainly has good sides to it. The King and Queen belong to it, after all. But we're

Low Church. We consider God's too great for us to go trying to show His likeness in images and statues. It's proper to look for Him only in our own hearts."

"But you look for Him through music and your hymns are the most beautiful on earth."

I didn't argue much longer. I barely saw the door close behind her as she tiptoed out. And as at Dauphin at the station master's, it seemed I'd only just gone under when I was being wakened again.

"Gabrielle dear, tea's ready. It's nice out still so we'll have it in the garden."

Today, so far from those enchanted moments, I make myself think I'm telling a fairy story when I talk about them. Yet this is really how it was. I do at times have trouble keeping my imagination from intruding, touching up, improving on my recollections perhaps, but in this case there's nothing to improve. It was all I could possibly desire.

The little back garden was perhaps even more delightful than the one in front. It had a vegetable garden with flowers and delicate herbs growing among the vegetables, a vine-covered garden shed, and an orchard of five or six trees. The tea-table was set in a small open space down at the end, half in sun and half in shade, under a twisted old apple tree whose largest bough was so low I had to bend to reach my place. A tall, elderly man with a smiling face and a beard as white as his hair rose to greet me. Esther must have told him who I was, to the extent she herself knew, because she said simply, "Father, our dear new friend who's just arrived, Gabrielle." And he just as simply said, "May you be happy in our house."

When I spoke to him, I addressed him, of course, as "Mr. Perfect", while Esther with great tenderness called him "Father". I soon felt I was being terribly formal and awkward in the warm familiarity at the table in the shelter of the old apple tree. Yet I couldn't start calling him "Father". Then suddenly I found the name "Father Perfect" on my lips.

The old man gave me a mischievous smile which creased his wrinkled cheeks in a thousand tight little folds and reduced his twinkling blue eyes to tiny slits.

"Generally," he said, "only God the Father gets called anything like that. He's the only father that's perfect. But it's not irreverent, the way you say it, and I'd like to try to be a kind of Father Perfect to you, my dear, dear child.''

Before long he ceased to be Father Perfect just for me. How the name I'd found for him in affection came into general use I have no idea, but pretty soon no one in the village, at the manor house, or in the countryside around called him anything else. I even believe that this is what is written on his tombstone in the little churchyard surrounded by yews.

A few minutes after the three of us sat down to tea, Father Perfect wiped his fingers carefully and turned to the old family Bible which Esther had just brought to him. He opened it at random as he always did and read aloud. As I recall, the passage was about Joseph's sojourn in Egypt. The air around us hummed with a song of thanksgiving from the insects foraging among the flowers. It also bore the fragrance of the three precious herbs, thyme, rosemary, and marjoram, one of which was for faith, Esther taught me, and the other two associated with which two virtues I now can't for the life of me remember. When he had finished reading, Father Perfect joined his hands before him and said an impromptu prayer, as he did each day.

First he prayed the Lord to take from us the threat of war which appeared to be hanging over Europe. I remembered then the sultry wind of fear that had blown over London not so long before, something of which I'd been barely conscious, absorbed as I'd been in my own selfish misery. So the terrifying shadow creeping over the world really began to reach me only then, at the bottom of the little garden full of flowers, the buzzing of insects, and the most delicate fragrances of summer. But the old man continued his prayer and peace dropped its fragile mantle over us again.

''Lord,'' he said as if talking to a friend sitting beside him, ''from faraway Canada, which, you remember, our John dreamed so much of visiting, you've brought us today a young friend whose heart is sorely troubled, perhaps. Help us, gentle Saviour, to know how to help her. She could have gone to a thousand other places, knocked on many other doors, but she came to ours. We can't help seeing in this a sign that you were giving her into our care. Now that she's part of our household, protect her, dear Lord, as you protect my dear Esther and myself.''

Silence fell. I could no longer see anything in the distance by the remaining light under the branches of the apple tree. While Father Perfect was praying, memories of the months since the day I met Stephen welled up in my throat, threatening to stifle me. But they didn't have the same bitter taste as in recent weeks, and even threatened to dissolve in tears, a few of which fell though I managed to hide them, I think. But I did take a while to clear my eyes enough to see the comforting landscape again.

Since we were at the top of the slope on which Upshire was built, we overlooked the countryside around. Just beyond the old apple tree that marked the end of the little back garden lay a succession of pastures and fields lying fallow, less attractive than the downs in front but broad and open, hardly closed in at all by the faint line of the forest reappearing in the distance.

Beyond this the sky, so pure elsewhere, appeared murky, darkened as though infected with a kind of sickness or sorrow.

"What's that making the sky so dark over there?" I asked.

"London," Esther replied.

"London!"

I already felt as though I'd been away from the city for years. It was still much on my mind as the scene of my feverish entanglement, then such unhappiness I didn't want to live, but I sensed that here I was protected from this confused memory, it was dormant, and as long as I stayed it wouldn't hurt too much.

Esther had hurried to the kitchen and now came back bearing a tray with a steaming teapot in a woollen cosy and a plate of her scones straight from the oven. She was right when she said their smell would revive my appetite. I devoured three or four one after the other, buttered and spread with local honey or plum jam. The wasps were given their little share on a saucer a short distance from the table.

Suddenly something warm and alive brushed against my leg. I lifted the tablecloth. A small black cat with incredibly sad eyes was looking at me.

"Your cat, Esther?"

"Yes and no. She arrived not long before you did, we don't know where from. She doesn't belong in the village or anywhere round, anyway. There are cruel people in this world. Sometimes they come all the way from London just to leave pets they don't want any more. She came and cried at the front door. I went to see what it was. She seemed hungry. Now it looks as if she wants to stay."

"That's because your welcome is so warm, Esther. Have you given her a name?"

"Not yet. I haven't had time. Why don't you give her one?"

I bent down and stroked the little lost creature.

"I think Guinevere would suit her."

"Guinevere! That's a very grand name for a little cat from the worst slums of London like as not! But then, why shouldn't she have a name that'll put her up a notch or two."

The homeless little animal rose on its back feet, put its front paws on my knee, and rubbed its head there, murmuring a kind of thank-you in the back of its throat.

The heat of summer had arrived. At moments a breath of cool air wafted under the branches of the apple trees, freshened by the broad reaches of the meadows beyond the garden. When we'd eaten our fill we stayed talking peacefully in the advancing twilight. I learned that Father Perfect had been garden boy, then assistant gardener, and eventually head gardener to the squire of the manor, primarily at an estate in Norfolk before being brought to the smaller manor of Upshire. He'd been retired for some years and had the use and enjoyment of the house and a small pension for himself and Esther as long as they lived, as well as certain rights, for instance to gather dead wood and take small game in the part of the forest still belonging to the manor. He still liked to go to the forest every day, partly to help the gamekeeper, who couldn't be everywhere at once, and partly for his own pleasure. He'd bring back mushrooms, bundles of good dry firewood which burned well, and sometimes just flowers. As I listened I came to understand the source of his serenity and goodness of heart, his uncommon gentleness, something like an original innocence preserved for all time. It must have been that he'd spent his whole life just looking after things that make the world more beautiful. "The roses in our rose garden in Norfolk, now...," he said to me, "I wish you could have seen them. They held themselves like queens standing in a row waiting for the daylight. You'd not even be surprised to see them bow to it...imagine!... Though they're proud, roses are...they don't bend much, even in a storm."

Eventually he seemed very weary from revisiting his earliest memories, perhaps also from the concern aroused by my arrival. He rose, wished us good-night and blessed us both, then went inside to retire for the night.

I offered to help Esther clear the table.

"Oh no!" she said with feeling. "Not yet. Let's stay and talk a little longer. I love listening to Father. You can see what a dear he is. But every evening it's the same, the roses in Norfolk, the hen pheasants that know him in the game preserve and follow him.... What else can you expect? He's lived in a kind of Garden of Eden and the woes of mankind haven't touched him as they have most people. And there really isn't much left to say about Eden once the story's been told, is there? Stay a bit, it's been so long since I had someone to talk to about all sorts of things, at a time of day when words just seem to come by themselves...you know, round twilight, for instance."

To me, twilight was more a time for silence and thinking thoughts that spread out in circles till they disappeared in perfect stillness, as in a pond at night. But this meant that she and I would get along beautifully. She could open her heart and talk, and I could stay quiet and listen.

In fact, she didn't talk very much...a few words at a time between long spells of thinking. But each little phrase rang so true, showed such pertinent reflection, contained so much wisdom, and was so articulate that each time I listened carefully.

"Where did you learn so much, Esther?"

"Well, certainly not in school at any rate. I stopped school at twelve to go into service in the master's house. They had lots of books, the family did. When the young ladies sat in the garden in their chaises longues they sometimes dropped their books and when I picked up after them there were times when I could open one and read a bit. I was surprised they were so careless of such treasures, even then. Later they gave me books, perhaps to be rid of them. Often I'd read by candlelight in my room at the top of the house till I couldn't stay awake."

"What books have you read, Esther?"

"I was so lucky! The master and mistress insisted their young ladies read the best...and the governesses saw to it they did.... I read all of *Paradise Lost*. I still know long parts by heart. I read *The Pilgrim's Progress* too, but I thought some of it rather boring,

I'm ashamed to confess. Then the Brontë sisters, Jane Austen, *Gulliver's Travels*, nearly all of Tennyson, Browning, both Robert and Elizabeth, and of course most of all the Bible, the Book of books, where there's everything we need to know, dearest Gabrielle. But I like to open my Shakespeare every day too, just anywhere, the way I do the Bible. It's a rare time when I don't come across a sentence that delights me, and then you might say it keeps me company all day long. Or one that tells me something I've been thinking but haven't known how to say, so I know I'm not the only one that thinks it. Then my small lonely life begins to open up, and I feel as if I'm rich and suddenly not lonely any more. Is it the same for you, Gabrielle dear?''

I was moved to hear such deeply personal thoughts and didn't know how to reply. Guinevere lay at my feet, asleep but still purring now and then. In the distance, where the sky had been so murky an hour before, lights were beginning to appear, though faintly still. Everything was different now. London had lost its power to terrify me, as had Paris when I stood on a chair and through the open skylight saw it at my feet in a gentle mood. How I've loved big cities when I've seen them not too close, at the approach of darkness when their lights are coming on, telling as nothing else does of brotherhood among men. Minute by minute the lights of London multiplied. Now they were beyond counting.

"I never thought I'd be sitting with London in the distance like this," I said, "as if it's a sweet, quiet friend I'm spending an evening with.''

"I go up to London once a year with Father to visit my sister Heather," said Esther. "You can't imagine sisters more different than Heather and me. She left when she was young to make her life there. She's not a bit shy, she's chic and always dresses in style, wears crazy hats and high heels, goes to the theatre and reads magazines that are a bit bold to my way of thinking. I feel very old-fashioned beside her. But I wouldn't change my life for hers any more than she'd change hers for mine, most like. I always come home all worn out. Besides this we go once a year to the seaside, Father and I do. You need a day by the sea every year, don't you, so you won't forget what it looks and sounds like. Father soon gets tired, so we just go to Bradwell-on-Sea because it's nearest. And we just go to sit and look at it, you know, just look and listen."

At last we went in. Esther wouldn't hear of my helping her.

"Tonight you're like some of my flowers," she said, "wilting suddenly at the end of a day. For them a day's probably like a whole life for us."

She lit a candle for me. As we crossed through the sitting room, I could see by its wavering light some of the books she'd told me she'd read. They seemed to be part of this room there on their shelves, like guests arrived long ago and still welcome.

"Are those the books the master and his family gave you?"

"Not all of them. Father and I manage to save a bit out of our small pension by scrimping on the coal in winter and not going anywhere except London and the seaside, and we've bought a few more modern ones to keep ourselves up a bit with what's going on in the world. We do lead a nice life as you can see...though perhaps there's one thing missing: I've never seen a single Shakespeare play, can you imagine? What's it like? Is it really wonderful?"

"You'd never forget it, Esther!"

"That's what I thought."

One behind the other, we climbed the stairs leading to the narrow landing onto which our three rooms opened, Father Perfect's, Esther's, and mine, which was the biggest and had the finest view.

Esther handed me the candle.

"There's a lamp all ready by your bed, and matches and some books in case you'd like to read a while. But do get to sleep as soon as you can. I'd like to see you looking better in the morning, and specially to see less unhappiness in your eyes."

She kissed me on the forehead, and as she would do many times again when I spent a night under her roof, now and later when I was almost happy and later still when I was less happy again, she said tenderly, "Night-night, Gabrielle."

I blew out my candle. I just had time to marvel that my rudderless little ship had reached such a kindly port, and I was asleep on the breeze off the downs whose crests rolled away to meet the crests of the sea.

XII

WHEN I WOKE I was perhaps more at peace than I had been since the Little Water Hen. No, since long before that – since the days of summer holidays at the farm when I'd wake on my first morning in my uncle's house not knowing where I was; then I'd recognize the inside and outside smells and know for certain I was happy again in the house I loved so much, where I'd known only peace and happiness.

From the big brass bed I could follow the sweep of the downs. In the soft morning light they had a green, silky sheen that made them even lovelier than the day before, I thought. I picked out the stone marking the spot where the queen of the ancient Britons had died. When I craned my neck a little I could see the small manor house, which had been bequeathed to charity and was now an orphanage, Esther had told me; the squire and his family had moved to another house almost hidden in the forest beyond the end of the village I'd arrived by, but down another road.

With the return of this peaceful feeling so long absent from my life, I discovered just as suddenly a burning urge to write. This had happened before. I would wake up happy to be alive, in a tranquil, receptive mood, and there in my head would be a story, ready and waiting, which I was eager to write. I've almost always harvested my best ideas, images, and stories on waking in the morning, as if they were produced by rest, sleep, darkness, or some long quest pursued unknown to me during my dreams. But I've always had to grasp them quickly if I wasn't going to lose them, for though the riches I find on waking are the most precious, nothing slips away more easily.

I hurried to a small table under one of the big windows where there was something to write on. Carefully I detached a few pages from the middle of a school copy-book so as not to damage it in case Esther was using it for keeping accounts, which seemed to be the case. This table clearly served as her desk. I took a pencil as well and went back to the bed. Propped against a stack of pillows in sight of the marvellous downs, I began to write.

The story I began with such enthusiasm that morning doesn't count for much today. If I dwell on it at all it's because it was at least better than anything I'd written before. It flowed well and, most important, it was irresistibly absorbing, restoring me to a state of contentment I hadn't known for a long time. As I recount this, it occurs to me how curious it is that one can only be happy when one is pleased with oneself. I'm sure it must be the same for everyone.

The story I found waiting when I woke and which flowed so well was coming in my mother tongue, in French. For a time I had thought it might be a good thing to write in English; I had tried with some success and I was torn. Then suddenly there could no longer be any hesitation. The words coming to my lips and from the point of my pen were French, from my lineage, my ancestral bonds. They rose to my soul like the pure waters of a spring filtering through layers of rock and hidden obstacles.

I wasn't surprised that it was in England, however, in an obscure little hamlet in Essex under the roof of people who had been strangers the day before, that I should waken to my destination, perhaps, but certainly to my own identity, of which I would never again have the slightest doubt.

The reason for what happened that morning was crystal clear, a miracle in a way, though the miracle would occur many times in my life. When I arrived the previous afternoon I had found myself with people who loved me instinctively. Where I've felt loved and have loved in return I've felt safe, and where I've felt safe I've found courage. Only affection can bring me such confidence that life no longer frightens me, I've known this for a long time now. Then I'm brave enough to throw myself into the work of writing, which never ends and has no real goal, an ocean without shores. Feeling such support this morning, perhaps I also felt duty bound to return in my own way the love the old man and his daughter were so freely giving me. I had seven or eight pages written when Esther came in with my breakfast tray.

She put it on my knees, brushing aside some of the papers littering the covers. It was such a huge meal I was sure I could never eat it and protested, only to get the same lecture I'd had at Wickendon Street, "A good day begins with a good breakfast."

Now that my mind was distracted briefly from my story, I thought about the long road I had travelled since leaving that dreadful street; I had so often reproached myself for going nowhere with my life since then. But tracing the route, I inevitably encountered a memory that brought back the wrenching pain provoked by the merest thought of Stephen; suddenly the downs, the vista I had been admiring, disappeared. Now I could see only myself, alone, bereft, and defenceless. Esther was as quick to read the changes in a face as in the sky which she studied constantly to foresee the weather.

"There you go, back in the dumps again," she said reproachfully. "A minute ago you were as happy as a child in a sandbox. Do come back. And first of all eat up this lovely kipper I've brought you. I went to get it this morning from the fishmonger in Walthamstow, specially for you. Then if you really must you can scribble some more for a while. But don't forget, the beautiful days God is giving you right now won't last for ever. This afternoon we'll go for a walk in the forest if you like...or on the downs...whichever you'd like best."

"Oh I'd love that, Esther! But I really feel I have to earn my joys, and when I woke under your roof this morning I found one of the greatest joys of my life."

WHEN THE LUNCH dishes were done and put away and Father Perfect had gone for his afternoon rest, Esther and I left for the downs. We climbed over a stile and up a little slope and were already alone in an expanse I was sure belonged only to the wind and the clouds. Distant farm sounds reached us now and then, the bark of a dog, the squeal of a pulley, the crow of a cock, just loud enough to keep us pleasantly in touch with the inhabited world. I was amazed how a country considered to be so small and densely populated could have such broad and beautiful spaces – useless spaces one might say, except for contemplation.

The moors of the north were much more rugged, Esther told me. More rugged and more enchanting too. She still missed them. She remembered being strangely carefree and light of heart for hours on end on long walks over those wild grey expanses, which were desolate yet noble, she said.

She knew everything about the downs, even their most humble plants. At any minute she might bend down and pluck a sprig of some wild herb or grass or a little flower, and tell me its name and what it could be used for, like forage, a medicine or just for making winter bouquets when there weren't many fresh flowers for brightening the house. She made it so easy to learn all these things that I decided to start my first book of pressed flowers that very afternoon. I'd have enough to fill several pages just with what we brought home from this first walk. As soon as I set to work, Father Perfect kept bringing me a veritable harvest day after day: cocklebur, catnip, a specimen of shepherd's purse (which interestingly becomes *bourse-à-pasteur* in French), and many more. Soon he was taking almost as much satisfaction as I myself in seeing the most characteristically English plants as well as the rarest represented in my collection. I worked at it with much pleasure night after night by the light of the lamp in the parlour with Esther helping me, showing me how to dry my specimens and then glue the stems and flowers to the pages. Alas, in the course of my frequent moves I must have lost it. I still grieve over it. With this collection I lost a tangible reminder of a time of most innocent pleasure.

We came home by a path through the forest. By habit Esther was now thriftily gathering pieces of fallen wood for burning rather than flowers. They would do to make the kettle boil for tea and even to build a cosy fire for the first chilly evenings of autumn, she said. It meant buying that much less coal, which was very dear, and even less of the firewood with which the shed would be stocked before winter came. Besides, without much effort on her part she was helping her father, who often felt he had to bring home much heavier bundles of wood from the forest than he ought to. With my inclination for mimicry, I also began gathering wood from the ground. I kept looking for bigger and bigger pieces, even tackling half-trees complete with branches and getting my feet tangled as I dragged them behind me. We entered the village by the upper end, I burdened like a little burro almost invisible under a bristling load of faggots. We passed the vicarage just as the lady of the manor was coming out. She greeted Esther rather briefly, I thought, then gave me a hard, perplexed look. I've often mused that my overenthusiasm may have embarrassed Esther that day, giving the impression that we at Century Cottage were in the direst straits. But Esther said not a word, perhaps so as not to spoil my pleasure in thinking I was being useful. However, in future when we came home loaded with wood, which was often, unless it was the dead of night we arrived by the back fields and the little gate under the apple trees.

I must have piqued the lady's curiosity, for before long she sent a message inviting us to tea. Esther seemed rather vexed.

"I'll have to get out the same old dress again," she said. "It was already out of style when I fixed it up a bit three years ago for the last invitation to tea at the manor. And isn't it a coincidence that I had someone with me then too, who milady couldn't imagine belonged to my social circle."

We were barely inside the cottage when I scurried to my room to pick up the thread of my story while Esther put the kettle on to boil for tea over a fire made from the sticks we'd brought home.

The fire burning in me was inextinguishable. I didn't care if it wasn't yet producing anything of worth despite its ardour, though I suppose I didn't know then that my writings were worthless. I wrote several pages before realizing Esther was calling me.

I came down and took my place at table in the garden. Twilight was rising gently like a peaceful tide at the bottom of the pasture. In the rather misty distance the myriad lights of London would soon be coming on. Closer there were groupings of lights I had learned to recognize as nearby towns: Walthamstow, where Esther often went by bicycle to do her shopping, Waltham Cross, and perhaps part of Waltham Abbey where I'd be going shortly to visit the squat little old abbey, one of England's truly exceptional churches.

It hadn't dawned on me until then that in my too-great contentment here I had forgotten to let Gladys know where I was. I realized she might be desperately worried not to have heard from me for two days.

I hurried at once to the phone booth outside the post office next door.

Perhaps she really had been frantic with worry. When she heard I was alive and apparently well she flew into a frightful rage, loosing such a torrent of reproach I couldn't get a word in edgewise. What kind of girl was I to have left like that without so much as a word?

Would it really have been too much trouble to at least have told the neighbours? She hadn't slept a wink last night. Geoffrey had been all over the place asking if anyone had seen me. And they had been on the point of calling the police when at last I condescended to telephone.

I might say in my own defence that with Geoffrey absorbed in his repairs or off for the day on some errand and Gladys herself in refuge at Hampton Court without giving any sign of life, they quite often went several days without even noticing whether I was there or not. But I felt guilty enough not to try to defend myself. I just said I was terribly sorry to have been a bother and a worry to her and Geoffrey, and I'd be back soon to get my things.

Early next morning I left for Wake Arms by a short cut Esther had shown me. At the bottom of the village hill I was to turn right at a junction which was easy to miss, so I had to be very careful. I was to walk beside the stone wall surrounding the manor house till I came to a big ploughed field. I had to skirt the edge of the field on a kind of beaten path made by people who knew the short cut. Unless I kept to the path I'd sink into the heavy clay soil at every step, which would be exhausting. Then I'd have only a short distance through the forest to the main highway, and I must walk it singing at the top of my lungs because, according to Esther, nothing keeps villains away in a lonely place like a song from a fearless heart, or one trying to appear so. I don't remember whether I sang as I walked along that dark stretch of path or not, but on the way back from London I may have sung with joy to be coming home to the only place in the world that felt like home at this time.

GLADYS WAS STILL in a towering rage. She followed me around while I gathered my belongings, telling me over and over that it was my own fault I'd lost Bohdan and probably Stephen too, such an attractive young man, and my fault I'd lose everyone unfortunate enough to love me like as not, ungrateful girl that I was. What gratitude had I shown her, who'd done so much for me?

But when I'd stuffed practically everything into my two suitcases I'd forgotten my beret, so I put it on my head, and when Gladys saw me looking much as she'd seen me for the first time her attitude changed completely. A tear came to her eye. What would become of me now, poor child, why didn't I stay, all would be forgotten, and anyway she was much more to blame than I was, leaving me to get along by myself so much of the time while she was off finding some peace and quiet.

I pointed out that I couldn't afford two places at once. She said I could stay at least a little while for nothing. I told her I could never accept that kind of arrangement. She was on the point of turning against me once more but softened and offered to come as far as the bus at least to help me put my luggage on. I was so afraid she'd take it into her head to come all the way to Esther's that I turned her down, assuring her I was quite capable of managing by myself. Then she did another about-turn. Well then I could go to the devil! If I'd come from Canada all by myself and gone running round Epping Forest all by myself, I certainly ought to be able to put my two suitcases on the bus by myself.

Geoffrey, however, came and met me halfway down the stairs and carried the suitcases to the waiting taxi. And he'd keep my wardrobe trunk in a corner of the bicycle shop till I sent for it.

"Bye-bye," he said rather kindly. "Don't take Gladys's temper too hard. She's like the wind, you know, the way she keeps changing, but she can't carry a grudge."

Indeed, she came running to beg me to write, at least to give her my address, to stop and have a cup of tea whenever I came back to Lillie Road.

I left without a single regret, or so I believed at the time. In fact my thoughts would return often to the neighbourhood, for it left me some of my most persistent memories.

THE TAXI RIDE was the most absurd extravagance, but I was in too much of a hurry to get back to Upshire to take the city bus and risk missing the earliest possible Green Line departure for Epping Forest. Miss it I did, however. I descended from the taxi just in time to see my dear little bus reach the end of the square, driving gaily away to the fresh green countryside. I sat down on the same bench I'd sat on the day I sprinted to the bus as it pulled out. I could have cried. I would only be held up for an hour, but another hour away seemed like an eternity. I sometimes wonder if I wasn't so possessed that if the bus I'd just seen disappear had been the last of the day to Epping Forest I would have set out to walk the distance, as I'd once set out for my uncle's farm in the snow and rain. Such is the pull of the place on this earth where we've felt the peace and happiness of home, however briefly.

THE FIRST THING I saw when I got off the bus at Wake Arms gave my heart a tug. Under the open sky with his fine white hair blowing in the wind, Father Perfect had probably been waiting for me for hours. Beside him was a crude pushcart I imagined he'd made himself years ago, on which to load my belongings. We set off immediately, almost without a word since the old man was saving his breath for pushing the cart when the ground was rough. He said only that he'd thought of bringing the cart just as he was leaving to meet me, in case I'd brought things back from London. I offered to help him push but he shook his head.

We came to the big ploughed field. Twilight was creeping over it. All you could see was a broad space filled with something vaguely blue and fluid, so ethereal it made you think more of a world beyond the visible than of a piece of unused farmland. Here the old man put down the shafts of the cart for a rest and gazed at the field. It was bathed in such gentle, soft light I thought it looked like happiness wrapped in a half-transparent package, yet close and accessible if only we knew how to get inside. He told me that he and Esther had found the day very long, they'd missed me, there were some people you became attached to very quickly and if you lost them you'd probably grieve all your life. Then he took up the shafts again and we continued. When he lowered them a second time to rest and had caught his breath, he told me light-heartedly that Esther was keeping my share of the shepherd's pie in the oven for me, and this time she'd made a particularly good one.

We came to the end of the field and were about to start along the path beside the manor house grounds. We both stopped for a last look back at the mysterious space, by now half dissolved in the gathering darkness. I saw this field in the first light of day when I was leaving for London, I saw it often near nightfall, and in full sun. I think now it must have been a perfectly ordinary field. I've certainly seen bigger and handsomer. How is it that no other has moved me this way, and why do I still treasure its memory as one of life's rare and precious gifts? Perhaps because each time I came to it I felt lightened, purified, though why this should be I simply can't say.

We emerged from the deep shadow of the trees into the feeble light of Upshire's two streetlamps...or were there three? From the pub, still some distance away, we heard men's voices, a kind of low growl. On weekdays there were rarely more than twelve or fifteen men there from the farms around, but they were soon warmed by the beer they drank and then they talked very loudly and apparently all at once.

On nights before Sundays and holidays, in echo to this rough chorus, from the little church surrounded with yews you could hear the choir practising its hymns line by line, expressing a most tender love of God and His creatures.

These tipsy voices and angelic ones were the only sounds I really ever heard in Upshire after eight or nine at night.

Esther was waiting for us at the gate with Guinevere rubbing about her legs.

"She's been looking for you all day," Esther told me. "I had to speak to her quite crossly. She wasn't giving me a minute's peace, wanting me to go out the front door to watch for you."

We sat down at the big table in the dining room in the soft light of the lamp with the écru shade. The best dinner service gleamed on the sideboard, ready for the meal. Though tired out, to celebrate my return Father Perfect had put off going to bed till later so he could have supper with us.

At his place at the end of the table he adjusted his glasses, opened the Bible, and read a passage, then closed his eyes, joined his hands in front of him, and said simply, "We thank thee, O Lord, for bringing back our Gabrielle safe and sound."

Now I no longer had any doubt. These people loved me as tenderly as I loved them. But why? What had I done to deserve the precious gift of their confidence?

THE VERY NEXT morning my day resumed the pattern it had taken before my return to London. I'd get up early, splash my face with cold water from my water jug, then hurry to the window to look fondly at the downs while I untangled my hair. Then I'd get back into bed and, sitting propped against my heap of pillows, I'd immerse myself in my writing. I had brought my light portable typewriter back from London and worked with it balanced on my knees.

More piquant than profound, my phrases weren't very demanding so I wasn't having much trouble with them. They just came more often than I had to hunt for them. Any time I had to wait for them to come I'd lift my eyes instinctively to the downs, and though I was so absorbed I barely saw them, they seemed to give me encouragement. This is the way it has always been, in fact. In order to work I always have to have a window in front of me and the window has to give me a glimpse of sky and space – curiously, instead of *espace* (space) just now I almost wrote *espérance* (hope). Concentrating on what I'm doing, I don't see the landscape, but it doesn't matter. As long as I know it's there I feel refreshed, lightened, perhaps freed of the bondage that is every human being's lot, a condition which probably, whatever people think, weighs most heavily on a writer. Because a writer, an interpreter of human dreams, doesn't always have access to them at will and must often wait hungrily at the door, like a beggar.

When Esther appeared with the breakfast tray I'd often have a dozen pages written, littering the bed. She'd scold me, telling me it wasn't healthy to work on an empty stomach like that.

One day I scolded her in return for tiring herself bringing up my breakfast, and announced that beginning the next morning I'd come downstairs and have breakfast with her at the kitchen table. She forbade me to, saying she liked to have the house to herself in the morning because it was always a bit of a mess and she could take her own good time putting things in order and getting lunch started.

Was this the truth? In the clear light of morning, if I took the time to really study her face, she always looked older than she had in the soft glow of twilight the evening before, sometimes even very tired. With my typewriter put aside and my breakfast on my knees in its place, she didn't linger now to talk at length as she had at first, since, as she said one morning, she could see I was more in my stories than in real life.

"But it's the same thing, Esther!" I retorted indignantly.

"The same thing? In certain very exceptional books, almost, yes. But in spite of all I've got from books, I must say there aren't many that have spoken to me the way life has."

Her perspicacity left me in confusion and disarray, I sensed there was so much truth in this. Was I wasting my time all over again?

Chasing illusions? Three or four cups of tea in quick succession made me feel better, however, my confidence restored; my creations, whatever else they might be, were at least lively.

I finished the long story I'd begun soon after I arrived at Esther's and at once began another. There seemed to be no end to the material coming to my mind and I expected to keep on living in this heady state of excitement. I tackled a series of short articles on Canada, an idea that had occurred to me when I was answering questions from Esther about what it was like, how we did things, what winter was like, and summer, and the people and so forth. I had barely finished three of these without a pause when on an impulse I put them in an envelope addressed to the editor of a Paris weekly I knew only through having bought an occasional issue in London. Then I ran at once to post them for fear I might change my mind if I hesitated even for an hour.

Sometimes I still shudder to think of my nerve at the time. I had no one to advise me or edit me and I hardly even reread anything myself, so my writing must have read like what I consider today to be a first draft and wouldn't dare show to anyone. But on reflection, the path I chose almost unconsciously is an exacting one, and perhaps one ought to set foot on it with a measure of thoughtlessness. Otherwise who would ever take this endless road?

AFTER LUNCH, which was always copious and which I had difficulty swallowing because I was still tense from four or five hours of work, Esther would send me to have a rest while she washed up, again refusing my offer of help, saying she liked to have this time to herself so she could practise parts of the hymns to be sung on Sunday or plan the next day's menu. Then she'd come upstairs and lie down for a rest herself in the bedroom next to mine. About three-quarters of an hour later she'd knock lightly at my door, saying "Ready?" very softly in case I was asleep, and we'd go for the happiest of walks. For Esther, whose life was all prayer, seriousness, and duty, I think they came to be a kind of reward, and I think now that they were this for me as well.

Most often we'd go out onto the downs as we had the first time, but now we went much farther, sometimes so far that we'd come home very late for tea and find Father Perfect waiting famished and worried at the gate.

"Forgive us, Father dear," Esther would say, "but you used to go on much longer walks than you intended yourself, remember?"

We went as far as one of the farms I'd been able to identify in the hazy distance only by the barking of a dog. We brought back some sweet butter and heavy cream, but I still think Esther took me there mostly to let me see a particularly beautiful view. It lay beyond a broad undulation. Below us was an old house with a blue slate roof cradled in some enormous trees, and beside it a fast-flowing stream with a turning water wheel, a mill race, and a moss-covered mill. A chubby-cheeked, half-naked child was sitting in the water playing with the barking dog.

I finally saw the moor of red heather I'd heard about from the bus driver. Esther knew it well and never failed to go there at least once a year when it was prettiest. It was much farther than I expected, though, and that day we didn't get home until nearly nightfall.

On some days Esther was kept at home tending her incomparable suet pudding which took so long to cook, or writing her "ramblings", interminably long letters like the ones to her old aunt in Malvern, for instance, or a friend she'd met thirty years earlier on a trip to Scotland, or a missionary somewhere up the Zambezi — like the many she would write to me later, in my case (since they came by airmail) all consisting of four sheets of onionskin covered on both sides and all the way to the edges with a tiny, crowded hand almost impossible to decipher. Something helpful I discovered was that each paragraph dealt with a particular subject, always in the same order. First came the Upshire weather. It was really astonishing what she could find to say about this, particularly the wind, which she might say was "soft and balmy, a sweet breath laden with the scent of the hayfields," or in autumn like "a nasty, vindictive soul shrieking across the land." Though some might think nothing ever happened in her life she always had countless little pieces of news to give, about each of her flowers for example: "The big pale blue delphinium by the door is as high as the door knocker; a single stalk of Canterbury bells has eighteen bells." Also about the birds, whose songs she knew and transcribed very well in syllables. And in almost every letter there was something about the old plum tree, which was decidedly showing its age. This year it had given practically nothing, but neither she nor Father Perfect could bear to replace it with a young tree when they remembered all the pots of jam it had given, and there were still some left on the pantry shelves. Thinking of this, she was reminded of a parable in the New Testament which she'd always felt was incompatible with the goodness of the Lord, about the sterile fig tree that was cut down although it had done its best. How unfair! At the very end of her letter, she would express thoughts about God and His mysterious designs for us and the world around. And since by now she'd have come to her last page, she would wind her final sentence around the rest, a minute line in the almost nonexistent margin, shrinking still further, twisting, weaving in and out and ending up written over other words among which, with a magnifying glass, I'd finally discover her signature. What she thought about God, from her letters in any event, I never really managed to make out. Despite her faith, I'm left with the curious impression that when she tried to throw light on her beliefs she became entangled and confused.

ESTHER SHOWED ME another short cut, this one across the fields adjoining the little orchard where we used to have tea. It led to a local road along which a bus ran every hour, serving the neighbouring towns. I went alone this way to Walthamstow and then Waltham Cross, where I found a cross beneath a delicately columned roof, identical to the one at Charing Cross and ten others, all erected by Edward I to the memory of "his dear Queen" wherever her funeral cortège stopped for the night as he brought her remains across England to London: Lincoln, Grantham, Stamford, Diddington, Northampton, Stoney, Shatford, Dunstable, St. Alban's, Waltham, Tottenham, and finally Charing Cross, the word "Charing", according to what I was told in London, being a corruption of "*Chère Reine*".

I also went alone to Waltham Abbey. The very ancient church was deserted when I entered. I sat down under its low vaulted arches and stayed for several hours in a state of peace I've felt nowhere else, even in the semidarkness of centuries-old romanesque churches in Provence. Here I found something even more ancient, cruder also, more primitive, something reaching out to God which gripped my heart but without hurting, reassuring me on the contrary. I went to Beechwood finally, to see the magnificent beeches to which Tennyson is said to have raised a contemplative gaze one day.

Thus time went by, so well filled and happy that I didn't notice it pass.

As soon as I was back from London I concluded a kind of agreement with Esther regarding my room and board. I told her my money was almost gone and I could only offer her a pound and a few shillings a week. Could she keep me for this ridiculous sum? If ever it should become possible, I promised, I would double and perhaps triple the amount, though I didn't expect this to happen.

"Why yes," she said, "a guinea's quite enough for food and light, for you don't waste any. And even if you had nothing to give us you could stay and we'd manage. After all, Father can snare hares if necessary. He can get eggs in exchange for mushrooms, too. And then, what you think will feed two will always feed three."

Time kept going by with life so sweet I found myself thinking this couldn't be real everyday life but some likeness of things as I'd subconsciously willed them. And yet I'd still sometimes feel a stab from the memory of the days of happiness and torment I'd known with Stephen. The days of happiness perhaps hurt the most. So happiness prepares the way for sorrow, I told myself rather naïvely. But now I was spared the steady ache I'd thought so unbearable for a time, because I was rediscovering the excitement and pleasure of telling a story. Or because all of a sudden I was filled with emotion to see some splendid aspect of the downs that I hadn't been conscious of just an instant before.

I couldn't have totally broken off my drama studies, at least my lessons with Madame Gachet, because I remember going to London about once a week and reciting lines from Racine and speeches from Molière in the woods on the way back. Now when I stopped reciting and looked around, it wasn't tombstones but great gnarled trees I would see, surprised to find them disapproving of my behaviour, as it seemed.

One day Mrs. Stone the postmistress called to me from her house next door to Century Cottage, "A letter from Canada for you, dearie!" and came and handed it to me over the picket fence between the properties.

It was from my mother. I began to tremble as soon as I recognized the writing. I always trembled when her letters came, not because

I was afraid of reading reproaches or complaints – there never were any – but because seeing her writing was enough to open the door to memories of all the suffering culminating in me. Surely I shouldn't be the only one to escape, I would think, and I'd feel condemned to suffer, as if it were a duty.

I tore open the letter. This time Maman hadn't really been able to hide her anxiety. Why had I come to this insignificant little village, she wanted to know. Was I discouraged? Had I completely run out of money? If only she had a little to send me!...

When I'd read and reread her letter I looked up at nothing in particular and saw – I imagine by one of those miracles of normal life which happen more often than we think – I truly saw my mother, on the other side of the earth, sitting at a wooden table writing to me, a bottle of ink nearby, her glasses slipping down her nose, her face showing anxiety at being unable to help me and determination at least not to upset me. At this, I was so ashamed of having been happy when she was so sad that I was really upset. Dragging my feet, I went where only yesterday the trees had watched me recite and gesticulate, this time to weep in silence.

How long it took me to accept my mercurial nature! Or life itself perhaps. One day all song and freedom from care, the next all torment and distress!

Not long after, the postmistress called across the picket fence, "Another letter for you, dearie! This time from Paris. My, but you're popular!"

What this letter contained was enough to make me jump out of my skin: a cheque and a few electrifying lines. The first of my articles was accepted – for an upcoming issue – and the two others would be published shortly. I thought I would die of excitement. I don't think I've ever felt as truly like a real, honest-to-goodness writer as I did that day in the little yard among the dandelions. I ran and waved the cheque under Esther's nose and I think was piqued that she didn't go as wild with excitement as I was. The sum wasn't large, about five dollars, but none I would ever receive later would seem as fabulous, or arrive more opportunely. For want of human company to appreciate the magnitude of my glory, I went to the forest to dance and sing and perhaps even try a leap or two among the stern trees. I think I really learned then that of all that comes our way, the hardest to bear in solitude is triumph.

Around this time the threat of a second world war began to filter through to Century Cottage, far removed from the world though it was.

Father Perfect came home from the forest with a long face one evening. He'd been talking to both the gamekeeper and the squire, with whom he'd crossed paths separately. Both had been of the same opinion: war seemed imminent. Day by day Hitler's demands were becoming more intolerable and Britain and France weren't going to give in much longer.

Before tea at the bottom of the little garden that evening, the air strongly scented with thyme and rosemary, Father Perfect, his voice breaking, implored the Lord to spare humanity from the scourge of war. "Thou who hast taken our John from us, my only son, dear Lord, who in Thy wisdom caused him to depart this world so soon...so soon...." Then very close, perhaps in the old damson tree, a bird began to sing and its song was so pure and sweet it could only have sharpened the pain in the old man's broken heart. And trying to hide her face with her hand that tender summer evening, Esther wept silently.

But the next day the sun rose on a radiantly beautiful day. Light streamed over everything – the neatly clipped yews beside the church, the grass on the nearest rolling slopes of the downs, the line of shimmering poplars around the old manor house. War no longer seemed possible.

"In such a beautiful world it can't be," declared Esther. "God won't allow it."

In any event, Esther and I were going to take advantage of this incomparable day to embark on a real expedition, taking our sandwiches because it was a long way. We were going to Copped Hall, Henry VIII's estate, whose manor house was destroyed long ago but whose gardens had been maintained over the centuries and that day would likely be at their most magnificent.

According to legend, Esther told me as we strode along, it was at Copped Hall that the dreadful man waited impatiently for the messenger who was to ride in all haste from London with the news that poor Anne Boleyn's head had indeed rolled – God rest her soul! We observed with a certain awe that the roses blooming in this place, inhabited since those days only by that gory memory, were perhaps the most beautiful in the whole kingdom.

And so, despite the rumours of war that rumbled more ominously every day, despite the painful memories that invaded me from time to time, within a certain radius of me all suffering seemed to have ceased. Nothing happened to break the spell for several weeks. Then from my window one morning, whom should I see approaching, already close, but Stephen.

XIII

HE MUST have taken the long way through the forest past Felicity's, as I had the first time, for he seemed to be tired and suffering from the oppressive late-morning heat. Also, he was carrying so many packages they reached his chin; he'd always hated carrying packages. It seemed they were intended for me. Besides all the boxes and bags apparently from candy and pastry shops, he was awkwardly holding a little bunch of flowers that were half-crushed by the packages.

As I had done when I first arrived in Upshire, he was looking above the doors of the cottages for their names, the only way they were identified.

He came to our gate and paused to rest his laden arms on it. He'd been smiling, or rather his eyes had sparkled at the sight of the exuberant little garden. Now he seemed to be far away in his thoughts.

From where I was standing I had an excellent view of his face, though he didn't know he was being watched. As almost always in such circumstances, I saw things I never could have seen otherwise. I thought briefly that I wasn't looking at Stephen's face at all, it was showing so much that I didn't recognize. Signs of sorrow, perhaps to think he'd lost me, perhaps for some totally different reason. How could I tell? Signs of uncertainty in a man who'd always been so decisive. Perhaps even a bitter, touching kind of regret. I wanted to warn him that I could see him exposed like this and it was unbearable, but the shock of seeing him at my mercy in a way was so great that I couldn't speak. He'd always sparkled so with vitality, but now I thought he looked thinner, almost exhausted. I was even more surprised to discover what had happened to my own feeling about him. Spying on him from the window so to speak, I felt none of the pathetic magnetism that had passed between us across Lady Frances's drawing room, as though we were hunted creatures exchanging signals leading us to one another. But there was no trace of my harsh resentment towards him either. What I was feeling at the moment seemed to be compassion, regret that he'd suffered because of me; a new and indulgent feeling, the germ of tenderness at last, perhaps.

I was so relieved to discover this kinder feeling in me that I put my head out the window and called cheerily:

"Stephen! Hello there!"

He looked up. Such a wonderful radiance came over his face that suddenly he was as beautiful to me as the downs behind.

I ran downstairs and out the door and threw my arms around him, flimsily tied packages and all. Our first kisses were sweet and grateful. We were both overjoyed, he that I should welcome him so warmly and I that he should be so happy to have found me again.

I relieved him of part of his burden and led him through the house looking for Esther. When we found her she was washing vegetables in the scullery, the small room behind the kitchen for household chores too dirty to do elsewhere. One day I'd said, "What's the point of it? You have to clean that too." She'd answered, "How right! It's most annoying how often you're right!"

She liked Stephen immediately. I saw it in the tenderness of her smile and the light in her grey-green eyes. And he liked the gentle old spinster immediately, I think almost to the point of adoration. He told me she reminded him of a beloved Ukrainian great aunt, of whom he carried a small photograph at all times.

Though always so natural, after a few minutes she said she was embarrassed to be seen in her apron by a visitor and sent us both to the garden to give her time to finish her vegetables and clean herself up a bit, she said. "But come back for lunch in an hour, an hour and a half at the latest," she reminded us.

By then she had put on a clean dress, redone her hairband, put carefully chosen flowers on the table, and as we arrived was carrying in a fragrant minted leg of lamb the like of which I've eaten only at her table.

Lunch was cheerful and lively. Father Perfect shook Stephen's hand with the same ready warmth he'd shown when he first met me. He enquired of him regarding events in the world, the country, and London with the deference due to someone who certainly had intelligent views on these matters. Naïvely, he and Esther were delighted to find me less alone in the world than I might have seemed, and their eyes kept straying from me to Stephen and from Stephen to me as if to show me they approved of my choice. Stephen could be such a charmer and cajoler, it was undoubtedly easy for him to win them over, but that day I think there was real affection rather than artifice behind his efforts to please under this roof.

When lunch was over Stephen went to the old harmonium at the end of the room, ran a hand over the keys, then sat down on the bench and, pumping at the pedals covered with worn old felt, began to play and sing a hymn, reading from the open book on the music stand. I knew the simple tune well. Esther used to sing it softly as she went about her dusting with a towel around her head to keep the dust out of her hair. Since she kept losing the key she'd go often to the harmonium to find it again, all of which I could hear in my room. Now she sat smiling at her place at table and as if unconsciously soon began to sing along with Stephen. I thought I must be dreaming to hear their voices in unison, one pious and fervent and the other sincere perhaps only for the moment.

The cow's in the meadow,
The sheep's in the pasture,
God's in His Heaven,
All's right with the world....

Abruptly Stephen dropped the song of praise. His hands seemed to be groping for an air he'd remembered. Then suddenly he was playing the beautiful but ominous Song of Destiny. I shuddered and dark forebodings crossed my mind, evil things, huge, inscrutable, faceless things. Then the uneasiness passed. He had begun another tune, a brisk and cheerful one for all the instrument's solemnity. It was amusing to hear the wheezy harmonium producing almost rollicking sounds. Guinevere was terrified by such unaccustomed noises and ran to hide under an old cupboard. Once again Father Perfect had tears in his eyes, tears of laughter this time. Finally Stephen swung his feet nimbly up and over the bench and turned to face us, smiling broadly.

Esther said, "It's such a lovely afternoon, you two had better hurry out for a walk in the forest."

Stephen looked at me in that burning, intense way of his. I looked down at the floor, Esther must so surely have seen and understood. But Stephen's desire to please came to the fore. He'd wash the dishes, he said, while Esther and I went and sat in the garden.

"The very idea!" said Esther. "You haven't come all the way from London to spend the best part of the day scrubbing pots. You ought to be out under the trees where it's cool, both of you. Go on now!"

I had an idea of my own. The moment had come to show Stephen my first finished story, I thought, and especially the cheque from Paris.

When I put the cheque before him the delight he showed almost outdid my own. I must keep it for ever, he said, because it marked the beginning of my literary life. He'd get it framed for me if I liked.

"Are you crazy?" I said. "I need that money for all kinds of things. Shoes to begin with, or I'll be going barefoot pretty soon."

He relented but was still sad at the thought of this memorable cheque coming to a very ordinary end as money, thus vanishing without trace.

Then I told him I had something better to show him, and produced my manuscript. I wanted so badly to get an opinion on my work at last that I think I was trembling with trepidation and hope.

Stephen took the manuscript from me, scanned a few lines, and at once expressed even greater enthusiasm than he had over the cheque.

Esther suggested we go into the parlour, which would be cool to work in since the sun had now moved to the back of the house. The room was rather reverently preserved, making it somewhat intimidating when we first entered, but it turned out to be a pleasant setting, for it was on a level with the front garden and with the window open the air was fresh and fragrant.

At first Stephen tried to kiss me after every sentence but soon became so absorbed in my story he forgot about me, making me happier than he ever had before.

He read aloud with a pencil in his hand, correcting typing errors as he went, and soon, with my permission, grammatical and careless mistakes. I had known he had an admirable command of French, but not to the point of being able to pick up all kinds of little errors at first reading, even awkward expressions for which he proposed substitutes that suited my text so well I was as pleased as if I'd found them myself.

Eventually he observed that I was inclined to use far too many adjectives. The noun, according to him, being the strong element in the sentence, could do without qualifiers if it was an adequate one. It didn't occur to me at the time that when writing his tracts with their abrupt, incisive style he had developed a manner of writing totally opposed to mine. That day, however, I was so subservient to his views that for a long time I strove to purge almost all adjectives from anything I wrote. That is, until I realized I was making my writing dry and parched, for a well-used adjective makes a phrase live, makes it touch a chord inside a person.

But Stephen wasn't only interrupting his reading to propose corrections. Much more often he'd exclaim, "That's good! That's very good!" with a pride that lifted me as if on the crest of a wave. And afterwards, with the conviction of someone certain of seeing a piece of the future, he told me as Bohdan had once, "You've really got talent. You're going to write something remarkable one day." His confidence in me was encouraging such confidence in myself that I believed it, too.

Later, however, I saw that what he had praised most highly was perhaps not the best in my writing but the facile, the provocative but shallow, the playful, a tendency to caricature, all things I would try to rid myself of later. Still, this hour of work in the little old-fashioned parlour, a cricket singing intermittently outside among tall flowers which seemed almost to be coming in through the window, had a major effect on my life thereafter. In this little room I discovered what a delight it is for two to work side by side at something both truly enjoy. There is no greater delight, in fact. The caresses bestowed by eyes and hands, which are pretty much the same for all lovers, are so banal beside the encounter of two minds, the part of us we keep most ferociously to ourselves most of the time. I think also I was vastly relieved to feel that however solitary the way ahead of me might be, having companionship at least for a while on occasion wasn't out of the question after all.

We had never been as truly united, Stephen and I, as during this hour when both of us were so intently focused on a common goal you'd think we'd forgotten each other. His eyes shining with something quite other than desire, he kept saying things like, "You really have a gift. You'll see, one day you're going to be a well-known author." And I kept laughing, pretending I didn't believe it, thinking he was exaggerating, too. But his approval encouraged me to want to do a hundred times better and so be more deserving.

Around half past three Esther came and almost drove us away from our work, saying it was criminal to stay inside at our scribblings with a summer afternoon like this just begging us to go outside.

At first we stayed walking decorously from one end of the village to the other, but it wasn't long before I'd shown Stephen all there was to see. It was very hot on the road. A footpath led into the forest near the gates to the manor house grounds. After taking a rather long loop it returned behind the village and ended almost in the fields adjoining Esther's little orchard. This was where I'd gone to weep among the unsympathetic trees over my mother's heart-rending letter. This was where I'd gone to dance and shout my triumph which so quickly turned to a kind of emptiness. We stood at the foot of the path and Stephen looked at me questioningly. I resisted, suggesting we go to Waltham Abbey. We could go and be back by tea-time and it really was worth seeing, I told him.

"Some other time," he coaxed.

I walked down the path with him into the forest. It was cool and pleasant. I tried to remember how he had hurt me, I tried to remember as well how the flesh can sometimes bring happiness but can also assuredly bring all manner of woe. But it didn't occur to me to think twice about Stephen's feelings, he had inspired me with such confidence in them this day.

He took my hand. He laced his fingers between mine. All the sadness, all the bleak despair I had known in human love faded from my mind. We reached the sanctum of the oldest trees. In the deep shadow of their raised, still limbs, suddenly we were entwined, clinging to each other as though we were the last of our species left together on earth.

338

EVERYTHING SEEMED to have changed by tea-time. An almost chilly mist was rising from the pastures that extended towards Walthamstow from the bottom of our orchard. Esther had thrown a sweater around her shoulders when she came out of the house, and now she pulled it closer. "It'll soon be the end of summer," she said, surveying the countryside around, and the sadness in her voice wasn't like the Esther I knew. "It's been such a splendid summer," she went on. "We should give thanks for having received our share, though pretty soon we'll be complaining about it being taken away."

Then she thought to ask us if we'd had a nice walk. Stephen's eyes as he looked at me shone in a way Esther couldn't possibly mistake. She blushed a little and looked away. Her expression wasn't disapproving. I think she was rather worried for me, and in fact she told me later she'd had a very strong feeling at this moment that Stephen and I were going to do each other great harm.

Father Perfect, so animated and talkative at lunch-time, seemed deeply disturbed. He leaned towards Stephen and asked him if it was true that nations were once again getting ready to kill each other. Was it possible they were on the point of starting the slaughters of the Great War again?

Now Stephen's face also changed. Only when he'd confessed his secret political activities had I seen this worried, haggard look that made him seem so much older than he was. Now I couldn't help thinking how often he must be really unhappy, and it made me feel more sorry for him than he had made me feel for myself.

"Yes," I heard him tell the old man, "war is possible. The Germans are arming for it in any case. As for the Allies, they've got their heads in the sand. They're trying not to see the danger, which couldn't suit Hitler better today, or Stalin tomorrow probably."

"Hitler, Stalin," said the old man softly, "are they as bad as all that? Isn't there some good in them if we can only reach it? In all my life I've never known anyone whose heart you couldn't reach if you tried. Hitler, Stalin...and that other one they say is just as bad...Mussolini...is that his name? Couldn't we come to an agreement with them?"

In the old face, the eyes the colour of forget-me-nots had never been more like two innocent little flowers growing in parched ground.

Stephen smiled at their naïvety and now made an effort to re-assure the old man. All the bets weren't in yet, he said. Things could still work out so war could be avoided, at least for a while.

Though Father Perfect was quick to be alarmed he was just as quick to recover, and soon he was talking affectionately about his old damson tree. They'd been going to cut it down in the autumn but it had come to be part of their lives and they'd decided to keep it a little longer, and the birds that loved it so would be back again to make their nests in it.

Several times I'd seen Stephen glance at his watch. Now he jumped up and announced he'd have to leave immediately if he wasn't to miss the last bus back to London.

Esther offered to put him up for the night on the sofa in the parlour, which was narrow and rather hard but he was most wel-come if he thought he could sleep on it. Stephen replied that nothing would please him more than to spend the night amid all the good smells of the garden, lulled by the song of the cricket which he preferred to any music, but he had urgent business in London and had to be there first thing in the morning.

Esther then looked at me and asked if I didn't think it would be a good idea to go with him to the end of the village to show him the short cut; it would take him less than fifteen minutes to reach Wake Arms if he took this path rather than the long way past Felicity's, which was all in the forest and would soon be dark and worrisome. I think she had a feeling we had something important to settle between us and wanted to give us a chance to be alone a few minutes more.

As we left by the front garden, Stephen bent down and picked one of the smallest flowers, a blue one, and put it in his buttonhole.

There was total silence in the village. The pub patrons had no doubt fallen silent all at once, as happened now and then. Without making a sound ourselves, we walked hand in hand in the soft blue semidarkness, which deepened over the downs not far away.

Suddenly I remembered to ask Stephen how he'd found me. "Was it Gladys who gave you my address?" I had told her she mustn't.

It had been much simpler than that, he said. He'd only had to enquire at Canada House, where I'd left a forwarding address for some of my mail.

I imagine we must have laughed heartily at ourselves because I seem to remember our merry voices ringing incongruously in Upshire's sedate silence.

But as soon as the burst of laughter was over, there was tension. As we passed beneath one of the streetlamps, Stephen turned to me in the wan light and took hold of my wrists. His face was grim.

"Go!" he said. "Leave England. Go back to Canada. I didn't want to talk about it seriously in front of Esther and the old man, he's so emotional, but I don't see how we're going to avoid war. It's almost certain, and it will be very soon."

"But how about you?"

"Oh, me.... I'm still a Canadian citizen and there's a good chance I'll find myself in the Canadian army to fight the Germans sooner or later. I'll leave before that if I have to because one of these days you'll find it's Stalin more than Hitler who'll be the enemy we have to destroy. The two of them may go through the motions of a pact but it won't last, and while I'm no friend of the Nazis I'm even less a friend of the Bolsheviks. So if there's war between them I won't be for the Soviets, I'll be for Hitler, because in order to get the Ukraine on his side he'll give guarantees of freedom for my poor country."

"You'd trust Hitler?"

"For a while at any rate – or I'd pretend to. He'll arm us against the Russians. It's already begun, in fact. Then we'll use those arms to free ourselves from the Nazis."

I listened, overcome by the same horror and revulsion I'd felt sitting beside him on the bench in the faintly lit little square when he first revealed his militancy. The shock was worse this time than the first. It hit me just as I'd renewed my trust in him, when I was freshly recaptured. So he had come and played the game of passion with me, I thought with deep resentment, while the only passion he ever had was for some ridiculous utopia. I studied his haggard face, feeling no pity.

"You might even stoop to terrorism, I suppose."

His eyes flashed briefly but fiercely.

"If I had to...perhaps...yes. My people have suffered far too much over the centuries."

But he wanted me as well. He begged me to keep trusting him... until the day when, if the bloody mêlée didn't end in apocalypse, he'd move heaven and earth to find me, because then he'd have no other thought than to live happily ever after with me.

My only reply was to point out that if he didn't leave soon he'd miss his bus, and perhaps his rendezvous with his Nazi allies tomorrow too.

The look he gave me was pained and reproachful.

I walked with him a little farther without speaking. In these minutes I really thought I hated him and would never stop hating him. I pointed briefly to the path beside the wall bounding the manor house grounds.

He started down it. Several times he turned around and raised a hand. I stood motionless, watching him go out of my life. Soon I lost sight of his form in the deeper darkness under the trees. I stayed for a time waiting for goodness knows what. I no longer heard his footsteps. After a few minutes I imagined him reaching the big ploughed field that had lifted my spirits so mysteriously. The first stars were still rather pale but they'd be brighter down there above the treeless space. Was his heart also touched by this? Was he still moved by the beauty of the world? Could a man's heart have room for a consuming political passion and also tears, laughter, and an unaccountable attachment to a lonely piece of field in a forest? It's strange how often I've wondered whether this field I loved so much didn't in some way establish a link that night between Stephen and me which has endured, though Stephen himself was gone for ever.

Now, I thought, he must be coming out onto the road. He's reaching Wake Arms. He's getting onto the bus this very minute perhaps. I knew I would never see him again.

XIV

THERE WAS NO CLOSING one's eyes any longer. War was coming. Sometimes in those last days of August one would imagine one could hear its horrible breath blowing across the calm, untroubled sky.

David had found my address as well, perhaps also from Canada House. He sent me a note saying he was worried about me and inviting me to have lunch with him two days hence. Lady Frances was also concerned about me, he wrote, and had asked him to let me know she thought I should go back to Canada. We would talk some more about this. He asked me to telephone him at the Admiralty to confirm that we'd meet outside Selfridge's.

I was there at the appointed hour. I wore my navy blue white-flowered linen dress. David had already seen it but I didn't have anything else suitable to wear when going out with him. I carried a small straw handbag which was also navy blue and went well with the dress. To complete the ensemble, I'd just squandered almost my last pennies for the month on a pair of very nice shoes of exactly the same blue, made of latticed strips of raffia; in the first heavy rain they unravelled before my eyes, leaving me practically barefoot in the middle of Oxford Street.

A City gentleman came into view, identical to a thousand others at this hour, a tall, elegant figure in tasteful and impeccably tailored tweed, walking with brisk, light taps ringing from the metal tip of his oh-so-tightly-rolled umbrella. For the hundredth time I asked myself what on earth this flawless product of British civilization could possibly see in me. Who knows, perhaps he was asking himself the same question. In any event, there was a camaraderie between us which seemed to satisfy a part of each of us, for we always fell easily into our familiar pattern of light joshing and superficial repartee, exactly as we'd left off several months earlier.

Spotting me in the crowd milling about the department store entrance, he greeted me with, "Ah, I say, hello dear girl!"

Without wasting a second he whisked me off to a well-known restaurant. I wonder if it wasn't the Trois-Pruniers, unless lunch at the Trois-Pruniers was another occasion. My memories of this lunch with David and almost everything else about these troubled weeks are rather muddled.

We'd hardly sat down at the table before he let me know, in his fashion, that he was really concerned about me. He'd brought me to London because he wanted to see me, yes, but more important to persuade me to book passage for Canada without delay. I mustn't risk having to go home on a liner converted for troop transport. Or getting torpedoed on the way.

Understatement was so much a part of his nature that I thought I was dreaming, hearing him talk this way.

"Come on David, you're telling me a story! I've just read in the paper that there's no cause for alarm."

He leaned forward so he could speak very quietly.

"Listen! The instructions are to avoid mass hysteria at all cost. If Londoners got wind of how vulnerable they are at this minute they'd lose their heads. You've seen those balloons in the sky over the city that are supposed to form an aerial barrage. Well, they might as well be balloons at a country fair that you could pop with a pin. The truth is we haven't got a single anti-aircraft gun that works, or any other kind of weapon that can do anything worth talking about to protect us from a surprise attack. If it came tonight the city could be wiped out."

The fine meal, the exquisite décor, the sparkling crystal, the attentive maître d'hôtel, the murmur of voices mingling with what David was saying created an atmosphere of confusion in which I felt myself sinking as in a fog.

"You realize," said David, "that as an Admiralty employee I shouldn't be talking to you this way. We're supposed to bend over backwards to reassure the population, but I think it's my duty to warn people who are in a position to leave...and who I care about. I've been in a stew about you, you know," he chided me with a brief smile. "Lady Frances too. Last time I saw her she told me again, 'You must try to get in touch with our little French Canadian and tell her she should leave.' ''

Now at last I was feeling remorse over not having kept in touch with people who were genuinely fond of me, who might have thought I'd come to some terrible end when I was really just preoccupied, avoiding all contact with the outside world, even the least suggestion of contact, trying to preserve the fragile spell I was using as a refuge – a serious sin of omission towards others of which I've been guilty many times in the course of my life.

We'd hardly touched our meticulously prepared food. David brought the meal quickly to an end by swallowing his coffee before dessert. He was tense, to the extent that such a thing was ever apparent with him. When we left he apologized for not taking me wherever I was going. He had to get back to the Admiralty as soon as possible. They were working night and day at present. Doing nothing more, he whispered to me in confidence, than preventing people from getting the wind up.

A taxi answered his signal and drew up to the sidewalk. He stepped in, rolled down the window, and said:

"Just in case we don't see each other again, don't forget to leave me your address in Canada."

Thinking I'd be going back to Manitoba and the prairies if at all and trying to keep the tone light between us, I said, "If I do, will you ever come and see me on my steppes?"

He kissed me lightly on the cheek. It was the first kiss he'd ever given me.

"I shall come and sit on your steps."

His taxi pulled away. In the press of people around, I began finally to see the dejection and bewilderment on all the faces. I went my way to wander alone around London.

IN HYDE PARK they were digging trenches. They were already so deep you couldn't see the men, just their shovels as they tossed out the globs of clay they were mining beneath the world's most lovingly nurtured lawns. Sometimes a shovelful would splatter into a bed of flowers. Children brought there by their nannies were hugely entertained by the transformation of the gardens into a battlefield. Playing at throwing grenades, they were hurling lumps of mud in one another's faces. Adults went this way and that, saying and seeing nothing. Now I was all attention to this strangest of spectacles, the sight of people going about their business though not believing in it any more. The eyes of the whole city were blank. It hurt more to see this blankness than to see pain, which is at least a sign of life.

In Mayfair as elsewhere, as everywhere I went that afternoon in fact, I saw morale-boosting signs at every streetcorner and arrows pointing the way to the nearest air-raid shelter. In the magnificently cloudless, exceptionally clear blue sky I saw the balloons David had mentioned, whose only purpose was to make people think they were protected. There were posters exhorting citizens to go to the nearest distribution centre and get equipped with a gas mask. Some would be adaptable even for babies. I went and picked up one myself, though today I wonder why. I wandered on for hours, through streets so silent you could hear the lightest footstep. Car drivers were no longer honking their horns. Coming back to the shopping districts, I noticed finally that nobody was going in or out of the shops. In curiosity I went briefly into Selfridge's and roamed through a dozen departments without seeing anyone except salespeople standing motionless behind their counters, as if hypnotized. Even in Piccadilly Circus, people and traffic, still as dense as ever, were moving at a snail's pace, like an old merry-go-round getting ready to pack up and depart. In this city I'd found so affable, gay, and ready to joke and banter barely a year before, I hadn't garnered a single smile or even a glance.

I returned late to Upshire and left again two days later with some of my things, intending to come and get the rest little by little. London was drawing me, I think, with the intense fascination worked on the mind by the approach of tragedy. I had just come to realize that the summit of high tragedy is war.

Thus London, where I was becoming acquainted with the world's greatest scourge, was where I would experience human solidarity as never before.

I rented a room in Chiswick. Why did I choose the extreme western edge of London, so far from its centre? Perhaps because the street where I'd be living was a mere step from Kew Gardens, which for some time I'd longed to be able to visit often and at my leisure, I had been so delighted on the few occasions I'd come there all the way from Fulham. So now I could and did go there almost every day, learning the names, origins, and characteristics of hundreds of trees transplanted from every corner of the world. Yet today I've been robbed of almost all this knowledge acquired so lovingly. What a waste! I must have spent days and days learning thousands of fascinating things about rare trees I'd never have a chance to see again, about others less exotic, about flowers from the remotest corners of the earth, and what have I left to show for it except the rather painful memory of having been enchanted without knowing exactly why?

Perhaps I also chose Chiswick because it was served by the Green Line, and Epping Forest was one of the destinations shown on the bus-stop marker at the end of my street. I could get to Esther's without a transfer on the way, perhaps faster than if I left from a more central point. And then it must also have been because living here was less expensive than in the heart of London.

The house in which I took a room was clean and bright, on a quiet street, and my room was big and comfortable though without much sun. However, my landlord and landlady were of the sort I'd known on Wickendon Street. If they were on their doorstep or in their tiny garden when I went in or out they'd greet me pleasantly enough, adding a word or two about all the beautiful weather we were having, for as this dramatic summer drew to an end we were blessed with invariably sunny skies. I didn't see them at all any other time and never saw the three other boarders in the house. Little by little I fell into the same unsociable habits as on Wickendon Street.

To tell the truth I don't remember much about how I spent my time in this period. I read a lot, I think, getting my books from the municipal library, which was just as well stocked as the one in Fulham. I roamed a great deal around Kew Gardens where I learned almost everything I ever knew about trees. I think I remember a marvellous corner where all the plants of Malaysia were collected together, and how pleasantly removed from reality I felt while there. But most of the time it was as though I was suffering pain and was only half aware of what was around me, even the books and trees perhaps, which may explain why I remember so little about them. The monstrous calamity brewing was carrying per-

Gabrielle Roy

sonal calamities away in its path, but not only these. It also thrust
all enjoyment of life away into the distance, perhaps for ever; it
even seemed to remove all meaning from life.

September came. In this house they put my breakfast tray down
outside the door and called, "Your breakfast, lady!" If I had the
misfortune to go back to sleep, I'd find it stone cold thirty minutes
or an hour later. One morning, however, I heard a prolonged
rapping at my door and an excited voice announcing, "Great news!
Chamberlain and Daladier have gone to meet Hitler. They may
still come to terms."

I hurried downstairs to hear more, and my landlord and landlady
were suddenly almost friends. They invited me to listen to their
small wireless with them. With my own ears I heard that Chamberlain and Daladier were on their way to undertake negotiations
with Hitler in hope of preserving peace.

I had the impression that the whole city was holding its breath
that day for fear of snuffing out the flicker of hope on the horizon.
Then all the newspapers were announcing in front-page headlines
that peace had been obtained in exchange for the cession of the
Sudetenland to Germany.

There was an explosion of joy in London the like of which I've
seen nowhere else. That is, if it can really be called joy to be
returning to one's self, one's personal life, one's own interests in
the grim knowledge that the event that has made this possible is
bringing tears in another country.

Strangers hugged in the streets. Women threw their arms around
tipsy sailors' necks. Conga lines formed and wound singing and
shouting through parks hitherto reserved for contemplation. The
bars were full night and day. A few souls wept in silence. "Those
poor, poor unfortunate Czechs!" exclaimed rich ladies at their garden parties. And with rings and bracelets pulled from their fingers
and wrists they filled baskets passed from table to table in smart
restaurants in aid of the "poor, poor Czechs."

But a few voices cried in the wilderness that England had covered
herself with shame by selling out her former friends, thereby encouraging Hitler to make more and more outrageous demands and
merely postponing the day of reckoning feared by everyone. It was
then, or perhaps a little later, that Churchill said prophetically in

his thundering voice, "If to avoid war we accept dishonour, we shall have war...and dishonour."

They laughed at him then. They said his speeches were purple oratory. They said he revelled in an atmosphere of gloom and doom, that he was never happier than when all was turning to disaster, fulfilling his prophecies. And they kept dancing and getting drunk and celebrating. I think it's since then that every time I see a city rejoice I feel uneasy. Too often, I've observed, the cause for rejoicing is having escaped an evil that has befallen someone else. Later, London in its agony showed a nobler face.

THOUGH THE THREAT of war seemed to have abated, the anxiety it had imparted to me stayed. I had been too frightened by my first glimpse of the monster to forget it so soon. I was also having quite frequent memories of the day with Stephen in Upshire which had begun so beautifully and ended in such bitter parting. Still, I no longer saw his face as clearly, nor heard his voice as plainly in my head. While I knew I'd probably remain scarred for the rest of my life by this unfulfilling love affair, I also knew that I could now envisage life without Stephen — which I had found the most dreadful prospect to accept.

I really had no heart for anything. I couldn't write a single line. I wasn't interested in any of the stories I might have written. I'd lost almost all interest in drama studies, though I still went to the theatre occasionally. When autumn came I may have continued my lessons with Madame Gachet for a time. I have the curious impression of not remembering much about this period. Yet when I stop trying, a fair number of memories do come back, though they're hazy and uncertain. When the weather was mild I must have spent most of my time in Kew Gardens, walking among trees from Ceylon, in tropical forests and through desert oases, where each plant and tree grew in a little soil brought from its native habitat. I loved these trees so much I could recognize them from a distance, like friends, though since then they've fled from my memory.

I missed Century Cottage every minute of the day; Esther had written to say that the lady of the manor had decided to paint the cottage inside and out before it lost too much value. The house

349

was all upside down as a result. Then she told me Heather was coming to visit, which she hardly ever did, and it was difficult to keep her from coming when the fancy took her. And of course she'd be occupying "my" room.

I just let myself drift, I think. Then I took fright. I began to struggle, looking for a current to take me to shore, any shore. One day I made myself go back to Cadogan Gardens. The drawing room was full to bursting, as on that far, far distant day when I had entered, immediately met Stephen's dark, bright eyes, and been hopelessly caught. I almost turned back, my heart gave such a leap for fear of finding him there with the others and having the torture of ecstasy and doubt begin all over again. But there was Lady Frances coming towards me with her hands outstretched.

"My child! At last! We've missed you so! Why didn't you come and warm your soul with us during those awful days before Munich? Now, listen to me. You must come out of that solitude of yours; you've been far too much alone, if you'll allow me to say so. Your stay in England will be coming to an end before long, I imagine, and like so many other Canadians you'll be leaving without having seen much of our country. I've two marvellous invitations for you – or rather you'll be getting them formally once you've accepted in principle. One is from Lady Curre in Monmouthshire. You'll have to have a long dress for dinner there... but don't worry, it can be anything at all, a sack will do providing it's long. Then before coming back you'll stay with a charming elderly lady in Dorset. You'll get a letter from each of them shortly telling you when you're expected and how long you're invited to stay."

I was astonished – and would be even more astonished later – to be invited as if I were a friend into the homes of people who knew me no more than I knew them.

I accepted because I was too weak-willed to refuse and also out of friendship for Lady Frances, she seemed so anxious for me to go and visit with the gentry; perhaps I was also too surprised to realize what I was agreeing to.

XV

IT WAS STILL warm and lovely that day in November when I took the train for Chepstow. I had a suitcase with me in the compartment. My wardrobe trunk, which was holding up well despite some hard knocks, was travelling in the baggage car. It was a very big piece of baggage to be taking when all it held was my red taffeta dress which had attended the event at Baron Frankenstein's and hadn't been out since, my other evening dress in peach mousseline with a little bolero, matching shoes for both and a few other small things. I probably seemed rather ignorant of the ways of society to have arrived with so much baggage for a week's stay, from the evening of the seventh to the evening of the fourteenth as the letter had said. Lady Curre must have been startled to see it, which she did only as I was leaving, in fact. I really made a great deal of trouble for myself, dragging the bulky thing around just about everywhere I went. I don't know why I was so determined, unless it was because I'd paid a lot for the trunk and wanted to be sure I got my money's worth. And perhaps it gave me courage in a way, as though the two of us seemed more important together.

In late afternoon I got off the train in the very pretty and ancient town of Chepstow. The massive towers of a ruined castle of William the Conqueror's time are still standing there.

An interminably long black automobile was parked in front of the station. A liveried chauffeur got out and approached me with his cap in his hand.

"You the young lady for Itton Court?"

I thought I was and told him so.

He introduced himself. He was Ward, and he presented milady's apologies for not coming to meet me in person. "She was asked at the very last minute to act as judge at a country exhibition, one of those duties one just can't escape."

In no time we left the historic town behind. We drove up the valley of the Wye, one of the most surprising rivers I ever had occasion to see. At low tide it's an ugly ditch with practically no water, just dreary grey mud all pocked as if with the footprints of large, strange beasts come to wallow there. But when the tide rises the Wye becomes a broad and peaceful river, lending a gentle, pastoral air to the valley.

In the distance I could see sky through some high, ancient arches. I asked what those magnificent arches were over there against the horizon.

"Tintern Abbey," replied Ward. "They say it's the oldest church in England."

Lines I had learned at school from Wordsworth's poem on the ancient Cistercian abbey returned to my mind, and more than ever before I was struck by the marvel of the things that were happening to me. I had wondered what this abbey was like that the poet loved so much, and here I was gazing at its ruins as the red of the setting sun beyond began to filter through.

On a peak surrounded by meadows which were still green I could see what looked to me like a castle. It dominated the whole countryside, in fact.

"What's that?" I asked.

"That's ours," said Ward proudly. "Itton Court, where we're heading, Miss."

My heart sank all the way to my boots. I think if there'd been a chance of bribing Ward I would have done it, begging him, "Take me back to the station...," or "Leave me somewhere on the way...," but his steady eye told me he was above that sort of thing. So I abandoned myself to my fate in a state of panic I've rarely exceeded since.

We turned onto a long tree-lined road leading uphill to the mansion. From the front it reminded me rather of Versailles seen from the gardens, but we drove around and pulled up behind where a squat, ancient tower formed an angle. Under a low archway were two postern doors. My suitcase and battered old trunk were whisked away through the smaller of the two by a servant I didn't have time to see. I myself entered by the larger, and inside was greeted by the butler, who, waving grandly to indicate the direction, enquired with a solicitude which almost seemed sincere if I had had a good trip, and if I wasn't too tired after the train ride on that most wretched of secondary lines.

He left me at the door to a huge room – the sitting room, drawing room, or music room, I don't remember which. It took me so long to distinguish one from another, except for the morning room, which was flooded with sunlight in the morning, that I still wasn't very sure when the time came for me to leave, as I'd arrived, by the postern door.

A little old lady rose and advanced towards me with tiny steps, blinking as if to see me through a fog. I hadn't noticed her at first because she'd been sitting in a high-backed armchair facing the other way. Thinking she must be my hostess and that it would be nice if I immediately showed myself to be both grateful and affectionate, I too advanced and in a trembling voice spoke as warmly as I knew how.

"So glad, dear Lady Curre! How very kind!"

Which merely irritated the little old lady, for she was a governess or penniless cousin or one of those undefined companions harboured in all great houses like Itton Court.

"Lady Curre will be here later, child," she muttered reproachfully. "Please follow me. I'm to show you to your room."

We walked through endless corridors intersected by other corridors, they also intersected by other, slightly narrower corridors, and finally came to my room. By itself it was nearly as big as any dwelling I'd ever lived in. There was an enormous fireplace at one end, in which practically a whole tree trunk was burning. Straight ahead beyond the high window lay the formal gardens with fountains and statues, for my room was on the "Versailles" side.

"Hope you like your room," said the little old lady. "Dinner's at eight. We dress for dinner here. The dinner gong will sound to call us. To find the dining room, just follow the sound. Now try to have a little sleep."

And she disappeared.

Left to myself, I began by sitting on the end of the huge four-poster bed. The chambermaid had been there before me. She'd unpacked my suitcase and arranged my humble little belongings, my hairbrush with the worn bristles and my slippers and dressing gown which were now far from crisp and new, I noticed.

In an angle of the room I spotted the prettiest little desk I ever had the use of. If I can trust my jumbled memories of that day, I'd say it must have been a Sheraton. Inside I found ink, pens, and some handsome pearl-grey writing paper imprinted with a crown. I sat down and began to write to almost everyone I knew. I began with Maman, telling her not to worry about me, I was fine and at the moment was living like a princess.

IF I HAD TIME it would be no hardship to describe my experiences during my week at Itton Court. For dinner one night I would put on my taffeta dress and the next the red-flowered peach mousseline, another night adding a red sash to the peach dress and the night after a red bolero. This way I imagined I looked different each night and appeared to have quite a varied wardrobe. I was certainly better equipped for dinner than the diffident little old lady – governess, penniless cousin, or companion, I never found out which – whom I saw night after night always in the same long plum-coloured sack.

There were twelve of us at dinner – I forget their names except for two, captains Wolfe and Fox, which were so appropriate to the hunt, Itton Court's principal activity. We sat at a huge table in a huge room at each end of which there were whole trees burning in cavernous fireplaces, each bigger than a country cottage.

We were all in a hurry to arrive because we were coming from distant wings of the house and froze as we navigated the endless glacial corridors. Indeed I lost my way the first time because the sound of the gong seemed to come from everywhere at once, perhaps because it kept echoing. I tuned my ear to it, however, and more important, I established some reference points in the form of lords in wigs and ladies in little lace bonnets along the way to the dining room.

While we were at table the butler and his footmen hovered behind us, so attentive to our every wish that we would hardly wet our lips and put down the glass before a hand would reach forward to fill it again.

Lady Curre was quite the opposite to the wizened little creature I'd mistaken for her. She was a tall, statuesque woman with broad shoulders and a booming voice, and she walked with a long stride. Very much a horse woman, as I believe was the term in those circles, not because she looked like a horse, heaven forbid, but because she spent as much time with horses as she did with people, and probably liked them better too. She took part in all the hunts in the region, often hosted them, and took me along on one so that, as she said, I could tell people how it was done one day when I went back to Canada. Among my mementos of this time I still have a little photograph of the hounds and riders, with footmen bringing glasses of sherry to the mounted riders before the start of the hunt. The Versailles side of the house is in the background.

One night at dinner two of the guests, writers and supposedly friends of Chesterton whom they called "G.K.", were conversing with a poetess whose hair was tinted pale mauve, and I suddenly thought how extraordinary it was to find myself in this circle. I suppose my mind wandered off totally for a few minutes. I've often been amazed by my experiences – who doesn't think his or her own life is more surprising than anyone else's? But that night I was astounded. I felt as though I were watching myself from a few steps behind, observing myself sitting here among the upper crust, and I couldn't believe my eyes. There must have been bewilderment on my face because Lady Curre suddenly interrupted the poetess and barked quite loudly at me from the far end of the table:

"Child! Lost in your reveries again! A penny for your thoughts!"

I loved this expression. Esther had often said it to me when she saw I was lost in "the ramblings of that wandering mind." Though a little disconcerted I couldn't hold back a smile for Lady Curre, because I had a feeling she wasn't as fearsome as she might seem and possibly no one had ever talked to her spontaneously. To her servants she was "Milady", and if their manner was superficially familiar when they spoke to her, it was always deferential. Her freeloading guests, some of whom she kept under her roof for long periods for want of something better, lavished endearments on her, which made their "dear Geneva" frown a little, I observed. I don't know what made me tell her what I'd really been thinking.

"I was seeing myself as if from a faraway part of my life," I told her, "back in my little prairie city in the Canadian West, and I couldn't believe I was really here with you, Lady Curre. I'm still not sure."

She smiled and told the others that at last she'd heard some talk under her roof that wasn't just chit-chat and what I'd said was so right, nobody really believes the things that happen to them are true.

From this moment she became so attached to me that it made me apprehensive; she talked of keeping me when my week was over so I could attend a ball she was giving the following week, when I could meet the young people of the region. I said I was expected in Dorset next week, which was nothing less than the truth.

Before leaving I sent the chambermaid, a young German girl who'd been assigned to look after my wants, to take my thank-you note and a little goodbye gift to Lady Curre's room. At Cadogan Gardens Lady Frances had thoughtfully let me know it would be considered good manners to leave some little thing as a mark of gratitude to my hostess, anything at all, it was the thought that counted. I'd wandered around Harrod's for hours looking for something for two dollars at most which wouldn't look too cheap. In the end I bought a spray of handmade lily-of-the-valley to wear on a lapel or as a corsage. I thought it was rather lovely, in fact, and I'd had it wrapped in a nice box. However, the moment I finally met my rather horsey hostess I was pretty sure she wouldn't be thrilled with my present.

So I nearly fell over in surprise when I arrived in London and found a note from Lady Curre waiting for me, thanking me effusively in letters at least six inches high for my charming gift. She'd keep it and cherish it all her life, she wrote, for it was "the one and only gift of the kind I've ever been given. So very sweet of you, child!" For a while I thought she might in a way be making fun of me, or else had been writing any old words just to fill up a sheet of her lovely pearl-grey paper. Then gradually I began to wonder if she mightn't in fact have been quite enchanted to receive flowers that weren't real for once in her life. "Only an imaginative girl like you," she'd written, "would have thought of such a gift."

TO GET FROM Chepstow to Dorset it would almost have been simpler to return to London and take the train direct to Weymouth or some other southern town. I had decided to travel cross-country, however, burdened with my trunk as always and changing trains at little out-of-the-way stations, wasting time in each waiting for the connection. Still, this way I had a glimpse of a profoundly rural part of England which I would never have known otherwise, and despite its inconvenience I have marvellous memories of this bewildering journey.

My hostess was waiting for me at Bridgeport Station, brought by her chauffeur, who was also the gardener and general factotum. She was a short, elderly woman in stout walking shoes and shapeless tweeds, with a face covered in warts and an enormous plush hat pulled down over her ears. She looked so ugly and frumpy that riding in silence beside her in the back of the car I said to myself, it's not going to work, I'll never be able to spend a week with this woman. But when she lifted her face and I saw her eyes under the rim of her enormous hat, I was so struck by their kindness, good humour, wit, and intelligence that I ceased then and there to find her ugly.

She had been born in England and brought up in Australia, where her father had made a fortune raising sheep. When he died she'd come back to settle in England and had chosen Dorset quite simply because this was where she had found and been able to buy an old cottage in pure Elizabethan style, which was just what she'd wanted all her life. With the help of a cook and her chauffeur-gardener she led a peaceful life, entertaining guests like me from time to time to brighten her days, and also to do her share to foster good feeling throughout the Empire.

This was more or less what Miss Shaw told me as we drove towards Matravers Cottage. Every now and then she called me "my lamb", which I thought at first was just a habit, rather natural for someone brought up among sheep. I soon realized that for her it was a term of affection. Soon, in fact, she began referring to me as "my niece", since her favourite "lambs" became family to her, she explained, her own family not amounting to much, consisting in all of a single real niece.

This was how she introduced me to the vicar, the squire of the village, the squire of the uplands we crossed on horseback, and everywhere she took me to have me seen and heard.

We arrived at the most charming cottage I think I ever saw in England. Together perhaps with a farmhouse with a roof of massive red tiles nestled in the foothills of the Alpilles near St-Rémy-de-

Provence and another old house in the Gaspé Peninsula, it was one of the few dwellings in which, the minute I set eyes on it, I imagined I could live all my life without ever wanting to look for something better.

It was a pleasingly proportioned house, built of grey stone rounded by time, rain, and wind, the walls pierced at precise intervals by small-paned windows framed in white. It stood on a kind of natural platform covered with rather stubbly grass, overlooking an expanse of downs which were perhaps even more beautiful than those at Upshire, for in the far distance was a bright line sparkling in the sun, which was the sea. Sometimes I was even sure I could hear it pounding on the very shores from which Robert Louis Stevenson made the *Hispaniola* set sail in search of Treasure Island.

My room was magnificent, big enough but not too big, and through its small-paned, double-casement window I discovered the downs, a vastness of landlocked waves which this time met the waves of the ocean within eyesight. For the first time in my life I slept between linen sheets. The cook-chambermaid had put an ancient stone hot-water bottle in my bed; it had a little woollen cover so it wouldn't burn my feet. Miss Shaw came to see if I had everything I needed, accompanied by her Scotch terrier, whose eyes, behind all his bristly hair, showed almost as much wit as his mistress's.

I've come upon so many oases in the course of my life, it seems to me now that I've only had to set out boldly and follow my nose in order to find one on the horizon and immediately feel at home.

THOUGH IT WASN'T the season at all, Miss Shaw was determined I should see Bath, the renowned watering place of Regency times. Perhaps she really wanted to see it herself, to revisit a scene from her youth. In any event, one fine morning we were on our way to Bath, driven by Jeremiah, who also found us hotel rooms, posted our postcards, and generally looked after us in all manner of ways. From Bath we continued to Bristol where Miss Shaw had a friend she wanted to see, who kept us overnight. Across the Bristol Channel was Wales, which Miss Shaw spotted me straining to see in the distance, probably looking wishful, because she told me that that was where we would go next time.

She asked me which way I'd like to return, by the coast road or by the moors. I'd already seen much of the coast with David and his hypercritical mother. I said I'd like to go by the moors. We took a long detour to get to Broadmoor and then Exmoor.

These wild reaches with their coarse grass, without a single house or cultivated field, where fierce winds blow incessantly beneath tormented skies, quite exhilarated me. Why do sterile, treeless, disturbing landscapes immediately seem to release pent-up tensions in me, set me free in some way? It happened in Brittany when I saw the moors of Lanvaux, which I felt I never wanted to leave; their desolation so fascinated me I stayed to look and muse for hours. It happened too when from the Col de Vence in Provence I discovered a sweep of whistling grasses raked by the wind from the mountains and inhabited only by great black rocks raised in most enigmatic poses. Why have these rather mournful landscapes almost always lifted my spirits more than vistas considered cheerful, harmonious, or charming? Miss Shaw, who'd been brought up in the Australian outback, seemed to understand this and agree in any event. Many was the time as we drove along, even before I asked, that she would tell Jeremiah to stop the car so I could get out and walk by myself on a path through the brambles towards some dramatic horizon.

No sooner were we back at Matravers Cottage than she took me to see the town of Dorchester, where the cruel Judge Jeffreys presided over the "Bloody Assizes" and sent people by the hundreds to the gallows. We came back through the pretty town of Weymouth. Miss Shaw always had some story to tell me about each place we visited. The stories never seemed very likely, but this didn't matter; I would watch the old lady light up with pleasure to be pleasing me. I thought she was so ugly when I arrived but now I'd come to think of her as quite lovely, her eyes would sparkle so with delight to have a companion through whom she was rediscovering her own youthful enthusiasm. "Those poor, half-dead old souls," she said of neighbours, most of whom were younger than she, "they aren't interested in anything and don't read anything or feel anything any more."

Seeing how much I loved to roam over the downs, she finally let me leave alone in the morning with sandwiches for lunch, but on two conditions: I mustn't be a minute late getting back for tea, and I must take a walking stick to use as a weapon in case I should have a disagreeable encounter. She even showed me how to use it; to get the better of an assailant, one had to give him a sharp blow to the side of the head. She'd learned this when very young on the lonely sheep station in Australia.

I think I was really always back in time for tea, which she would have been very disappointed to have alone. As for the walking stick, as soon as I was out of sight I'd hide it under the end of a hedge and then retrieve it on the way back; I'd lean on it heavily at each step if I spied Miss Shaw's face at the window. She'd come out to meet me, beaming.

"Good girl! Good girl!" she'd say. "Nothing like a good stick when you're walking rough ground, eh?"

IN RETURN for such generous hospitality, she asked nothing more than for me to listen to her telling me about the glorious hours of her youth, when she'd do twenty miles on horseback without a stop to get to the nearest neighbouring station. She loved it too when I made her laugh by imitating the curious accent of the local people in my own accent, which was already curious enough. "Give me a lilt from your youth," she'd say, "you have some to spare." It was partly from her that I learned how essential we are to each other, old souls who grieve less for their heyday when they have young people near, and young souls who are less afraid of old age when they see the old still capable of enjoyment and delight.

After a copious dinner, Miss Shaw also liked me to play a game of Australian rummy with her, having taught me the game. We would pull the card table almost into the flames of the fireplace, and the little Scotch terrier would come and lie beside us with his nose towards the fire. It was bad for his eyes, said his mistress, but he couldn't be prevented because he was as fascinated by the flames as we were.

We'd begin our game. Almost every night I'd win and she'd be cross. "May you be thoroughly bedevilled!" she'd exclaim. Though she'd learned much about the nature of people and about Nature itself in the Australian outback, she'd also learned habits of speech that set her somewhat apart from her rather starchy social circle in Dorset. From under his mistress's skirt the scottie would growl, scolding me in his own way for beating her.

This was the only shadow on the easy relationship developing between us, Miss Shaw and me, in our lonely abode out there on the downs. The crusty little dog was not inclined to be friendly at all. If I invited him to go for a walk with me, though he loved walks he'd shake his head angrily as if to say, "Keep your distance if you want me to keep mine." I was all the more hurt by his surly manner when Miss Shaw declared him to be the best judge of human nature she'd ever known.

"He's never been wrong," she said. "Whenever he's refused to be polite to someone who's been here, I've been sure to learn nasty things about the person sooner or later. I've found out a good many false friends this way. If he's nice to a guest under my roof on the other hand, I know I can sleep in peace because then I'm sure the person is straightforward and honest."

"That's not a very good sign for me," I protested.

"Ah, but Alec's far from being done with you yet. He takes his time. He takes longer to make up his mind about some people than others. Besides, you mustn't forget Alec's a Scotchman. He's dour. And cautious. All this time he's been studying you deeply, don't you doubt it."

Which made me even more uneasy about my relationship with the scottie, whom I'd renamed "Alec the Intellectual", to the delight of his mistress.

"That's just what he is," she said, "an intellectual! I've been looking for the right word for ages and now you've found it. Come here, Alec-the-Intellectual!"

By nine o'clock or nine-thirty, Miss Shaw would be sleepy and she'd leave for bed. I didn't know how old she was. Later I learned that she must have been about eighty-seven. "Come along, Alec," she'd say. "We're getting old, you and I, it's time for bed."

Halfway up the stairs she'd stop and look back at me curled up in an easy chair with a book I'd just taken from a shelf beside me. She had an extraordinary set of books recounting the most gruesome crimes from all ages and in every country. Once I'd begun to read those books, I was almost impatient for Miss Shaw to retire for the night so I could get back to the horror that kept me in breathless suspense.

Miss Shaw suspected as much and resented it, though she understood my engrossment for she must have read all those books, since she'd taken the trouble to bring them back from Australia, all thirty gold-edged, heavy red-covered volumes.

This was the hour when the wind over the downs and the wind from the sea met in howling combat around our lonely hilltop.

One night Miss Shaw listened to it with her hand on the banister.

"I've lived in ten houses in my life," she said, "and this is the only one where the winds buffet from all sides at once this way. There's a mystery about it no one can explain. Something evil surely happened in this old house at some time in the four hundred years it's been here. You know, I wouldn't be surprised if there was a skeleton hidden somewhere in these thick walls."

I realized she was dramatizing, hoping to get me to leave my book and take to the upper floor with her. But the sound of the curse-driven wind just deepened my contentment to be absorbed in my grisly story beside a gently crackling fire.

Then she flung at me, like a malediction from the top of the stairs:

"May you be thoroughly frightened! Shaken to the bones!"

MANY HOURS after she'd left me one evening, when I was carried away and read on and on into the night, I thought I heard a small sound. A second later I felt a gentle tongue lick my hand. Through all the hair over his eyes, Alec the Intellectual was looking at me kindly, tenderly, lovingly, but also a little mischievously as if to say, "We mustn't let her know. She wants to be the only one I love. She hasn't got many other real friends, and I love her too much to risk making her the slightest bit jealous." And he rested his muzzle trustingly on my knee while I stroked his forehead trying to reassure him.

WHEN MY WEEK was up Miss Shaw invited me to stay another week, and this had hardly begun when she suggested I stay till the end of the month. This time I felt I shouldn't abuse such generous hospitality, and anyway it was time I was getting back to London. But why? I didn't have anyone really waiting for me. I was even afraid of going back, as if the grief, misery, and loneliness I'd known there were just waiting for me to return before falling upon me again, whereas here at Matravers Cottage I was protected, even happy in a way. What surprised me most about myself at this time was how often I'd been happy despite an almost constant undercurrent of despondency, and how often I'd made other people think I was naturally gay and light-hearted – and no doubt I was, whenever my melancholy waned.

A little scene occurred before I left which I would have given a great deal to have avoided, though it left me with a very touching memory. The Intellectual and I had been observing our agreement; I never patted him and he would even give me a pretend growl as I passed.

But when he saw me come from upstairs with my coat after Jeremiah had brought down my trunk and suitcase, he lost control and threw himself at my feet to lick them, then pawed at my knees trying to scramble up, crying and whimpering inconsolably it seemed. Through his crying I thought I heard him say, "What's to become of us, my mistress and me? We're both very old and lonely in this windblown house." I wanted to comfort him and I didn't dare.

I met Miss Shaw's eye. It showed a kind of satisfaction at seeing the Intellectual confirm her judgement of me...but also shock and disappointment to find me receiving some of his love when she was supposed to have it all.

In the end she came round and laughed, though perhaps not heartily.

"He had our number!" she said. "He fooled us properly, the little scottie devil!"

XVI

BEING BACK in Chiswick was even worse than I had expected. There was no sky, no open country to look at, no voice of the wind in the trees to listen to, not even a sad or raging wind – none of the things that have always most helped me to endure life. My despondency returned and took hold of me even more firmly than before. Everything I'd done to be rid of it, my week at Itton Court and my two weeks at Miss Shaw's, seemed only to have left me feeling more desolate than ever.

It rained almost without pause that late November. We didn't see the sky for two whole weeks. It was too wet to look for solace among all the incredibly beautiful trees and plants in Kew Gardens. How it rained!

I hardly ever saw Bohdan any more. I'd gone to live a very long way from my friends, it's true. Bohdan scolded me for this on the few occasions we met, always at some middle point so as not to take too much of his time when he had a program on the BBC or a rehearsal with the London Symphony. Sometimes he'd take enough time to invite me to an ABC for a quick cup of tea. He did his best to cheer me up, he who had barely three more years to live; you'd have said he sensed this, he seemed so restless, in such a ferment, never relaxed.

We had no word from Stephen. Bohdan thought he must be away on one of his clandestine visits to militants in countries bordering the Ukraine, where some day he'd probably leave his bones. Bohdan was of Ukrainian descent himself and was very attached to the culture of his forefathers; he thought it absurd for a handful of fanatics, as he called them, to dream of liberating the country. After a few brief meetings, I wouldn't see him again for weeks.

I was back in touch with Phyllis and we went to the theatre

364

together a few times. It says much about the state of mind I must have been in that I don't remember any of the plays we saw. There are whole segments of my life that have disappeared from my memory, I suppose quite simply because I myself had disappeared. I was just drifting across the surface of things, retaining nothing. Still, as in Paris, I must have been unconsciously registering certain moments from this part of my life, for at times some of them do come back, as though rising to the surface from a deeply buried dream.

Phyllis and I were living in opposite ends of London and we both had to take an interminable bus ride in order to meet at Kensington halfway between. Phyllis was very busy with her studies too. She was persevering at the Guildhall, without showing signs of any greater talent I believe. After I stopped hearing from her, I often wondered if even so she'd managed to make a career for herself in the theatre, if you can call it a career when all you ever play are the rather unrewarding little roles that must be played by someone, and whether in the end she felt she'd somehow achieved what she had hoped. But then, why shouldn't she? There are plenty of writers who never write anything but clever banalities all their lives, yet they've probably put as much effort and perseverance into them as others have put into great works. There's no reason why they shouldn't feel a little pride in what to them is an accomplishment.

For my part, I had heard of an experimental theatre not far from Chiswick where they guaranteed registered students small roles under the guidance of a professional director, as well as whatever might be learned by attending rehearsals of a play being prepared for staging. This was almost exactly what I'd had for nothing from the Pitoëffs, but here one paid handsomely for it. Like an idiot I registered and very soon discovered I'd been fleeced. I went to lodge a complaint at Canada House with some other Canadians in the same predicament and we retrieved half of what we'd paid to this so-called drama school.

I wasn't really writing any more. I couldn't even imagine I would ever have anything to say. I had only one persistent desire throughout my last month in London, and that was to return to Upshire. I knew the cottage was cold and damp at this time of year. Esther had told me she couldn't ever heat it adequately and always had a cold all winter long. Her father's longstanding bronchitis was back,

worse every year. I didn't care. I couldn't picture Century Cottage
except surrounded with flowers and overlooking perpetually sun-
drenched downs. Even if it was cold and miserable I thought I'd
be better off with people I loved and who loved me than anywhere
else. I wrote to Esther asking if I could come and spend a few weeks.

Two days later she called me on the telephone. In my present
boarding house it was rare to hear someone calling up the stairs
that I was wanted on the phone. I was seized with apprehension,
as though the call could only mean terrible news. I was even more
worried when I heard Esther's voice, for she had to telephone from
the booth outside the post office and hated it so much she'd only
resort to it in the direst circumstances. She sounded far away at
the end of the earth, perhaps because of the resonance in the closed
booth.

"Dearest, there is nothing I'd love more than to have you here
but my dear old aunt in Malvern, Father's sister, is in a very bad
way. Father and I are leaving tomorrow to go to her. I wasn't sure
we should. Father's not well. He coughs a lot and even has a little
fever in the evening but he insists on going to be with his sister.
She's the only one left in his family. They need each other at this
time."

"But Esther," I protested, "your father's too frail for a trip like
that, particularly when it's so damp. He'll be ill when he gets there
and then what help will he be?"

"I'll wrap him up in lots of woollies and watch him so carefully
he won't be any worse off on the trip than here. Anyway, it's a
risk we have to take. Father would never forgive himself if he didn't
go to his sister when she's dying."

I don't know what possessed me to keep arguing with her when
she must have been shivering with the cold in the icy phone booth.

"But Esther, haven't you told me a hundred times that our
immortal souls will meet in ineffable bliss when this life is done?
Since they're sure to be reunited then, why expose him to all the
fatigue and emotion of the trip? He could die himself as a result."

She was silent for so long I began to be frightened and called,
"Esther! Esther!" Finally she spoke in that gentle, reproachful
voice.

"Of course we'll meet in bliss when we're gathered to the Lord
and our suffering will be forgotten. But I want you to know,

Gabrielle, that I've thought all of this over many times and I feel it's important for people who are going to be separated to meet again one last time in this life...with all their suffering...."

"But since it's going to be forgotten forevermore, as you say...."

"With all their suffering," she repeated gently, compassionately, "and also to say goodbye properly...on this earth."

When I went back upstairs to my room I reflected on these words. They kept ringing in my head. I couldn't get rid of them. I've never been rid of them since. I hear them every time I'm about to lose someone I love.

"Important to meet one last time...in this life...with all our suffering...and say goodbye properly...."

But why, when suffering will be wiped away by happiness in the end? Perhaps so that a trace may remain for us to reflect on.

I thought about my mother, who might this very minute be sitting with pen in hand, trying to compose the difficult words that would leave me free but still bring me back to her. I realized that she'd been in constant fear for us both since Munich. She never said so outright but she was sure that war would break out soon, that I might not be able to return to Canada, that we wouldn't meet one last time, she and I, with all our suffering...and it was clear to me that the prospect grieved her more than all she had suffered in her life.

FINALLY I fell ill. Was it a real physical illness or was I giving up because everything I'd been trying to do seemed so fruitless? Both, no doubt. In the evening I'd have a little fever. My throat was terribly sore. I didn't even go out to eat in the neighbourhood tea-shops and my landlady brought me practically nothing. Phyllis came all the way across London many times to bring me a big jar of soup and biscuits, fruit, and medicines. At times I could have laughed to see myself. Yesterday I'd been living in a grand house, being pampered by a maid who attended to me almost exclusively, running my bathwater, laying out my freshly ironed dress for dinner...and today I was helpless and alone in a single icy room.

Phyllis insisted I consult a doctor. In the end I gave in, too weak to resist. I think it was she who made the appointment. Perhaps she was acquainted with one of the famous Harley Street doctors but I really don't know. All I remember is that one fine day I found myself in the consulting room of one of London's leading specialists in otorhinolaryngology. He examined my throat, upper throat, and sinuses at length with a head mirror, as was the practice then.

He informed me that my sinuses had probably been infected for years and my mucous membranes were badly damaged. How, he asked me rather severely, could I have allowed this to happen at my age? I thought of the icy rooms I'd slept in, particularly at Cardinal where I'd had to break the ice in my water jug in order to wash myself, but also at Deschambault Street in our most difficult years, when Mother had to turn down the heat as far as possible, even on nights when it was thirty degrees below zero Fahrenheit.

He told me that he didn't want to alarm me unduly, but if I wasn't careful I'd be in for some very serious respiratory problems later.

At this time when my condition was still quite mild, how far I was from taking his warning seriously! How far I was from thinking that these minor aggravations would give rise to the dreadful disease which finally caught up with me six years ago, from which I've suffered ever since. Often when it wakes me on the brink of suffocation at night, I tell myself that this is no doubt what I'll die of, like my brothers Joe and Rodolphe, who died of asthma. Most of all, since it keeps reminding me I'm mortal, this is what has made me want to write this book, because I'm able now to see so much I never saw before, as if when life is threatened – though when, in fact, is it not? – it throws a light on itself which illuminates every nook and cranny.

"But besides," continued my specialist, "you must have been putting a terrible strain on your throat. What kind of work have you been doing to tire it so?"

I told him I'd been a teacher for eight years. He gave me a smile in which there was compassion, and even more, I think, satisfaction in having been right. Since then I've often seen the same curious mixture of reactions on the faces of other doctors.

"Ah yes," he said, "eight years of talking almost constantly from morning till night, and almost always with your voice raised a bit because of the noise, and chalk dust in the air, that's hard on the throat."

One did indeed write on the blackboard a great deal in the days when I was a teacher.

"Now," he went on, "tell me what you're doing in London. The climate, you must realize, is one of the worst in the world for the respiratory passages. What brought you here?"

As he questioned me, I had the eerie, painful impression that everything I'd ever done had been wrong. I'd practised the wrong profession, I was in the wrong city....

I said I was studying drama.

He shuddered, incredulously perhaps, then after studying me at length conceded that I might have a gift for the theatre...in a way, as long as....

"You're not hoping for a career on the stage, I trust," he said abruptly.

I admitted that I might have considered it...vaguely...though I wasn't sure I really wanted it.

"Put the thought out of your mind for good," he said categorically. "Your throat can't stand that profession. Before long you wouldn't have any voice at all."

Then he tried to qualify what he'd said, thinking he'd probably dealt me a blow and upset me.

It was quite the contrary. His words had just lifted a weight from my shoulders that I'd never really known was there. He'd closed the door for ever to something else that was going to be wrong, something I'd felt obliged to keep exploring even after it was clear I wasn't cut out for it. So now there remained the other road, which was really the most frightening one.

I had already made many forays in this direction, yet the way was still anything but clear. I kept pondering this while the doctor was making an attempt to help me.

"Are you planning to go back to Canada soon? The climate here, I repeat, is very bad for you."

"Probably soon," I said, "because I'm going to run out of money."

"Before you do, would you have enough to go and spend a few weeks where it's warm and sunny? In Provence, for example?"

Had he been there himself and liked it, or in the constant oceans of fog that inundate London had he just dreamed of going? In any event, to lure me out of my total indifference he couldn't have done better than to remind me of one of the great delights of my childhood, discovering the stories of Alphonse Daudet. He must have seen my eyes light up. I'd kept them obstinately fixed on the carpet while he talked about unhealthy climates and occupations I couldn't pursue.

"Why don't you go?" he urged. "You can live there for practically nothing. You'll manage with no trouble at all, I'm sure of it. The sun and *joie de vivre* will do more to cure you than all the medicines I could prescribe."

I found myself outside in a very curious state of mind. Alexandre Chenevert's impressions on leaving the doctor's office as I described them many years later were exactly like my own feelings when I left my distinguished Harley Street doctor. Hearing myself advised to obey my dearest wish had cost me a pound, an enormous sum for me.

I hurried to Cook's travel agency. What I had left in the bank – almost all of it – was enough to pay for a third-class return fare to Nice and two weeks' room and board with a family in Beaulieu-sur-mer. Why there? No doubt because I was dealing with an agency employee who was very persuasive or perhaps just very obliging, a characteristic of Cook's in those days. While on holiday himself he had tried this boarding house; it was inexpensive and he could recommend it to me in all good faith.

Early in January 1939 I left with my wardrobe trunk, which once again was to be more hindrance than help but I couldn't face a decision to part with it. I probably felt it had been too much involved with all the ups and downs of my life. Two railway employees loaded it onto the baggage car. I kept a close eye on them from my compartment in the train, for I was always very careful to make sure it didn't go astray.

I embarked on the Dover-to-Calais ferry in early afternoon. The weather was as grey, wet, and miserable as one could imagine. The cries of gulls reached me from the foggy sky as they had when I'd left the coast of France just over a year before, reinforcing my impression of not having advanced a single step since then, of feebly groping still, in my life as on this mournful day, for an impossible path through the fog and rain, listening to eerie, muffled cries coming from somewhere I couldn't identify and against which they were trying to put me on my guard.

XVII

THE CHANNEL was in the grip of one of the worst storms of the winter. Our small, flat-bottomed ship kept climbing to the crests of monstrous waves which then let us drop abruptly as if to the bottom of the sea. I've never endured such pitching except perhaps in the Aegean, when we were taken from our cruise ship in frail caïques to visit the islands of Delos and Mykonos, against the world's most tumultuous winds. But these were crossings of ten or fifteen minutes, whereas the crossing from Dover to Calais took two hours in those days.

In no time almost everyone was seasick. You'd see passengers turn pale, then green, and finally leave the dining room in haste, holding their hands over their mouths. There was an adjoining room full of little camp cots which one might think had been set up in anticipation of sudden seasickness. I was soon stretched out on one of these, surrounded by other moaning bodies. The ship creaked from stem to stern. Its groans mingled with those of humans and the haunting sound of an errant wind imprisoned in the gangways.

At one point I imagined I was locked inside one of those frightful little vessels of olden days which took months to cross from Europe to North America – a gasping, retching immigrant who probably wouldn't survive the voyage. It was a taste of the incredible sufferings with which our country was built, with each tiny foothold won from the deep silence of coast and forest.

I'd left London with bronchitis and probably a fever. My stubborn cough, splitting headache, and appalling nausea, and even more perhaps the helpless feeling of not being able to pull myself together, all these had combined to defeat me utterly. Harmless though it may be, seasickness can make us believe we're going to die and even hope we do. I was reduced to a mere bundle of misery and indifference. Still, beneath the indifference I remember observing bleakly that, all things considered, life seemed such a waste of dreams, efforts, enthusiasm, and hope. I've sometimes wondered what would have become of me that day if someone hadn't suddenly been there to save me, as on so many occasions when I've been most in need. I suppose I could have let myself be taken back to England on the same ferry, or simply stayed aboard until I was removed by force.

Out of the moaning all around me came a placid voice. "Come on now, make a little effort! Swallow a sip of this cognac. Nothing makes one feel better than a steady stomach, you'll see."

I opened my eyes. I could just make out the face of a young woman I'd met on deck shortly before leaving port. I'd heard her from a distance speaking to a porter and by her accent had recognized an English-speaking compatriot from Toronto. I'd gone over to greet my fellow Canadian and we'd exchanged a few pleasantries. She was Ruby Cronk, she told me, and she was a nurse. I found the name so odd I remembered it without difficulty this time. She'd just finished a period of training in London and was going to the South of France for a short holiday before returning to Canada. We'd parted, each to go her own way, with a "Bye-bye now, see you later," which might have turned out to be never. Now here she was beside me, intending to force her care on me if necessary. I don't think I made it too difficult for her. In the hopeless condition I was sure I was in, I simply put myself into the hands of the young woman with the kind, calm round face and swallowed the medicines she was insisting I take.

It seemed only minutes later when she was shaking me to get me up.

"We're going to be getting off soon. The crossing's over. We have to be ready."

I tried to sit up but my head spun and I fell back again. I didn't want to leave that wretched little cot for anything in the world. So Ruby opened my handbag, found my passport, and took charge of my affairs as well as her own. She held me up as we went through customs. Instead of my many other potential worries, the only one that came to the surface of my muddled mind was once again about my trunk. I'd so often been afraid of losing it; of all my fixations this was certainly among those which caused me the most problems. I mumbled a word or two about it to Ruby. She retrieved it, found the key, and opened it for inspection.

With our baggage checked, we left in mid-afternoon on the fast train to Paris. Already it was almost dark. It was pouring. Rivulets of rain streamed down the windows. Nightfall, blotting out all trace of the dark landscape outside, made them seem more doleful still, like floods of tears. Ruby made me take another capsule and I went to sleep with my head on her shoulder as if she were my dearest friend.

It always moves me deeply to remember the tenderness, care, and kindness I've received from so many strangers. It renews my faith in humankind but also makes me sad. For I think people I've barely met have shown me more affection than many of my close relatives, who, it's true, have had to suffer me over a much longer time. Perhaps everyone finds this to be so.

In Paris we had to change stations, retrieving our baggage in one and taking it to the other. How Ruby managed with only the three or four words of French she knew I have no idea; all I could do was follow her. I remember vaguely hearing her shout at the top of her heavily accented voice, *"Porteur! Porteur!"* which made everyone turn around but not come to help, and seeing her pivoting my trunk on its corners towards the taxi at the curb. With everything swimming in my head, I thought I was arriving in Paris for the first time again and it was my other compatriot who had taken charge for me.

On the Paris–Nice express, Ruby took command of an empty compartment. She had me lie on one of the seats with a rolled-up sweater for a pillow and covered me with my coat and hers too. After this I wasn't conscious of anything else all night. While I slept, she told me next day, she mounted guard at the door. When passengers tried to enter she'd gesture at my sleeping form and with a sorrowful but authoritarian face beg their compassion saying, "Poor girl. Very sick. Perhaps contagious!" Our would-be companions would retreat hurriedly and squeeze as best they could into compartments already full. Some remained standing outside in the corridor, leaning on the handrail and gazing out at the darkness flying by. These I still have on my conscience. After Lyon, our only stop on the way, I think, where she had to beat off some last attempts at invasion, Ruby lay down on the other seat and she too slept like a log. Even the conductor, who came in twice to punch our tickets, as he told us the following morning in his delightful lilting southern voice, couldn't bring himself to wake the "two sleeping beauties so deep in the arms of Morpheus."

When I opened my eyes it was broad daylight. Everything was flooded with light. The sea was very close and sparkling. I thought it was a dream playing tricks on me and began to rub my eyes. I'd left London in a filthy pea-soup fog. I hadn't seen the sky for months. Perhaps I hadn't really seen it since leaving my native Manitoba and my nostalgia for the tall, boundless sky of the prairies had prevented me from really seeing almost any other. I took my hands from my eyes and all the blue was still there, sky and sea together dazzling me. Among the tamarisks, which I recognized from my walks in Kew Gardens, the aloes holding high their single long-stemmed flowers, and the palms, orange trees, and early-flowering mimosas, I kept catching glimpses of pretty villas in glorious colours nestled in their gardens. It was as if they were for ever beyond reach of poverty, suffering...all the unpleasant things in life.

Had my illness run its course? Had Ruby's medicine taken full effect? Or was I cured instantly by the joy of seeing the world as it ought to be? Today I'm almost certain it was my joy that brought me back to life that morning.

Then Ruby woke and she too showed utter astonishment to find herself whisked as if by magic to such a beautiful world. In keeping with her less demonstrative nature, a more contained happiness than mine spread slowly across her wide, good-natured face. We looked at one another, each discovering the other with excitement, we rain-soaked, wind-whipped pilgrims of yesterday arriving to-gether in the mellow South of France. I felt a fondness for her already, and not merely from gratitude. She seemed drawn to me too, as one often is to someone one has cared for and restored to health. Besides, I'd barely recovered and already I was gay and exuberant. I suppose I delighted her as I had Phyllis and would many others on my way through life, people who haven't been granted my capacity for observation, laughter, and exhilaration, and have become the more fond of me for having caught a little

374

of this from me, as it were, while in my company. The Lord be praised for ever if I've been able to share this with others.

I don't know whether we went to the dining car or had coffee and croissants brought to us. I only remember that we enjoyed our breakfast, watching the endless garden of the Côte d'Azur unfold. I was ecstatic over the gracefulness of the shoreline, its coves, steep-sided inlets, and little fishing villages, and most of all the brightness of the sky which I'd never seen so brilliantly and abundantly diffused anywhere else. As the minutes passed I felt myself conceiving a love for this land that would remain with me all my life. But I was apprehensive also that my joy had been too immediate, and I told Ruby I was terribly afraid I'd find myself back in the constricting reality of just a few short hours before. She confessed the same feeling, afraid for her part that she'd find herself back in Toronto, sloshing through the mud and slush in the crowd on Bloor Street with a bitter wind blowing off Lake Ontario. Then we saw that we really had set foot in Paradise, and it was just as real as all the gloomy places where so many people have chosen or are forced to live.

Ruby told me about her hotel in Nice where she'd meet mostly English people and feel more comfortable, not speaking French. I told her about my boarding house in Beaulieu-sur-mer.

Suddenly I exclaimed, "We're crazy, Ruby! We're both going to be bored to death, you with all those old Englishwomen in big hats and sensible shoes and me in my fussy boarding house."

"What else can we do?" she asked, wide-eyed.

I held out my arms to embrace the delightful villages of the Alpilles, the parasol pines, the highway, the beach...the hillsides with ancient olive trees marching in orderly ranks to their summits.

"Hundreds of things, Ruby! It's all ours, if only we put ourselves out a bit. It's up to us. We can have all of Provence."

"How on earth...?"

"By walking it!"

"Walking?"

The idea had just come into my head, but I was already so enchanted I had a glowing picture to paint for Ruby.

"We won't take anything with us. There'll be nothing to tie us down. It's the best possible way to travel. You see everything, hear everything. And it won't cost much, either. Just look, the country's so rich and warm and inviting. We'll sleep at farmhouses for a pittance. We'll live on olives...."

Ruby stopped me in full flight.

"Oh, but I have to eat well, you know, to sustain myself...,"

I conceded this.

"We shall eat, and even if we eat well, with the money we'd have spent, you at your hotel and I at Beaulieu, we'll have enough to stay a month, maybe two...."

I saw she was wavering but was resisting the idea of walking.

"I've never walked in my life," she said, "and I've got sort of bad feet from years of standing on hard hospital floors."

"Well," I said, "it's high time you got those poor feet in shape, Ruby, and you know better than I do that there's nothing like walking for doing that. Anyway, we'll start out slowly, two or three kilometres a day at first, then working our way up to twenty, thirty...."

"Thirty kilometres!"

"Well, ten...fifteen.... Don't forget, a kilometre's a lot less than a mile."

"How much less?"

"Oh, an awful lot less!"

I felt her softening in my hands. As strong and determined as she was when it came to nursing, for example, she seemed pretty malleable as soon as you got the better of her in imagination and adventurousness. And I was brimming over with these, thanks to the excellent care she'd given me. Perhaps she was the kind who couldn't blow with the winds of chance but deep down had always longed to and was ready to follow as soon as there was someone to lead. She would suit me perfectly if this was the case. I could already see her confidence in me and this made me more daring by the minute.

"Of course," I said, "you can stay in Nice and spend your holidays playing cards with your nice old ladies. Or you and I can be roaming the countryside, getting to know shepherds and violet pickers, exploring the hills and seashore, seeing heathlands and mountains and Avignon, Arles, and Tarascon. There'll be no end of things to do once we're on the road."

I talked so much and so well that by the time we were nearing

Nice she was converted. We would go to her hotel for just one night and leave our baggage there. The next morning we'd set off on the open road in the good Lord's sunshine, free as the air, and go where the wind took us. My knight and saviour of the Channel had become my faithful Sancho Panza.

Had I gone about it with consummate skill, or had Ruby long been subconsciously ready for the role? So far, in any event, she was apparently as happy as could be with her commitment.

XVIII

EARLY NEXT MORNING we went to outfit ourselves inexpensively in the old city. Ruby was enchanted by the clothing and other wares hanging all along the dark, narrow streets. We bought ourselves good strong walking shoes and, to have done with it quickly, matching skirts and identical jackets and finally knapsacks to wear on our backs. In our knapsacks we stowed an extra sweater, a large-scale map, some chocolate bars, a baguette of bread, and some cheese. Scarcely more hampered than a pair of goats, we left Nice by the rail car known as the *micheline*, getting off shortly afterwards and continuing on foot. We were enchanted with everything we saw, no doubt because we were walking in step and our hearts were open to everything.

A kindly sun looked down, warming us just sufficiently through our jackets. Since Ruby was somewhat plump and sturdy and I was rather slight, we must have looked like ill-matched twins in our identical clothes, and all along our way people smiled at us. The air was fragrant with thyme, sage, and rosemary. The postman, a shepherd, and two old women in black greeted us cordially as they passed and we returned their greeting: " *'Jour, 'sieurs-dames.''*

I didn't know it yet, but that morning my real youth began. I had been so preoccupied with cares and worries I had never felt as totally young before and would never be as giddily young again. For the first time I was far removed from all the harm that had touched me, that was still touching others. I've so loved this dear land of Provence most of all perhaps because only here have I been truly free of anxiety, ambition, maybe even memories, blissfully living for the moment.

Towards the end of the morning we reached St-Tropez or Ste-Maxime, I'm not sure which. I looked up and there was the first

378

Saracen village I'd ever seen, perched on a rocky peak in the mountains of the Maures massif, its houses forming a rampart. At once
this was where I wanted to go. We enquired at a café. Yes, we
could get up there by bus, but it had left an hour ago and there
wouldn't be another until the day after tomorrow. I was pawing
the ground with impatience and couldn't wait that long.

"Come on, Ruby, let's go!"

"We're going to walk?"

"Why not? It can't be more than five or six kilometres. We'll
take it slowly. We've got lots to eat on the way. We'll sleep up
there tonight. The view must be magnificent."

And since I was beginning to know how she loved to eat, I added
an enticement, saying, "Tonight we'll ignore our budget for the
day if we have to and treat ourselves to a real feast. How about a
pepper steak or a sole amandine, with cream puffs for dessert?"

So poor fat Ruby was persuaded to tackle the rugged uphill road,
though she was already dead tired. We didn't see a soul on the
way up and passed not a single habitation, only a long-deserted
hermitage. She whimpered somewhat on the most difficult stretches
of the stony track. I did what I could to make her feel better.

"Just wait till you taste the air we'll be breathing on that peak!"

Alas, the village I'd guessed to be five or six kilometres from the
coast must have been fifteen at least. The farther we dragged ourselves towards it, the farther it seemed to draw away into the
mountains. At times we couldn't even see it, perhaps because we
were tired or it was hidden by a bend in the road.

Ruby began to limp. When she took off her socks we found a
huge blister ready to burst on each heel. Fortunately I'd brought
some adhesive tape. I made her some adhesive bandages, found
some fresh water for her to drink and even a stout walking stick.
When I discovered she'd eaten all her chocolate on the sly I gladly
gave her what was left of mine. What wouldn't I have done to
keep my Sancho by my side? Without her the adventure would
have lost almost all its tang. On the other hand, wasn't she already
so committed to her tormentor that she'd have followed me come
what might? In any event, when I pointed out that we wouldn't
arrive before nightfall at the rate we were going, she got to her
feet and followed me without too much complaint.

Years have passed since I lost Ruby. That we so quickly became inseparable still amazes me, still draws me to her in even greater friendship.

In late afternoon, the stronger of us leaning heavily on the weaker, with twisted ankles and dishevelled hair, we reached Ramatuelle and almost simultaneously the friendly doorstep of Chez Henri, its only inn.

When he witnessed the arrival of these dust-covered maidens, Henri himself – and eventually everyone in the village – was absolutely convinced we were a pair of eccentric heiresses. Who else would embark on such utter madness just for the fun of it? Certainly not honest-to-goodness poor girls, anyway. Thus was born some local lore regarding us which led to the most ludicrous misapprehension, a source of endless mirth for Ruby and me.

FOR THE PAST three months the inn had been giving shelter to an Irish baronet, Sir John Henry Dunn, Bart., who couldn't pay his bill and therefore couldn't leave. While it was customary not to pay until leaving, there was no exemption from an eventual reckoning and the longer the poor penniless blueblood stayed, the less able he was to pay. With Ruby's and my arrival, it appeared that his day of deliverance might have dawned at last. He invited us to a copious meal the like of which we'd not imagined even in our wildest dreams. Expense was no object, since this was simply added to his account; he'd been brought up to consider it unbecoming to forgo anything you didn't have to pay for on the spot.

Ruby was instantly restored by the feast, which she completed with two *savarins* in quick succession. I kept marvelling at the quantities she could consume, all of which seemed to be transformed into good humour and goodwill. That night I saw how I could make her follow me to the end of the earth if all other means failed.

That very night there was a *bal musette*, a dance to accordion music in the little village square. We attended, one on each arm of our baronet.

In the middle of the square, almost filling it, grew an ancient elm tree seven hundred years old, which was venerated as the ancestor of all in this eyrie. Around it was an enormous wooden bench, well rounded from years of use, on which the oldest villagers were already seated, the women together and the men smoking, their pipe-smoke rising into the dense arch of branches beneath the great starry arch of the balmy night.

Young and old came to meet us, see us up close, and congratulate us for having climbed all the way up their steep little mountain to come to their party. Though she didn't understand much of what they were saying, Ruby watched the movement of their lips and the expressions on their faces, smiling and showing her delight. Later she told me that she knew she wasn't charming or beautiful or attractive – ah yes, she knew it all too well – but that night for the first time in her life she felt wanted, accepted, liked, and she had to keep pinching herself almost constantly to believe that she was really the one creating this effect.

The accordionist struck up a lively tune. I whirled in the arms of Sir John Henry Dunn, Bart. He danced beautifully. He also had a way with words. He told me I had beautiful eyes, they'd pierced his heart the moment he saw me, he said. And a lot of other such things. I might have let him go on this way except that I wanted Ruby to have a dance too. For the moment she was sitting on the circular bench among the sages, delighted to be on such good terms with them.

"Ruby's much more beautiful," I said.

"The English girl? She's unattractive, poor thing, too short, nose too big, thick lips."

"But her eyes are beautiful, you'll see if you take the trouble to look, and she has a heart of gold."

I didn't yet know he was fortune-hunting, even dower-hunting perhaps, so what possessed me to fabricate at this point?

"And then, she's rich, very rich, which doesn't hurt."

"Oh, really?" he said with ill-concealed interest.

He danced the next dance with Ruby, his face wreathed in his most enchanting smile, and apparently he strung some kind of line to her too. She was quicker than I to see what he was up to.

"He's obviously looking for an heiress," she whispered to me before the next dance. "He thinks you're gorgeous and paid you a bunch of other compliments besides. I told him your father owns the Canadian Pacific Railway. Don't let on he doesn't. Your turn now!"

I said I thought the game was rather cruel but she retorted, "So what! He's probably fishing for some silly little ninny."

During my next dance with him he dropped what was meant to seem a casual question.

"So you say your delightful, entertaining friend Ruby's rich as well as charming?"

"Is she ever! Her father owns the three biggest pulp and paper mills in Canada. I think he supplies all the newsprint for the *Chicago Tribune*."

Between dances we kept comparing notes, agreeing on what our fathers owned and how far we could push our luck with our suitor.

Poor Sir John Henry Dunn, Bart. That surprisingly warm January night, on the little mountaintop beneath the twinkling stars and the equally twinkling gaze of the old folk sitting around the tree, how shamelessly we led him on!

Ruby was having the time of her life. When they saw how avidly she was being courted by the haughty baronet, the young men of the village also decided that she was desirable and flocked to ask her to dance. She had partners aplenty into the wee hours. Her eyes were bright and her face was animated; as I remember her in these moments, she was almost beautiful.

NOT MANY hours later, having arranged a magnificent picnic to take with us, Sir John led us by a goat path to another Saracen retreat tucked away even higher in the Maures massif, the incredible Gassin, so remote and isolated that Ruby and I may have been the first foreign women to set foot in the village.

From this height the view was breathtaking – the blue line of the Mediterranean in the distance and before us jagged mountain ridges, forests, terraces under cultivation. The air was so light, so intoxicating it made me as happy as if sorrow had never crossed my path.

I owed the discovery of all this to the Irish baronet and hated the thought of leaving him with a false impression of Ruby and me. We spent another day at Ramatuelle to give Ruby's feet time to heal before taking the bus to Ste-Maxime. We left behind an abashed Sir John; I had decided to end his awful suspense and confessed to him that we hadn't a sou to spend on staying an hour longer at an inn as luxurious as this. In an attempt to make amends, I said as we left:

"Why don't you write your memoirs while you're here? You've

got lots of time and the memoirs of princes in exile are always in great demand."

He gave me a look with a very Irish twinkle. Perhaps he was going to take my suggestion.

Two days later, I don't quite remember how, we reached the island of Porquerolles. Ruby took a final potshot at our suitor. She predicted that he'd languish in captivity for ever in his Saracen village, like the Man in the Iron Mask in the dungeon we visited on one of the small Lérins islands. Serve him right, too!

DAY AFTER DAY I was filled with joy, that mysterious visitor whose presence in us after crushing grief is the most puzzling of our experiences. At moments the memory of my tormenting love for Stephen passed through me, like the hoarse cry of a wounded bird, I thought, or I would recall a scene from the days of Deschambault Street and my mother's endless struggle to give us at least a distant glimpse of happiness...which I now possessed in such abundance. Tears of guilt would flow for having allowed myself such joy. Ruby was quite nonplussed, since she clung as if for dear life to my happy self.

She was knowing joy for the first time. Since she firmly believed she would never have found it by herself, she used to say that I had brought it to her by some kind of magic. I didn't realize how deeply grateful she was for this until much later. But already I was having little difficulty leading my Sancho almost anywhere the fancy took me to go. The only grumbling I ever heard from her was mild, for instance when I suggested that we stretch our hikes to twenty-two kilometres a day.

After Agay, Ruby's choice for once, for the odd reason that she had a cousin by the name of Agay in Peterborough, Ontario, where did we go next? Today I find it impossible to recall our whimsical itinerary, if one could call it that. Our rovings took us one day to Hyères, the next to Grasse and Vence, the day after that to the gorges of the River Var. Not even a pair of excited hares would have traced a more erratic route.

I remember a day with a fiercely blowing mistral when against everyone's advice we took it into our heads to rent bicycles. We must have pedalled for hours without advancing an inch, all the time beside the same property with a high bamboo hedge thrashing as if in torment. Two men passed us on the road, capes flapping, and kept looking back at us in disbelief. It seems we were watched from the tightly shuttered house, through some crack no doubt, because someone finally came out and offered to share the soup pot with us and give us and our bicycles shelter for the night.

Did I fall in love with Provence because I was hungry for consolation and received far more than I ever hoped? Or was it Provence itself that won my heart and made me happier than anywhere else, with its sparkling gaiety and mercurial moods so much like my own, droll one minute and sombre the next? Only here, I think, have I lived purely for the moment – well, perhaps at the Little Water Hen, but there I had to work. Here, my past with its crippling old anxieties might not have existed. The future wasn't important. I didn't care in the least what was to become of me. Have I ever been as free?

One evening in late twilight we came to Mouans-Sartou, a village of no importance except as the site of a boarding house kept by a Madame Viscardi which was so good and reasonably priced that we decided to make it our headquarters. From here we set out according to our whim of the moment, returning at night to a comfortable bed, the warmth of a massive stove, and the congenial company of a half-dozen boarders who immediately became a kind of family to us. I almost persuaded Ruby that we should become shepherds or goatherds and never leave Provence; it would be sheer folly to go elsewhere having found a land of happiness at last, I said, since no success, money, promotion, or diploma would ever bring us what we already had here for nothing. I didn't know enough about life to see that "nothing" was in fact almost everything: a light heart, bubbling enthusiasm, a spring in one's step, and above all – yes, above all – the ultimate injustice, just because you're young, healthy, and happy-faced, of having everyone love you at first sight.

One day when we had left early in the morning for no more than a long walk, having told Madame Viscardi that we'd be back for dinner, we took a succession of little roads of the kind that have always appealed to me, each lonelier than the last, and eventually realized we were lost. The country was wild and so deserted that the only hint of habitation we'd seen was a slim, handwritten sign at the crossing of two dirt roads announcing "Château de Besançon,

8 km." We'd already tramped farther than that, probably turning in circles, trying to find our way out of this wasteland with its impenetrable silence and circle of dark woods all around.

"We aren't in Provence any more," I said. "The devil's tricked us and we're in some godforsaken corner of Asia."

Ruby was cross with me and wouldn't laugh. This was one of the few times she rebelled openly, saying we were going to get what we deserved, that by just following my nose I'd end up leading us into some insoluble predicament. We seemed to have come to that now. In the tall straggly grass beside this dismal road there was a big flat rock. Ruby sat on the rock and, taking off her shoes to rub her sore feet, told me she wouldn't go a step farther with me. I sat down in the grass beside her. That morning we'd put on our identical flaming red pullovers, which could have been seen for miles across these monotonous meadows. I didn't know what to do to mollify her. I pulled a blade of grass and chewed it glumly. Who would ever expect a most unusual opportunity to be heading our way at this very moment? It would prove Ruby's dire predictions wrong and my luck dependable after all.

A car appeared far down the little road. We watched it come like a pair of vultures, heads and shoulders showing above the grass, as red as could be. When it reached us the car stopped and its driver put a smiling face through the window.

"*Mesdames?...mesdemoiselles?...* Pardon me, would you be local folk?"

"Local folk, indeed we are!" said I in my best imitation of the Provençal lilt.

"Well then, *mesdames...mesdemoiselles...*would you know a Château de Besançon hereabouts? It must be hidden away because I've spent two hours already looking and not finding it. I'm from Nîmes," he added with the obliging tendency in this part of France to anticipate and satisfy the curiosity of others. "I'm an agronomist, and I'd stop looking and go home, only they've got a sickness in their vines at the Château de Besançon and wanted me to come without delay."

"Besançon!" I exclaimed. "What a lucky thing, indeed I know how to find it! Keep on the way you're going. Less than a kilometre on you'll see the sign. Be careful though, it's written by hand and very small. You need good eyes to read it."

Then, to be authentically local, with firm conviction I added something I'd heard a thousand times in France:

"Can't miss it! It's straight ahead!"

When he'd left I began to shriek with laughter. Ruby, now more curious than resentful, wanted to know what the motorist and I had been gabbling about.

"He was lost and wanted directions."

"So?"

"So...I gave him directions."

Then she began to shriek with laughter too.

Our cheerful relationship was completely restored. Two hours later we'd begun to consider going to beg a meal at Besançon when we saw the agronomist's car reappear. We were still sitting in exactly the same place. The car stopped.

"*Mesdames?... Mesdemoiselles?...* You aren't lost, I know. So why do I find you here again in your lovely red sweaters, giving this country such a pretty bit of life?"

"*Eh oui!*" I said. "Red's cheerful, sure enough," and I enquired after the vines.

"Ah, very sick, poor things! They've waited too long to have them seen to. It's because the owners themselves are poor, poor things!"

"*Eh aussi*, I thought as much!..." I said compassionately.

"You have something like the accent of these parts," he observed, "but not exactly. Where d'you come from then?"

"From.... That is, from near..., Marseille."

"Marseille? Ah, no! I know the accent of Marseille, *allons!* Would you be from Norway? Sweden? No?"

In the end I told him the truth.

"Canada! The land of snows! Of Maria Chapdelaine! And come to think of it, Montcalm too. Your Montcalm, our Montcalm. Before he went and got himself killed in Canada, poor man, he was from Nîmes, you're aware perhaps. At least, from very close to Nîmes. *Allons, mesdames...mesdemoiselles...*you can't leave without coming to pay your respects to the birthplace of Montcalm. *Allons!* Come with me, *mesdames...mesdemoiselles.* I'll take you to Nîmes."

"What's he so excited about?" Ruby wanted to know.

"He wants to take us to Nîmes to pay our respects to Montcalm."

She said she'd rather go and pay her respects to Wolfe but she had nothing against Nîmes, and besides, she'd rather ride with the devil himself than walk all that awful distance back to Madame Viscardi's.

"He isn't the devil," I assured her. "Agronomists are serious people. And just look what a nice face this one's got."

We both sat in front with Monsieur Didier Laroche. He drove us through the prettiest villages, which I never saw again on later trips to Provence. They must have been on some relatively untravelled road. He made a detour through the radiant countryside near Nîmes to show us the ancient Roman aqueduct, tier after tier of delicate arches striding across a glowing sky. In the city itself he showed us several monuments and the amphitheatre known as Les Arènes, perhaps the best preserved in Europe, and glass in hand on the terrace of a café as the last rays of a golden afternoon fell across the table, invited us to keep a minute of silence in memory of Montcalm. He would find us an inexpensive hotel. The next morning he'd come and pick us up and take us to see parts of Languedoc where there were vines in need of his care. It was very tempting, but if we were going to stay we'd have to let Madame Viscardi know. The waiter brought us a pen, ink, and a kind of express card designed to travel at lightning speed. I composed a few lines assuring Madame Viscardi that in order to see as much as possible of the fair land of France we couldn't be in better hands, those of a physician to the Lord's vines, and advising her not to expect us for any particular day.

When I look back on all I've been able to see without spending a cent in the course of my travels, I realize I owe nearly all of it to the kind Monsieur Didiers I've met along my way.

When our card had been posted, he dropped us at the door of such a pitiful-looking hotel we hesitated to go in.

"D'you feel like going in there?" asked Ruby. "I'm sure it's full of fleas."

We waited till Monsieur Didier's car was out of sight, then turned and went to look elsewhere.

On the way Ruby said, "I don't know what I'd give to sleep tonight in my nice comfortable bed at Madame Viscardi's, after a lovely dinner of her sorrel soup, her sea perch cooked with fennel, and her chocolate mousse."

"D'you think we could still arrive in time?"

"If we run all the way to the station and catch the next *micheline*...."

When we arrived at the station, panting for breath, the *micheline* was on the point of leaving. The conductor saved us from being crushed between the doors, which were about to close. The same conductor had punched our tickets the day before and the day before that. He was a Corsican, a handsome man with a dark complexion and a sad face. He fixed an intense and despairing eye on me.

"Listen," he said. "I can't stand it any longer. I've loved you madly since I first saw you, now you know, I've told you. I've tried my best to forget you. I can't help it. You get on, you get off, you come back. Not a day goes by that you aren't there. Really, I can't stand it any longer. Marry me. I'll make you a good husband, I swear."

I looked at him and abruptly lost my initial impulse to laugh. The poor fellow wasn't joking. Without the least intention, even in fun, I'd cast some kind of spell on him.

He wasn't the only one. We were in an inn one evening finishing our dinner. A young man seated facing me hadn't stopped staring. He tore a page from a notebook, hastily wrote a message, and asked the waiter to bring it to me. It read, "I'm single – electrician – earn a pretty good living. I lay my life at your feet. I know already I'll love only you. You know, don't you? Your enchantment is irresistible."

Even allowing for the emotional Mediterranean temperament, I must admit I made more than my share of conquests along our path, which Ruby called "the trail of broken hearts".

What was going on? What was giving me the power I seemed to have over people, men and women alike? Wherever I went and at all hours of the day I made friends with people I'd barely met. It was partly the impulsive Provençal nature and its harmony with my own, yes, but there was more. What was it? In London too I made many dear friends among strangers who often passed very briefly through my life and then vanished for ever, but I have the impression that it happened there at times of heartache, loneliness, and melancholy, to which the hearts of Londoners are perhaps particularly attuned. Whereas here...!

Today, so far from what I was then, I watch this blithe creature move, live, laugh, and flit about, and can hardly believe it's myself

I see. I think I must have been radiant with happiness at being loved at every turn, and the radiance attracted more love, which made me still more radiant.

From the Mouans-Sartou stop to the boarding house, again we ran all the way, and were out of breath when we arrived just after nightfall. Madame Viscardi and the boarders were gathered around the shaded lamp reading our card, which had just arrived, with even more astonishing dispatch than the Fulham birthday card.

I can still hear Madame Viscardi's comically accented voice reading aloud: "Leaving with kind Monsieur Didier for a tour of Languedoc.... Perhaps the Cévennes.... Don't expect to see us for a day or two.... Or three or four.... Perhaps not until the end of the week...."

She raised her arms towards heaven and exclaimed, "Did you ever see such devilment, especially the little one that speaks French! She's the one who leads the other one on...."

They turned, saw us standing in the doorway, remained stunned for a moment, then opened their arms to give us hugs, rejoicing at our return as if we'd been away for a century.

XIX

THIS WAS the way things continued for more than a month. Life was so happy that today, after so many trials and bereavements, my face would turn red with shame except that I've learned that if you haven't at least briefly known real happiness, you can't feel for the suffering in this world either.

What made our days so rich, I think, was that everything was so unexpected. We never knew on one day where we'd be the next. We entrusted ourselves to each new day, and the day, like life itself, almost always took us by surprise, happy surprise, a never-ending delight.

At the end of the second week Ruby talked about leaving, arguing that she'd soon have to resign herself to getting back to "real life" and it might as well be now as later, when it would be even harder. I managed to dissuade her.

"A week more," I begged her, and when that was up, "One more, Ruby!"

It wasn't so easy, though, to persuade her to leave Madame Viscardi's nice comfortable bed and excellent table and move on, not knowing where we'd lay our heads each night until we found something almost as good in the little village of Castries in Languedoc, at the far side of the region. This was in a house where a Madame Paulet-Cassan lived with her shy spinster sister whom she always addressed as "*Ma-de-moi-selle Thérèse.*" We had asked an obliging gendarme where we might find a good but inexpensive room and he'd sent us there without hesitation saying, "At Madame Paulet-Cassan's, that's the place, no doubt about it.... But don't say I sent you.... I could be in trouble with the hotel, you know...."

At the very end of the village, in a big, pink, rough-plastered house with brown shutters, we each had a room that was unheated but huge, with generous windows overlooking a panorama of plains, gardens, and hillsides covered with vineyards. It was here one chilly morning, standing barefoot on the icy tile floor, that I opened the shutters and for the first time in my life saw the dazzling spectacle of an almond tree in flower. I'll always be able to see this young tree, its delicate pink flowers freshly unfolded with the daylight, standing against the clear blue sky of the vibrant South of France.

Our rooms with big brass beds and down comforters and our deliciously fragrant morning coffee cost us each about twenty-five cents a day in our money. Living with the people not only made our money go further but was also very pleasant, since we learned to adopt their customs and live the same peaceful, uncomplicated lives.

Madame Paulet-Cassan had a small vineyard a kilometre from the village, which it was her pleasure to go and tend almost every day. We left together early one fine morning, the little donkey with his bells ringing, Ruby and I, Madame Paulet-Cassan carrying the *serpe* or hooked pruning knife, her sister with bottles of wine wrapped in napkins in a basket, and the dog Fidèle trotting behind. We came to the field of vines in the midst of sweet-smelling *garrigue*, a kind of *maquis*, past the wondrous arches of the Roman aqueduct, where Ruby and I helped with the pruning and tidying up. In the mellowest of twilights, typical of this region, the donkey laden with faggots of pruned vine-shoots, we passed again under the delicate arches. Some old women drawing water in pitchers from the community source called cheerfully, "*Hé ben! Hé là!* So, Madame Paulet, that's what paying guests are for!"

Over a slow fire of the vine prunings we'd brought home, Madame Paulet-Cassan roasted *bouchées* – morsels of lamb, bacon, and cèpe mushrooms sprinkled with thyme – threaded together on a slender spit which she turned with infinite patience by hand, crouching by the hearth. The smell was enough to make one's mouth water for the rest of one's life.

"Madame Paulet-Cassan, keep us for dinner," I pleaded, "it's so much better here than at the hotel."

"I know why," she said. "At the hotel they don't have time to cook over vine shoots, or know how any more."

She had a plan for us.

"Go to the baker's and the grocer's, buy a bit of cheese, a tart.

Wherever you go, make sure they hear you say I let you do your cooking over my fire. They can't complain about that, the jealous things, all ready to send the gendarme round, they are, saying I haven't got a permit. Permit! Permit! Can't blow your nose without one! Go along now, girls. Do as I say and I'll make you *bouchées* you'll still remember when you've got no teeth left."

Before long she decided the daily price she'd fixed for us was too high. Because we were staying the week she reduced it considerably. The longer we stayed the less it was costing to eat better and better, since besides *bouchées* she soon began making us superb crêpes cooked deftly on a griddle heated in the fireplace.

"At this rate, Madame Paulet-Cassan, what's it going to cost us to live this well if we stay a whole month?"

"Why, nothing at all of course, because you'll be family! Which you are already, in fact. You help in the fields, after all."

Help? From me? Giving me any such credit was more than generous. We would barely reach the vineyard when I'd stray off into the *garrigue* nearby. It was warm and fragrant and alive with the chirp of young crickets, not yet their stridulant song of summer. I'd lie on the sun-warmed, rubbly ground. I'd watch the fluffy clouds float by. I'd dream aimlessly, questlessly, thoughtlessly, without remorse, perhaps even without memories. I surrendered willingly, innocently to the drift of time. This humble, stony field, like the big ploughed field on the path to Upshire, is one of the dearest places on earth to me, among those which I still see most often when I let my mind wander or try to picture the best of things in life. Yet the only memory I can attach to it is simply of well-being without apparent cause, indefinable and as vast and calm as the prairie or the ocean.

My radiant happiness was coming to an end, however. There were times now when it was tinged with sadness. I would have many more happy hours after this, more than I've deserved, perhaps, but never as then. It was perhaps because I sensed this end that during these last days I so often stayed hidden in the *garrigue*, as if it could keep me in this state of peace and torpor.

One day, finally, there was no holding Ruby back. She had become perhaps even more attached to the life we were leading than I was. Since she wasn't naturally dreamy like me, it must have seemed magical to her, more of a fairyland than it did to me, for in a sense I had expected nothing less. But her strong sense of duty made her feel she ought not to stay away from her nursing any longer.

We returned to Nice to collect our belongings. We parted at the station. At the very last minute she pulled down the window of her compartment and called to me with a most uncharacteristic display of emotion:

"Take care! Take care! And oh, Gabrielle, thank you, thank you for the lovely time! And mostly for making me feel young at least once in my life!"

We would never see each other again. We corresponded for quite a while. Perhaps one of our letters went astray. Perhaps Ruby changed her address and didn't let me know. I stopped hearing from her and she stopped hearing from me. Years passed. When *Street of Riches* appeared in English, *Maclean's Magazine* of Toronto published a picture of me on the cover. Ruby saw it and wrote me in care of the magazine. It was a very touching letter. She told me she had a cherished memory of my euphoric face of the days of Provence, but perhaps she liked the one of today even better, since according to the photograph it showed signs of wear, but still at our age seemed unstripped of illusions.

She had married and lived a rather dull life, she thought now, with no great trials or great happiness either, "a life of very ordinary days." If it hadn't been for our spree in the South of France she might believe she'd never really been young at heart. After that, the colour of everything had been very prosaic. She was therefore still grateful to me for having taken her "on the sideroads of enchantment", and always would be. Sadly, since she was such an unadventurous person, whenever she recounted our escapades no one would believe she'd had such experiences, much less with me since I'd become a "famous author". Saddest of all, she had even come herself to doubt that she'd had them. Perhaps she'd only dreamed those adventures in Ramatuelle, Castries, and Nîmes. Perhaps our dear Madame Paulet-Cassan had never really existed. Perhaps everything, the Saracen eyrie in the Maures massif, the brightest of blue skies, kind Monsieur Didier, had only been the product of long years of wishful thinking. Wouldn't I come one day to visit and reminisce with her? Then she could be sure it was true she'd been so happy to be alive at least this once; it wouldn't seem so much like something she'd made up. She would come herself to see me, she said, only her health was failing. At the very end, as if it weren't important, she mentioned in the briefest terms that she had cancer and didn't know how long she had to live.

I replied at once that I'd come very soon. Did I take too long, or was her illness already more advanced than she'd admitted? She died the day I was preparing to go and assure her that those happy times so long ago were real. And yet I had known since Anna's death and most of all since Dédette's that before dying everyone needs terribly to know that one had been happy occasionally, and how, where, and why. It's not so important to know that one has suffered; what counts is to know how it feels to hold happiness in one's hand, as if it were the key to love and the mystery of our existence. The people who die most alone are those who cannot remember being happy at least for a moment on this earth.

Like a great bird with dark outstretched wings soaring over a parched valley, Ruby's memory often haunts me.

With Sancho gone, Don Quixote wasn't half as enterprising any more. However, I did stay a little longer to roam about Provence, to Nîmes, Montpellier, and elsewhere. In the end I returned to my old ladies in Castries. Madame Paulet-Cassan welcomed me like a daughter returning to the fold. In a way this is what I'd become to her, for her own daughter lived in Marseille and hardly ever came to see her, and when she did come she spent the time scolding her mother for still cooking over the hearth with an iron cauldron and pans from the olden days. And perhaps seeing the face of Mademoiselle Thérèse all crinkled with joy at my return delighted me even more than her sister's effusions, because I'd never before seen a smile on this face that was as grizzled as a rennet apple.

Years later, when I felt the need to revisit earlier scenes of happiness – an incredibly persistent need for me – I went to introduce my husband to the two old sisters. They recognized me immediately, then examined him with great interest, like an object they were turning this way and that for better scrutiny. "*Hé hé*, Mademoiselle Thérèse and I often used to wonder which of your admirers you'd pick. You've chosen well, I'd say!" They went to the cupboard where they kept liqueurs and brought out the finest, one they had made themselves from oranges and kept for the most precious reunions. An hour later they'd already contrived to spread through the "jealous" village the news that I really had returned, bringing my husband to show them besides, and if that wasn't proof of faithfulness and heart in the right place, what was!

I have made so many unexpected friends in every corner of the world when I've sought affection from simple folk, and afterwards have rarely lost this affection.

ONCE THE MISTRAL had subsided I rented a bicycle and rode in every direction, as far as Béziers and to Sète to visit the *cimetière marin*, a cemetery for sailors by the sea. When I returned from my outings I recounted them to my two old ladies, who had never seen most of their own region and were delighted to learn something about it from me. One of my great and fairly frequent delights has been in helping others to see around them, feel their own happiness, sometimes dream their own dreams.

I went to Carcassonne and spent a whole day walking on the ramparts without once coming down. I missed Ruby quite beyond reason. It made me feel better if I pretended to be telling her about my most amusing discoveries. Sometimes I laughed out loud to myself, startling passers-by. This still happens, moreover, for instance when I'm doing my shopping on Cartier Street in Quebec City and instead of saying hello to someone I know I'll absent-mindedly laugh in her face. Some think it's a slight and hold it against me. I don't know how to make them believe otherwise.

One day I went by bus to Perpignan. Here I was reminded of the woes of the world and of how infinitely more massive and widespread they are than its ephemeral happiness. Yet for two months I'd hardly seen or given them a thought.

I knew indeed that Spain was torn by civil war, and knew that the forces on both sides were committing atrocities. The war in Spain had seemed unreal in the happiness of each new day I'd spent in Provence, but now the Catalan front had broken and refugees were flooding at the rate of ten, fifteen, and twenty thousand a day through a pass in the Pyrenees into the border village of Prats-de-Mollo not far from Perpignan.

This was where I went. Fortunate though I consider myself to have so often had the *joie de vivre* of others reflect on me, I must also hold it a great but painful privilege to have been near the greatest of the world's woes.

I had barely arrived in Prats-de-Mollo when I made friends with some young teachers who were working as volunteers for the Red Cross. They gave me a little badge which identified me as an assistant and allowed me to go everywhere with them.

Oh God! The spectacle I saw! The memory still haunts my nights with fragments of horror as in Picasso's *Guernica*.

The communal school had been turned into a hospital and the wounded lay on the floor, each wrapped in a single blanket. They watched us as we moved about, never complaining. I remember a tiny girl holding her dying mother's hand, calling to her softly as if not to wake her. Behind the barbed wire were the men who were still whole or at least able to stand, thousands and thousands of them. Grotesquely thin, emaciated, they looked back at us as we looked at them in alarm and curiosity, here also without a word of complaint passing their lips. What struck me most forcibly and still comes back with chilling immediacy was the silence that cloaked this gathering of lost souls. Only one uttered a sound, an old woman looking for her son, not knowing whether he was dead or perhaps alive somewhere in this sea of unrecognizable faces. She wandered ceaselessly from camp to camp, peering into the unvarying masses and calling, "Alfonso, where are you? Are you alive, Alfonso my son? Has anyone seen Alfonso dead or alive?" All one day we heard her voice through the cruel silence, like a stone dropped in a bottomless well.

The French government distributed a loaf of bread a day to each refugee. To this, people of the village added what they could, sharing most of their own food with the unfortunates. A drop in the bucket.

Night-time was still cold at the foot of the snow-covered mountains. The refugees beyond the barbed wire made small fires around which they could be seen trying to warm themselves, blankets over their shoulders, hunched motionless in circles as though in the flames they might discern the enigmatic strands of destiny.

Each day the pitiful flood kept swelling, streaming down from the mountain pass, the sorely wounded carried on stretchers of branches, a few slung over the backs of mules, others hobbling, a blood-soaked bandage around head or calf. Women who had given birth on the snow in the mountains the night before carried infants, some still alive, cradled in the folds of their skirts. All had the look of those who have seen death face to face and found it less unbearable than life. My young friends of the Red Cross assured me that the human herd straggling all the way from the border to the village had been pursued and attacked by Franco's planes, perhaps Hitler's.

Last of all came their wretched animals, cows with bony haunches, exhausted ewes, lambs newly born perhaps just the night before like the infants, horses with terror-stricken eyes. I saw a horse that was all white, blind, with festering sores for eyes, keeping well in the middle of the herd as if to be sure of not being abandoned. Only the animals whimpered. Rounded up in great haste, they had been brought along to be slaughtered one after the other on the way, cooked over meagre fires and used to nourish suffering a little longer. In their dim awareness, no doubt they sensed their fate.

There were two separate groups among the men who had escaped more or less unhurt to Prats-de-Mollo. One group hoped to be taken by ship to the Spanish coast with help from France, and put ashore near Barcelona to join the forces supporting Negrin, who was still resisting. The rest, trusting in the promised armistice, had chosen to return immediately to Spain. We could see them leaving in small groups to go back the way they had come, unarmed, each with his only possession, his blanket, over his shoulders. According to my friends of the Red Cross, who claimed to have it on good authority, they were being shot as soon as they reached the border. All night long we could hear machine-gun fire coming from the direction of the pass, this much is certain.

I, a stranger, could move about with total freedom through this inconceivable turmoil. I still wonder how it could have been possible. I think I remember there being as many as a hundred thousand refugees on some days, all crammed into the village of Prats-de-Mollo whose population couldn't have been more than two thousand. The efforts were phenomenal. The villagers took in orphans and mothers with small children. Whole convoys kept leaving with the severely wounded. I did my little bit to help. The suffering and hardship were too great for the best will in the world to make much difference. I wandered among these wandering souls a little like Pierre Bezuhov on the field of battle in Tolstoy's *War and Peace*, incredulous, confused, in the depths of my soul not believing what I was seeing. It was a long time before I believed I had seen it. But

397

I took some photographs with my little Brownie camera. My friends the teachers gave me theirs. I still have some of these photographs. They still make me catch my breath when I look at them. I can barely conceive that I was a witness – should I say a privileged one? – of those terrible hours in history.

Eventually the French security policy arrived and drove away everyone who, like me, had no business there. I returned to Perpignan.

The wind was now bitter, like the misery blowing from the Pyrenees. In my icy room I threw myself into my first writing dictated by indignation, pity, and the sorrow of belonging to the human race. I think I put my whole heart in it, though this alone has never produced anything of note. Not knowing what to do with what I'd written, in the end I sent it with some photographs to *La Presse* in Montreal. What a curious decision! In a period when not even André Malraux himself would have been allowed to defend socialist Spain in Montreal, I can imagine how promptly an article by an unknown expressing such sympathies was dropped into the wastebasket.

Now there was nothing left for me in Provence. To say the least, I no longer knew what happiness was and wouldn't for a long time to come. Looking back a mere matter of days, I couldn't believe I had been so moved to see an almond tree in flower. What was a tree with delicate pink flowers doing among my memories? The breath of war affected me here even more deeply than in London at the time of Munich. Henceforth one couldn't escape feeling that it was coming relentlessly closer. Even if I were inclined to stay a little longer, I couldn't in any event. I had hardly a sou left. I couldn't have stayed even this long without the few dollars Ruby had slipped into my handbag when I wasn't looking; I found them after she left.

I took the train to Paris, throughout the trip reviewing all the happy moments whose memory now seemed so incongruous. I needed years, almost a lifetime, to see all the beauty of the joys I'd known in Provence. It takes time to forgive ourselves for being able to be happy in this world.

I stayed a few days at Madame Jouve's on the way through, sharing the room with Charlotte who was still working hard at her piano, beginning at eight in the morning. I really believe she'd barely heard of the troubles in Spain. Nothing much about Madame Jouve's seemed to have changed. I looked around me with a kind of bewilderment. Madame Jouve observed me sympathetically, perceptively too.

"My child, you go and you come, you appear and you disappear, as though you can't settle down. I'm sure you're listening, looking, learning and absorbing, but what's it all for? Where are you going with it all?"

Did I know – that is with certainty and conviction? Have I ever known? Except during the months and years when I've been harnessed to the writing of a book, have I really felt like a writer? At this time I think I was in one of my muffled waiting states, unaware but available, someone waiting for the train. Occasionally while waiting I've briefly been given my freedom again and been almost happy, then the discontent with doing nothing has taken hold again. Then I've been unhappy not to be writing, or else I've been agonizing over having to begin again with no assurance of doing better this time.

Yet one day Madame Jouve would in a sense have an answer to her own question. After my Prix Femina I searched high and low and finally found her in a wretched little room, running a home for the aged and lonely. She who was so reserved took me by the shoulders and kissed me tenderly.

"You're the only one of my charming young ladies who's sought me out in my old age, my child, and in your hour of triumph too. I'm not really surprised. I always knew you'd go far because you never knew where you were going. But I was afraid you'd lose courage on a path so poorly marked."

Indeed, in the spring of 1939 I left in great perplexity.

I landed in London beneath the same low sky, heavy with fog and soot, as when I'd left nearly three months earlier. Hardly anything here had changed either. After the scare before Munich, it was as though dear old England had simply gone back to dozing over its cup of tea beside its little coke fire.

I had been worrying over whether or not to write to Stephen. I thought about him increasingly the closer I came to where we had loved so deliriously. In the end I wrote him a brief note saying I'd soon be returning to Canada. Did he get my letter? Perhaps it arrived while he was away on one of his crazy incursions into Soviet-controlled territory. Perhaps he was as much afraid as I of reopening freshly healed wounds.

I went to Century Cottage for a few days. What a distressing sight! The little garden I remembered as overflowing with fragrance and colour was sodden and cold, half of it lying on the ground, stems crushed and dead blossoms in the mud. A smell of swamp hung in the air.

Dampness oozed from the cottage too. Esther couldn't keep things dry inside with her little fireplaces here and there. With all the doors closed to keep in as much heat as possible, we sat by the stove in the dining room, which now seemed small and dark. Father Perfect had a cough. His sister was dead. After the Bible reading each evening, his prayer was still for me, his tears now for his dear departed Norah. He was glad at least to have gone to keep her company as far as one can go in this life, to the mysterious threshold, since otherwise she would have gone with less confidence to meet the Father. During this time he talked to me in words of great wisdom beneath their apparent simplicity, all of which I wish I could recall today. For example, that we must feel loved by our fellow men before we can feel loved by God and not fear death. Sometimes, not often, I could still make him laugh and even bring a smile to Esther's lips with my stories of Provence, which I made as amusing as I could, trying to cheer them up.

The morning I stepped into the taxi that was taking me to Victoria Station with my trunk and two suitcases, I turned my head for a last look. Beyond the rain-soaked garden I saw their pinched faces trying to smile encouragement. They waved through the pouring rain as if from a diluvial realm that was already half engulfed. We thought we would never see each other again.

And yet...life, which can be so cruel, can sometimes be surprisingly kind, leading us by unsuspected paths back to what we have thought was lost.

Nine years later, after *The Tin Flute*, weary of all the fuss, I came to Upshire from Paris to see if the peace, protection, and love I had known were still there.

Once again it was summer. The delphiniums, the sky-blue and the deeper blue so like the far horizon, had retaken possession of the front garden. We had tea in the back garden beside the old damson tree which had been spared once more, and watched the lights of London come on beyond the pastures. I found Father Perfect not aged too much, still able to set his snares in the forest and bring home mushrooms and flowers. Esther's face below her hairbands had hardly changed at all. And impossible as it seemed, there was Guinevere rubbing against my leg under the tea-table.

Again I had my big airy room with its windows wide open to the downs, which were even more exhilarating than in the picture I'd been cherishing, rolling away as before beyond the stone raised to the memory of Boadicea, beneath the big white clouds scudding to or from the Channel.

And one morning when I woke, calm and at peace in the big brass bed, I found my memories of the Little Water Hen ready for a book, filtered and transfigured by time, in the depths of my unconscious turned into elements of fiction, meaning elements of living truth, perhaps.

Esther came in with the big breakfast tray and put it on my knees, brushing aside some of the scattered pages.

She asked, "Are you pleased with your work this morning, dearest?"

I replied, half light-heartedly, half absently, "I don't know, Esther."

The only thing I've ever been certain of, in fact, is that I've never known and probably never will know what to think of what I find emerging from within me.

XX

I BOARDED ship in Liverpool. At the last minute a cabin boy knocked on my door. He had a long box of flowers for me. Trembling, I untied the string. My poor heart, which I'd thought was so well cured, tugged towards Stephen because he couldn't let me leave without sending a token of the feelings we'd shared. I seized the card. It was from David, whom I'd phoned on my way through London to say a simple goodbye. He was wishing me bon voyage and good luck in life and saying, among other nice things, that he hoped to come and see me one day in Canada. I tore the card into little pieces. I was vexed with poor David for the gesture I would rather had come from Stephen.

Long before we reached the estuary, the waters of the Mersey were tossing us about abominably. The weather was atrocious; rain, fog, howling wind. Almost every minute you could hear the chilling, mournful toll of a bell-buoy, no doubt marking the channel between reefs. On this apocalyptic note I left the shores of England. Sometimes, in the strange dark corner behind my conscious memory, I still hear the great strokes of iron clappers which I associate, I'm not sure why, with the thunderclaps and menacing tone of the Song of Destiny.

In the open sea, such furious waves battered the ship that the cabin boys quickly came to shut the portholes, while deckhands hurried to set in place the heavy panels that closed in the deck completely. I sailed for almost two days on a ship that was blindfold so to speak. I might have felt that nothing could be more depressing, but my heart was too full of its own misery to have room for more. Curiously, I was less seasick than I'd been on the Channel crossing with Ruby. But I was more heartsick.

When the panels were finally removed and we could go and

breathe the fresh air on deck, I remained for a long time, almost alone, gazing in a kind of bewilderment at the vast and disconcerting expanse of endless choppy water. I don't think I've ever liked the ocean when it's all around me, excluding everything except its awesome grandeur. What I love are its shores, gentle or rugged, the tide, seabirds, islands in the distance, harbours, all that the call of the sea implies for someone on land. But on the ocean itself, this vast moving surface, I feel lost. Perhaps it makes me feel something of the same anxiety that "this immeasurable space" aroused in Pascal.

There had probably been other times when I wished I could die. Perhaps everyone has wished this at least once, even in the course of a happy life and especially in one of perpetual adversity or discouragement. But this time it was not a vague wish. I kept looking at the choppy waves buffeting one another, the leaden clouds gathering on the pale horizon; my eyes blurred with tears, I wanted so much to leave this life. Where was it taking me? Nowhere, of this I was certain now. I had left my teaching, hurt my mother unbearably, given up all I had, crossed the ocean, squandered the money I'd so painfully saved, tried all manner of new things, and today was I any further ahead? I felt I had failed in everything, love, drama, writing. Yes, in everything. Why continue the struggle? What would I gain? All I could do now was go back where I had come from and dig myself in, stay quiet, and consider myself lucky in my lot, as most people must in the end. Or I could sink in the waves and let them carry away my grief, remorse, regrets – perhaps also good things to come, which now I would never know. I think my mind was set on this for several days. But would I have had the courage?

I was always alone at the stern of the ship, as though unable to do anything but gaze behind me. Finally a young man approached me, a Scot with a very attractive face and personality, all fun and good humour. His name was Jock. He had the most laughing eyes in the world while I, he chided me affectionately, had the saddest.

"And why is that?" he said. "At your age your troubles have only begun, and your joys besides."

I had no heart for flirtation or new friendship. The following day, however, he drew a smile from me when he said, "Gabrielle," (he must have asked the steward my name) "hold my hand and talk to me about myself, for isn't that what we all want most, each in our selfish self?"

Perhaps he helped me find my feet by helping me find my sense of humour again, which is the first step out of a persistent depression. I laughed with him a little after a while, though not heartily.

The sea was still very rough. We were going to sail up the St. Lawrence, and despite my mood I was looking forward to rediscovering the route in the steps of Cartier, Champlain, and Maisonneuve. I would be seeing the country from the river again, in reverse order this time, renewing my pleasure in the sight of villages along the shore with their brightly flashing church roofs, which were almost always galvanized in those days. From a distance you'd have thought they were sending friendly signals.

Shortly before the estuary, however, the ship entered a huge field of icebergs and was forced to reduce speed to a crawl. This was the month of April, early April admittedly, yet the Strait of Belle Isle was still icebound. The captain was ordered to go to Saint John, from where a special CPR train would take us to Montreal. So in the end I returned by one of the country's dreariest gateways. Endlessly bleak and lonely beneath a grey sky, what could have looked more forsaken from the moving train than New Brunswick at this unattractive time of year? In the background there were always the same still, monotonous forests, here and there the same little villages of humble, often colourless wooden houses, separated by interminable fields of old snow melting with the rain and leaving muddy puddles, tree stumps, and once in a while a shack, sometimes quite alone in this woeful landscape. How unloved our dear country seemed and still seems in comparison with the countrysides I had seen in Europe, all so tenderly cared for and kept so neat and clean.

MY JOURNEY ended at Windsor Station. During the night there had been a fall of wet snow. It melted under one's feet and made a dirty kind of mash which I quickly learned to call "slush" like everyone else. I soon learned to love this forlorn, lonesome urban landscape with all my soul, yet on this first day I felt as foreign as if I'd never set foot here.

I found a room as close as possible to the station, almost at the door, in fact, on Stanley Street. Strange though it may seem today, I had become such a wanderer that stations, railways, and railway tracks would feel almost like home to me for some time to come. I never lost heart as long as I could hear the puff of the fat locomotives of those days departing and arriving. I think I entered the dear old station several times just to listen to the powerful engines huffing and puffing by their platforms, and left feeling less alone. If I woke in a daze at night I could go back to sleep, reassured in a way to hear the long whistle of a train, thinking, "Well, the train's not far away, if life gets too difficult I can always jump aboard and in less than two days be back where I came from." I'd forget that I couldn't afford it for the moment.

But I had another reason for not living too far from the station. Since I might be moving any minute, I left my trunk in the checkroom, the poor old cumbersome companion to which I'd become so curiously attached. By now my feeling for it was perhaps what we often feel for certain people and objects we don't know how to part with. In any event, for once it was convenient to have it close at hand, for I could go and take out lighter clothes as the weather became warmer. To keep my tiny room uncluttered, I also had to put into it things I no longer needed, that is, at least as much as I took out. For a few weeks I kept going back and forth between my room and the Windsor Station checkroom. I always dealt with the same station employee who, as soon as he saw me coming, would go and fetch the trunk, pivoting it on its corners to within my reach. I gave him a twenty-five-cent piece for his trouble the first time, but the second, having seen me hesitate, no doubt, he adamantly refused it. It would be a crime when he had nothing to do for hours on end, he said, to accept a tip for a service so small it wasn't worth talking about. Since he had to go and bring it from the back of a huge room so full of baggage he could hardly move, I didn't think it such a small thing. He said he was already being paid anyway by my comings and goings, which entertained him hugely, for in all his years with the CPR he'd never yet seen anyone come and take a pair of beige shoes out of a trunk and the same day come back and put a pair of brown shoes in. The trunk stayed in his care for a little over a month, and by the end he knew its contents almost as well as I did. He was my first friend in Montreal.

It was he who suggested I move into a house on Dorchester Street next to his, where I had a better room for the same price I was paying on Stanley. We had neighbouring windows through which, since his house adjoined mine, he used to pass me a share of his Irish stew, always saying he had too much. Later still he encouraged me to take a room and board with someone he had found who made even better Irish stew, a Miss McLean. I owe it to Pat Cossack that in her house, compared to what I'd had before, I was in the lap of luxury.

BUT WHEN I first arrived I lived in the most horrid little room imaginable except in a prison. It was so cramped I had to turn sideways to pass between the grey metal bookshelf and the iron bedstead. The window overlooked the yard behind the principal bus station in Montreal, which was then on Dorchester Street. There dozens of buses were drawn up, always some with motors idling noisily, sending clouds of stifling fumes straight through my window. The loudspeaker never stopped announcing departures and arrivals. "Leaving for Rawdon, *traque numéro sept*, track number seven...leaving for Terrebonne, *traque numéro onze*, track number eleven...." Sometimes I used to repeat in my sleep, "*Traque numéro douze*, track number twelve...."

The atmosphere of wayfaring, confusion of tongues, and dizzy whirl of activity wasn't unpleasant. It suited my state of mind and was certainly more congenial, more friendly than some tranquil little street inhabited by equally tranquil people who have lived there for years. I always seem to have had the right place to stay at the right time.

Two letters arrived at the post office general delivery which I didn't dare open until I was back in the safety of my room, fragile haven though it was. One was from the St-Boniface School Board reminding me that I had been allowed a second year's leave of absence without pay and the privilege couldn't be renewed. I must therefore either return to work or resign. The second was from my mother. I can see myself reading her letter, holding it on my knees as I sat at the foot of my little iron cot.

"*Mon enfant*," it read, "so you're back in Montreal, not so far from home now. Home isn't a house any more, of course, but with the bit of money I have left and what you'll be earning we'll be able to live pretty well, you'll see. And with you so independent and me probably too possessive, I'll try to get used to letting you lead your own life. I imagine I can expect you home soon...."

I looked up and inches away, in the mirror on the little chest of drawers, I saw my distorted face. The flaws in the mirror? My own emotion? The old knot was in my throat again, just as in our days of greatest hardship, perpetual fears, and all that futile courage.

I looked at myself and knew that the time had come to make a decision from which, good or bad, there would be no turning back. I couldn't avoid it any longer.

I left the letter on the chest of drawers, the pages filled with the rather untidy writing which alone always told me better than anything else how strained and bruised Maman's nerves had been.

I went out. Aside from kind Mr. Cossack, I didn't know a soul in the city. I wandered the streets though I don't remember which. I must have walked some distance on St. Catherine Street, then up to Sherbrooke, for behind my agitated thoughts I remember the clanging of streetcar bells, then, as had happened once in London, a sudden intrusion which at first I didn't recognize, the rustling of early spring leaves. And as I had in London and Paris, I kept searching the indifferent faces in the crowd, hoping someone would at least glance at me. At last I walked downhill to where the lights were less bright, St. Antoine or Craig Street perhaps. Down here there was less traffic and less bustle on the sidewalks, and instead something like the murmur of a more private, friendlier sort of life. I wonder why I've always felt less lonely among ordinary people than in drawing rooms and society gatherings, however fondly I'm regarded by others present.

What shall I do? What shall I do? I kept asking myself as I walked. The question hammered at my mind, tormented me much as had the Song of Destiny and the mournful sound of the bell-buoy at Liverpool. What shall I do? Stay or go back?

I had no means of support nor assurance of even the most humble employment here, not even a friendly hand to reach out to me now and then. But could I live in Manitoba's suffocating French climate, its suffocating climate altogether, now that I knew there was something better? For it was misfortune enough to have been born French in Quebec, but infinitely worse, I now perceived, to have been born French outside Quebec in our little colonies of the Canadian West. Though I was lonely here, around me as I walked I heard French being spoken with what seemed a very heavy accent

407

after that of Paris, but with the words and expressions of my people, of my mother and grandmother, and I found this comforting.

Without knowing the way, I somehow reached the banks of the old Lachine Canal. I stopped short, intrigued. Barges were gliding slowly by, their sides scraping against the old timbers lining the canal. Their horns, requesting the opening of the lock gates, raised strange, repeated cries, like lamentations. I think I stayed for hours, dreaming of nothing in particular, as if abandoned by my own thoughts but not distressed by this. The night was rather mild as I recall, far from the miraculous spring of London but with the kindly feel of our Canadian spring. In the little streets of wooden houses and wide-spaced streetlamps where I went to walk, still aimlessly, I heard sounds of water trickling along the gutters, and here and there saw puddles of melting snow.

The bleatings of barge horns were not all I had for company. This district of St-Henri, whose name I had yet to learn, was constantly shaken by passing trains. First you heard a thin warning bell announcing the approach of a train towards each level crossing, then the long black-and-white-striped arms of the safety gates lowered and the crossing lights began to flash. The great trains bound for east and west came thundering down the track, shaking the ground, the windows of the houses, and perhaps something in the soul that remained quivering, in suspense, after the din had ceased.

Everything about the aura of departure and travel that I discovered in Montreal that night and subsequently made me want to stay. This atmosphere was like home to me for some time, consoling me in a way for not having another home, whispering that all of us are wanderers in this life and it's better to possess nothing if we want at least a clear view of the world we're passing through.

Less than a year later I returned deliberately to this district, listening, observing, sensing that it would be the setting and to a degree perhaps the substance of a novel. Already it gripped me in some curious way that I still don't understand. Its cries, smells, and reminders of travel weren't its only fascination. Its poverty moved me. Its poetry touched my heart, strains of guitars and other wistful scraps of music escaping beneath closed doors, the sound of the wind straying through warehouse passageways. I felt less alone here than in the crowds and bright lights of the city.

I walked up the long Atwater hill. I turned along Dorchester Street, passing, as it happens, in front of the house in which I would shortly have a room. After many wrong turns, I found my way back to Stanley Street. Sitting on my bed and leaning against the wall with the writing paper on my knees, I wrote first to the School Board thanking them for keeping my position open for me and herewith resigning. Then I wrote to my mother. What did I tell her? Probably to be patient, to expect me back in a year or two. She would soon be seventy-two. When I returned to St-Boniface after her death and searched among the pitiful remains of her belongings – practically nothing, cards from her children, small photographs – I couldn't find that first letter from Montreal in which I so hoped to have found words at least to soften the blow. Many of my letters were missing, though she kept little except letters in her last years – all, in fact, except the most recent. Some-one must have taken them to use them against me in some way. Or to prevent someone from using them against me. We were a divided family after Maman's death. She had held us more or less together with the strength of her love.

When I had written my letters I counted the money I had left. Fifteen dollars and a few cents. Enough to pay my rent for a week. I wrote to the two friends whom I thought the most dependable. I hated to borrow. I did it very rarely and never without the most agonizing scruples. In reply I received a long letter from one, full of praise for my talent, courage, and sense of initiative…and regret for not being able to help me because she'd had to buy a new fur coat and pay her tennis club fees, she explained, and really had nothing left, nothing! The other wrote hastily, "This is all I have to send you, alas, but I send it gladly…." She enclosed three five-dollar bills. Coming from the poorer of the two, it seemed like a huge sum. With this, I thought, I could hold out for several weeks and have time to see what lay ahead. Better still, because a friend had such confidence in me that she'd sent me her last pennies as it were, my courage was restored.

On the advice of a journalist at *The Gazette* to whom I had a letter of recommendation from a colleague posted in London, I made the rounds of a number of magazines and weekly papers. All I had to show a modicum of talent was the small collection of articles published here and there over the previous couple of years.

At *Le Jour* I was given to understand that they might, when there was room, publish a short column on a subject of my choice, for a fee of three dollars per column. At *La Revue moderne* they would pay up to ten dollars for a longish story if I could write it in the style the readers liked.

I went back to my room. I sat on the bed leaning against the wall with my typewriter on my knees, my thoughts invaded by relentless announcements – "*Traque numéro huit*, track number eight..." – terror-stricken to realize that now there was really no turning back; to earn my living, I would henceforth have to write and keep on writing. I suddenly saw how ill equipped I was.

I began with anecdotal accounts of my adventures in England and France. Alas, in my downcast state of mind, no longer stimulated by elation, I could bring forth only platitudes. It took close to a year before I began to write articles with some substance, given the opportunity by a farmers' publication, the *Bulletin des agriculteurs*, to write on subjects involving fact, reality, close observation.

It was even longer before I began to build on the reveries germinated beside the old canal that April evening, coming by stages to the major task whose prospect filled me with even greater terror than I had felt on Stanley Street when I began to write for a living. But now at least I was totally absorbed in my subject, helped and sustained by all the experience of human nature and other resources I'd acquired, as well as by my feeling of having come home, of oneness with my people, whom my mother had taught me to know and love in my childhood.

But back in my room on Stanley Street, I could only write insipid little pieces in which one would probably have searched in vain for traces of the torment and delight that have been with me since I was born, and no doubt will leave me only when I die.

Yet a bird, almost the minute it's hatched, I'm told, already knows its song.

The Author

GABRIELLE ROY was born in St-Boniface, Manitoba, on March 22, 1909. She was a schoolteacher from 1928 to 1937, the year in which she left on an extended trip of two years in France and England on the eve of the Second World War. Returning to Canada in 1939, she decided to settle in Montreal and became a freelance journalist with *Le Jour, Le Canada, La Revue moderne*, and *Le Bulletin des agriculteurs*, for which she wrote stories and several major series of articles. Her first novel, *Bonheur d'occasion*, was awarded the Prix Femina in France in 1947, and its translation, *The Tin Flute*, was chosen as the Book of the Month by the Literary Guild of America. While in Europe once again from 1947 to 1950 with her husband, Dr. Marcel Carbotte, she wrote her second book, *La Petite Poule d'Eau (Where Nests the Water Hen)*. She returned to live in Quebec, where she remained and wrote for the rest of her life. She died in Quebec City on July 13, 1983.

Gabrielle Roy wrote fifteen books besides this autobiography, comprising novels, short stories, children's books, and a collection of essays. She also wrote a number of other essays and articles. Her recognition as one of the leading figures in Canadian and Quebec literature is attested by the many honours she received, including three Governor General's Prizes (1947, 1957, and 1978), the Prix Femina (France, 1947), the Lorne Pierce Medal (Royal Society of Canada, 1947), the Medal of the Académie canadienne-française (1947), the Prix Duvernay (1956), the Prix David (1971), and the Canada Council Prize for Children's Literature (1979).

The Works of Gabrielle Roy

Second and subsequent Canadian editions listed are revised editions, excepting special editions as noted.

Bonheur d'occasion, Montreal, 1945, 1947, 1965, 1970, 1977; Paris, 1947, Geneva, 1968. Prix Femina; Book of the Month, Literary Guild of America; Medal of the Académie canadienne-française; Governor General's Prize; Lorne Pierce Medal, Royal Society of Canada. English translation by Hannah Josephson, *The Tin Flute*, Toronto, McClelland & Stewart, 1947. Retranslation by Alan Brown, Toronto, McClelland & Stewart, 1980. Spanish, Danish, Swedish, Norwegian, Slovak, Czech, Romanian, and Russian translations.

La Petite Poule d'Eau, Montreal, 1950, 1957, 1970, 1980; Paris, 1951, 1967; Geneva, 1953; numbered art edition with twenty prints by Jean-Paul Lemieux, Montreal, 1971. English translation by Harry Binsse, *Where Nests the Water Hen*, Toronto, McClelland & Stewart, 1951. German translation.

Alexandre Chenevert, Montreal, 1954, 1973, 1979; Paris, 1954. English translation by Harry Binsse, *The Cashier*, Toronto, McClelland & Stewart, 1955. German translation.

Rue Deschambault, Montreal, 1955, 1956, 1967, 1971, 1980. Governor General's Prize. English translation by Harry Binsse, *Street of Riches*, Toronto, McClelland & Stewart, 1957. Italian translation.

La Montagne secrète, Montreal, 1961, 1971, 1974, 1978; Paris, 1962; numbered deluxe edition illustrated by René Richard, Montreal, 1975. English translation by Harry Binsse, *The Hidden Mountain*, Toronto, McClelland & Stewart, 1962.

La Route d'Altamont, Montreal, 1966, 1979; Paris, 1967. English translation by Joyce Marshall, *The Road past Altamont*, Toronto, McClelland & Stewart, 1966. German translation.

La Rivière sans repos, novel preceded by three short stories, Montreal, 1970, 1971, 1979; Paris, 1972. English translation (novel only) by Joyce Marshall, *Windflower*, Toronto, McClelland & Stewart, 1970.

Cet été qui chantait, Quebec and Montreal, 1972, 1973; Montreal, 1979. English translation by Joyce Marshall, *Enchanted Summer*, Toronto, McClelland & Stewart, 1976.

Un Jardin au bout du monde, Montreal, 1975, 1981. English translation by Alan Brown, *Garden in the Wind*, Toronto, McClelland & Stewart, 1977.

Ma Vache Bossie (children's story), Montreal, 1976, 1982. Illustrated by Louise Pominville.

Ces enfants de ma vie, Montreal, 1977, 1983. Governor General's Prize. English translation by Alan Brown, *Children of My Heart*, Toronto, McClelland & Stewart, 1979.

Fragiles lumières de la terre, Montreal, 1978, 1980, 1982. English translation by Alan Brown, *The Fragile Lights of Earth*, Toronto, McClelland & Stewart, 1982.

Courte-Queue (children's story), Montreal, 1979, 1980. Canada Council Prize for Children's Literature. English translation by Alan Brown, *Cliptail*, Toronto, McClelland & Stewart, 1980. English and French editions illustrated by François Olivier.

De quoi t'ennuies-tu Eveline? suivi de *Ely! Ely! Ely!*, Montreal, 1979, 1982, 1984.

La Pékinoise et l'Espagnole (children's story), Montreal, 1987. Illustrated by Jean-Yves Ahern.